Gacha Gacha

THE NEXT REVOLUTION

1

Hiroyuki Tamakoshi

Translated and adapted by
David Ury

Lettered by
North Market Street Graphics

BALLANTINE BOOKS • NEW YORK

Gacha Gacha: The Next Revolution volume 1 is a work of fiction. Names of characters, places, and incidents are the products of the author's imagination or are used fictitiously. Any resemblance to actual events, locales, or persons, living or dead, is entirely coincidental.

A Del Rey Trade Paperback Original

Published in the United States by Del Rey Books, an imprint of The Random House Publishing Group, a division of Random House, Inc., New York.

Publication rights arranged through Kodansha Ltd.

First published in Japan in 2003 by Kodansha Ltd., Tokyo

ISBN 978-0-345-49233-3

Printed in the United States of America

www.delreymanga.com

9 8 7 6 5 4 3 2 1

Translator and adapter: David Ury

Lettering: North Market Street Graphics

CONTENTS

A word from the author

HOW DO YOU LIKE THE NEW *GACHA GACHA?*
I HOPE YOU'LL ENJOY THE CONTINUING
ADVENTURES OF YURIKA SAKURABA,
AKIRA-CHAN, AND AKIRA! IT KEEPS
GETTING SEXIER AND SEXIER.

Honorifics Explained

Throughout the Del Rey Manga books, you will find Japanese honorifics left intact in the translations. For those not familiar with how
the Japanese use honorifics and, more important, how they differ
from American honorifics, we present this brief overview. Polite-
ness has always been a critical facet of Japanese culture. Ever since
the feudal era, when Japan was a highly stratified society, use of
honorifics — which can be defined as polite speech that indicates
relationship or status — has played an essential role in the Japanese
language. When addressing someone in Japanese, an honorific usually takes the form of a suffix attached to one's name (example:
"Asuna-san"), or is used as a title at the end of one's name, or ap-
pears in place of the name itself (example: "Negi-sensei," or simply
"Sensei!").

Honorifics can be expressions of respect or endearment. In the
context of manga and anime, honorifics give insight into the nature
of the relationship between characters. Many translations into English leave out these important honorifics, and therefore distort the
feel of the original Japanese. Because Japanese honorifics contain
nuances that English honorifics lack, it is our policy at Del Rey not
to translate them. Here, instead, is a guide to some of the honorifics
you may encounter in Del Rey Manga.

-san: This is the most common honorific and is equivalent to
          Mr., Miss, Ms., Mrs. It is the all-purpose honorific
          and can be used in any situation where politeness is
          required.

-sama: This is one level higher than "-san." It is used to confer
          great respect.

-dono: This comes from the word "tono," which means "lord."
          It is an even higher level than "-sama," and confers
          utmost respect.

-kun: This suffix is used at the end of boys' names to express
          familiarity or endearment. It is also sometimes used by
          men among friends, or when addressing someone
          younger or of a lower station.

-chan: This is used to express endearment, mostly toward girls. It is also used for little boys, pets, and even among lovers. It gives a sense of childish cuteness.

Bozu: This is an informal way to refer to a boy, similar to the English terms "kid" and "squirt."

Sempai: This title suggests that the addressee is one's senior in a group or organization. It is most often used in a school setting, where underclassmen refer to their upper classmen as "sempai." It can also be used in the work place, such as when a newer employee addresses an employee who has seniority in the company.

Kohai: This is the opposite of "sempai" and is used toward underclassmen in school or newcomers in the workplace. It connotes that the addressee is of lower station.

Sensei: Literally meaning "one who has come before," this title is used for teachers, doctors, or masters of any profession or art.

-[blank]: This is usually forgotten in these lists, but it's perhaps the most significant difference between Japanese and English. The lack of honorific means that the speaker has permission to address the person in a very intimate way. Usually, only family, spouses, or very close friends have this kind of permission. Known as *yobisute*, it can be gratifying when someone who has earned the intimacy starts to call one by one's name without an honorific. But when that intimacy hasn't been earned, it can be very insulting.

Gacha Gacha

THE NEXT REVOLUTI

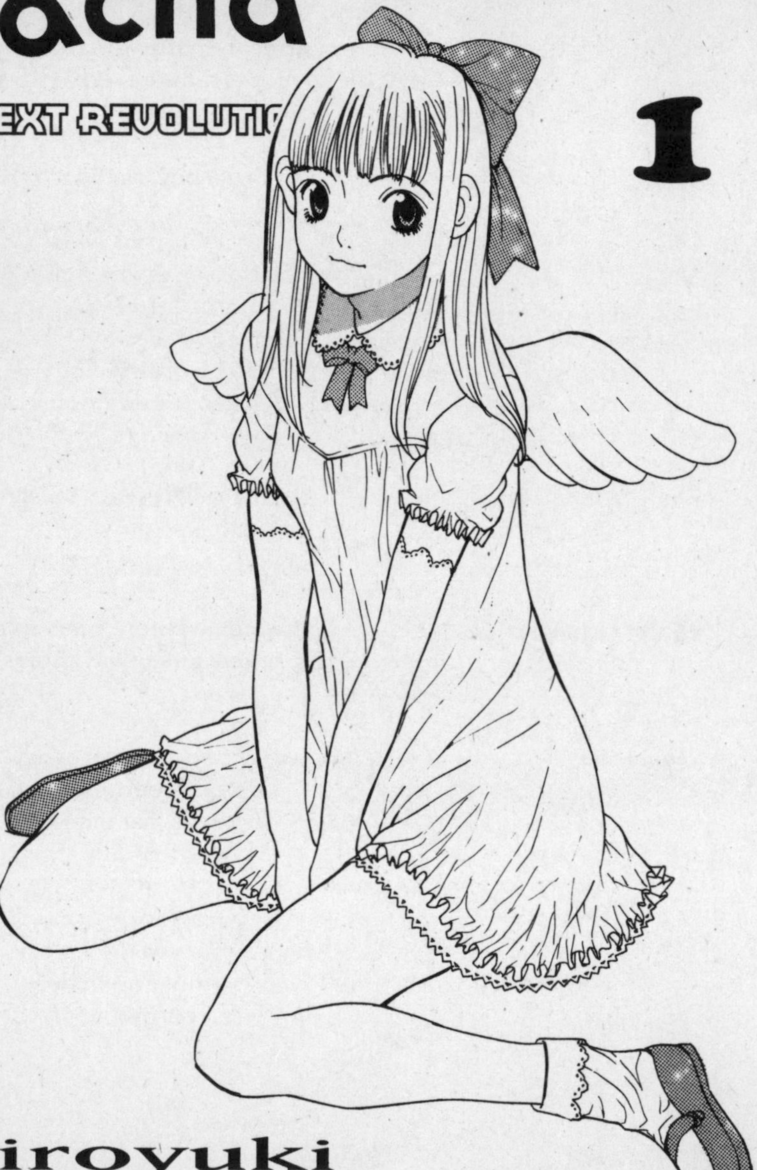

1

Hiroyuki Tamakoshi

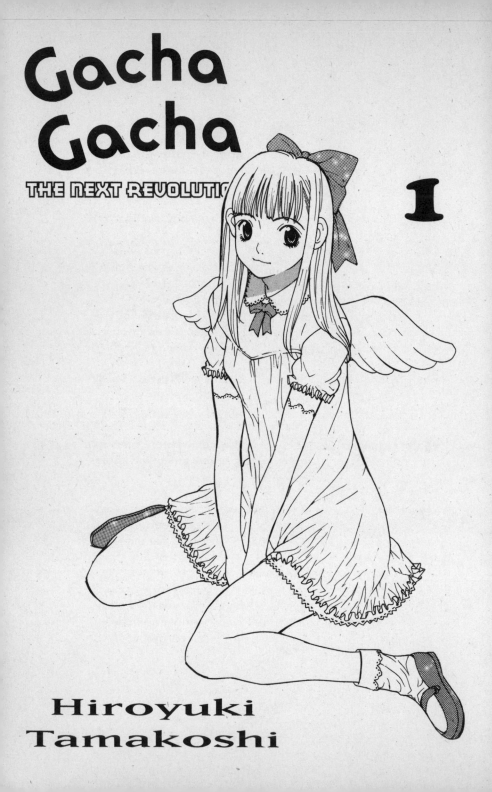

THE NEXT REVOLUTION

CONTENTS

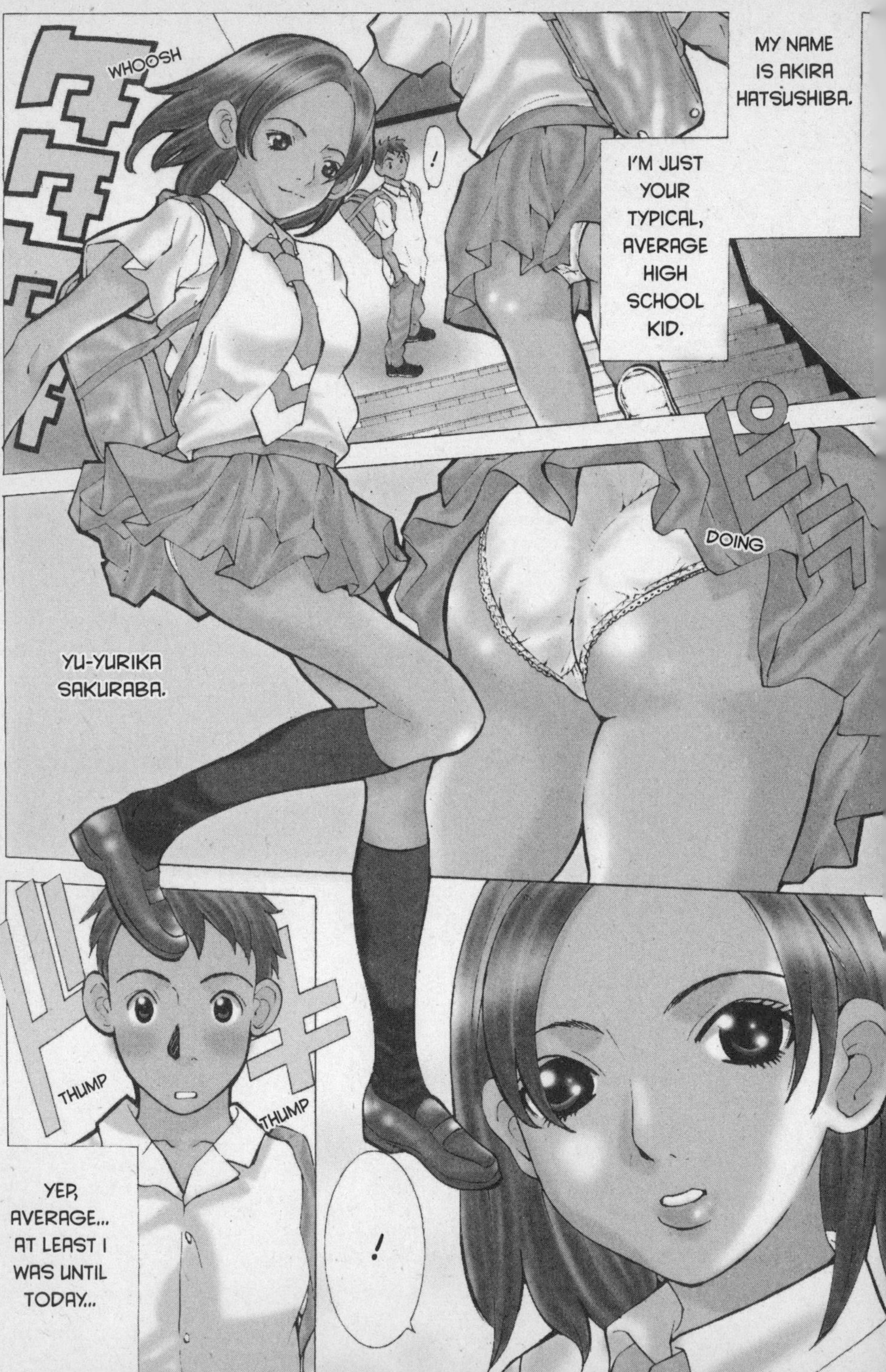
MY NAME IS AKIRA HATSUSHIBA.
I'M JUST YOUR TYPICAL, AVERAGE HIGH SCHOOL KID.
WHOOSH
!
DOING
YU-YURIKA SAKURABA.
!
THUMP
THUMP
YEP, AVERAGE... AT LEAST I WAS UNTIL TODAY...

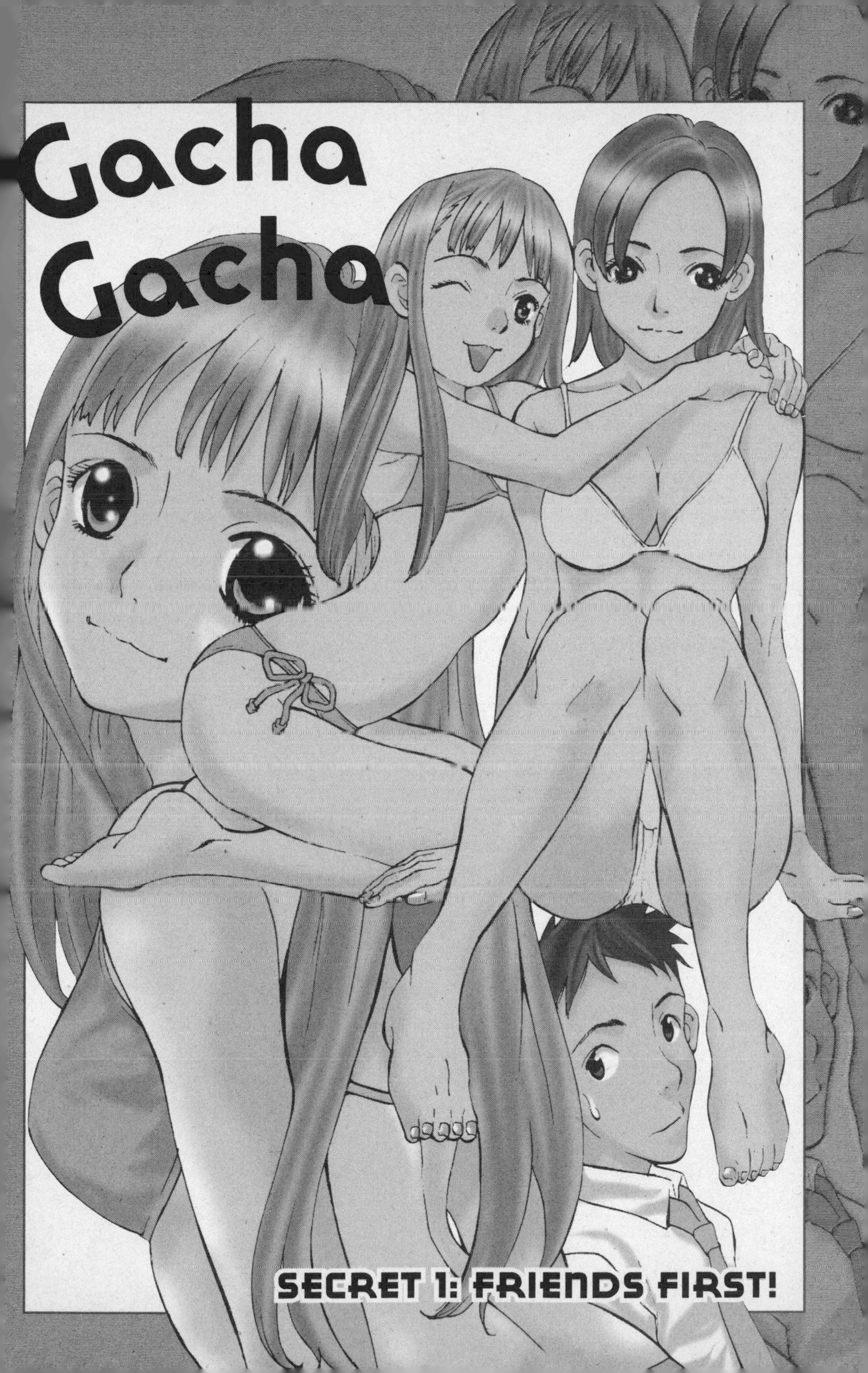
Gacha Gacha
SECRET 1: FRIENDS FIRST!

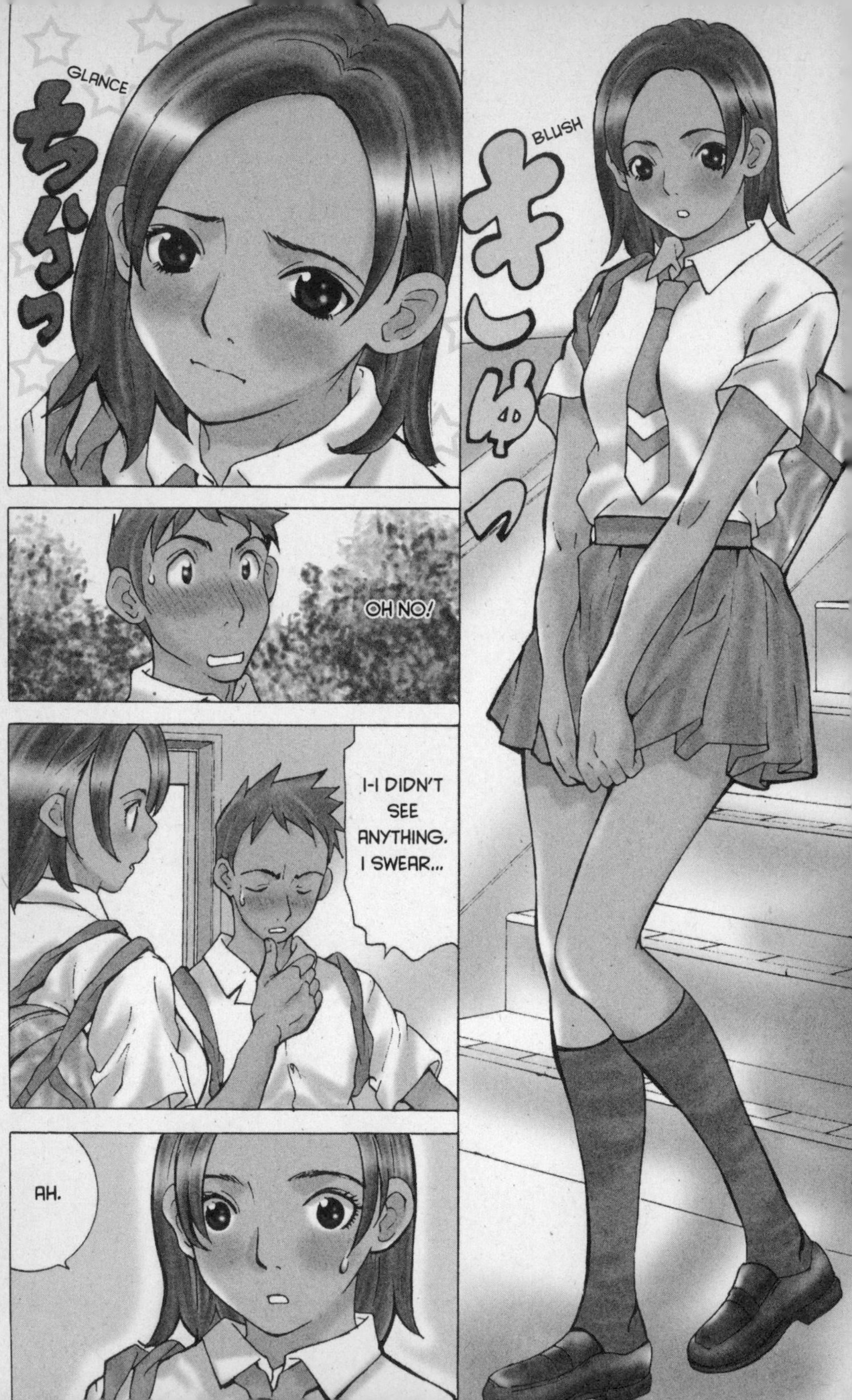
BLUSH
きゅっ
GLANCE
ちらっ
OH NO!
I-I DIDN'T SEE ANYTHING. I SWEAR...
AH.

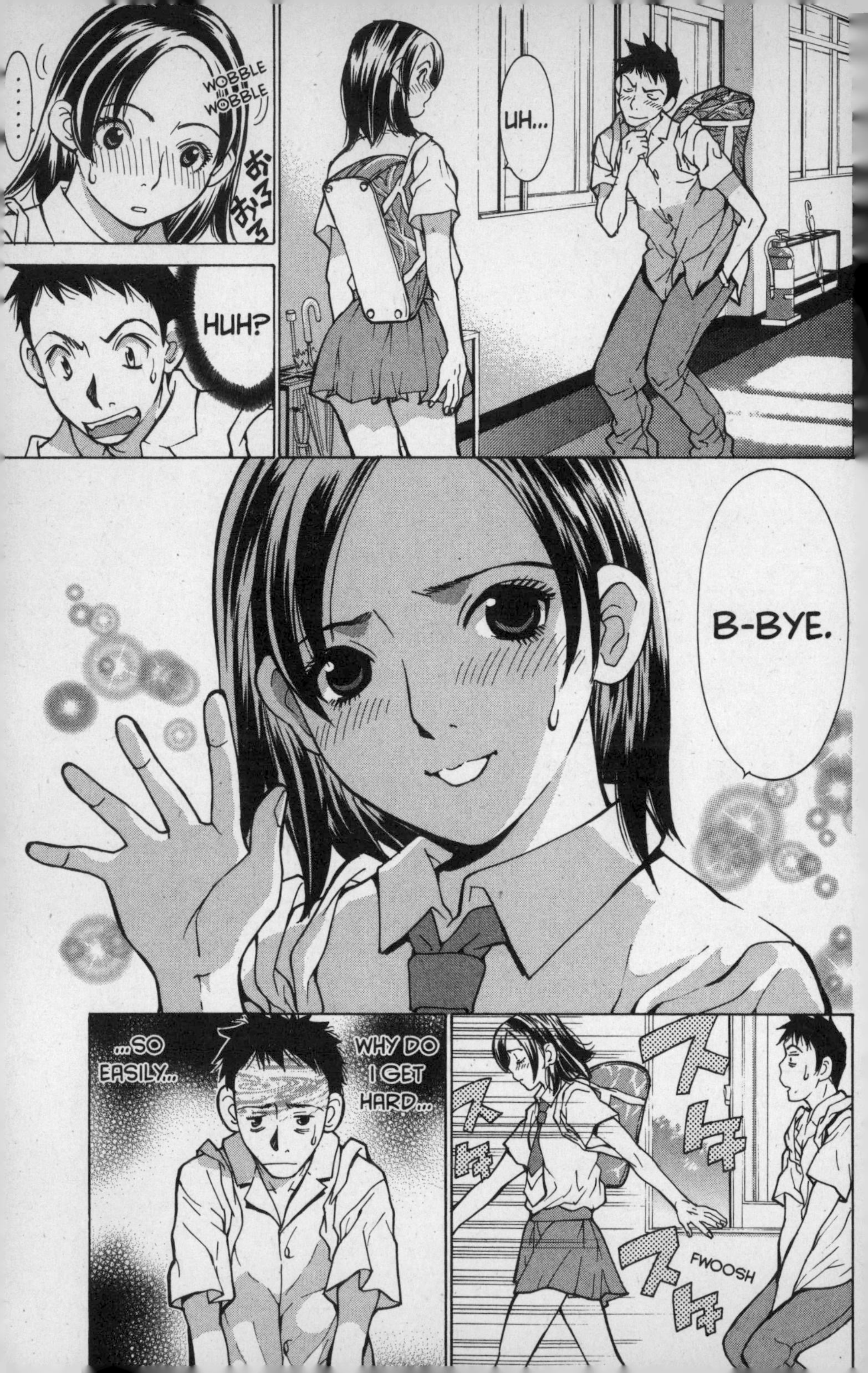
UH...
......
WOBBLE WOBBLE
おろおろ
HUH?
B-BYE.
FWOOSH
WHY DO I GET HARD...
...SO EASILY...

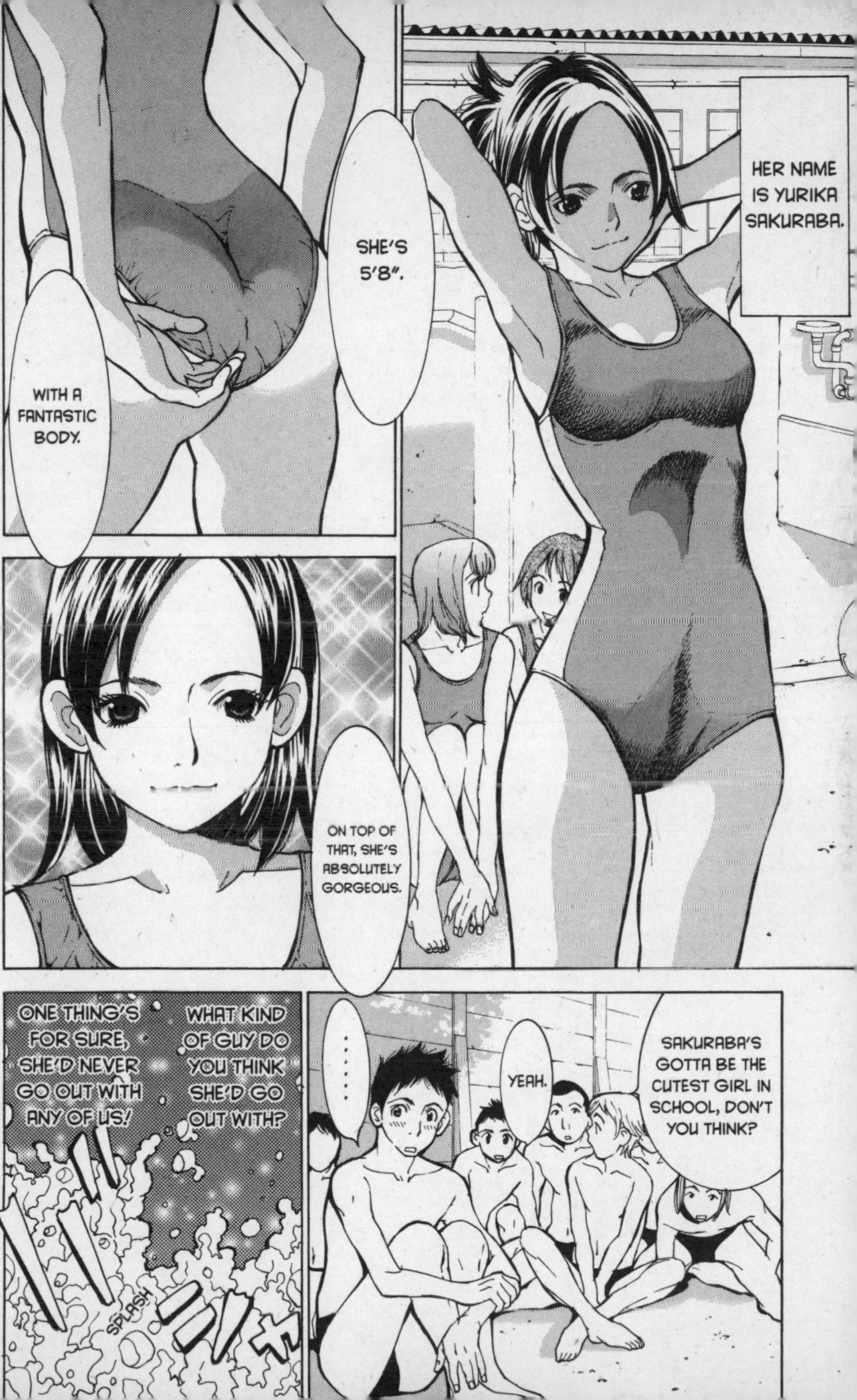
HER NAME IS YURIKA SAKURABA.
SHE'S 5'8".
WITH A FANTASTIC BODY.
ON TOP OF THAT, SHE'S ABSOLUTELY GORGEOUS.
SAKURABA'S GOTTA BE THE CUTEST GIRL IN SCHOOL, DON'T YOU THINK?
YEAH.
......
WHAT KIND OF GUY DO YOU THINK SHE'D GO OUT WITH?
ONE THING'S FOR SURE, SHE'D NEVER GO OUT WITH ANY OF US!
SPLASH

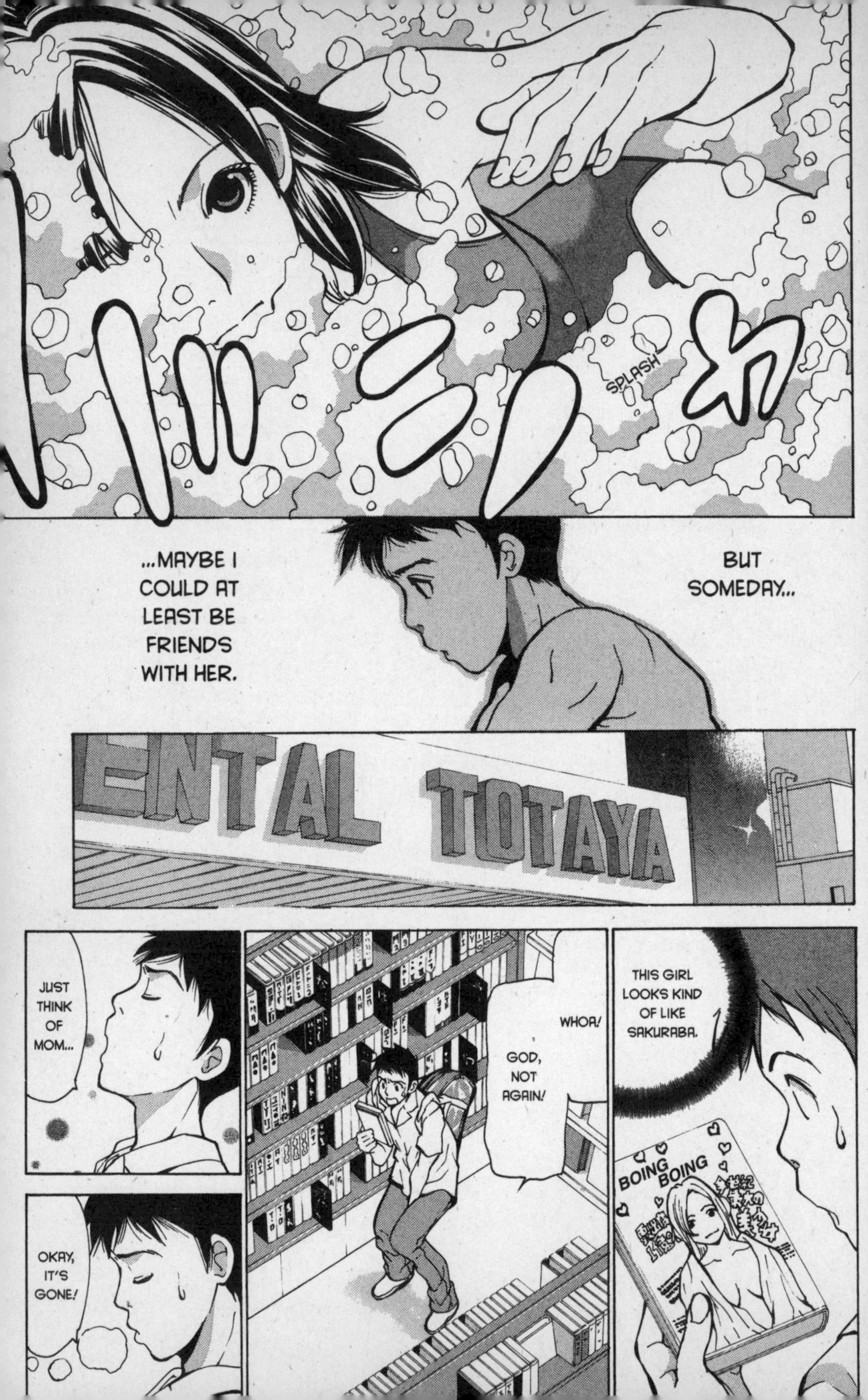
SPLASH
BUT SOMEDAY...
...MAYBE I COULD AT LEAST BE FRIENDS WITH HER.
ENTAL TOTAYA
THIS GIRL LOOKS KIND OF LIKE SAKURABA.
BOING BOING
WHOA!
GOD, NOT AGAIN!
JUST THINK OF MOM...
OKAY, IT'S GONE!

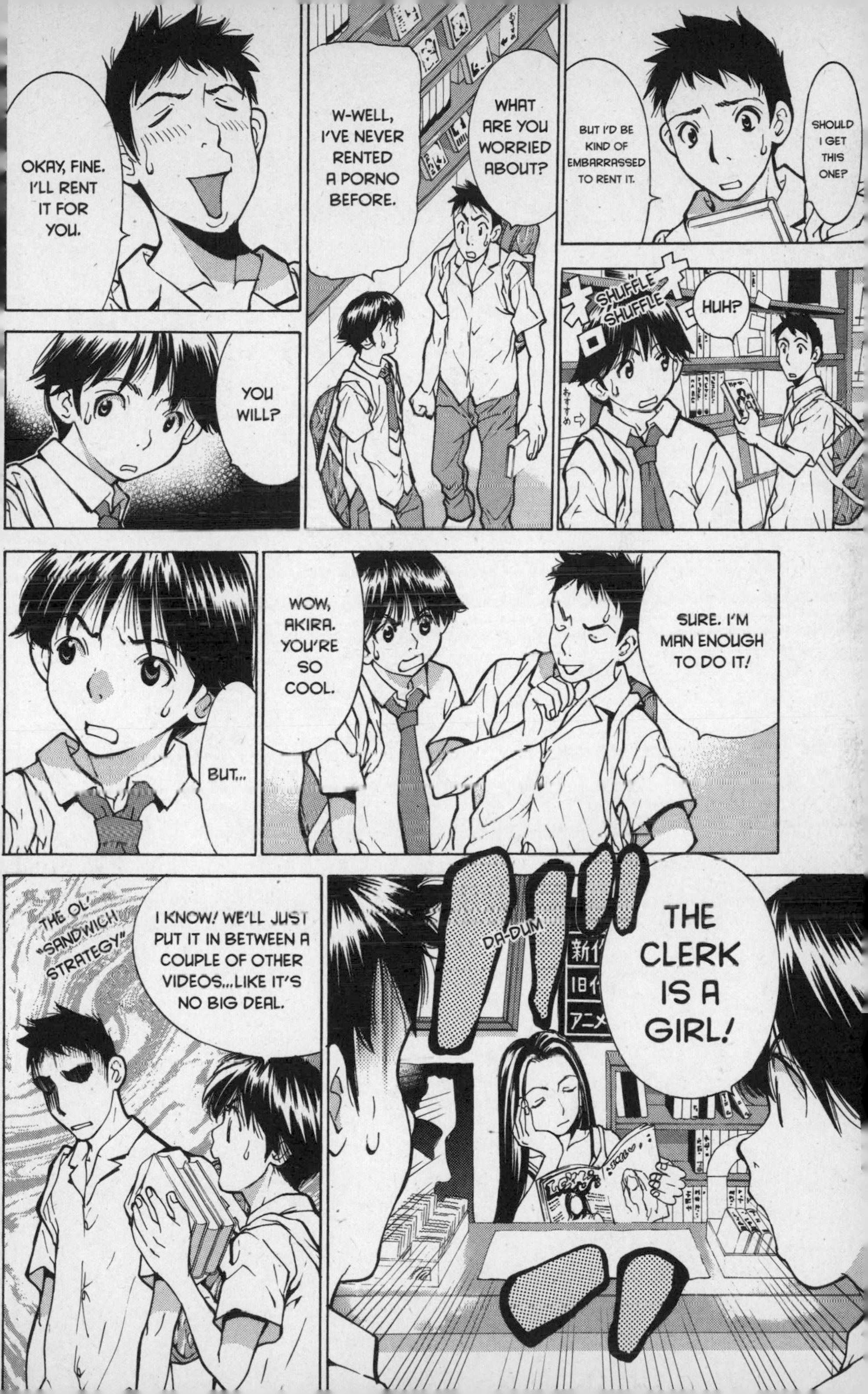
SHOULD I GET THIS ONE?
BUT I'D BE KIND OF EMBARRASSED TO RENT IT.
SHUFFLE SHUFFLE
HUH?
おすすめ
WHAT ARE YOU WORRIED ABOUT?
W-WELL, I'VE NEVER RENTED A PORNO BEFORE.
OKAY, FINE. I'LL RENT IT FOR YOU.
YOU WILL?
SURE. I'M MAN ENOUGH TO DO IT!
WOW, AKIRA. YOU'RE SO COOL.
BUT...
DA-DUM
THE CLERK IS A GIRL!
I KNOW! WE'LL JUST PUT IT IN BETWEEN A COUPLE OF OTHER VIDEOS...LIKE IT'S NO BIG DEAL.
THE OL' "SANDWICH STRATEGY"

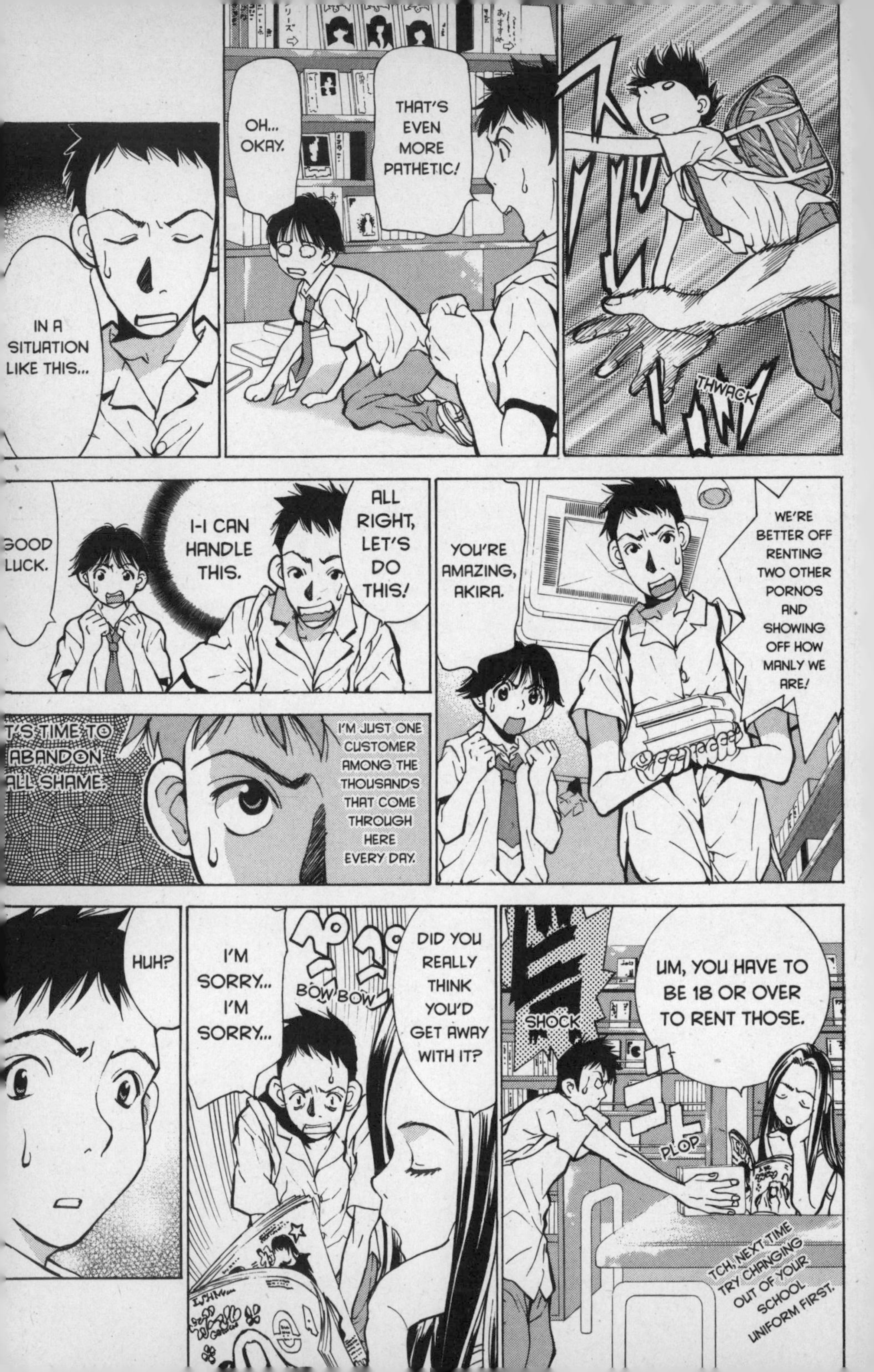
THWACK
THAT'S EVEN MORE PATHETIC!
OH... OKAY.
IN A SITUATION LIKE THIS...
WE'RE BETTER OFF RENTING TWO OTHER PORNOS AND SHOWING OFF HOW MANLY WE ARE!
YOU'RE AMAZING, AKIRA.
ALL RIGHT, LET'S DO THIS!
I-I CAN HANDLE THIS.
GOOD LUCK.
I'M JUST ONE CUSTOMER AMONG THE THOUSANDS THAT COME THROUGH HERE EVERY DAY.
T'S TIME TO ABANDON ALL SHAME.
UM, YOU HAVE TO BE 18 OR OVER TO RENT THOSE.
SHOCK
PLOP
TCH, NEXT TIME TRY CHANGING OUT OF YOUR SCHOOL UNIFORM FIRST.
DID YOU REALLY THINK YOU'D GET AWAY WITH IT?
BOW BOW
I'M SORRY... I'M SORRY...
HUH?

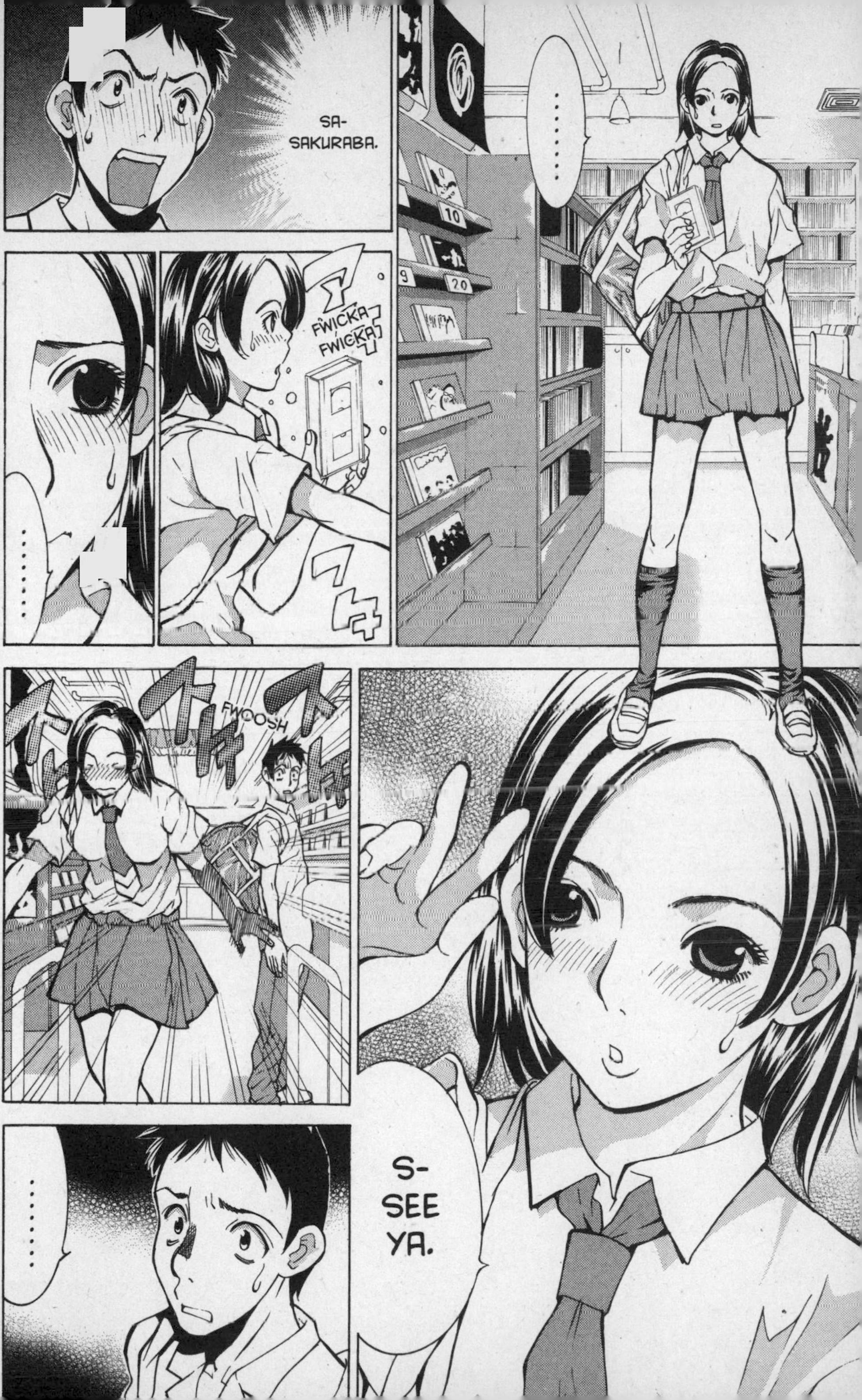
......
SA-SAKURABA.
FWICKA FWICKA
......
S-SEE YA.
FWOOSH
......

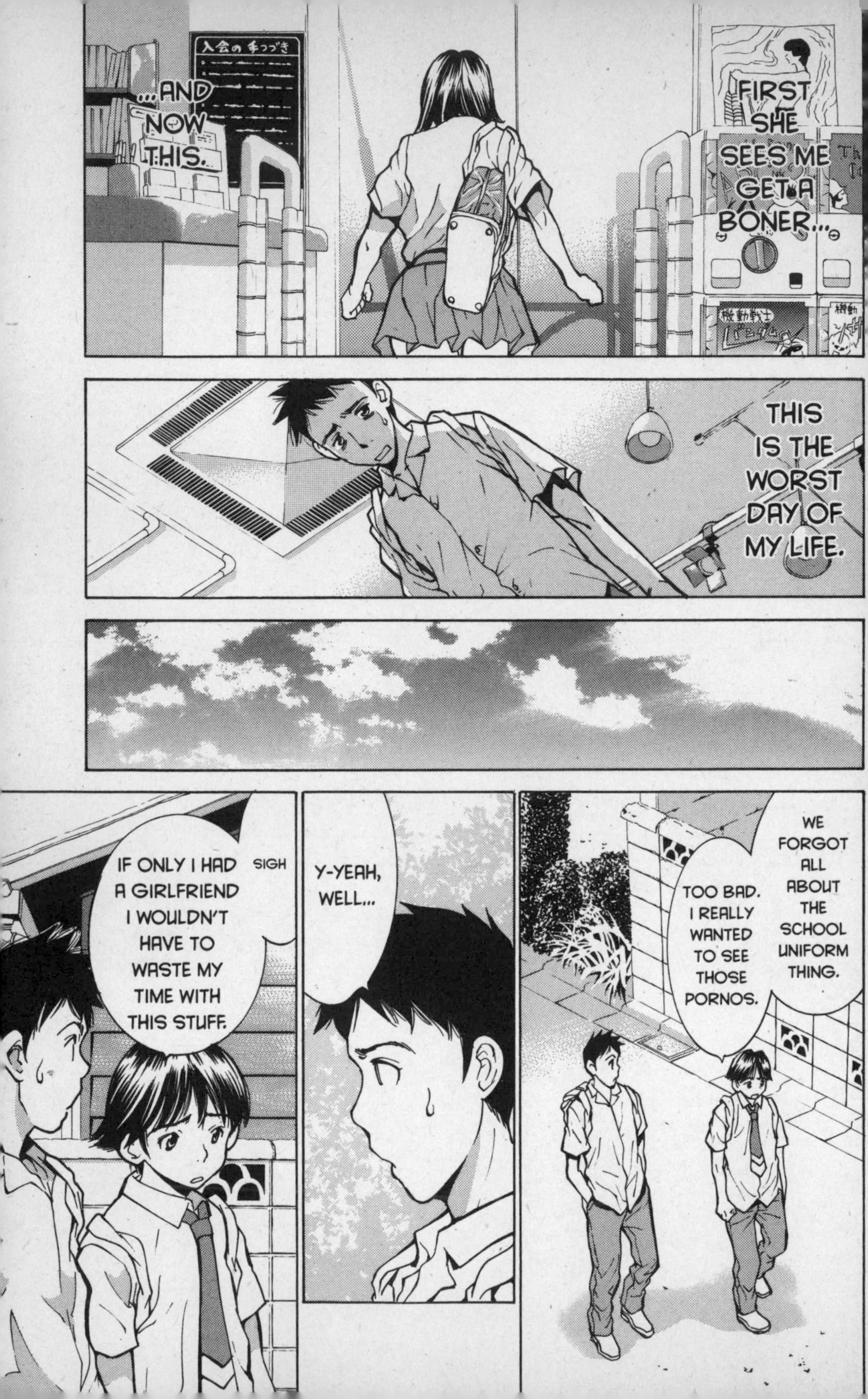
入会の手つづき
FIRST SHE SEES ME GET A BONER...
...AND NOW THIS.
THIS IS THE WORST DAY OF MY LIFE.
WE FORGOT ALL ABOUT THE SCHOOL UNIFORM THING.
TOO BAD. I REALLY WANTED TO SEE THOSE PORNOS.
Y-YEAH, WELL...
SIGH
IF ONLY I HAD A GIRLFRIEND I WOULDN'T HAVE TO WASTE MY TIME WITH THIS STUFF.

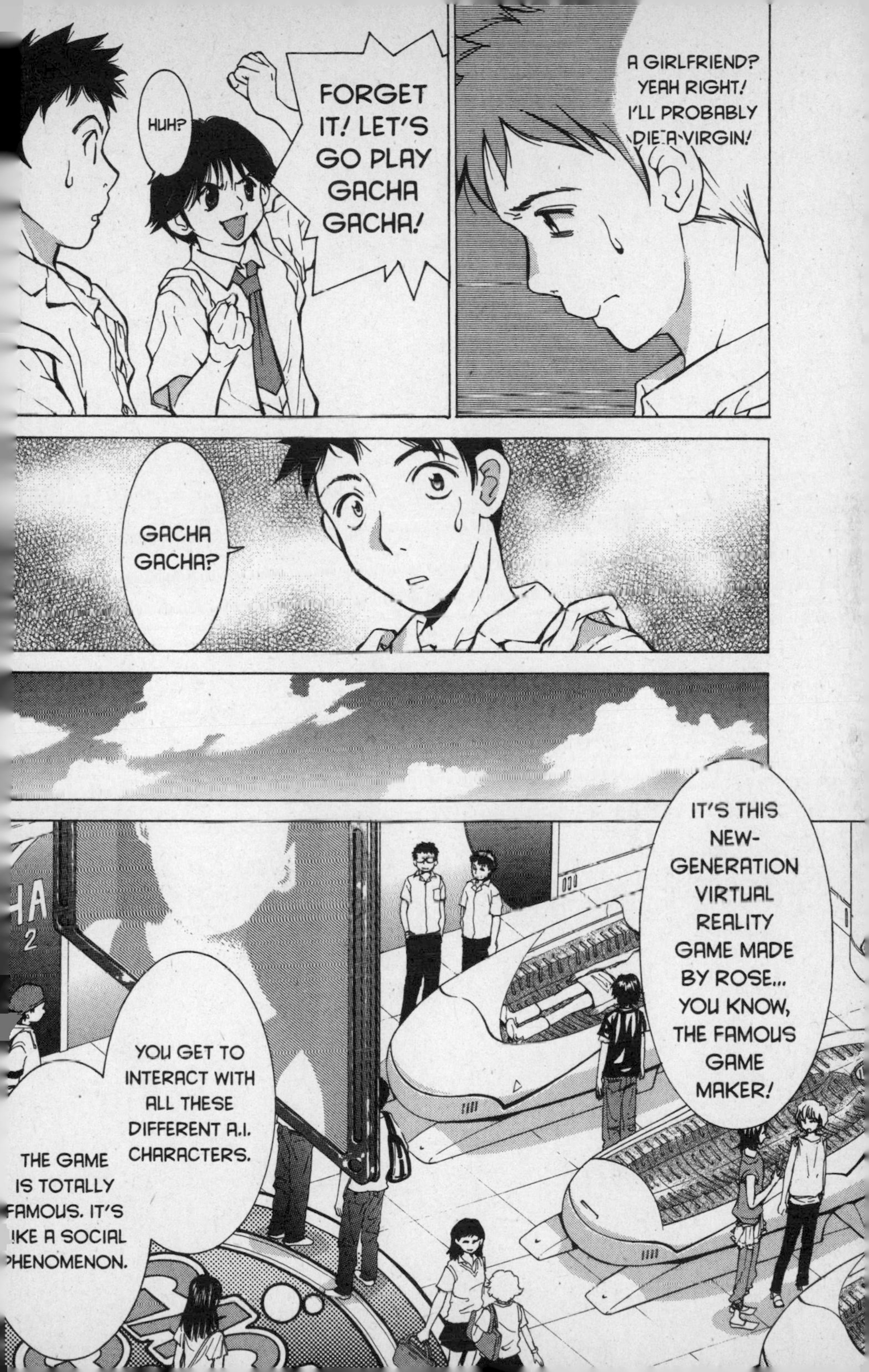
A GIRLFRIEND? YEAH RIGHT! I'LL PROBABLY DIE A VIRGIN!
FORGET IT! LET'S GO PLAY GACHA GACHA!
HUH?
GACHA GACHA?
IT'S THIS NEW-GENERATION VIRTUAL REALITY GAME MADE BY ROSE... YOU KNOW, THE FAMOUS GAME MAKER!
YOU GET TO INTERACT WITH ALL THESE DIFFERENT A.I. CHARACTERS.
THE GAME IS TOTALLY FAMOUS. IT'S IKE A SOCIAL PHENOMENON.

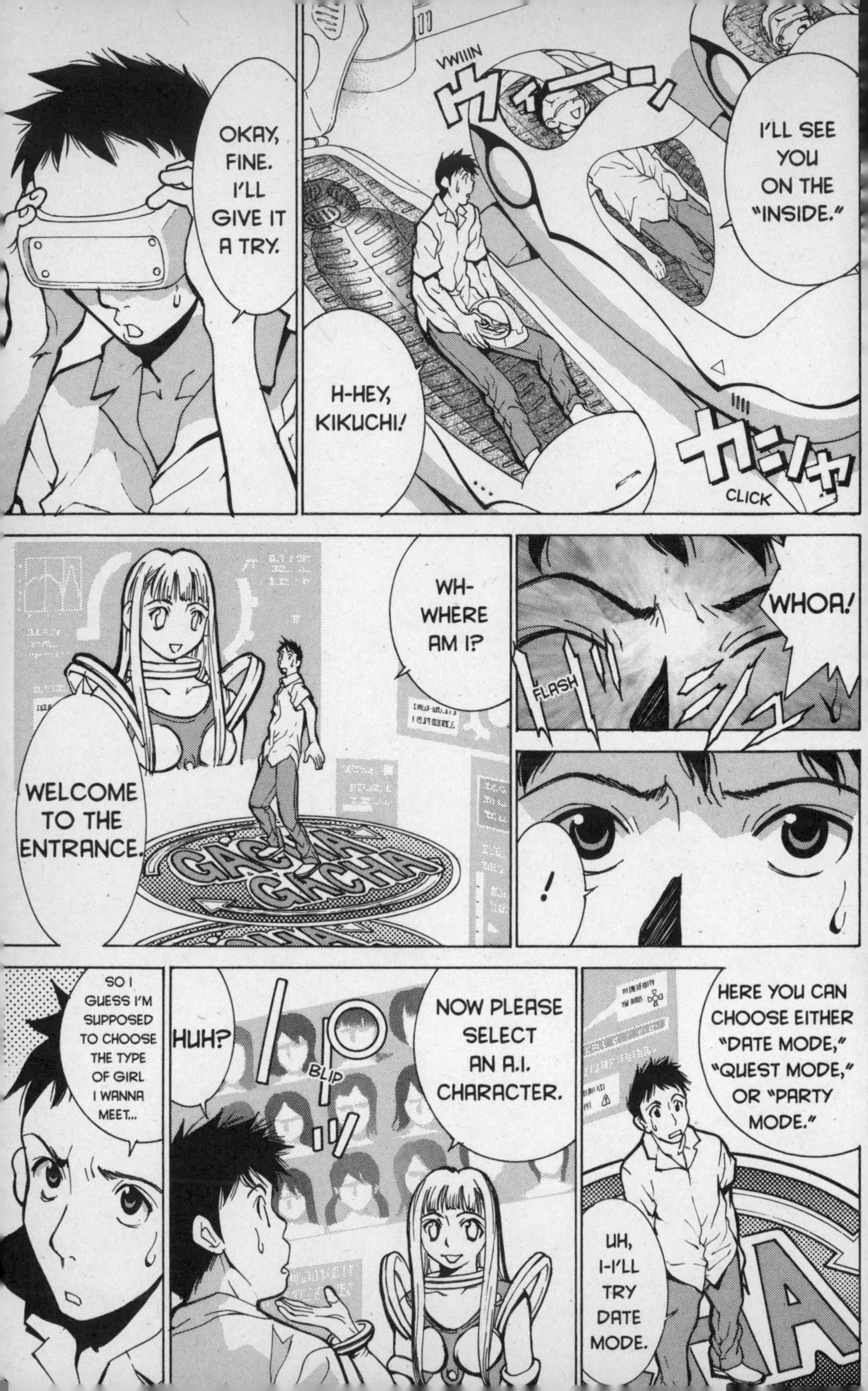
I'LL SEE YOU ON THE "INSIDE."
VWIIIN
H-HEY, KIKUCHI!
CLICK
OKAY, FINE. I'LL GIVE IT A TRY.
WHOA!
FLASH
!
WH-WHERE AM I?
WELCOME TO THE ENTRANCE.
HERE YOU CAN CHOOSE EITHER "DATE MODE," "QUEST MODE," OR "PARTY MODE."
UH, I-I'LL TRY DATE MODE.
NOW PLEASE SELECT AN A.I. CHARACTER.
HUH?
BLIP
SO I GUESS I'M SUPPOSED TO CHOOSE THE TYPE OF GIRL I WANNA MEET...

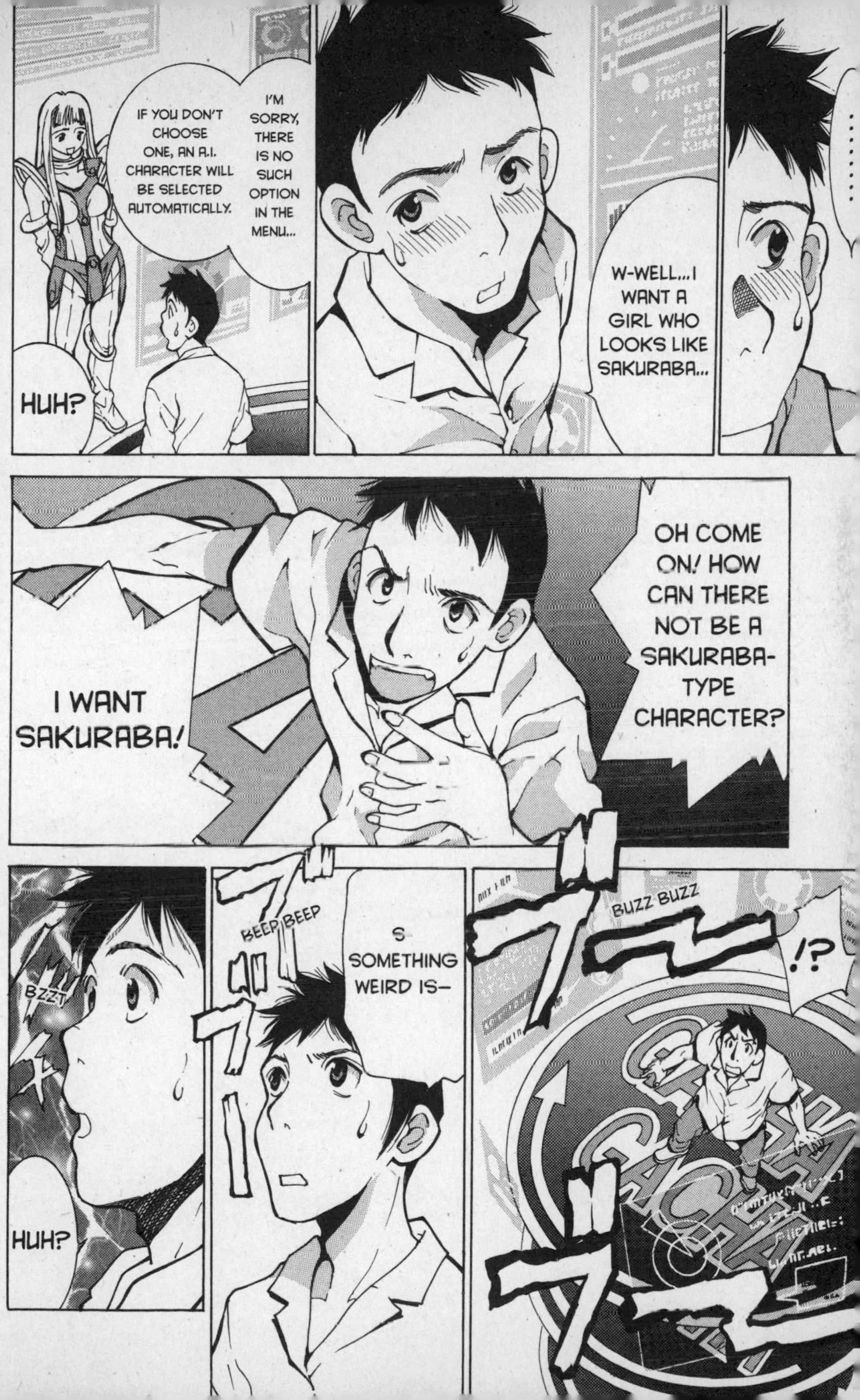
W-WELL...I WANT A GIRL WHO LOOKS LIKE SAKURABA...
I'M SORRY, THERE IS NO SUCH OPTION IN THE MENU...
IF YOU DON'T CHOOSE ONE, AN A.I. CHARACTER WILL BE SELECTED AUTOMATICALLY.
HUH?
OH COME ON! HOW CAN THERE NOT BE A SAKURABA-TYPE CHARACTER?
I WANT SAKURABA!
BUZZ BUZZ
!?
BEEP BEEP
S-SOMETHING WEIRD IS—
BZZT
HUH?

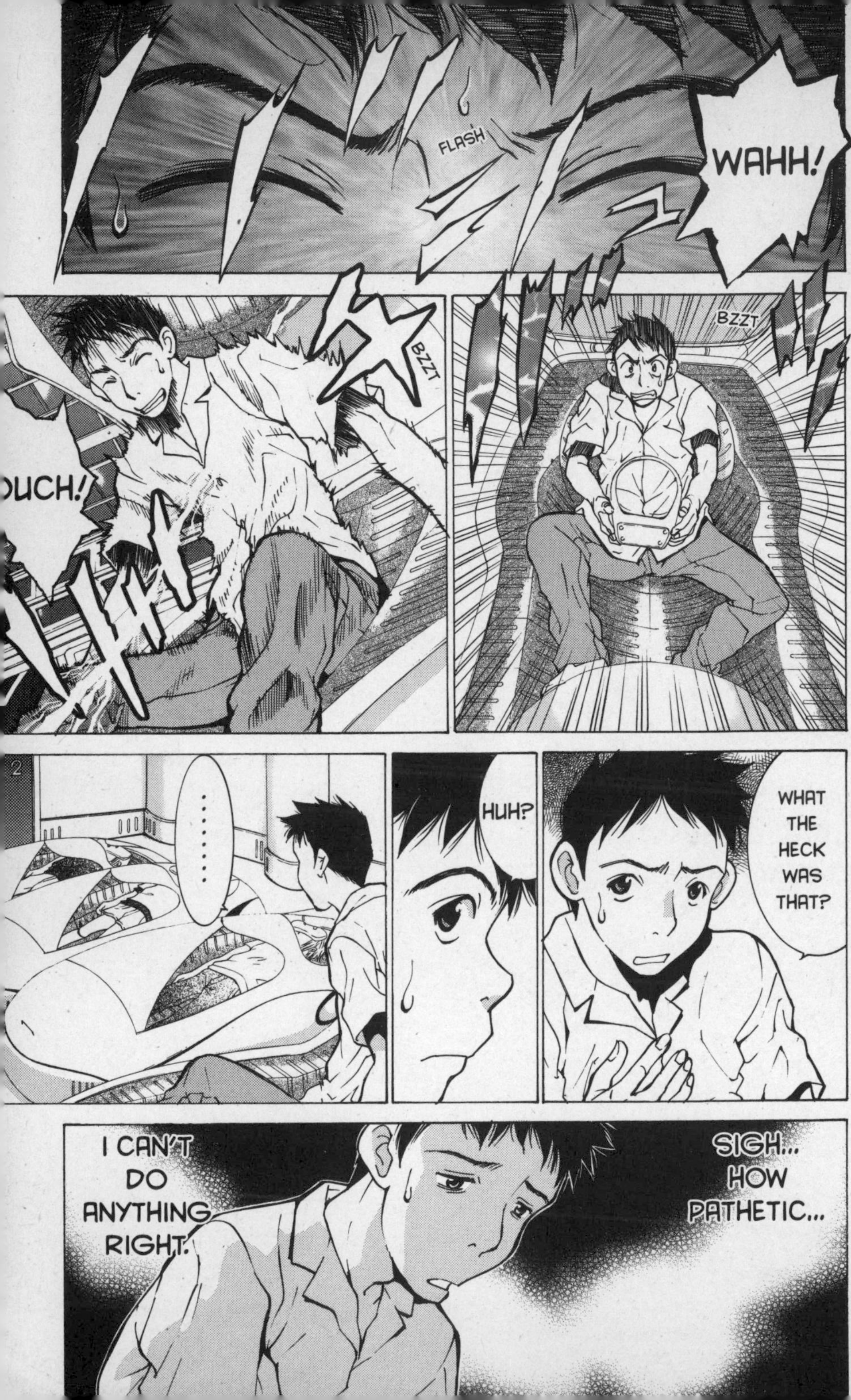
WAHH!
FLASH
BZZT
BZZT
OUCH!
WHAT THE HECK WAS THAT?
HUH?
....
SIGH... HOW PATHETIC...
I CAN'T DO ANYTHING RIGHT.

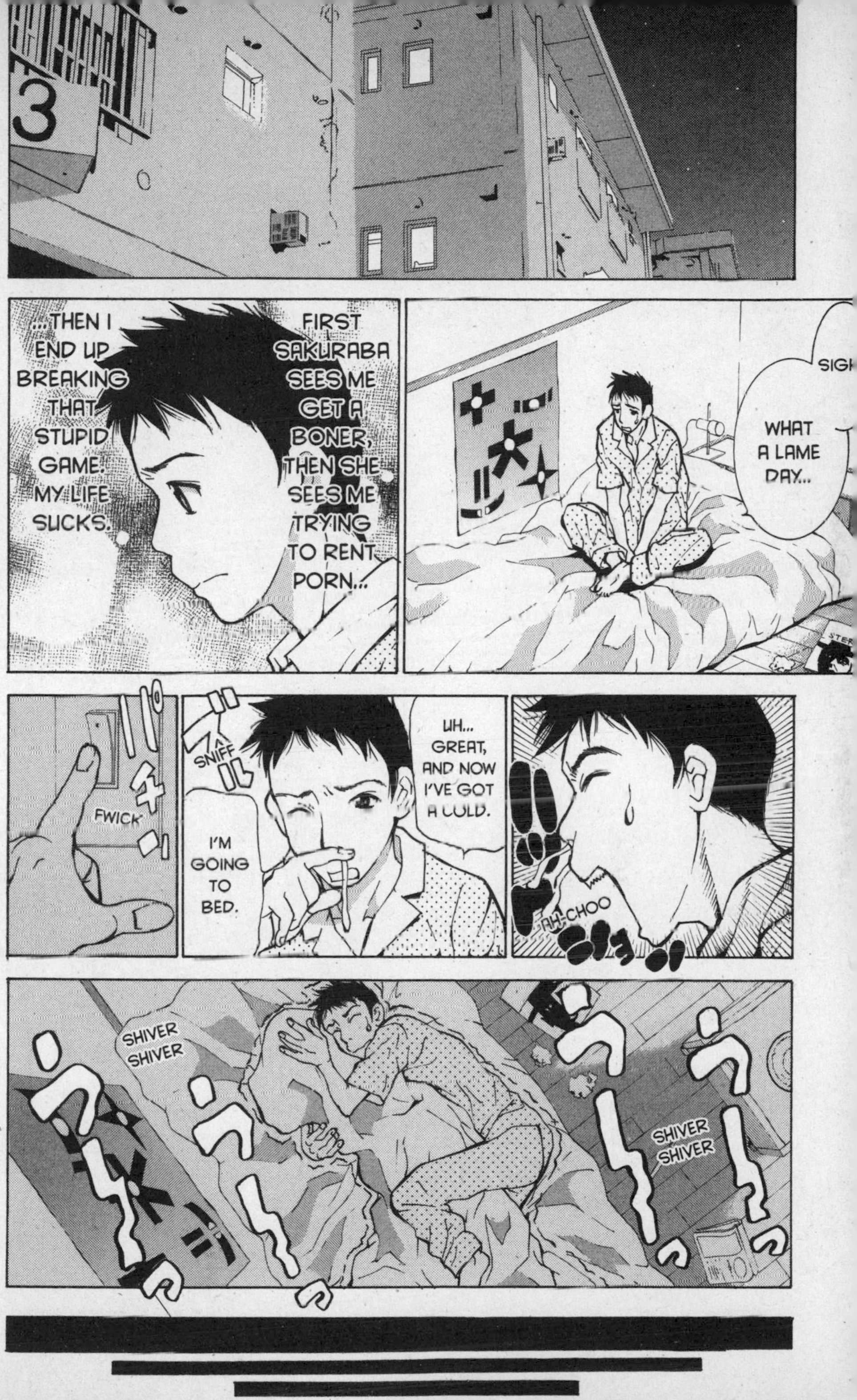
SIG
WHAT A LAME DAY...
FIRST SAKURABA SEES ME GET A BONER, THEN SHE SEES ME TRYING TO RENT PORN...
...THEN I END UP BREAKING THAT STUPID GAME. MY LIFE SUCKS.
AH-CHOO
UH... GREAT, AND NOW I'VE GOT A COLD.
SNIFF
I'M GOING TO BED.
FWICK
SHIVER SHIVER
SHIVER SHIVER

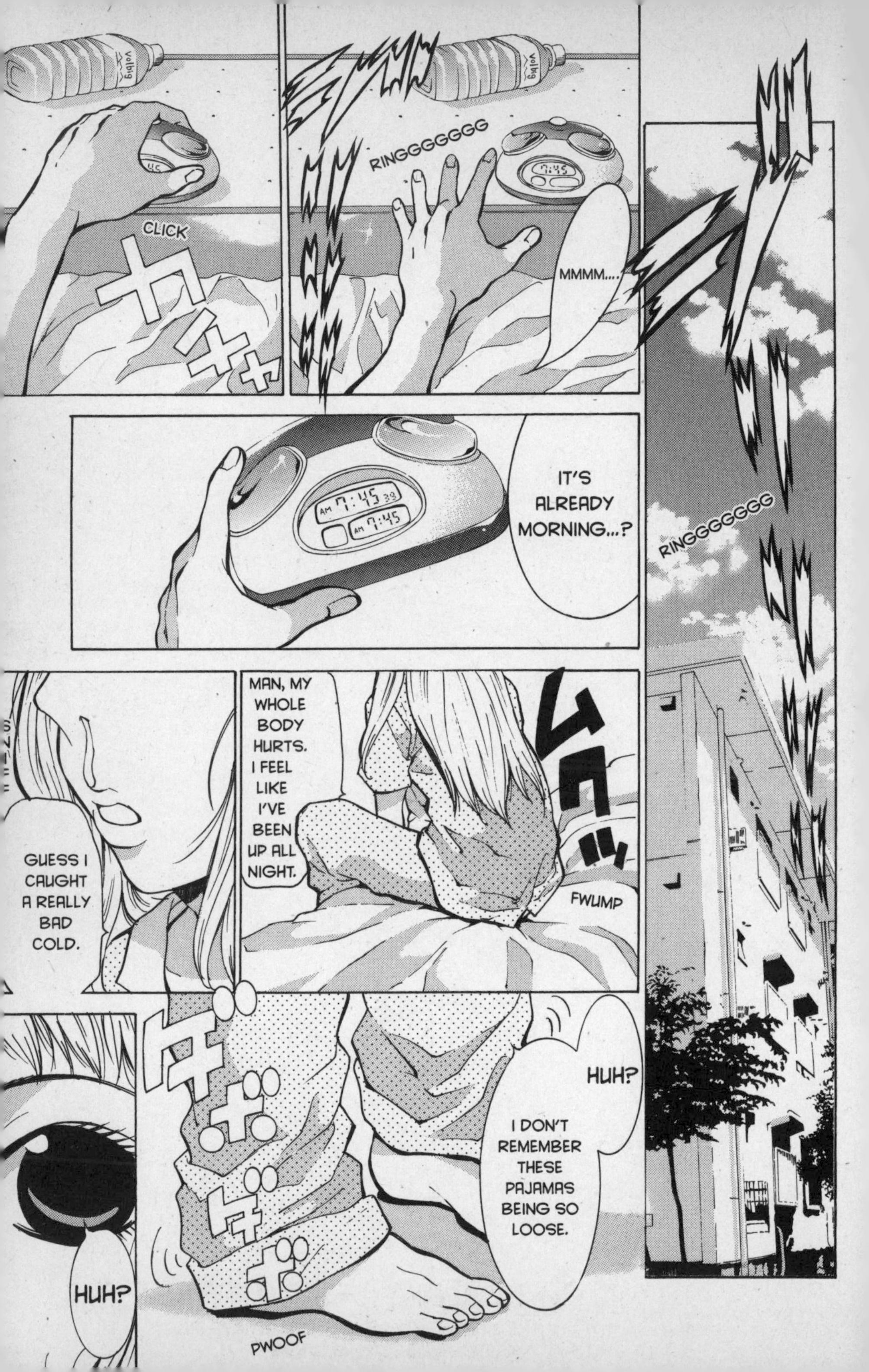
RINGGGGGGG
RINGGGGGGG
MMMM....
CLICK
IT'S ALREADY MORNING...?
MAN, MY WHOLE BODY HURTS. I FEEL LIKE I'VE BEEN UP ALL NIGHT.
FWUMP
GUESS I CAUGHT A REALLY BAD COLD.
HUH?
I DON'T REMEMBER THESE PAJAMAS BEING SO LOOSE.
PWOOF
HUH?

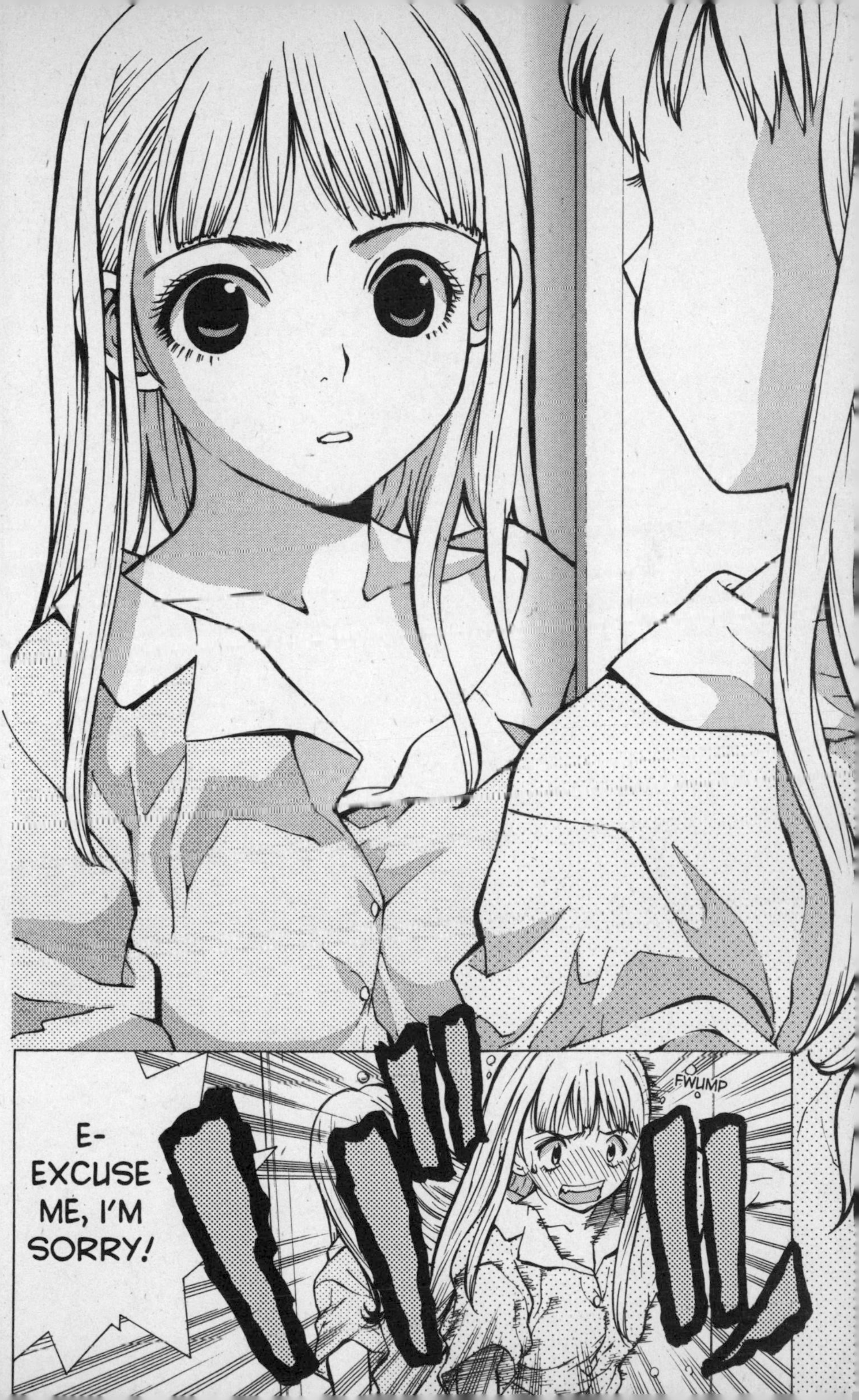
FWUMP
E-
EXCUSE
ME, I'M
SORRY!

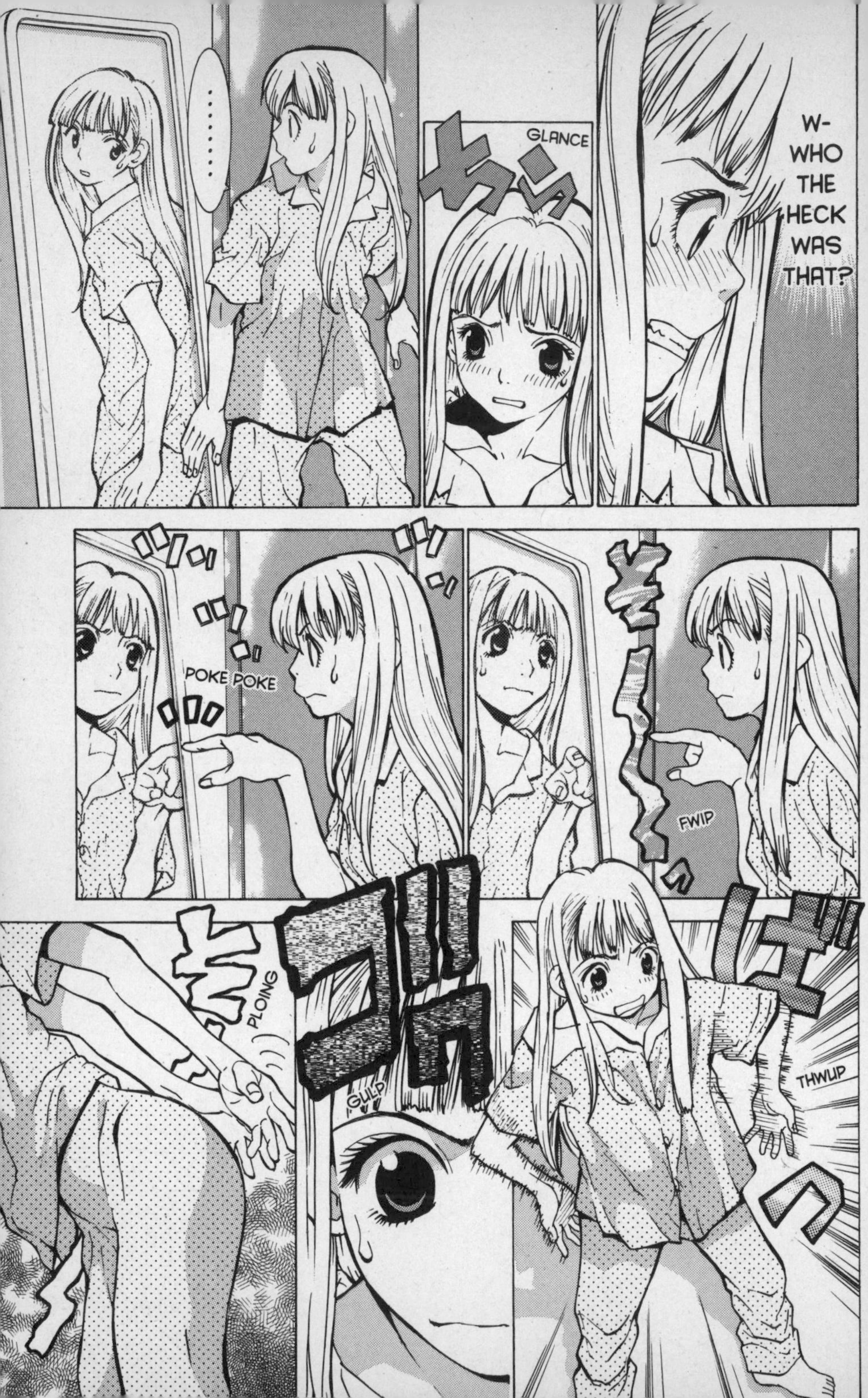
W- WHO THE HECK WAS THAT?
GLANCE
......
FWIP
POKE POKE
THWUP
GULP
PLOING

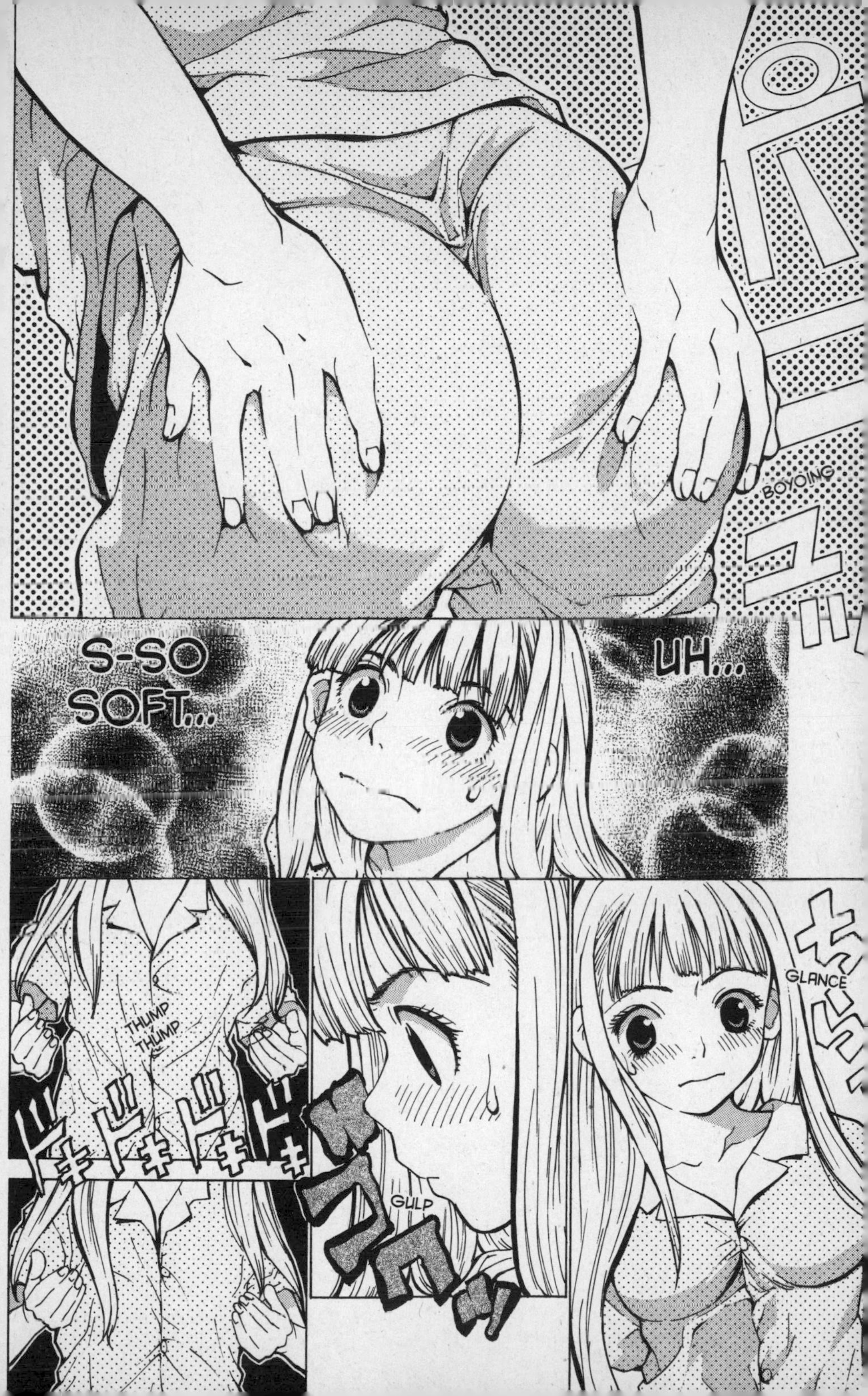
BOYOING
UH...
S-SO SOFT...
GLANCE
GULP
THUMP THUMP

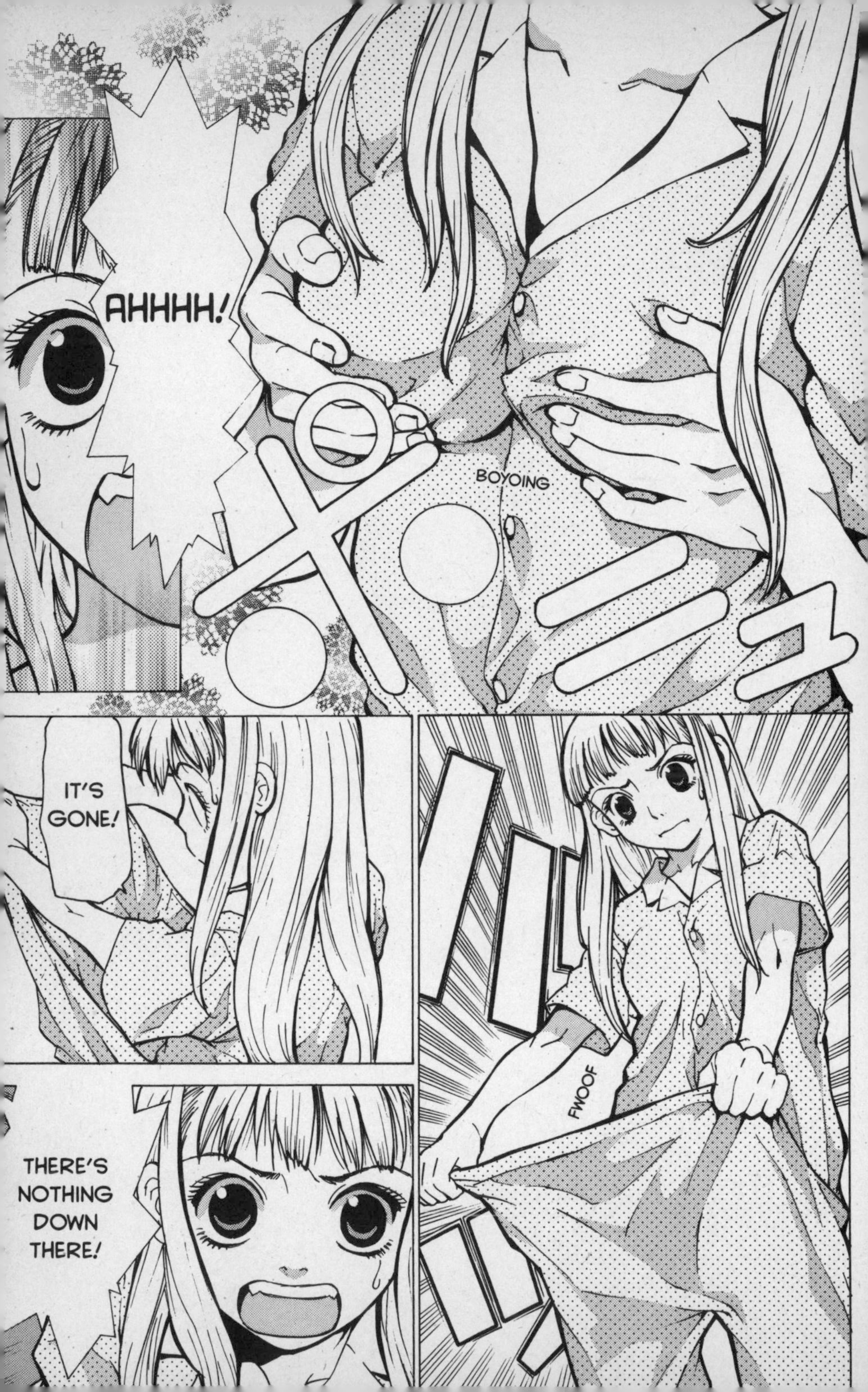
AHHHH!
BOYOING
FWOOF
IT'S GONE!
THERE'S NOTHING DOWN THERE!

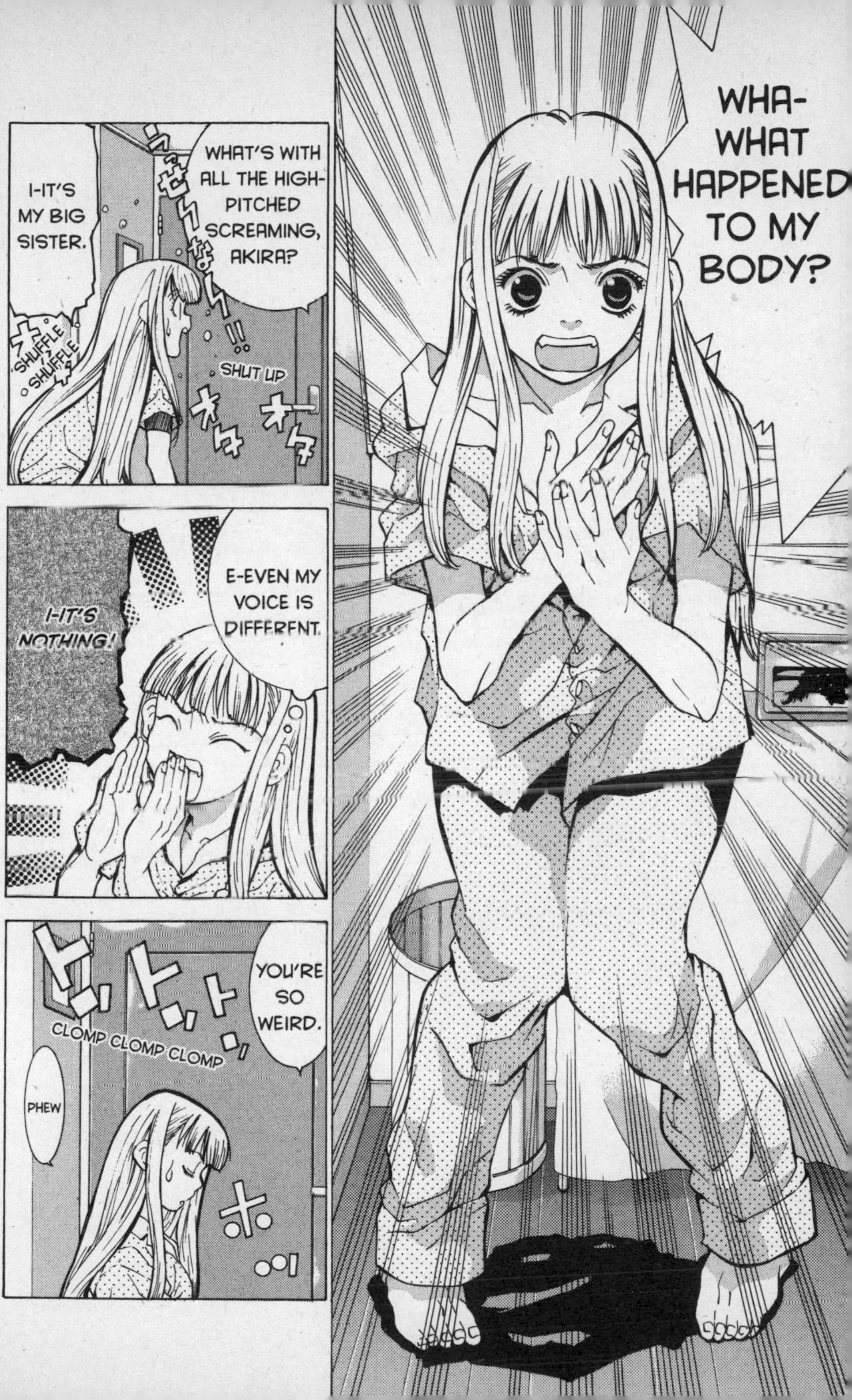
WHA-WHAT HAPPENED TO MY BODY?
WHAT'S WITH ALL THE HIGH-PITCHED SCREAMING, AKIRA?
I-IT'S MY BIG SISTER.
SHUT UP
SHUFFLE SHUFFLE
E-EVEN MY VOICE IS DIFFERENT.
I-IT'S NOTHING!
YOU'RE SO WEIRD.
CLOMP CLOMP CLOMP
PHEW

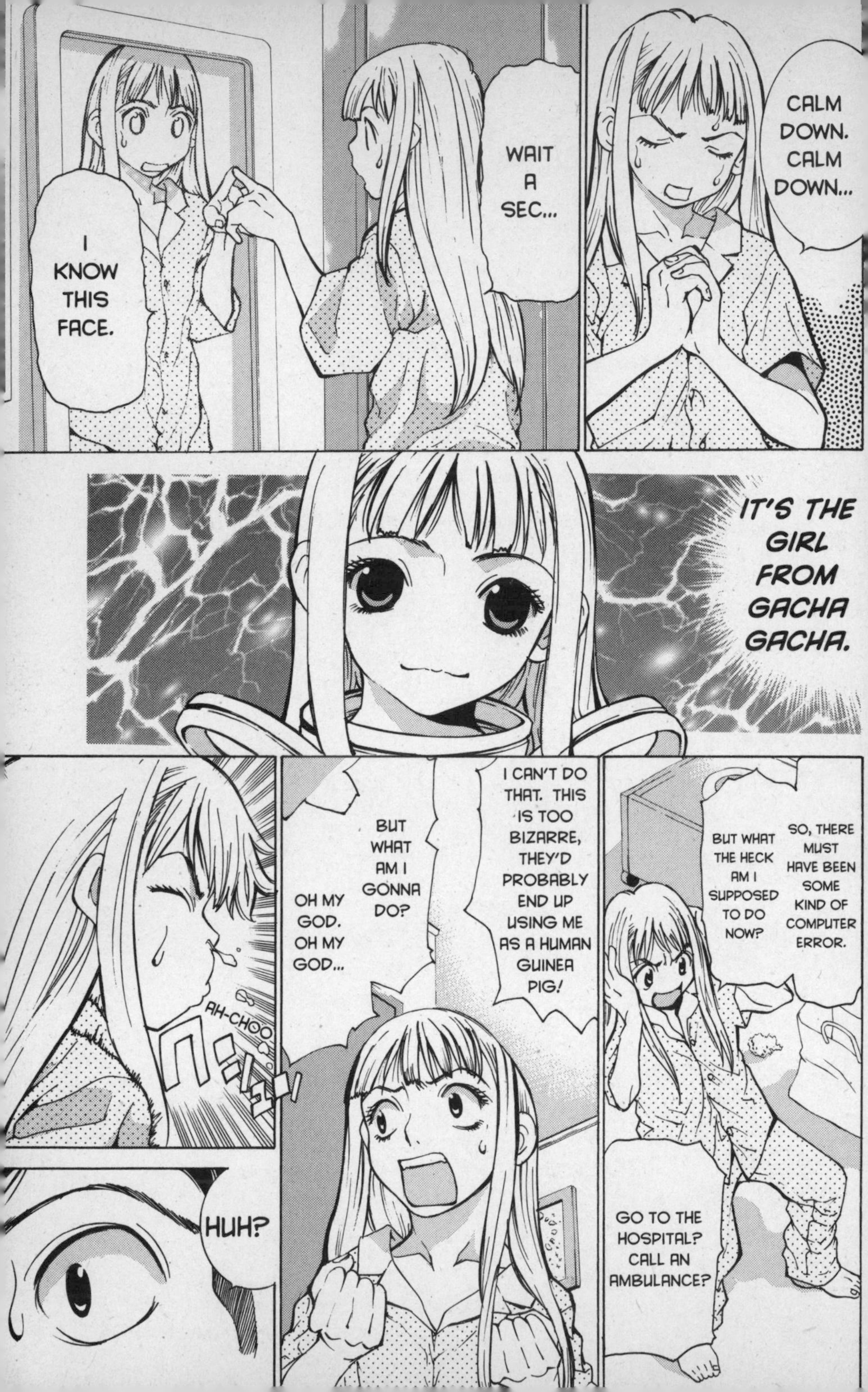
CALM DOWN. CALM DOWN...
WAIT A SEC...
I KNOW THIS FACE.
IT'S THE GIRL FROM GACHA GACHA.
SO, THERE MUST HAVE BEEN SOME KIND OF COMPUTER ERROR.
BUT WHAT THE HECK AM I SUPPOSED TO DO NOW?
GO TO THE HOSPITAL? CALL AN AMBULANCE?
I CAN'T DO THAT. THIS IS TOO BIZARRE, THEY'D PROBABLY END UP USING ME AS A HUMAN GUINEA PIG!
BUT WHAT AM I GONNA DO?
OH MY GOD. OH MY GOD...
AH-CHOO
HUH?

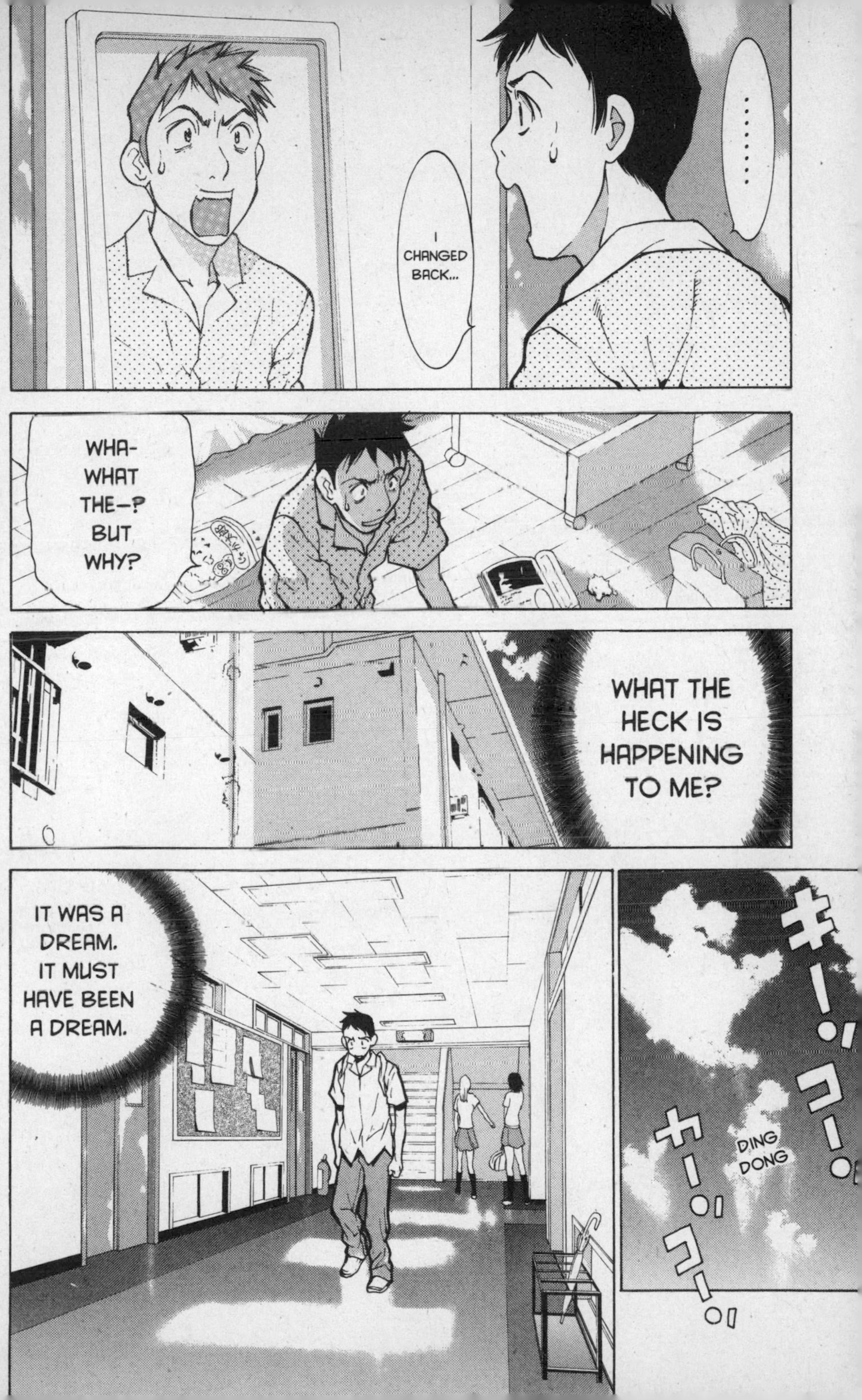
......
I CHANGED BACK...
WHA- WHAT THE-? BUT WHY?
WHAT THE HECK IS HAPPENING TO ME?
DING DONG
IT WAS A DREAM. IT MUST HAVE BEEN A DREAM.

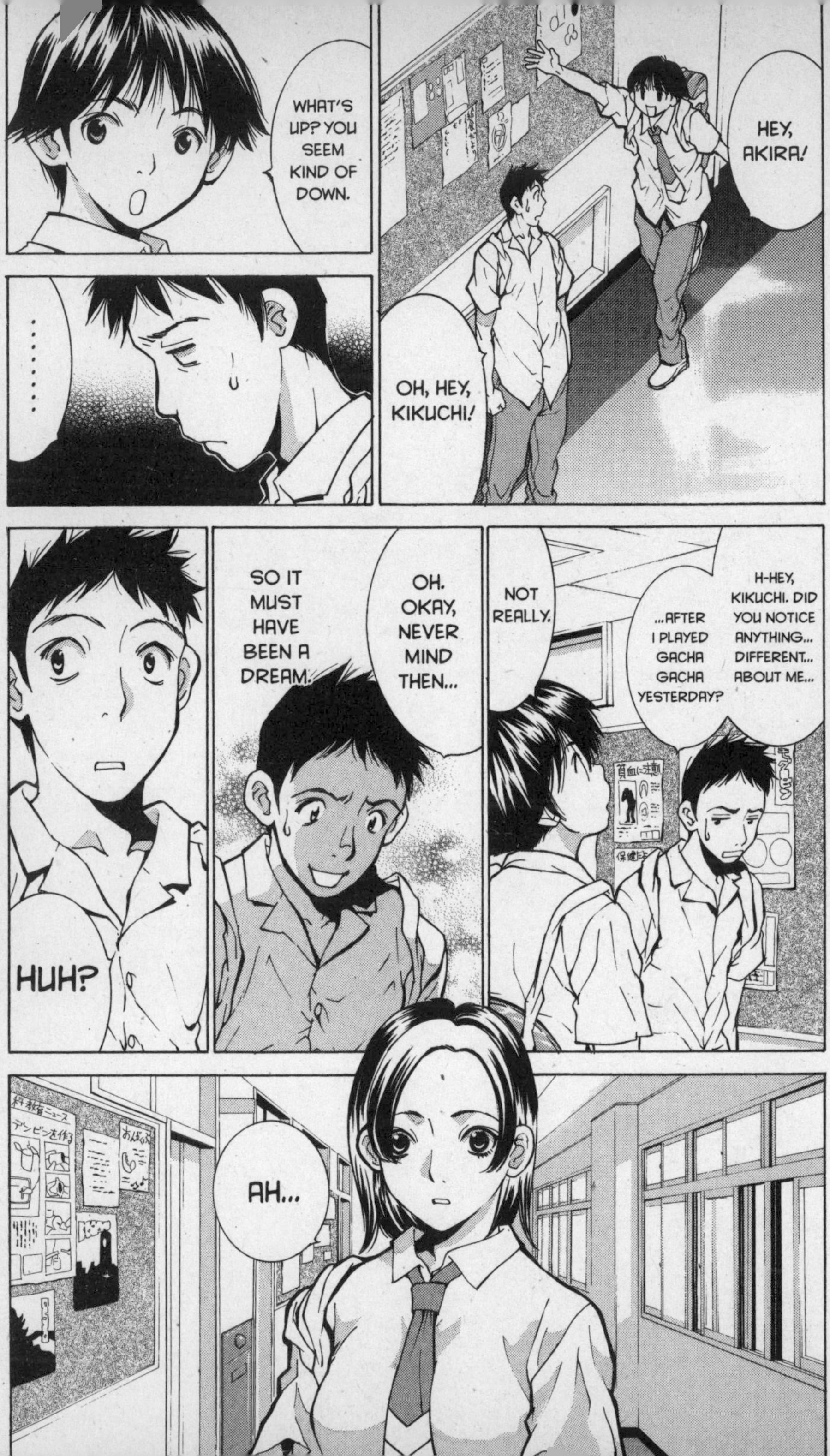
HEY, AKIRA!
OH, HEY, KIKUCHI!
WHAT'S UP? YOU SEEM KIND OF DOWN.
......
H-HEY, KIKUCHI. DID YOU NOTICE ANYTHING... DIFFERENT... ABOUT ME...
...AFTER I PLAYED GACHA GACHA YESTERDAY?
NOT REALLY.
OH. OKAY, NEVER MIND THEN...
SO IT MUST HAVE BEEN A DREAM.
HUH?
AH...

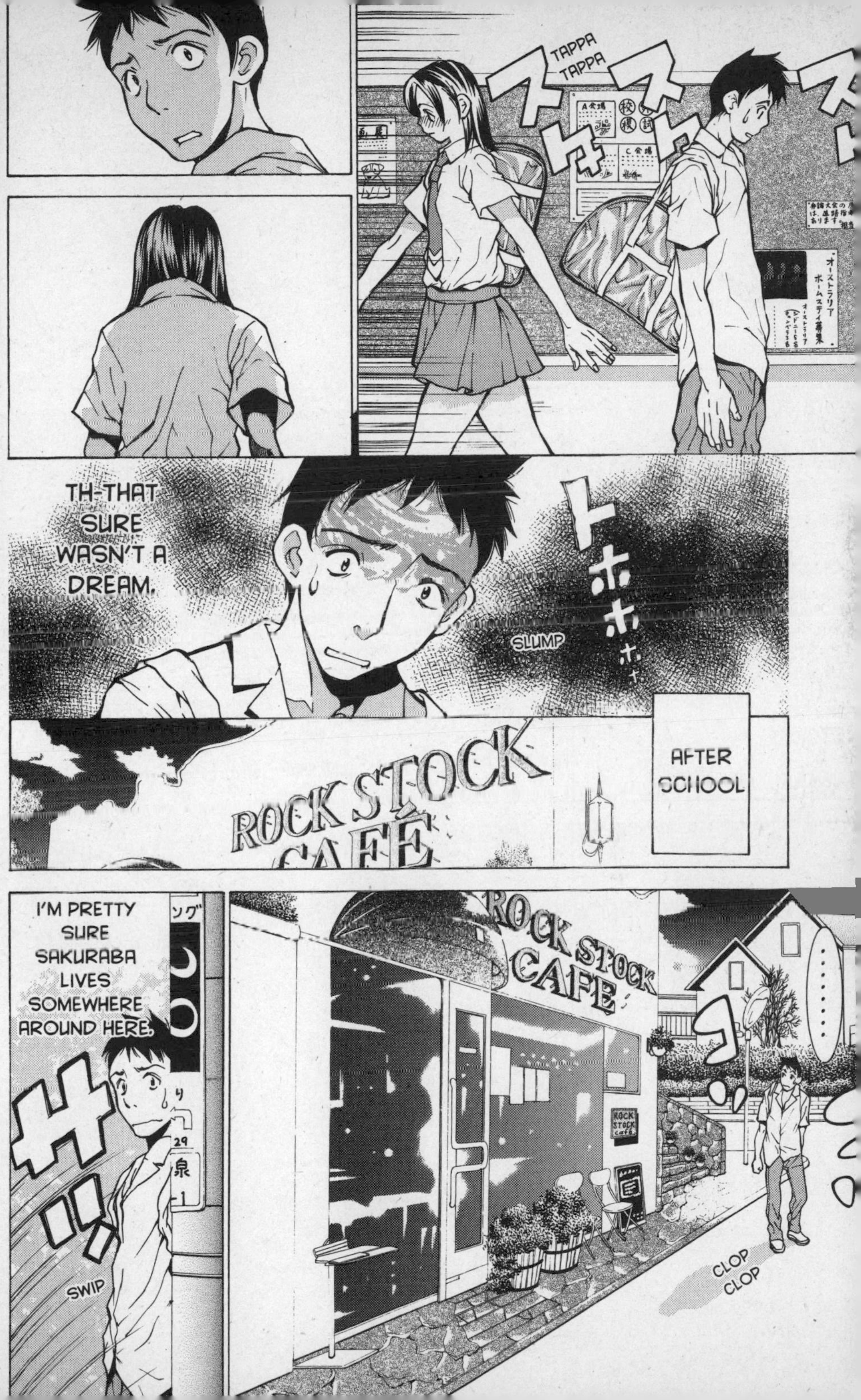
TAPPA
TAPPA
TH-THAT SURE WASN'T A DREAM.
SLUMP
AFTER SCHOOL
ROCK STOCK CAFÉ
ROCK STOCK CAFE
......
CLOP
CLOP
I'M PRETTY SURE SAKURABA LIVES SOMEWHERE AROUND HERE.
SWIP

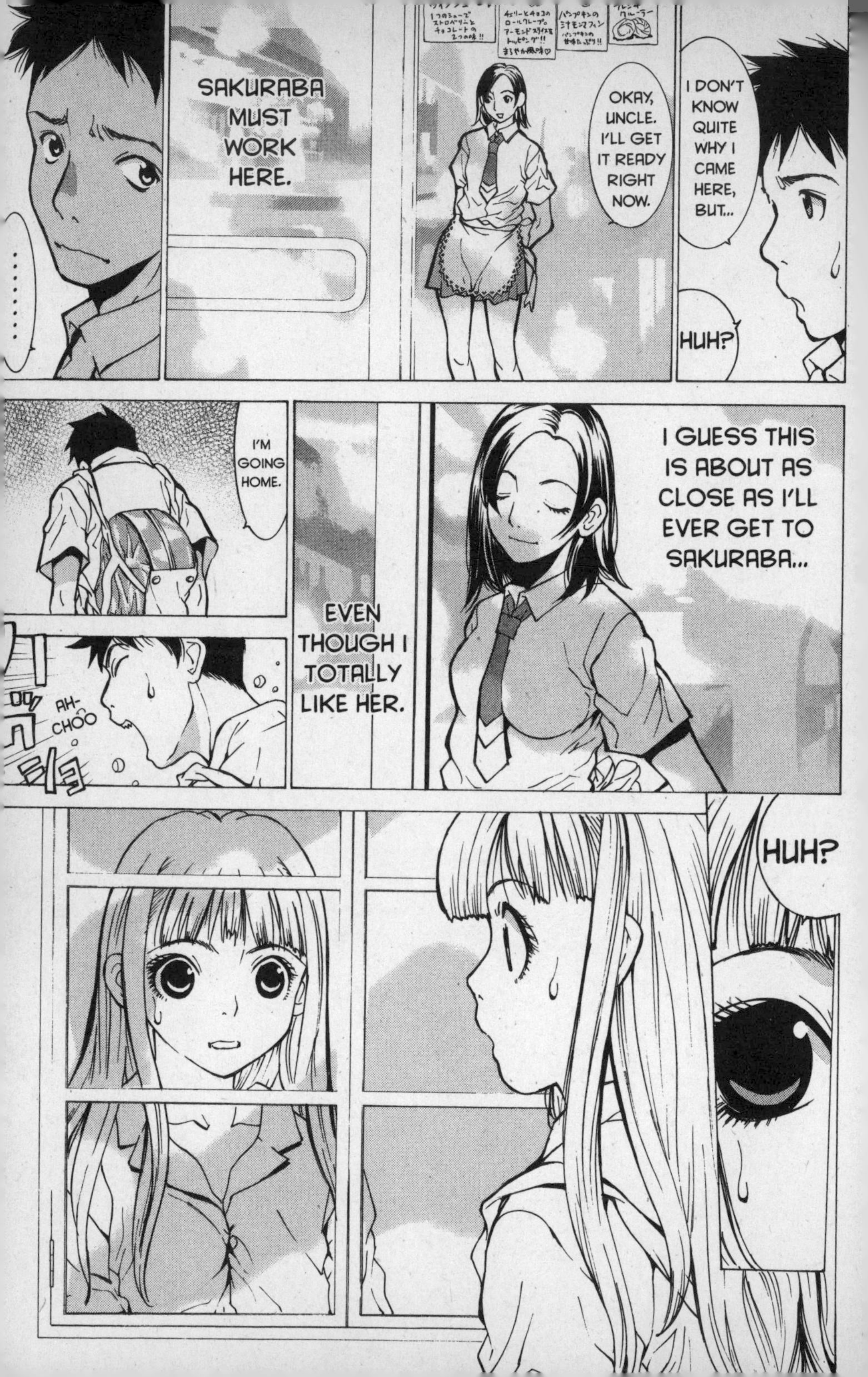
I DON'T KNOW QUITE WHY I CAME HERE, BUT...
HUH?
OKAY, UNCLE. I'LL GET IT READY RIGHT NOW.
SAKURABA MUST WORK HERE.
......
I GUESS THIS IS ABOUT AS CLOSE AS I'LL EVER GET TO SAKURABA...
EVEN THOUGH I TOTALLY LIKE HER.
I'M GOING HOME.
AH-CHOO
HUH?

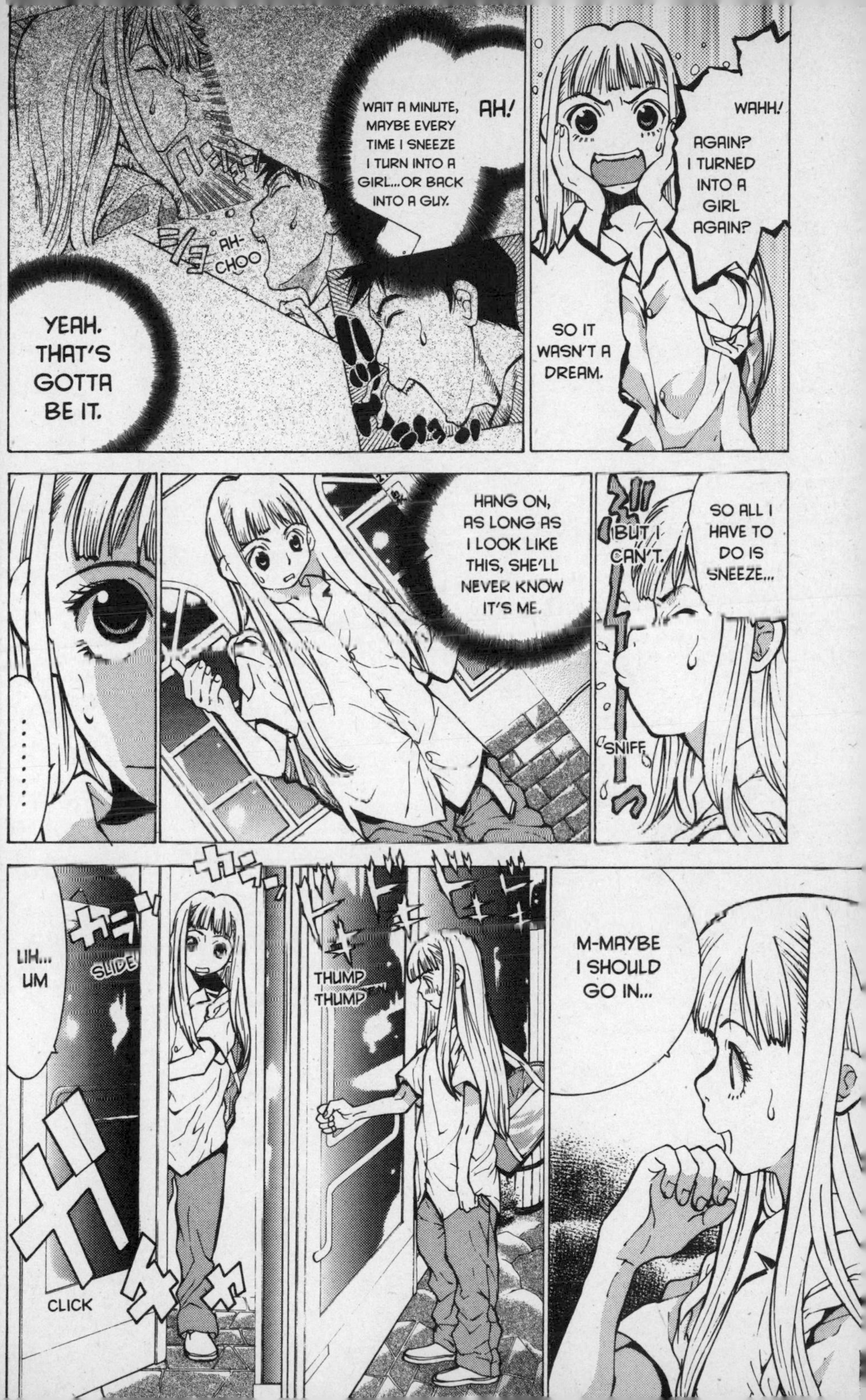
WAHH!
AGAIN? I TURNED INTO A GIRL AGAIN?
SO IT WASN'T A DREAM.
AH!
WAIT A MINUTE, MAYBE EVERY TIME I SNEEZE I TURN INTO A GIRL...OR BACK INTO A GUY.
AH-CHOO
YEAH. THAT'S GOTTA BE IT.
SO ALL I HAVE TO DO IS SNEEZE...
BUT I CAN'T.
SNIFF
HANG ON, AS LONG AS I LOOK LIKE THIS, SHE'LL NEVER KNOW IT'S ME.
......
M-MAYBE I SHOULD GO IN...
THUMP THUMP
UH... UM
SLIDE
CLICK

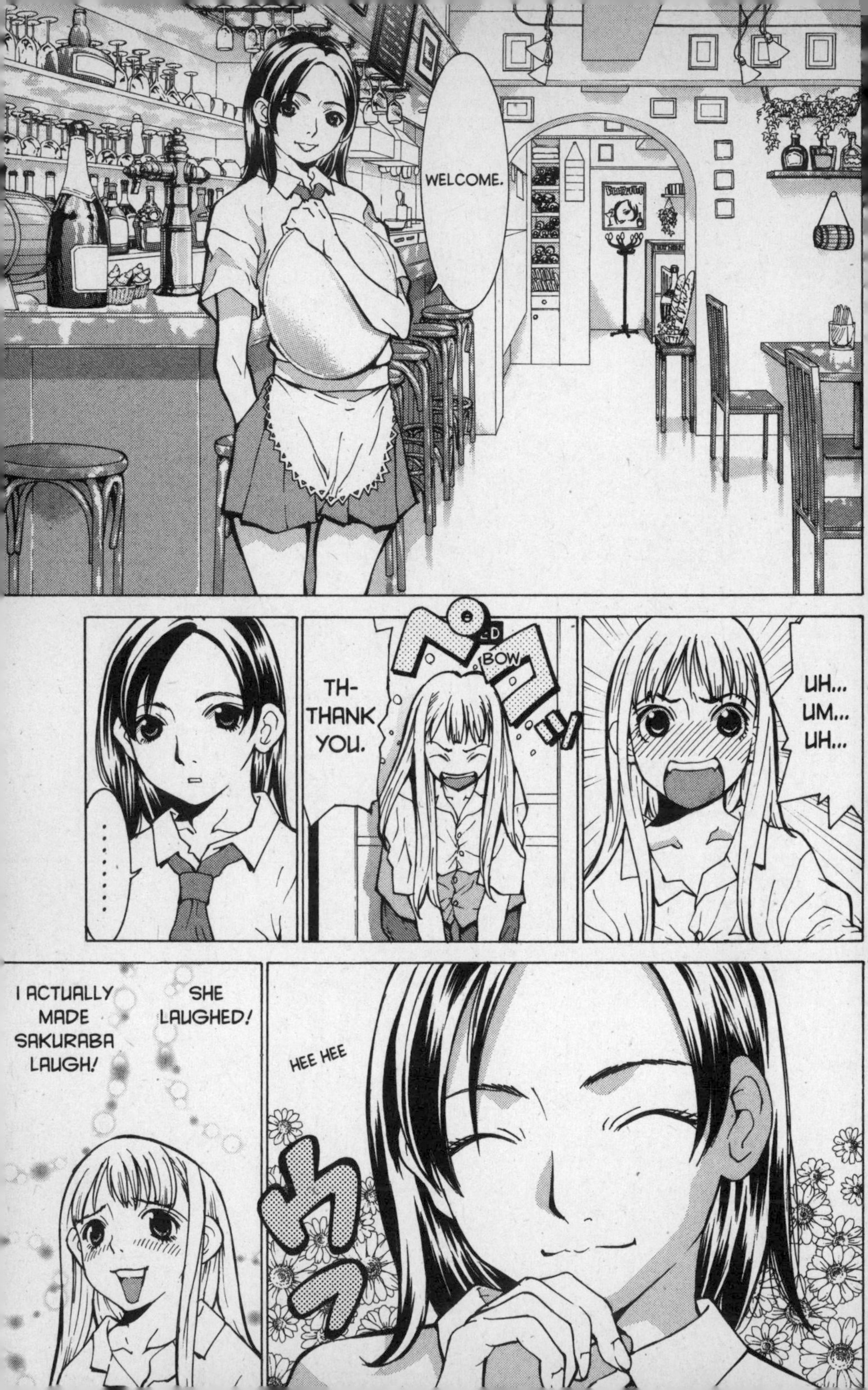
WELCOME.
UH... UM... UH...
TH- THANK YOU.
BOW
......
HEE HEE
SHE LAUGHED!
I ACTUALLY MADE SAKURABA LAUGH!

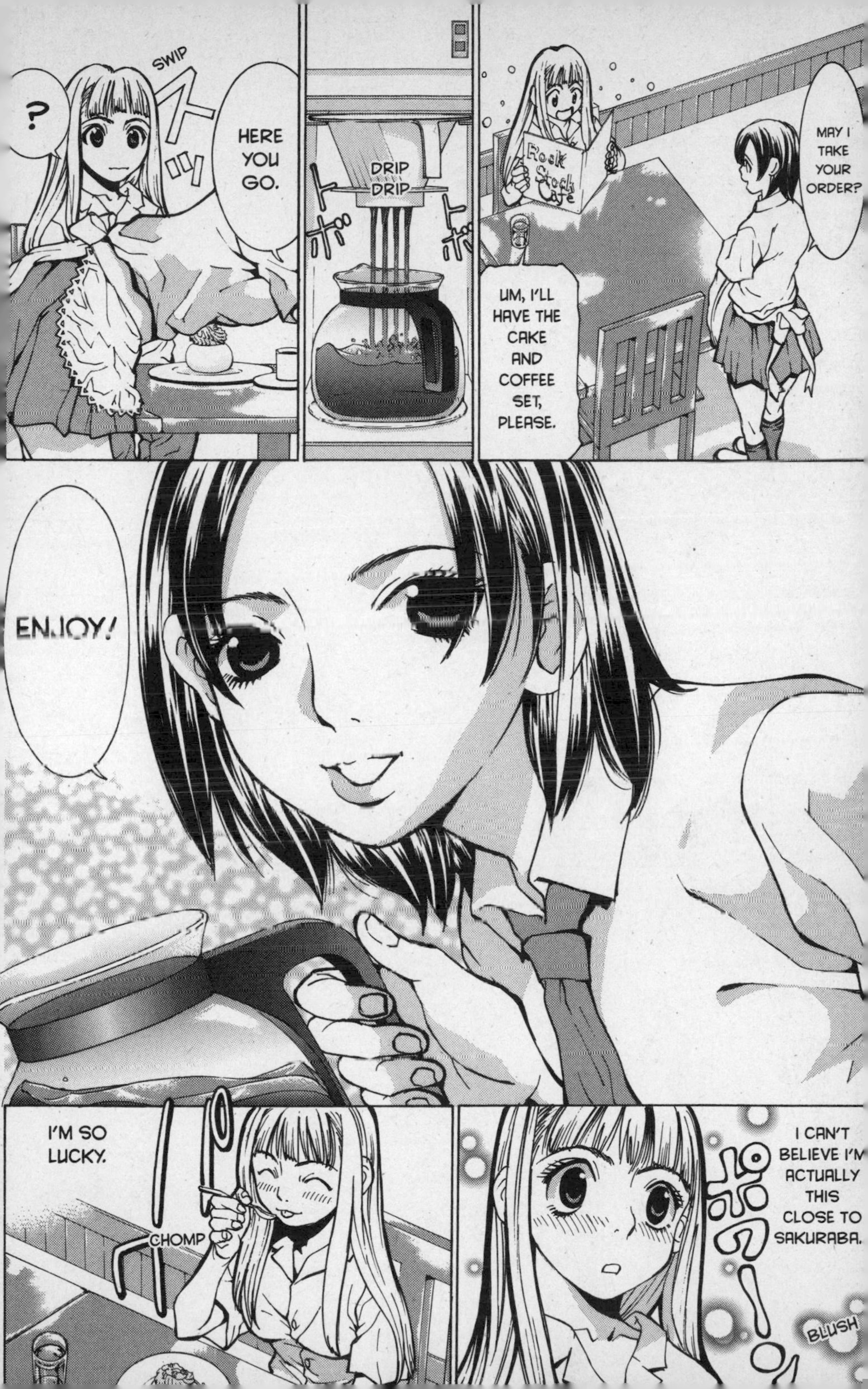
MAY I TAKE YOUR ORDER?
Rosik Stock Cafe
UM, I'LL HAVE THE CAKE AND COFFEE SET, PLEASE.
DRIP DRIP
SWIP
HERE YOU GO.
?
ENJOY!
I CAN'T BELIEVE I'M ACTUALLY THIS CLOSE TO SAKURABA.
BLUSH
I'M SO LUCKY.
CHOMP

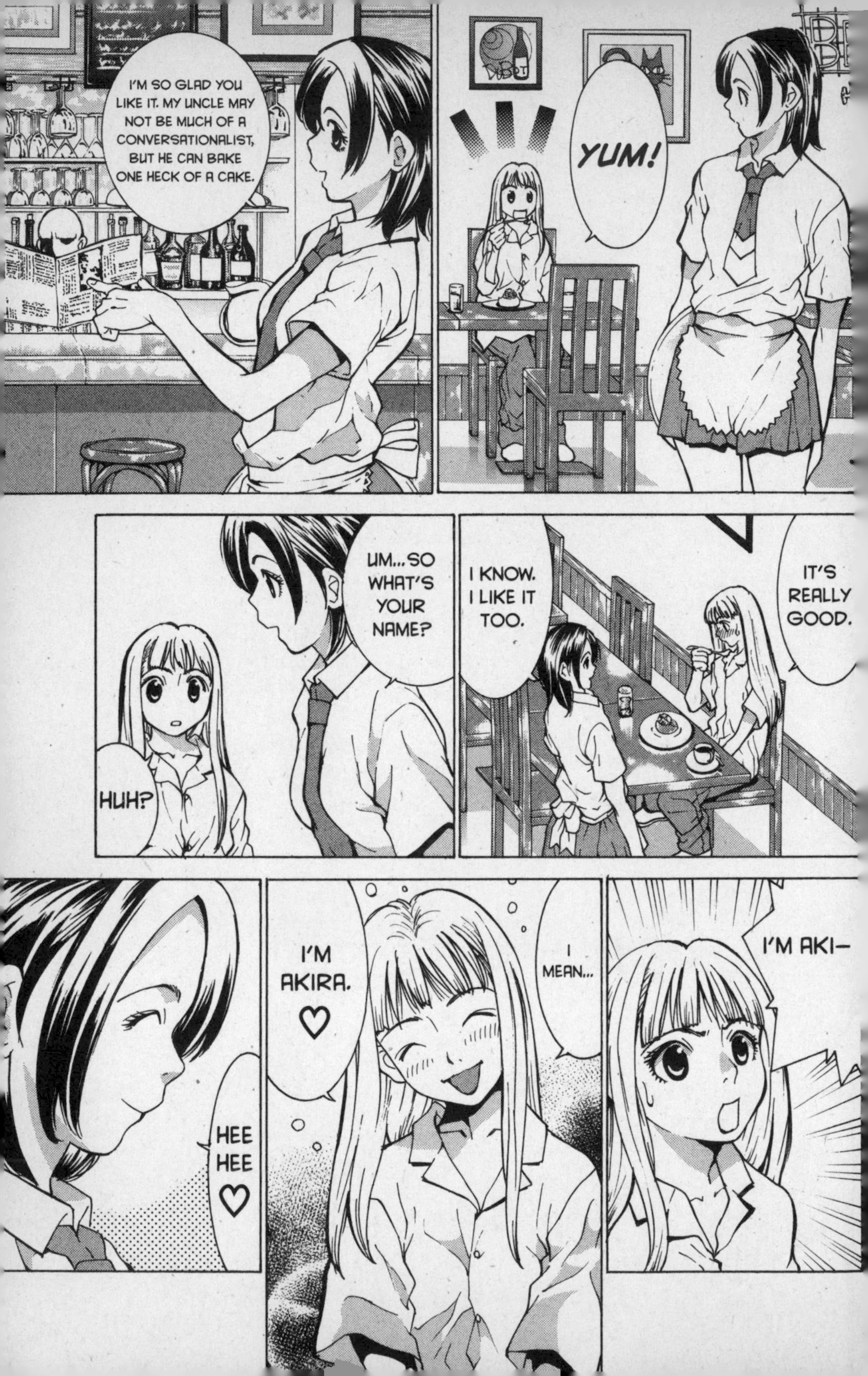
YUM!
I'M SO GLAD YOU LIKE IT. MY UNCLE MAY NOT BE MUCH OF A CONVERSATIONALIST, BUT HE CAN BAKE ONE HECK OF A CAKE.
IT'S REALLY GOOD.
I KNOW. I LIKE IT TOO.
UM...SO WHAT'S YOUR NAME?
HUH?
I'M AKI—
I MEAN...
I'M AKIRA. ♡
HEE HEE ♡

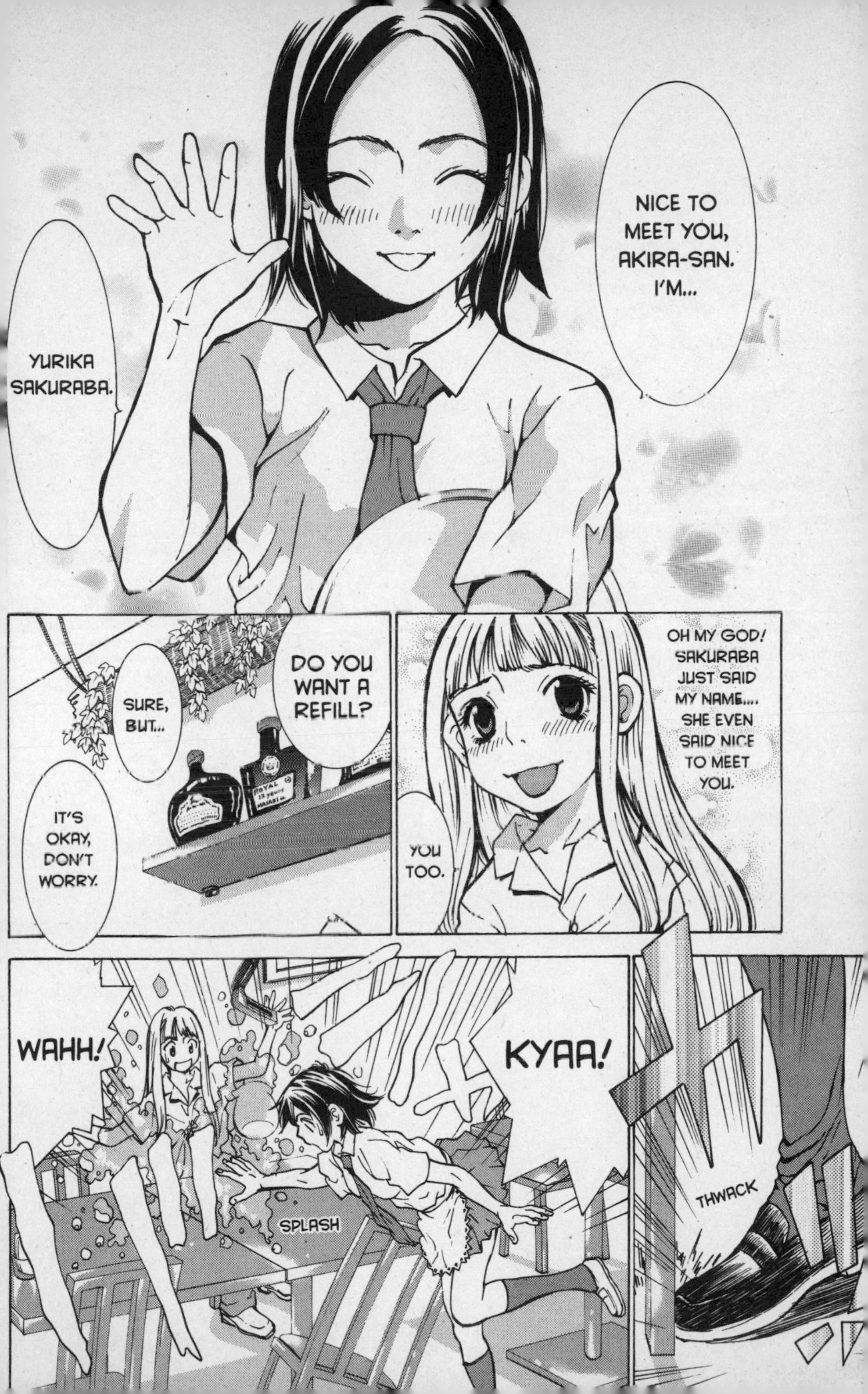
NICE TO MEET YOU, AKIRA-SAN. I'M...
YURIKA SAKURABA.
OH MY GOD! SAKURABA JUST SAID MY NAME.... SHE EVEN SAID NICE TO MEET YOU.
YOU TOO.
DO YOU WANT A REFILL?
SURE, BUT...
IT'S OKAY, DON'T WORRY.
THWACK
KYAA!
WAHH!
SPLASH

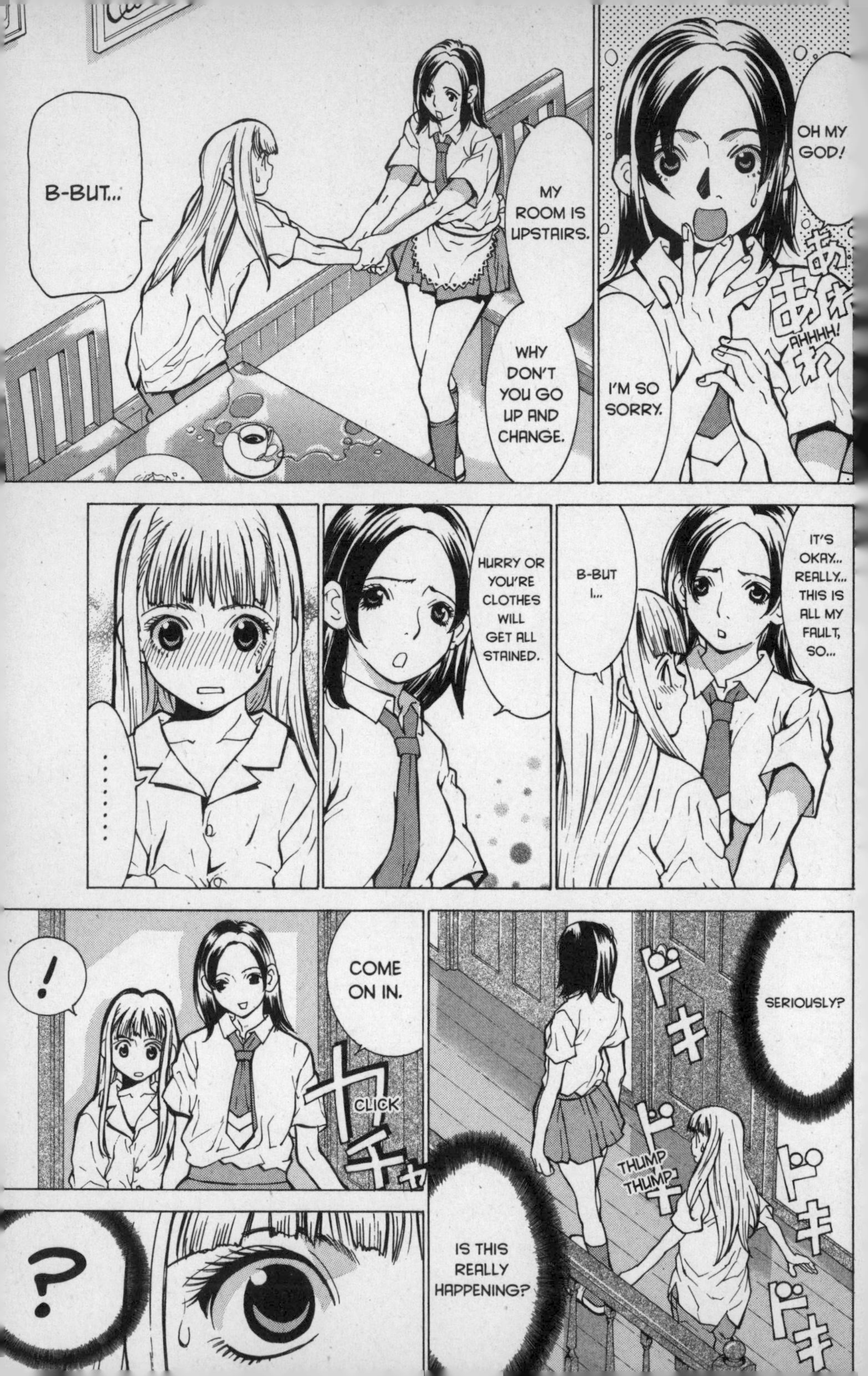
OH MY GOD!
あああ
AHHHH!
I'M SO SORRY.
MY ROOM IS UPSTAIRS.
WHY DON'T YOU GO UP AND CHANGE.
B-BUT...
IT'S OKAY... REALLY... THIS IS ALL MY FAULT, SO...
B-BUT I...
HURRY OR YOU'RE CLOTHES WILL GET ALL STAINED.
......
SERIOUSLY?
ドキ
ドキ
THUMP THUMP
ドキ
ドキ
IS THIS REALLY HAPPENING?
COME ON IN.
!
ガチャ
CLICK
?

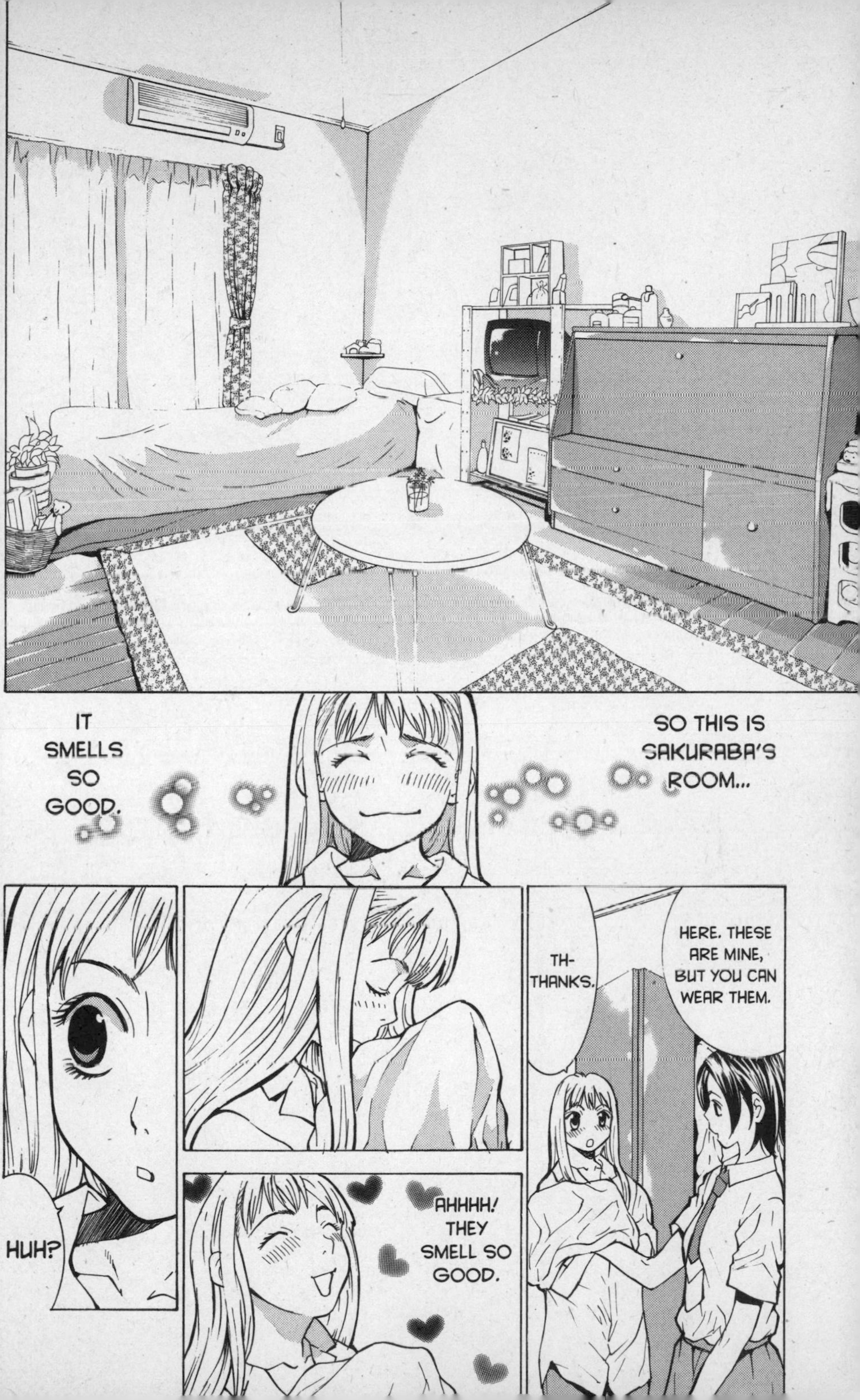
SO THIS IS SAKURABA'S ROOM...
IT SMELLS SO GOOD.
HERE. THESE ARE MINE, BUT YOU CAN WEAR THEM.
TH-THANKS.
AHHHH! THEY SMELL SO GOOD.
HUH?

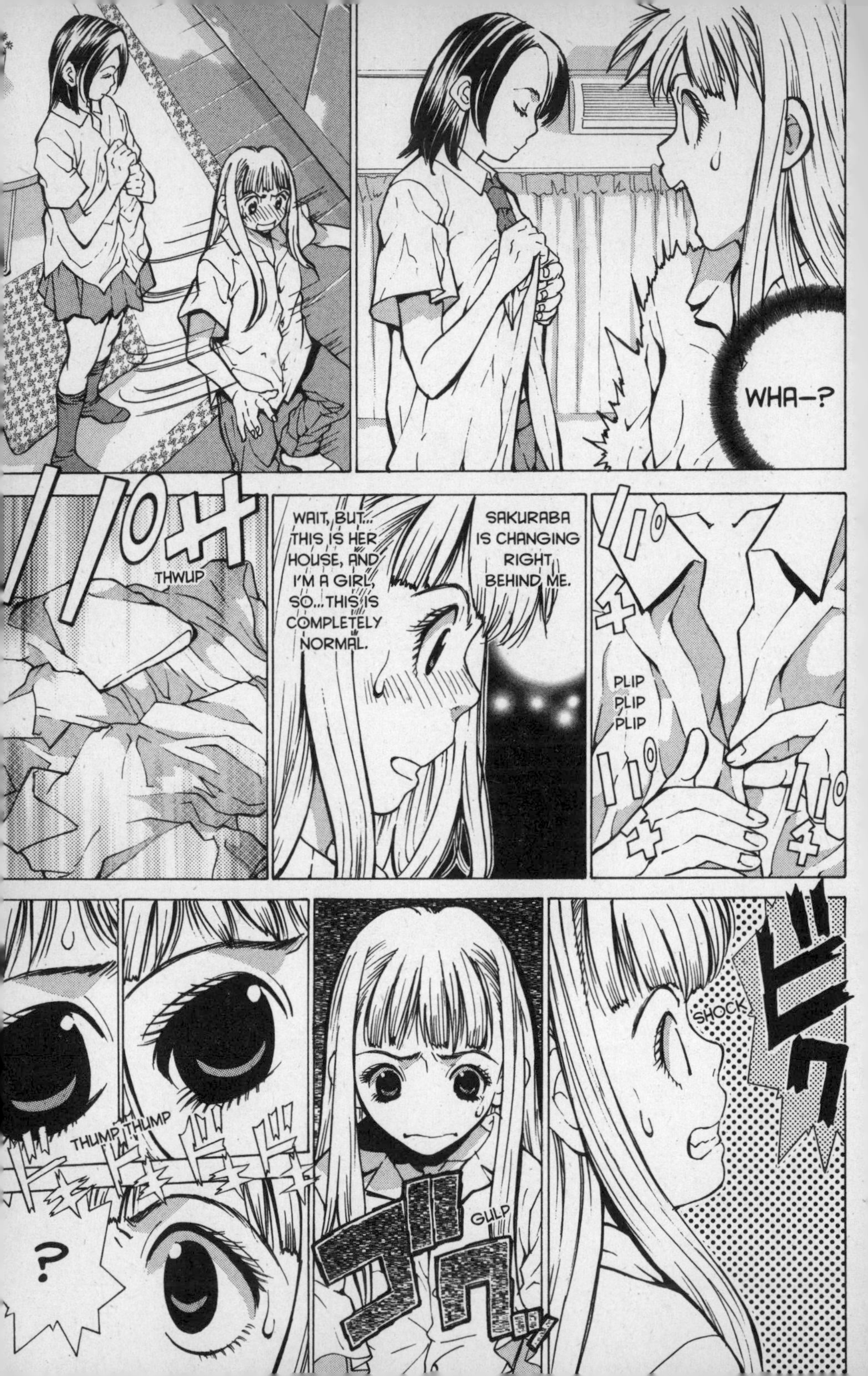
WHA-?
PLIP
PLIP
PLIP
SAKURABA IS CHANGING RIGHT BEHIND ME.
WAIT, BUT... THIS IS HER HOUSE, AND I'M A GIRL, SO... THIS IS COMPLETELY NORMAL.
THWUP
SHOCK
GULP
THUMP THUMP
?

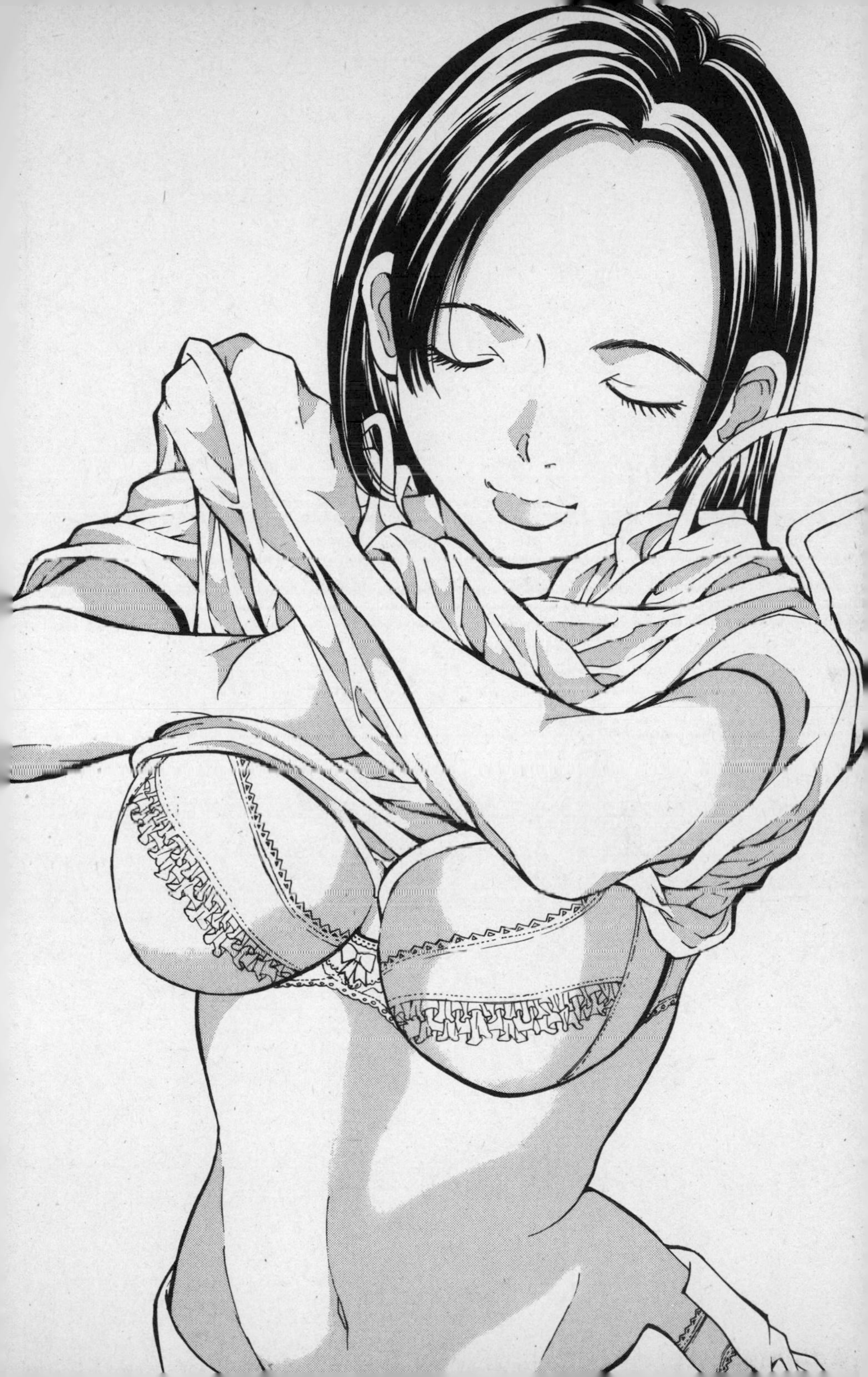

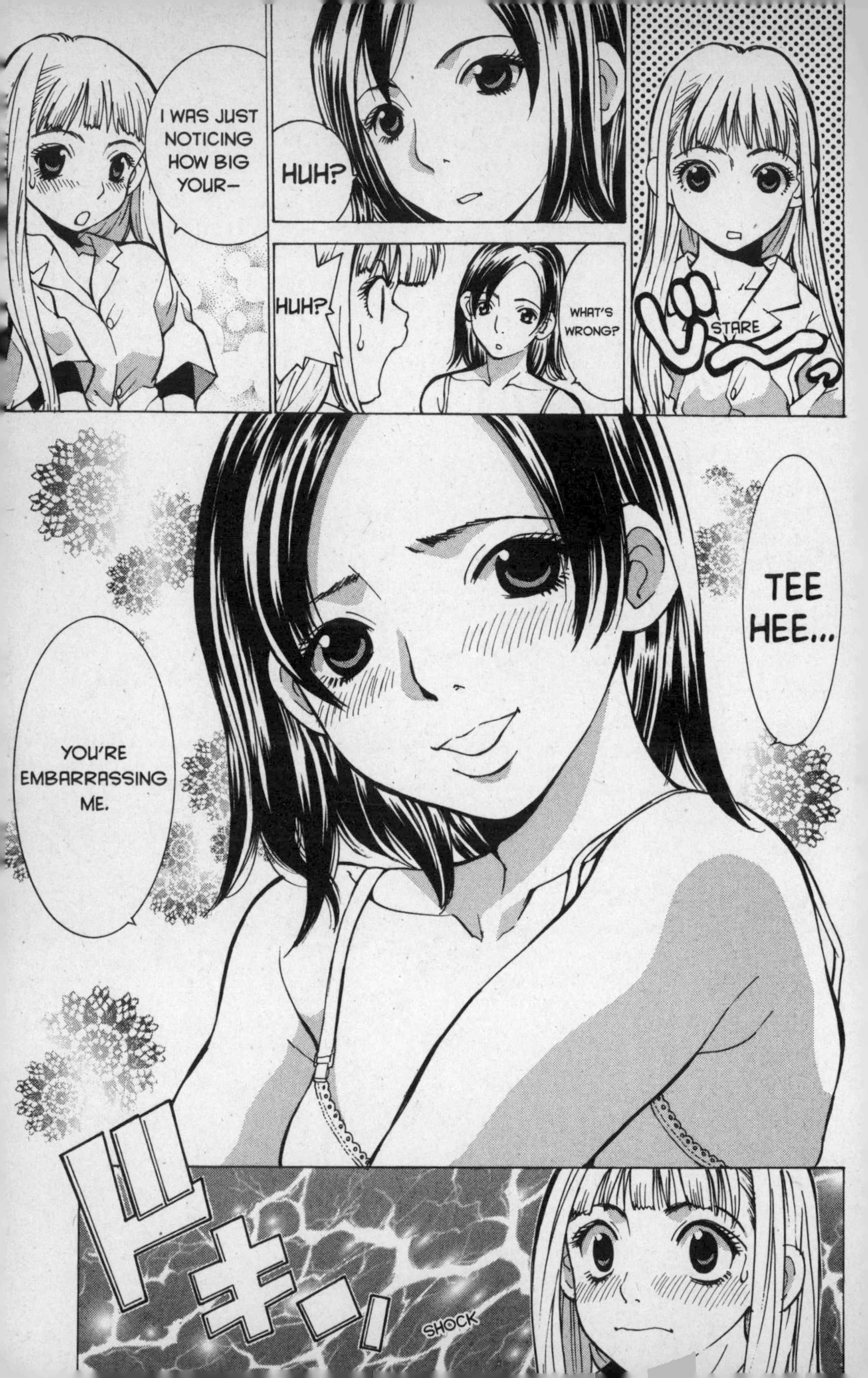
STARE
HUH?
WHAT'S WRONG?
HUH?
I WAS JUST NOTICING HOW BIG YOUR–
TEE HEE...
YOU'RE EMBARRASSING ME.
SHOCK

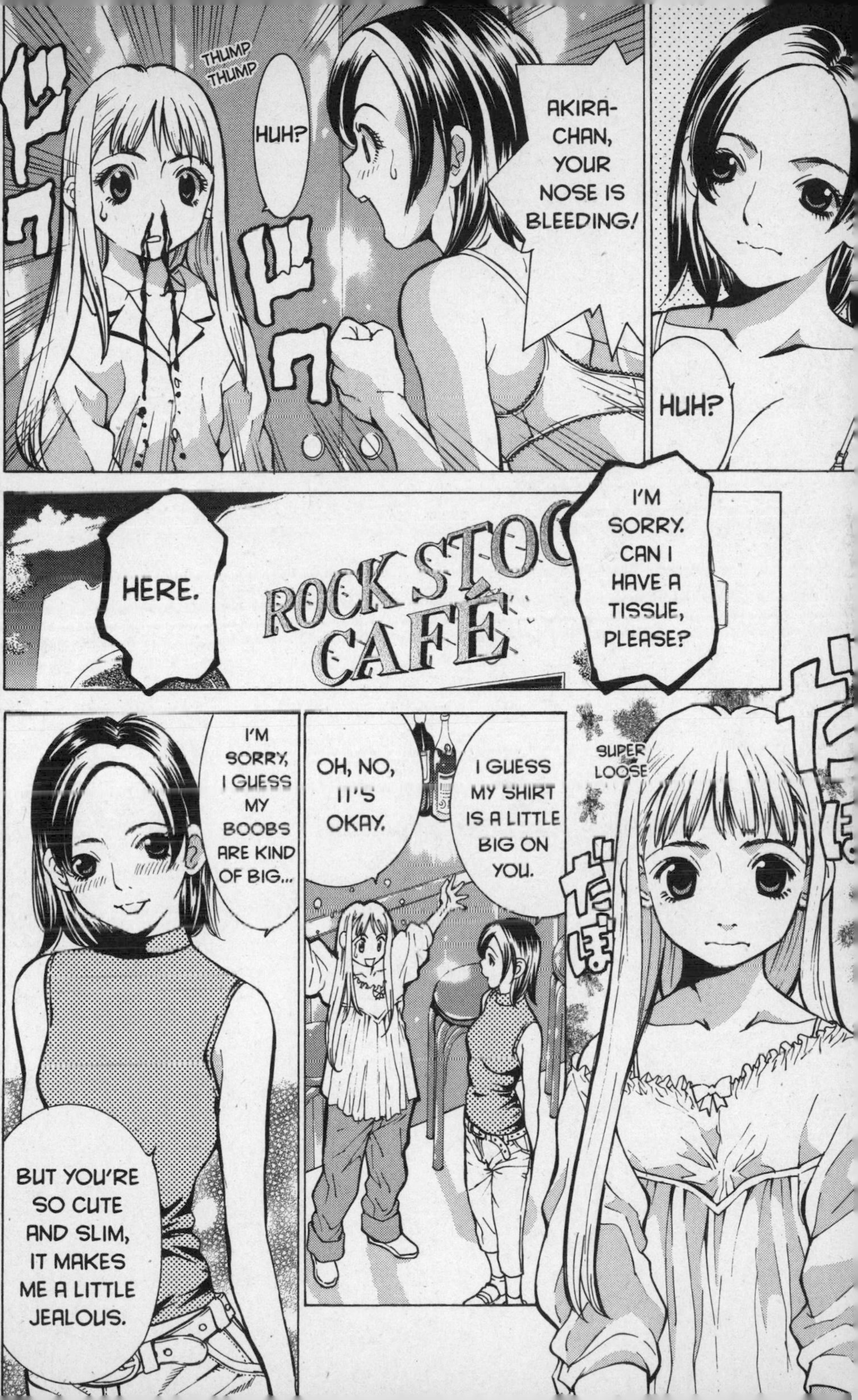
HUH?
AKIRA-CHAN, YOUR NOSE IS BLEEDING!
HUH?
THUMP THUMP
I'M SORRY. CAN I HAVE A TISSUE, PLEASE?
ROCK STOC
CAFÉ
HERE.
SUPER LOOSE
I GUESS MY SHIRT IS A LITTLE BIG ON YOU.
OH, NO, IT'S OKAY.
I'M SORRY, I GUESS MY BOOBS ARE KIND OF BIG...
BUT YOU'RE SO CUTE AND SLIM, IT MAKES ME A LITTLE JEALOUS.

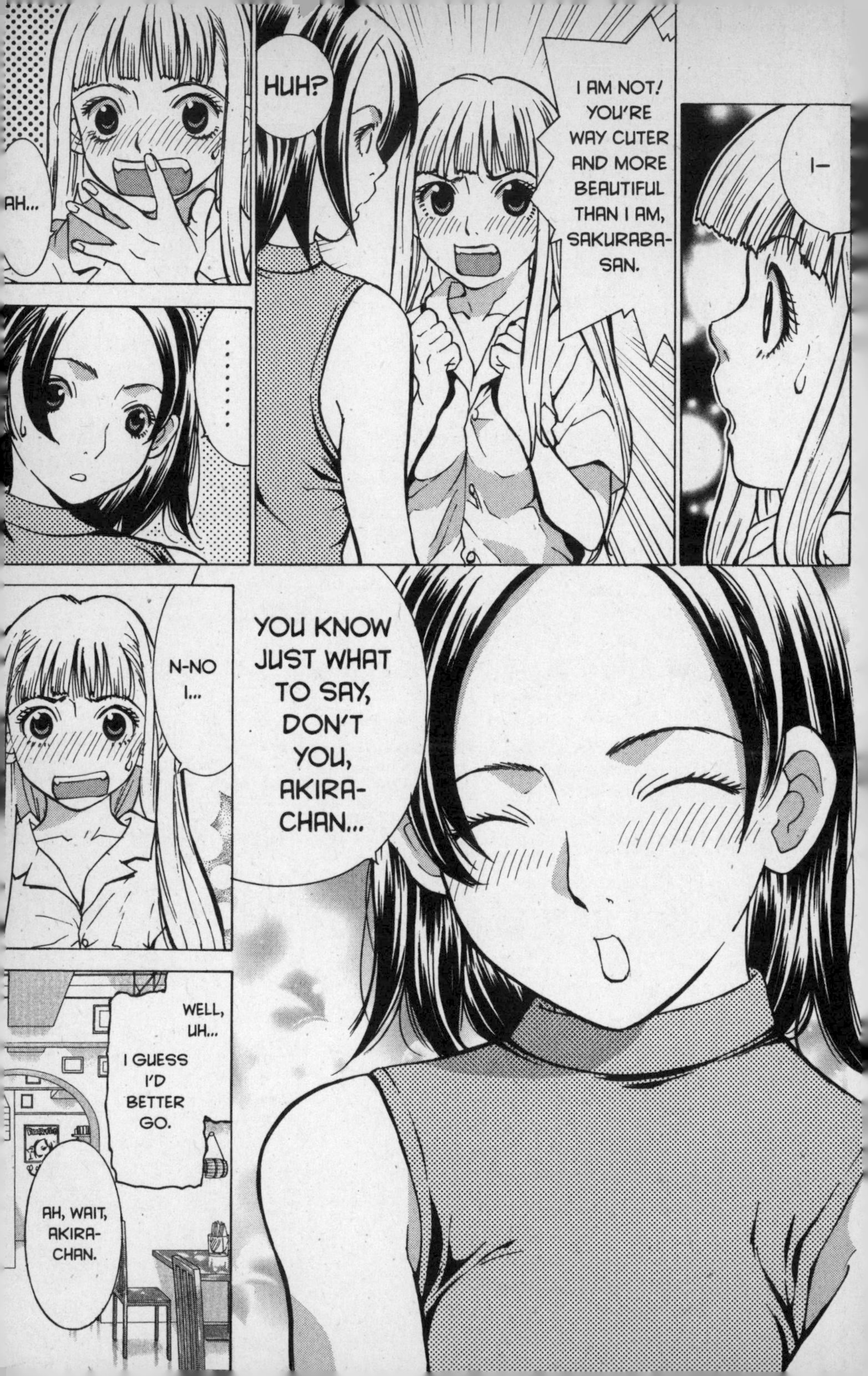
I–
HUH?
I AM NOT! YOU'RE WAY CUTER AND MORE BEAUTIFUL THAN I AM, SAKURABA-SAN.
AH...
......
YOU KNOW JUST WHAT TO SAY, DON'T YOU, AKIRA-CHAN...
N-NO I...
WELL, UH...
I GUESS I'D BETTER GO.
AH, WAIT, AKIRA-CHAN.

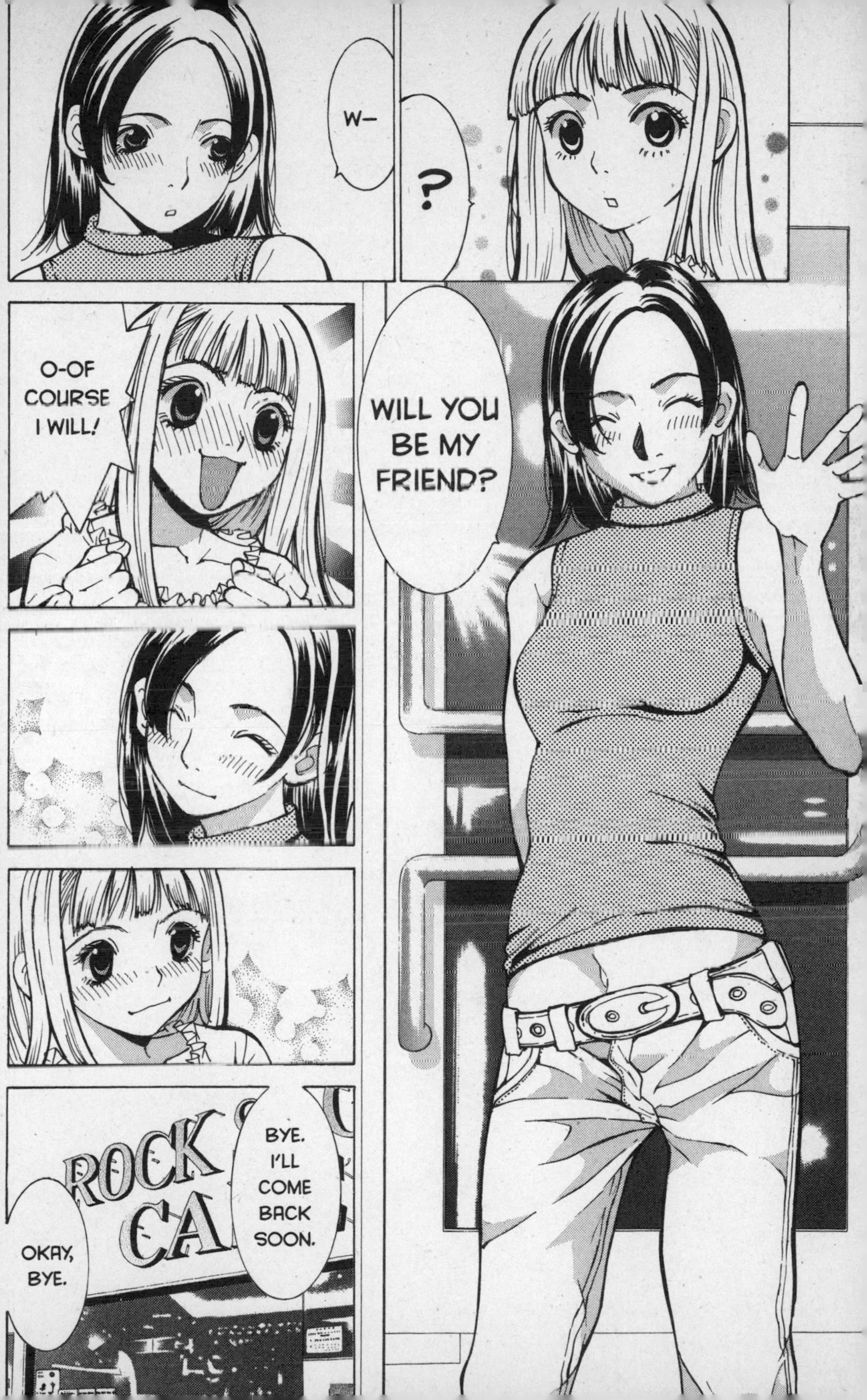
?
W–
WILL YOU BE MY FRIEND?
O-OF COURSE I WILL!
BYE. I'LL COME BACK SOON.
OKAY, BYE.

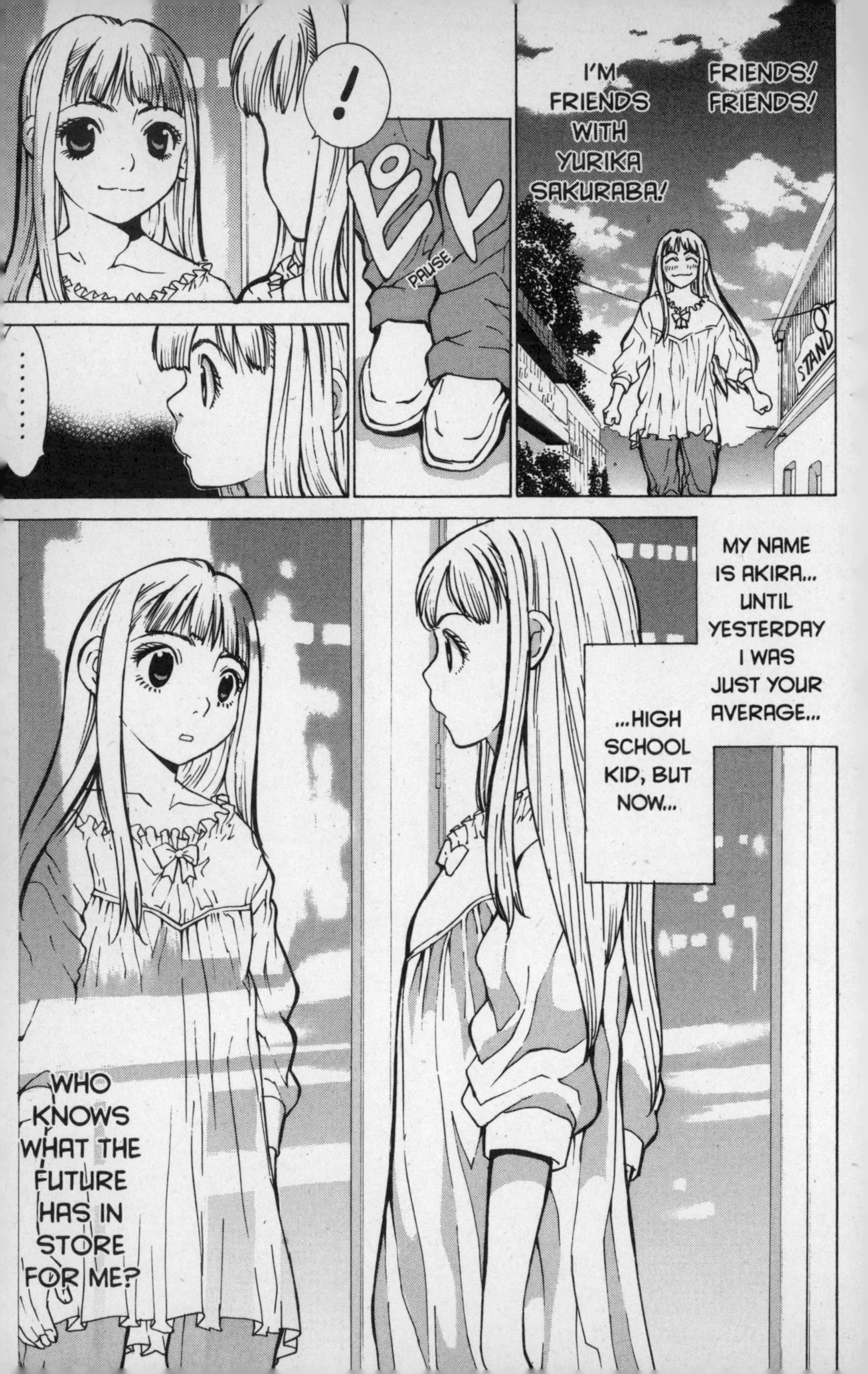
FRIENDS! FRIENDS!
I'M FRIENDS WITH YURIKA SAKURABA!
STAND
!
PAUSE
......
MY NAME IS AKIRA... UNTIL YESTERDAY I WAS JUST YOUR AVERAGE...
...HIGH SCHOOL KID, BUT NOW...
WHO KNOWS WHAT THE FUTURE HAS IN STORE FOR ME?

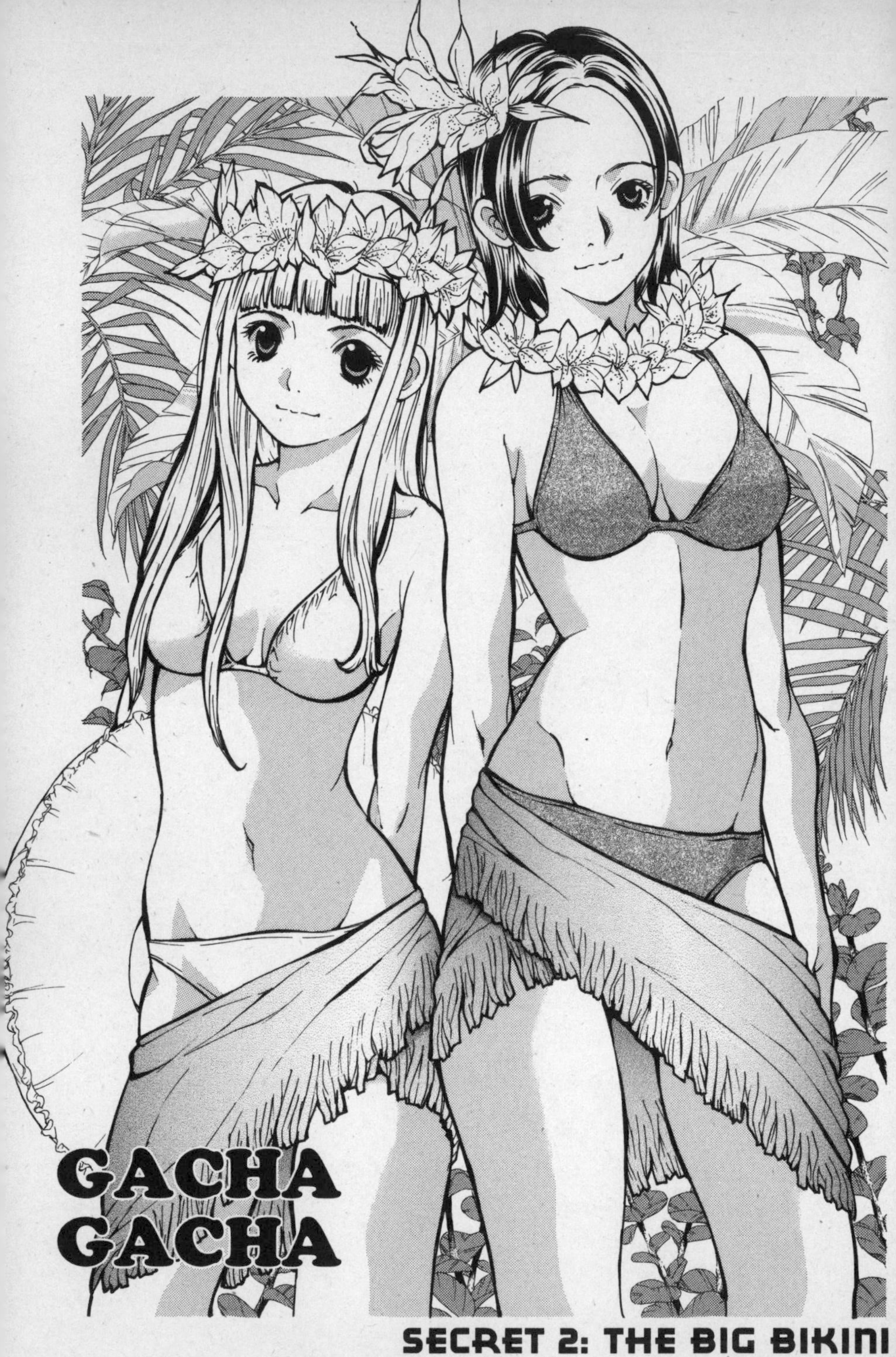
GACHA
GACHA

SECRET 2: THE BIG BIKINI

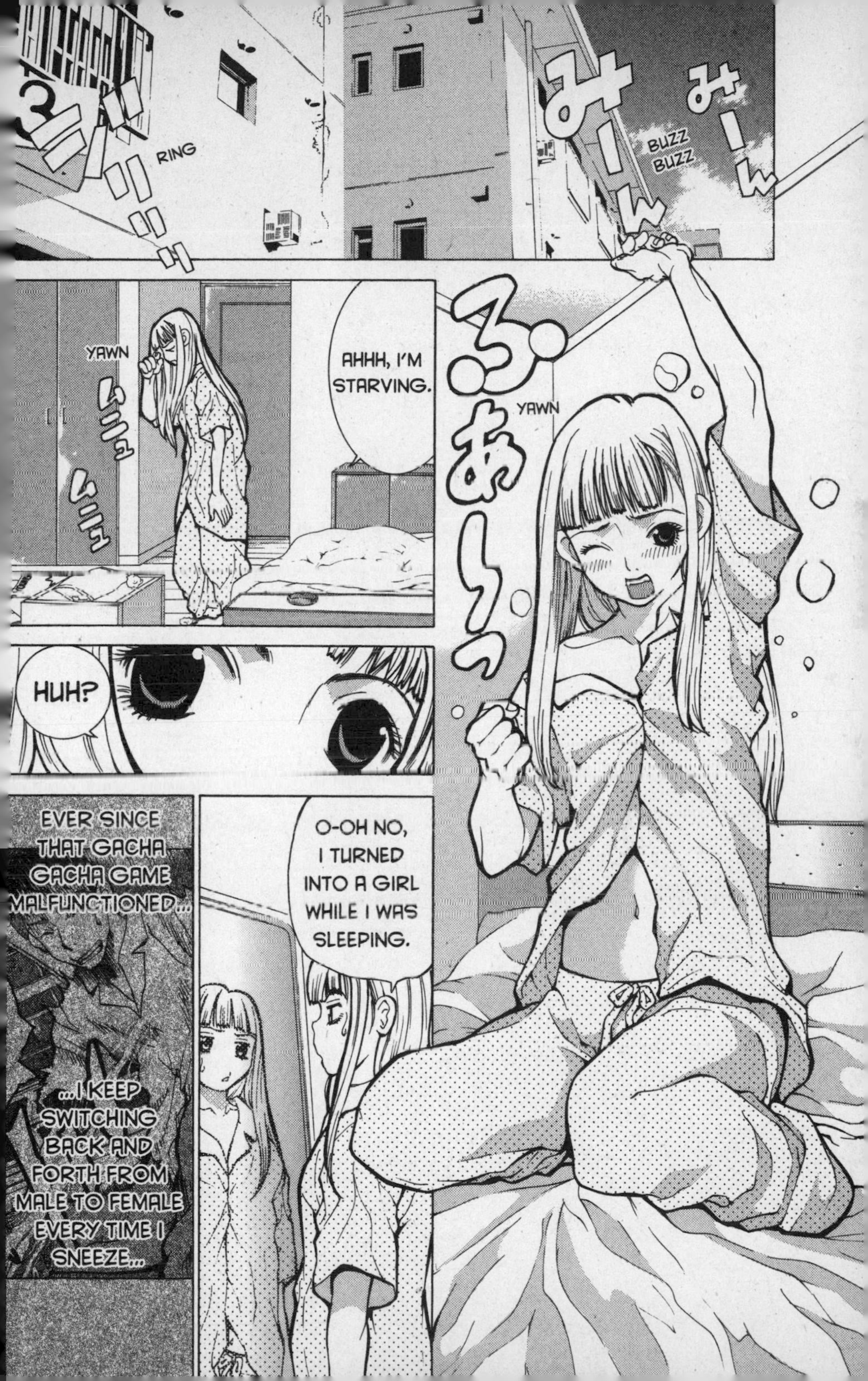
みーん
みーん
BUZZ BUZZ
RING
ふあ～っ
YAWN
AHHH, I'M STARVING.
YAWN
HUH?
O-OH NO, I TURNED INTO A GIRL WHILE I WAS SLEEPING.
EVER SINCE THAT GACHA GACHA GAME MALFUNCTIONED...
...I KEEP SWITCHING BACK AND FORTH FROM MALE TO FEMALE EVERY TIME I SNEEZE...

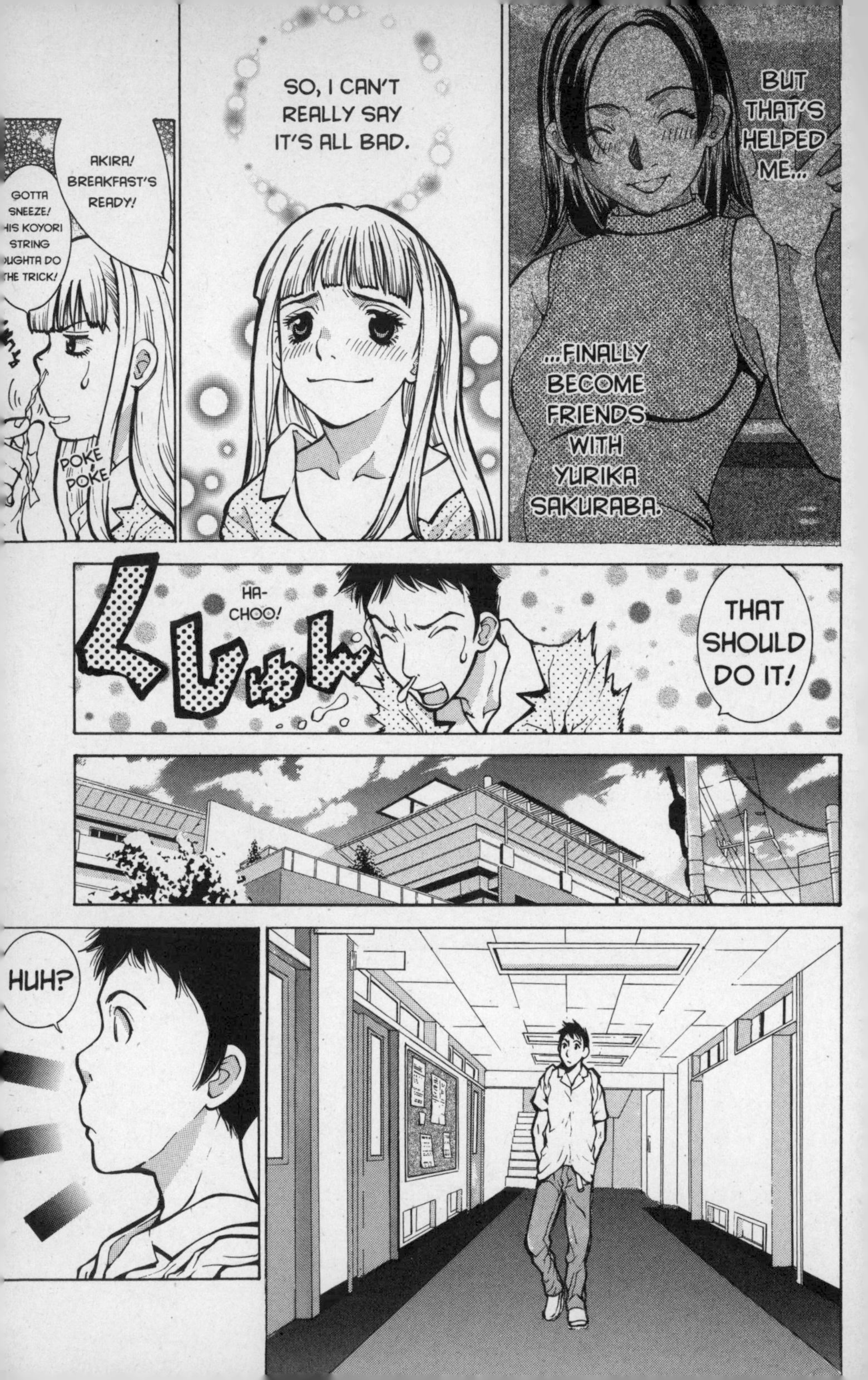
BUT THAT'S HELPED ME...
...FINALLY BECOME FRIENDS WITH YURIKA SAKURABA.
SO, I CAN'T REALLY SAY IT'S ALL BAD.
AKIRA! BREAKFAST'S READY!
GOTTA SNEEZE! HIS KOYORI STRING UGHTA DO HE TRICK!
POKE POKE
THAT SHOULD DO IT!
HA-CHOO!
くしゅん
HUH?

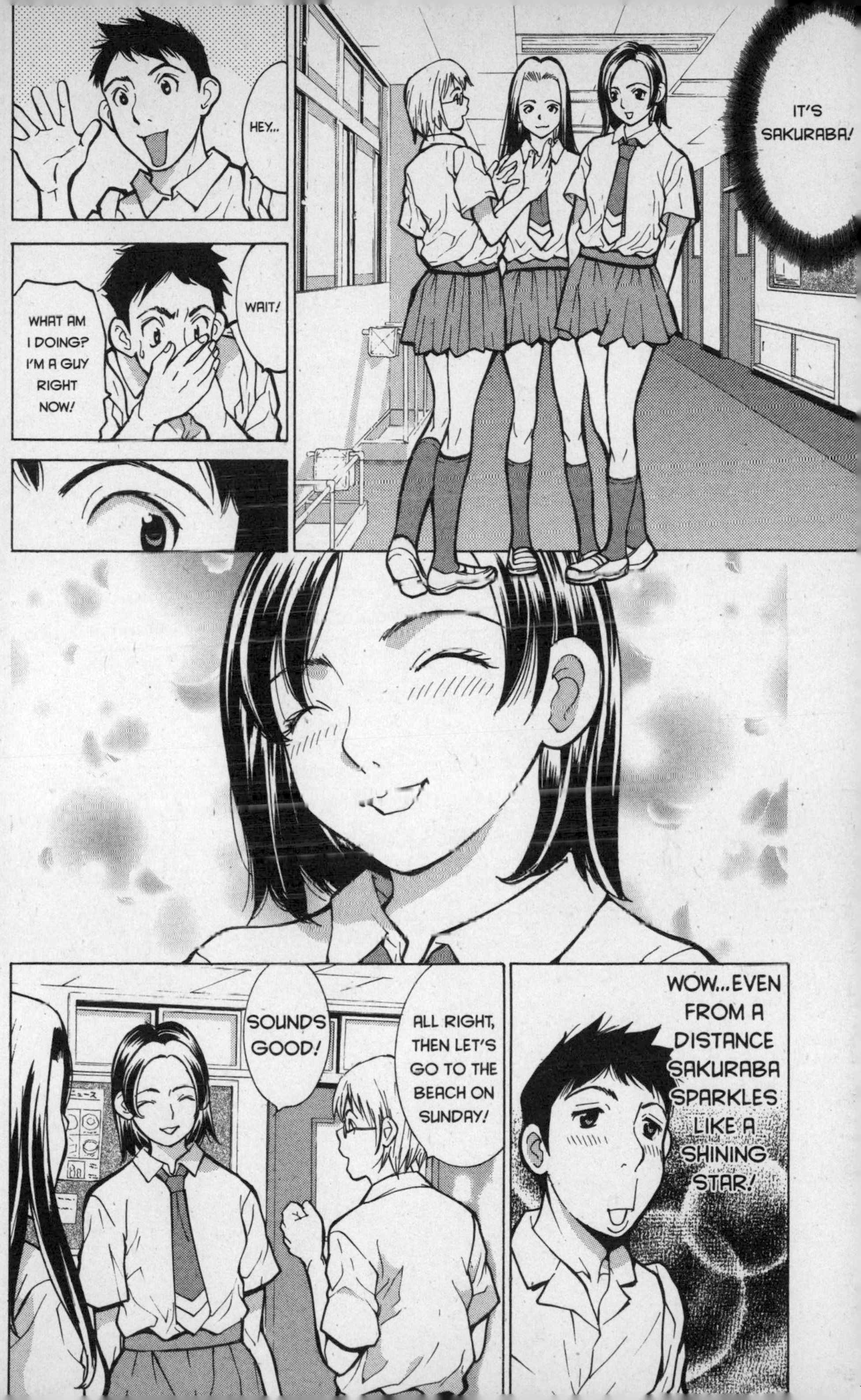
IT'S SAKURABA!
HEY...
WAIT!
WHAT AM I DOING? I'M A GUY RIGHT NOW!
WOW...EVEN FROM A DISTANCE SAKURABA SPARKLES LIKE A SHINING STAR!
ALL RIGHT, THEN LET'S GO TO THE BEACH ON SUNDAY!
SOUNDS GOOD!

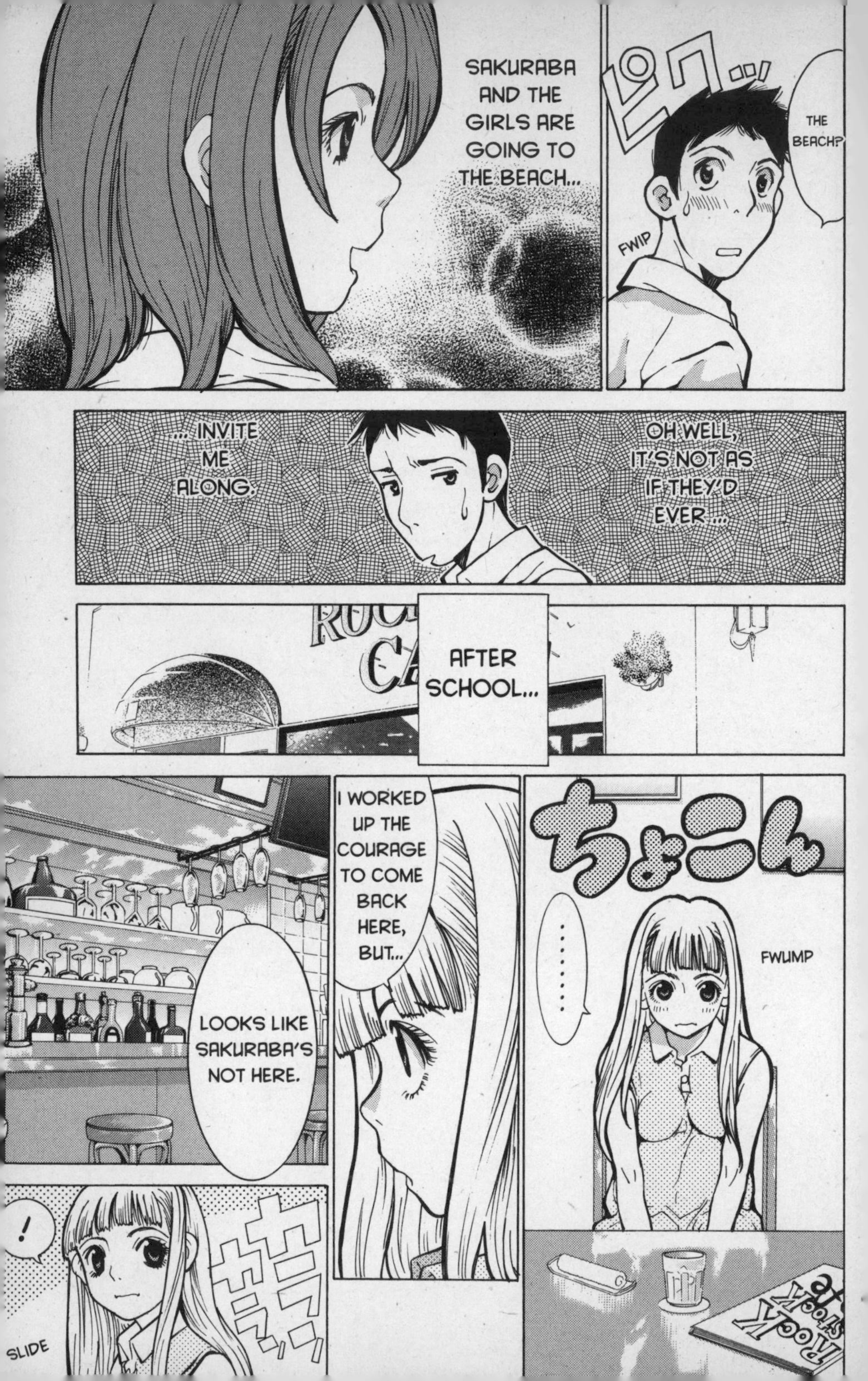
THE BEACH?
FWIP
SAKURABA AND THE GIRLS ARE GOING TO THE BEACH...
OH WELL, IT'S NOT AS IF THEY'D EVER ...
... INVITE ME ALONG.
AFTER SCHOOL...
ちょこん
......
FWUMP
I WORKED UP THE COURAGE TO COME BACK HERE, BUT...
LOOKS LIKE SAKURABA'S NOT HERE.
!
SLIDE

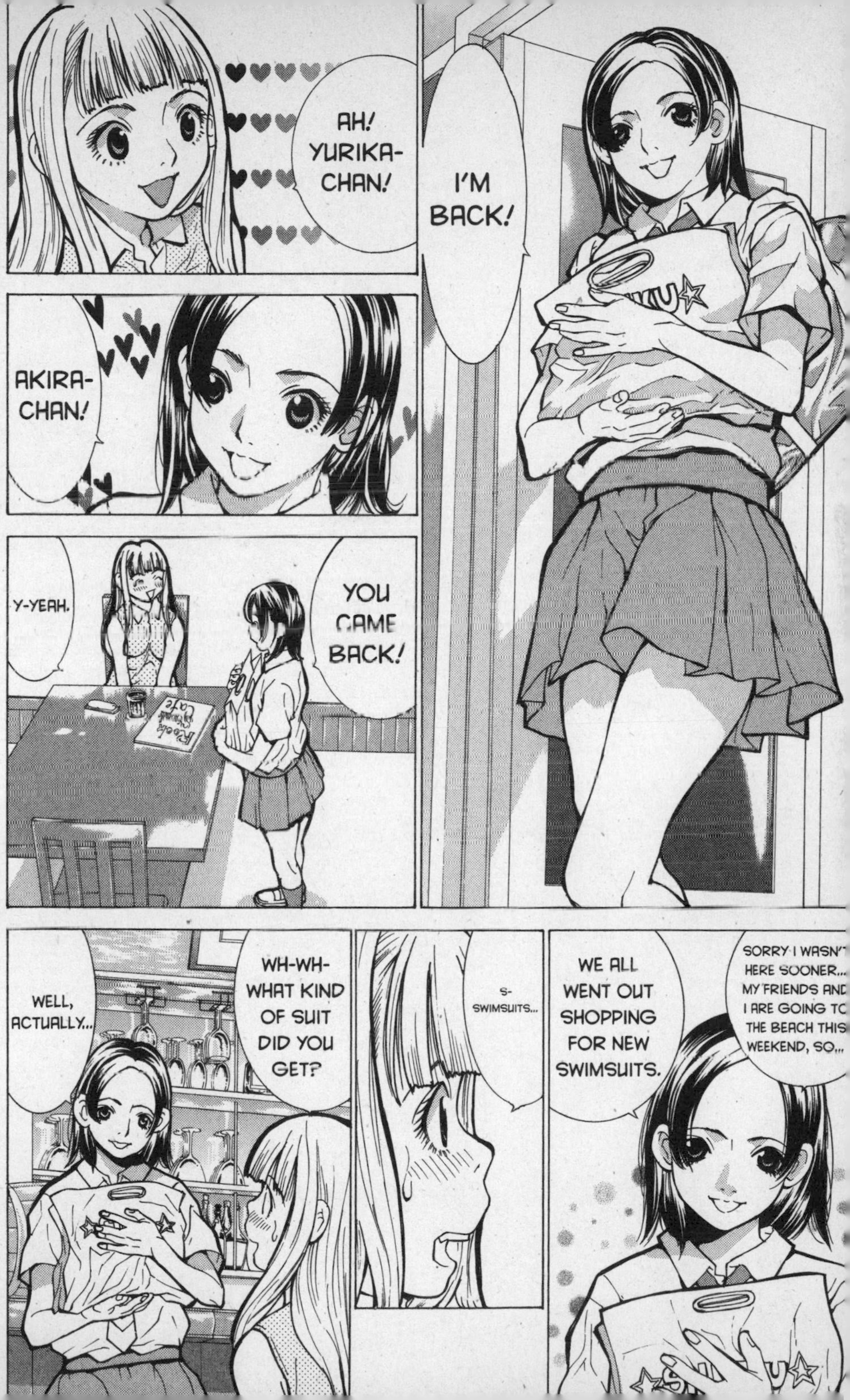
I'M BACK!
AH! YURIKA-CHAN!
AKIRA-CHAN!
YOU CAME BACK!
Y-YEAH.
SORRY I WASN'T HERE SOONER... MY FRIENDS AND I ARE GOING TO THE BEACH THIS WEEKEND, SO...
WE ALL WENT OUT SHOPPING FOR NEW SWIMSUITS.
S-SWIMSUITS...
WH-WH-WHAT KIND OF SUIT DID YOU GET?
WELL, ACTUALLY...

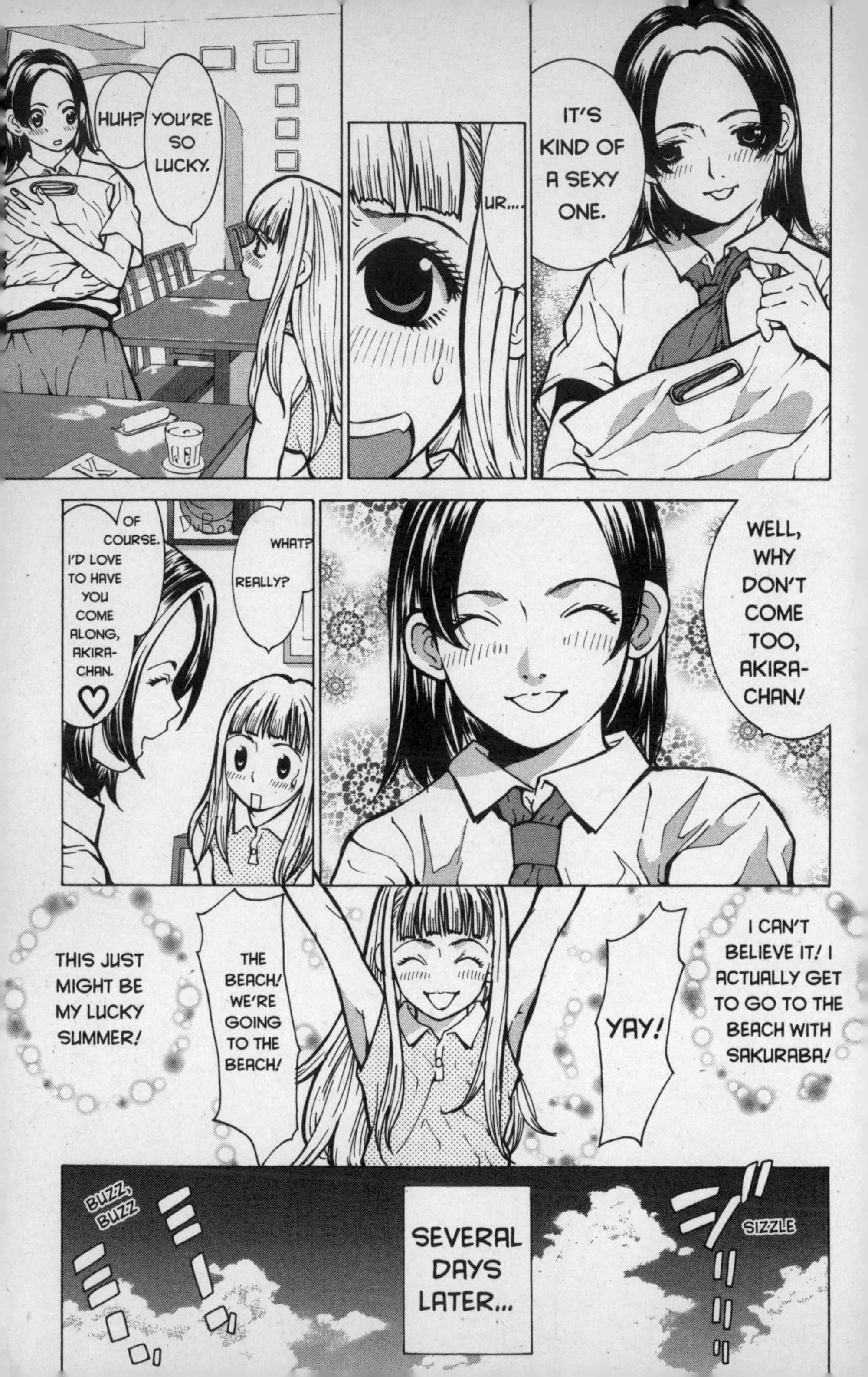
IT'S KIND OF A SEXY ONE.
UR....
YOU'RE SO LUCKY.
HUH?
WELL, WHY DON'T COME TOO, AKIRA-CHAN!
WHAT? REALLY?
OF COURSE. I'D LOVE TO HAVE YOU COME ALONG, AKIRA-CHAN. ♡
I CAN'T BELIEVE IT! I ACTUALLY GET TO GO TO THE BEACH WITH SAKURABA!
YAY!
THE BEACH! WE'RE GOING TO THE BEACH!
THIS JUST MIGHT BE MY LUCKY SUMMER!
SIZZLE
SEVERAL DAYS LATER...
BUZZ, BUZZ

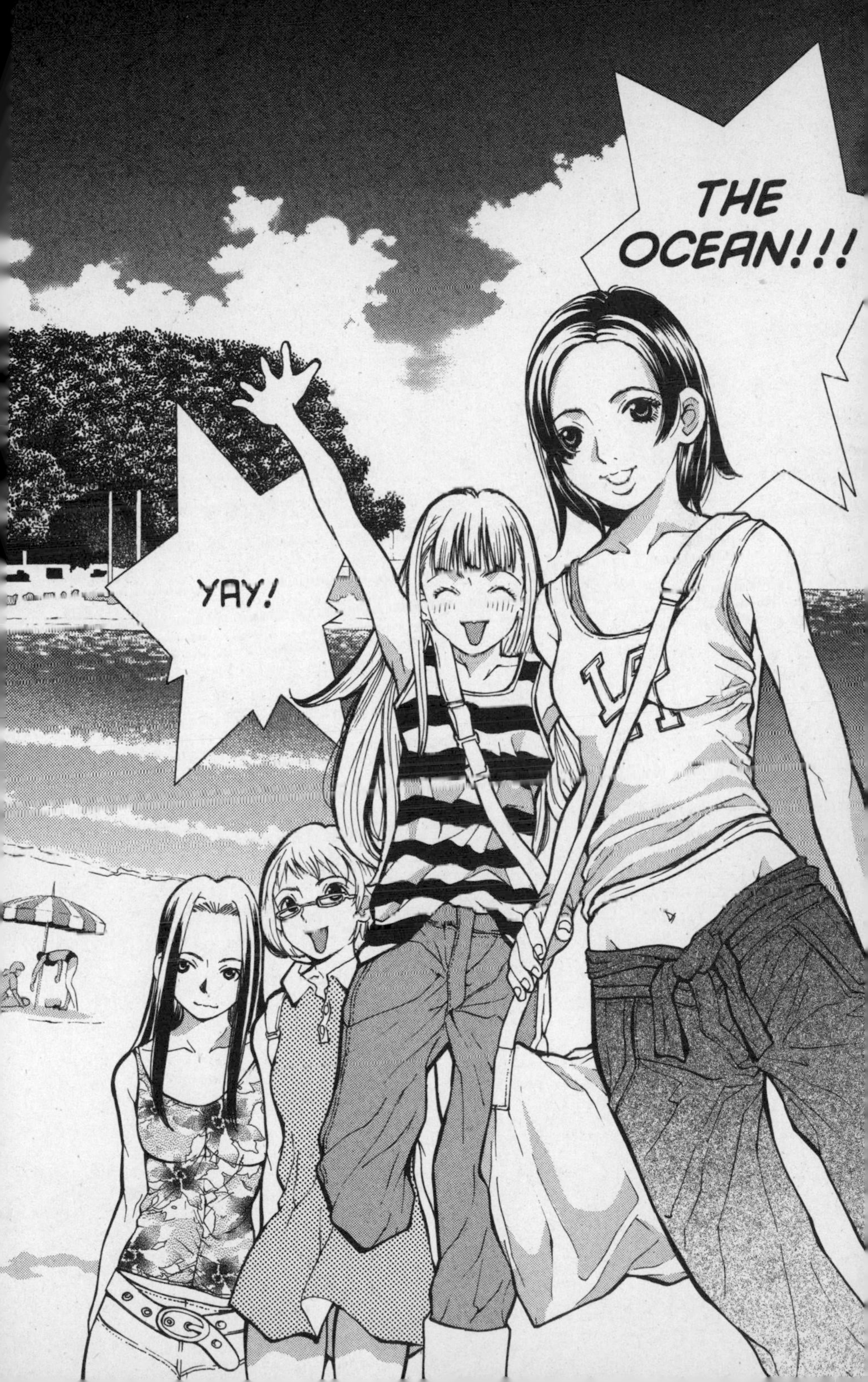
THE OCEAN!!!
YAY!

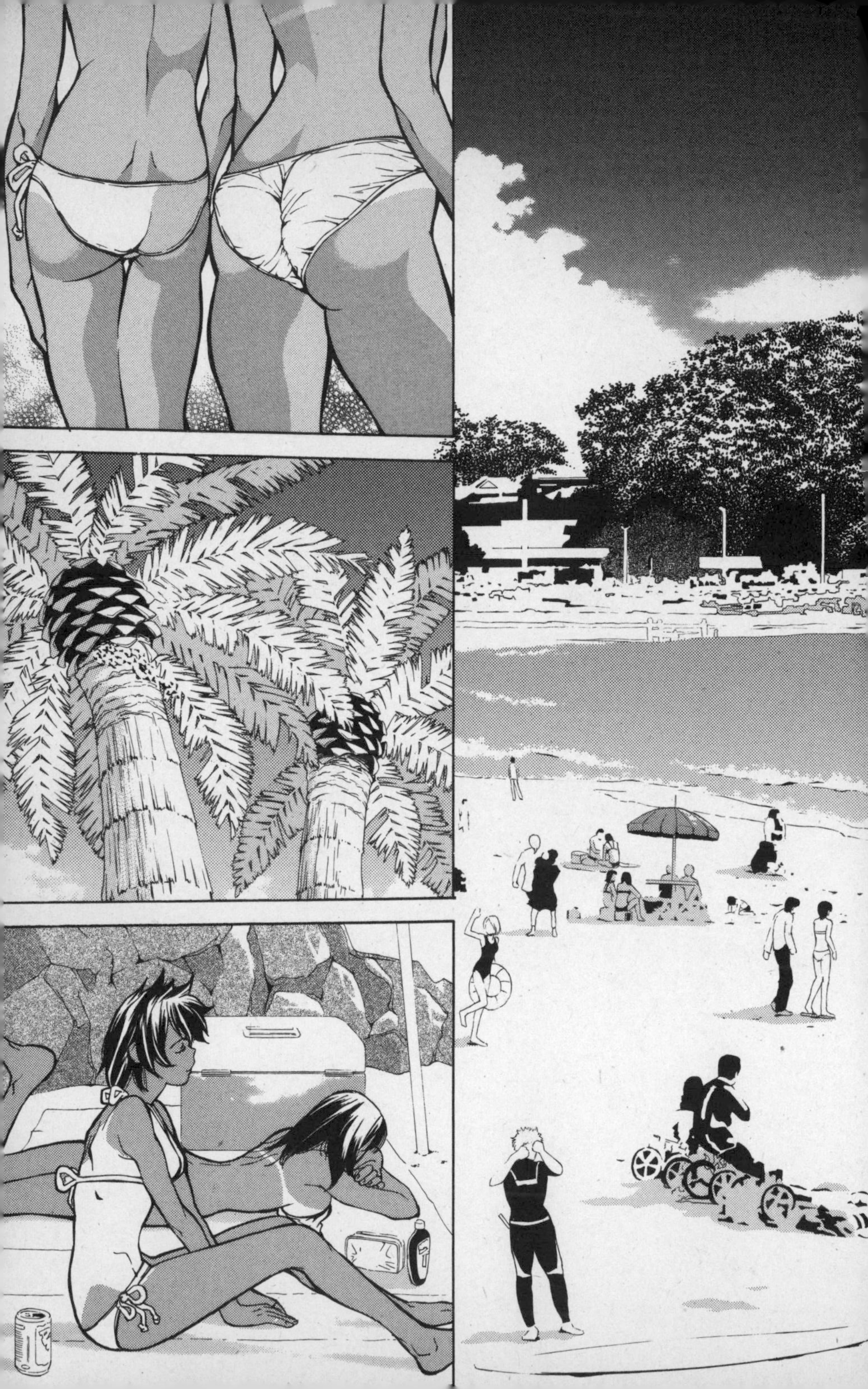

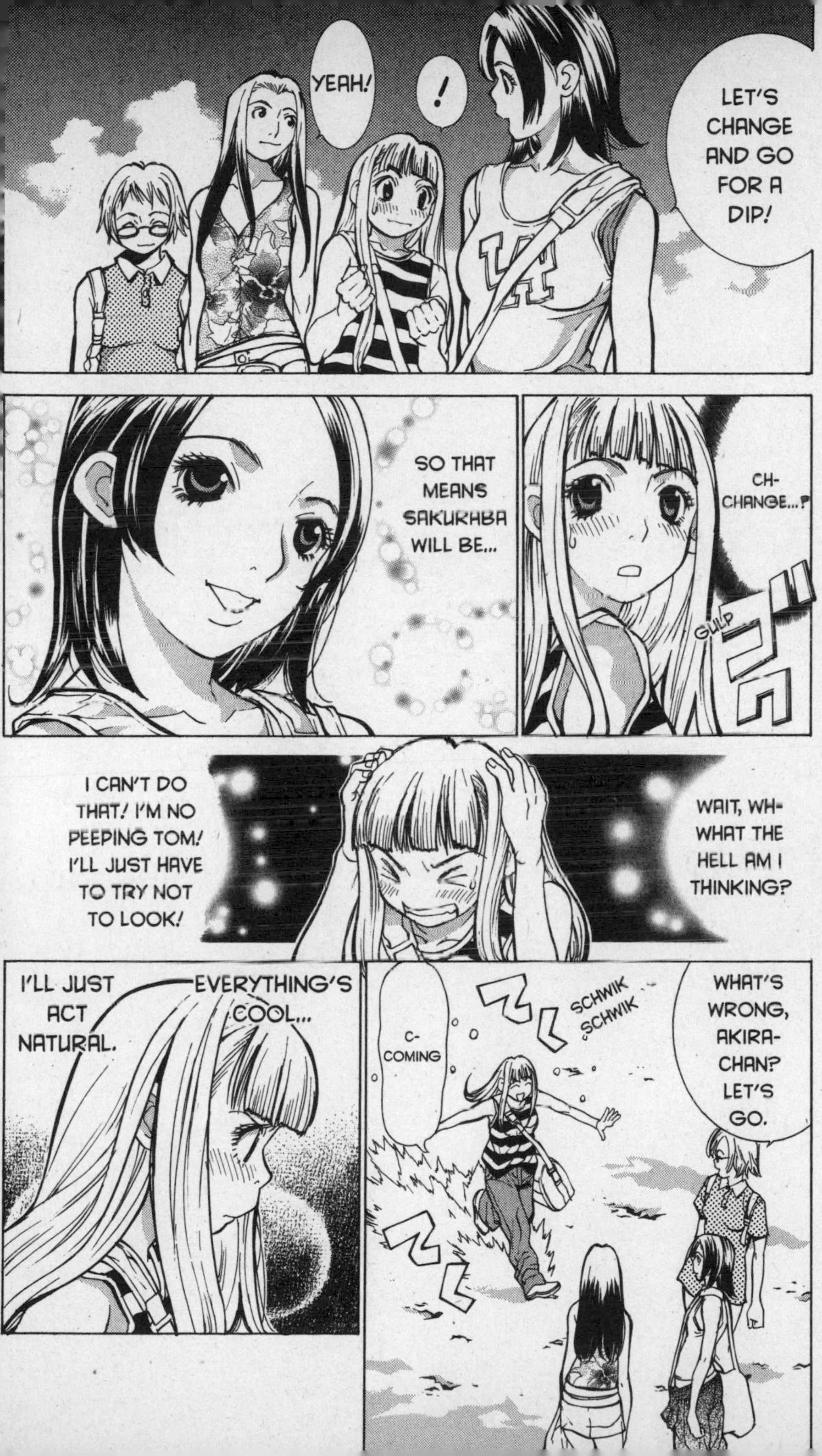
LET'S CHANGE AND GO FOR A DIP!
!
YEAH!
CH-CHANGE...?
GULP
SO THAT MEANS SAKURABA WILL BE...
WAIT, WH-WHAT THE HELL AM I THINKING?
I CAN'T DO THAT! I'M NO PEEPING TOM! I'LL JUST HAVE TO TRY NOT TO LOOK!
WHAT'S WRONG, AKIRA-CHAN? LET'S GO.
SCHWIK SCHWIK
C-COMING
EVERYTHING'S COOL...
I'LL JUST ACT NATURAL.

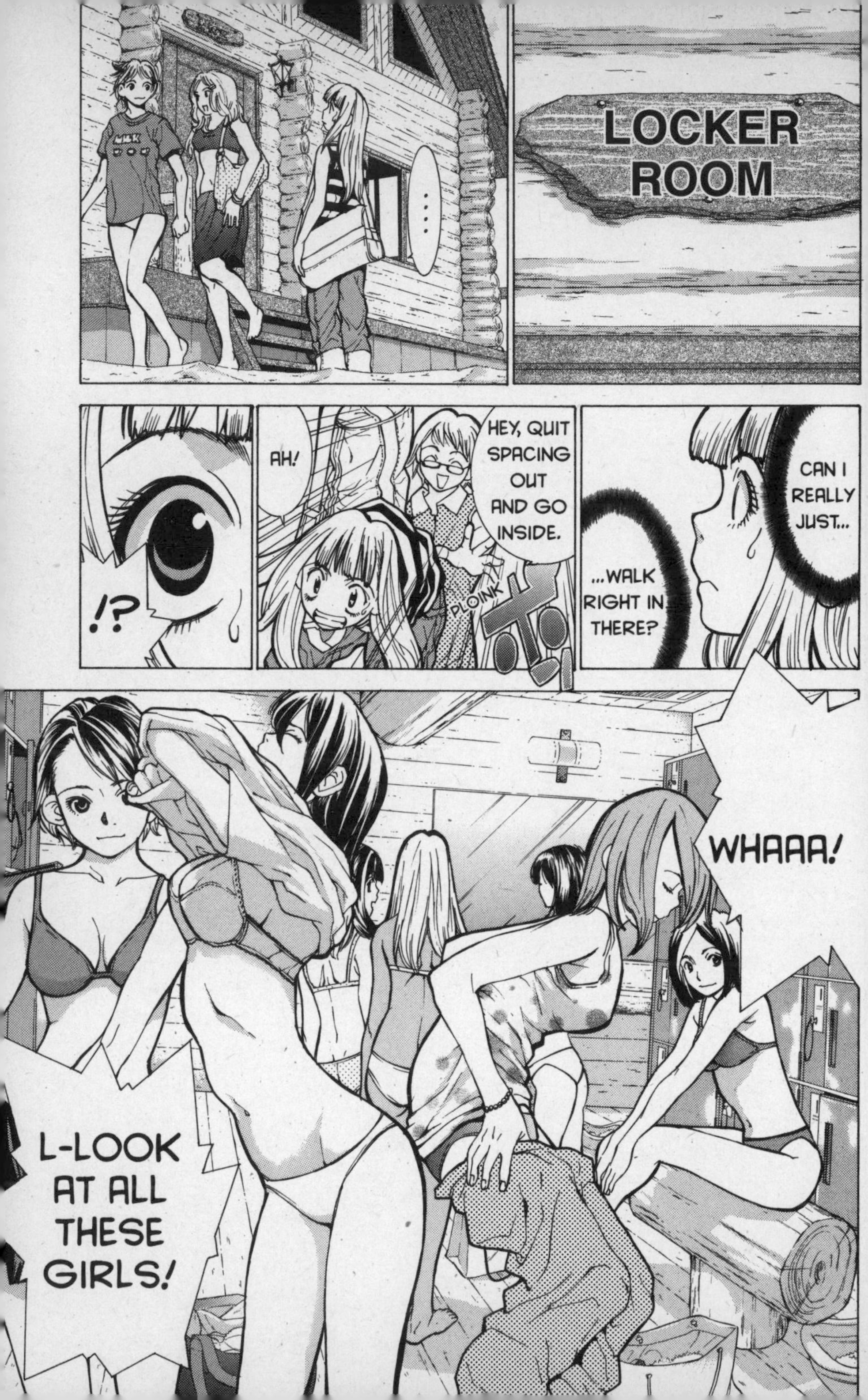
LOCKER ROOM
....
CAN I REALLY JUST...
...WALK RIGHT IN THERE?
HEY, QUIT SPACING OUT AND GO INSIDE.
AH!
PLOINK
!?
WHAAA!
L-LOOK AT ALL THESE GIRLS!

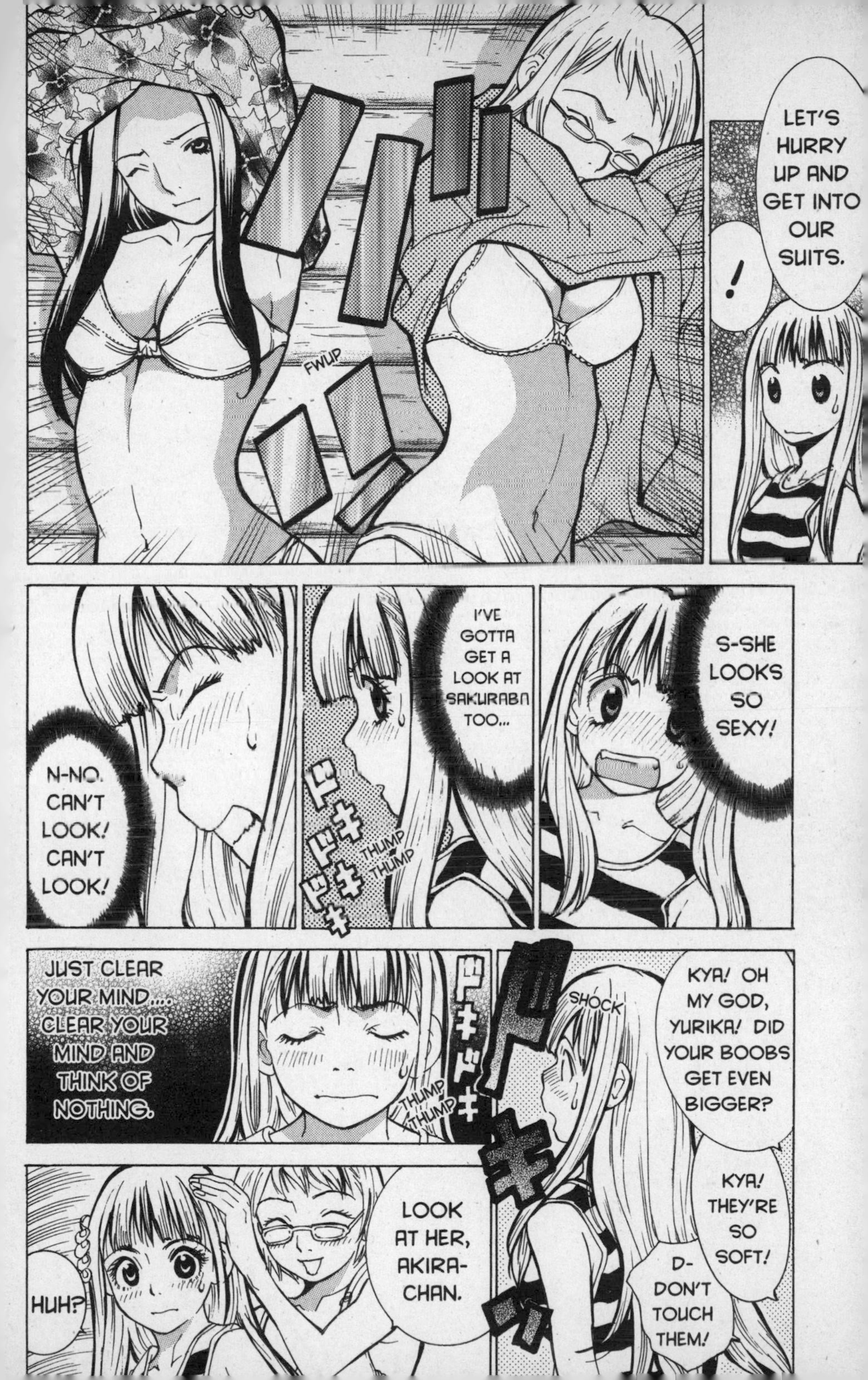
LET'S HURRY UP AND GET INTO OUR SUITS.
!
FWUP
S-SHE LOOKS SO SEXY!
I'VE GOTTA GET A LOOK AT SAKURABA TOO...
THUMP THUMP
N-NO. CAN'T LOOK! CAN'T LOOK!
SHOCK
KYA! OH MY GOD, YURIKA! DID YOUR BOOBS GET EVEN BIGGER?
KYA! THEY'RE SO SOFT!
D-DON'T TOUCH THEM!
JUST CLEAR YOUR MIND.... CLEAR YOUR MIND AND THINK OF NOTHING.
THUMP THUMP
LOOK AT HER, AKIRA-CHAN.
HUH?

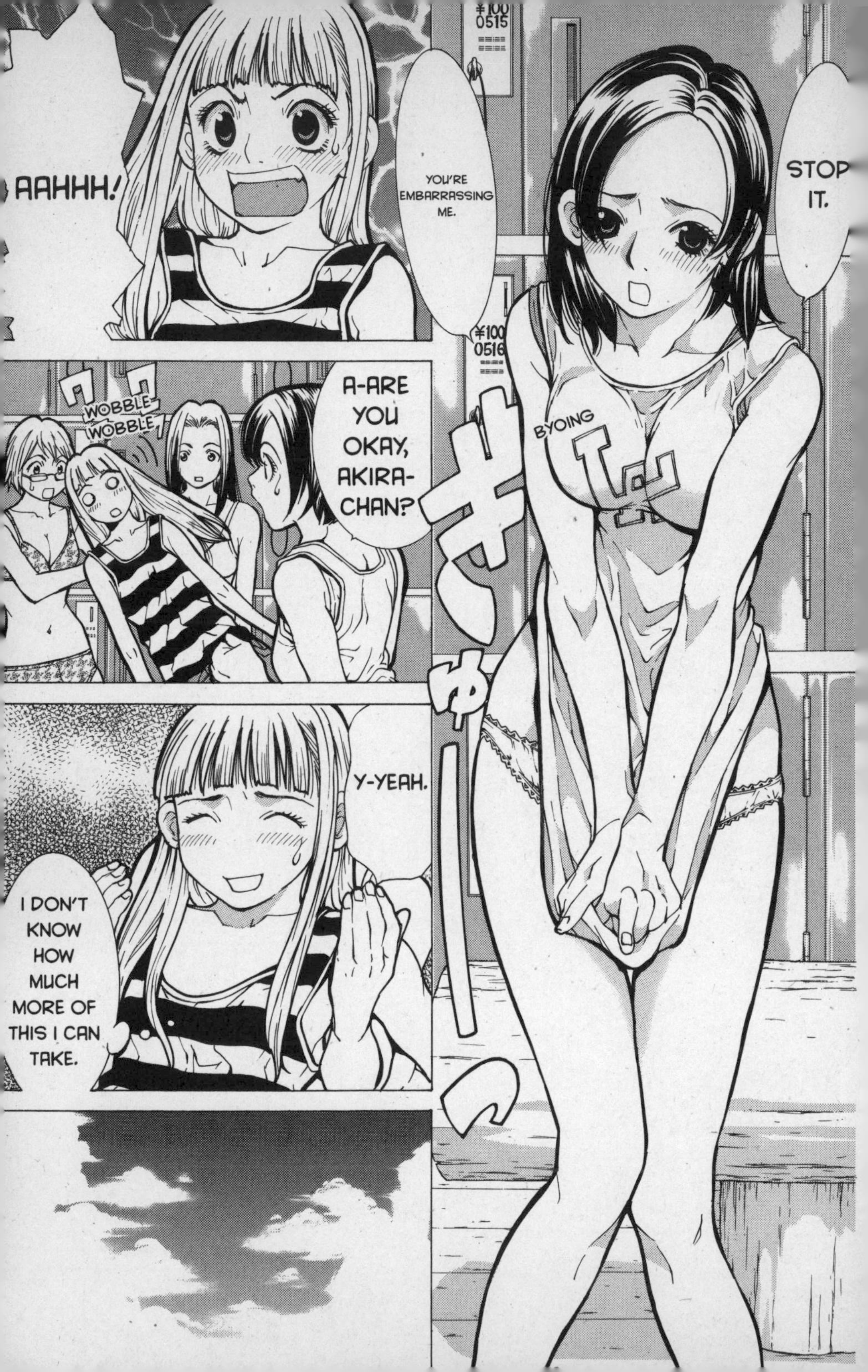
¥100
0515
STOP IT.
YOU'RE EMBARRASSING ME.
¥100
0516
BYOING
AAHHH!
A-ARE YOU OKAY, AKIRA-CHAN?
WOBBLE WOBBLE
Y-YEAH.
I DON'T KNOW HOW MUCH MORE OF THIS I CAN TAKE.

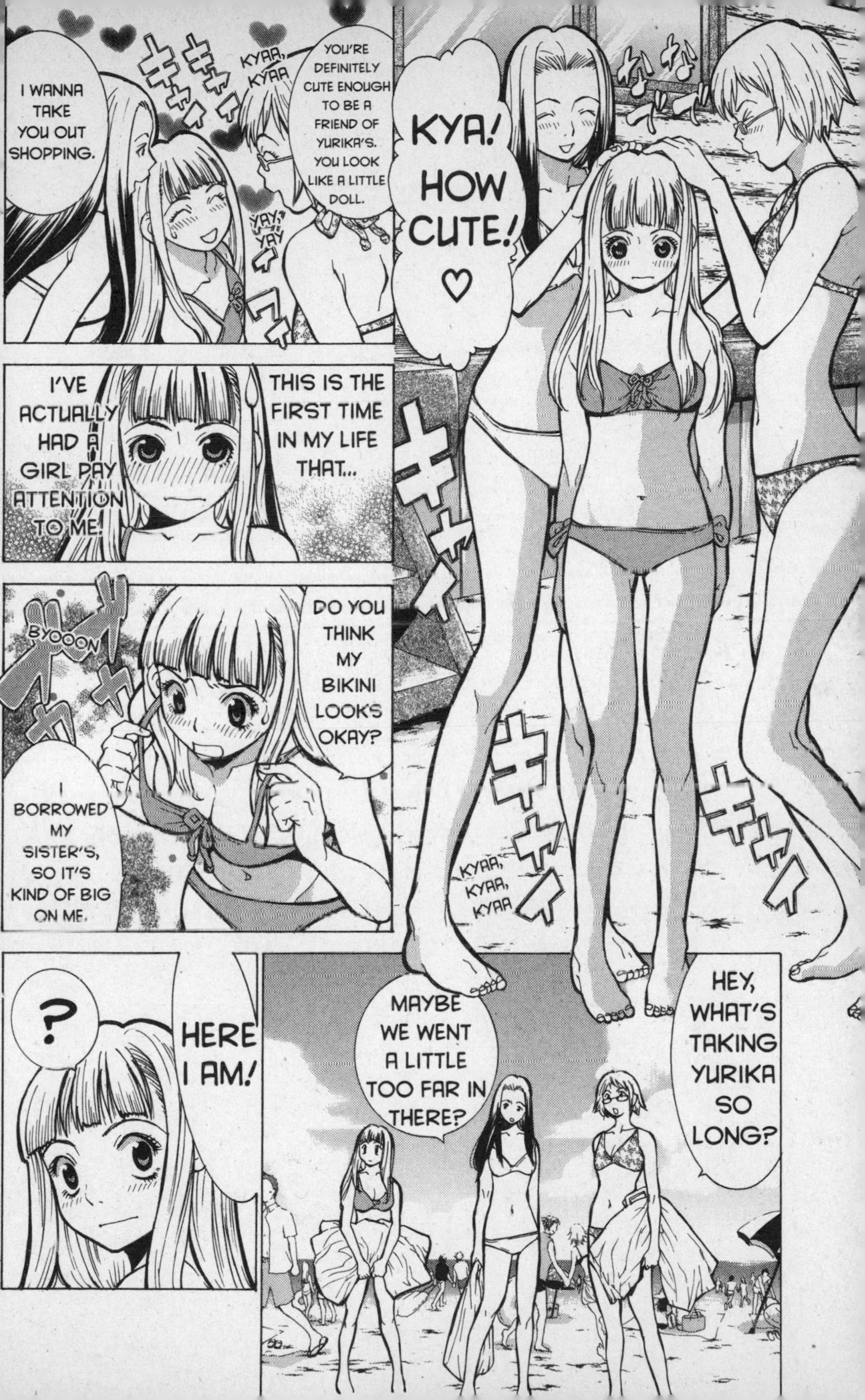
KYA! HOW CUTE! ♡
KYAA, KYAA, KYAA
YOU'RE DEFINITELY CUTE ENOUGH TO BE A FRIEND OF YURIKA'S. YOU LOOK LIKE A LITTLE DOLL.
KYAA, KYAA
I WANNA TAKE YOU OUT SHOPPING.
YAY, YAY
THIS IS THE FIRST TIME IN MY LIFE THAT...
I'VE ACTUALLY HAD A GIRL PAY ATTENTION TO ME!
BYOOON
DO YOU THINK MY BIKINI LOOKS OKAY?
I BORROWED MY SISTER'S, SO IT'S KIND OF BIG ON ME.
HEY, WHAT'S TAKING YURIKA SO LONG?
MAYBE WE WENT A LITTLE TOO FAR IN THERE?
HERE I AM!
?

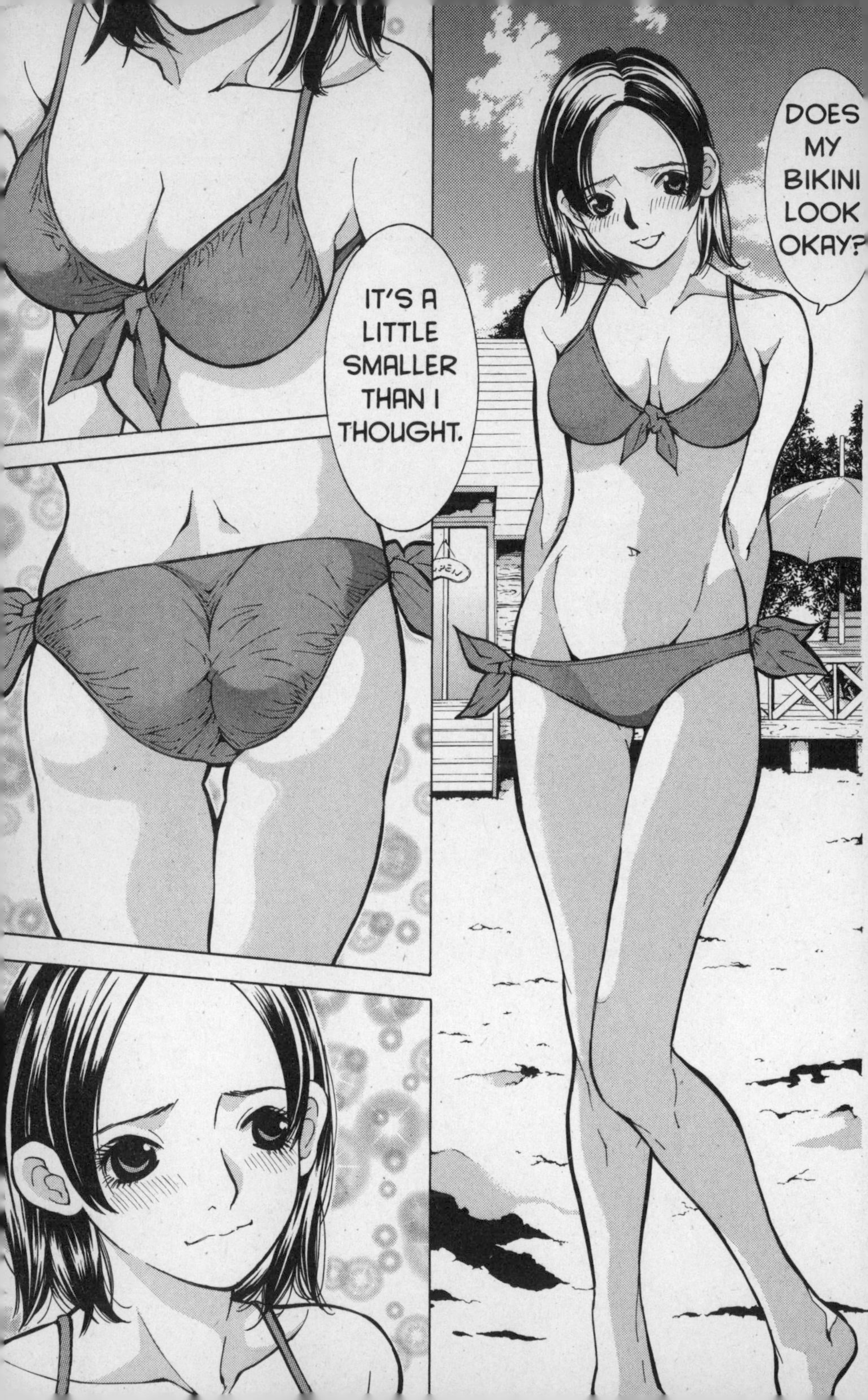
DOES MY BIKINI LOOK OKAY?
IT'S A LITTLE SMALLER THAN I THOUGHT.

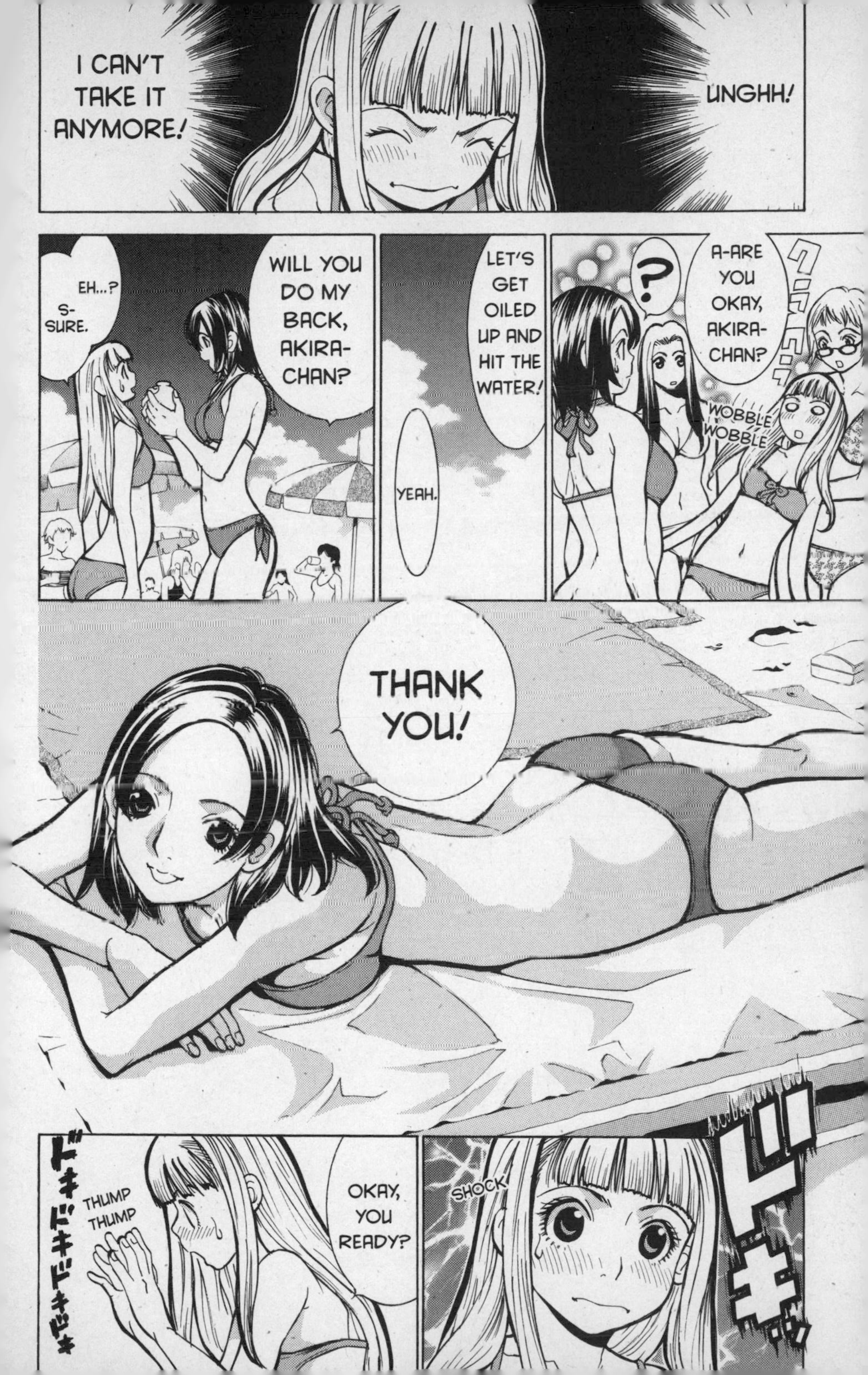
UNGHH!
I CAN'T TAKE IT ANYMORE!
A-ARE YOU OKAY, AKIRA-CHAN?
?
WOBBLE WOBBLE
LET'S GET OILED UP AND HIT THE WATER!
YEAH.
WILL YOU DO MY BACK, AKIRA-CHAN?
EH...? S-SURE.
THANK YOU!
ドキ
SHOCK
OKAY, YOU READY?
THUMP THUMP
ドキドキドキドキ

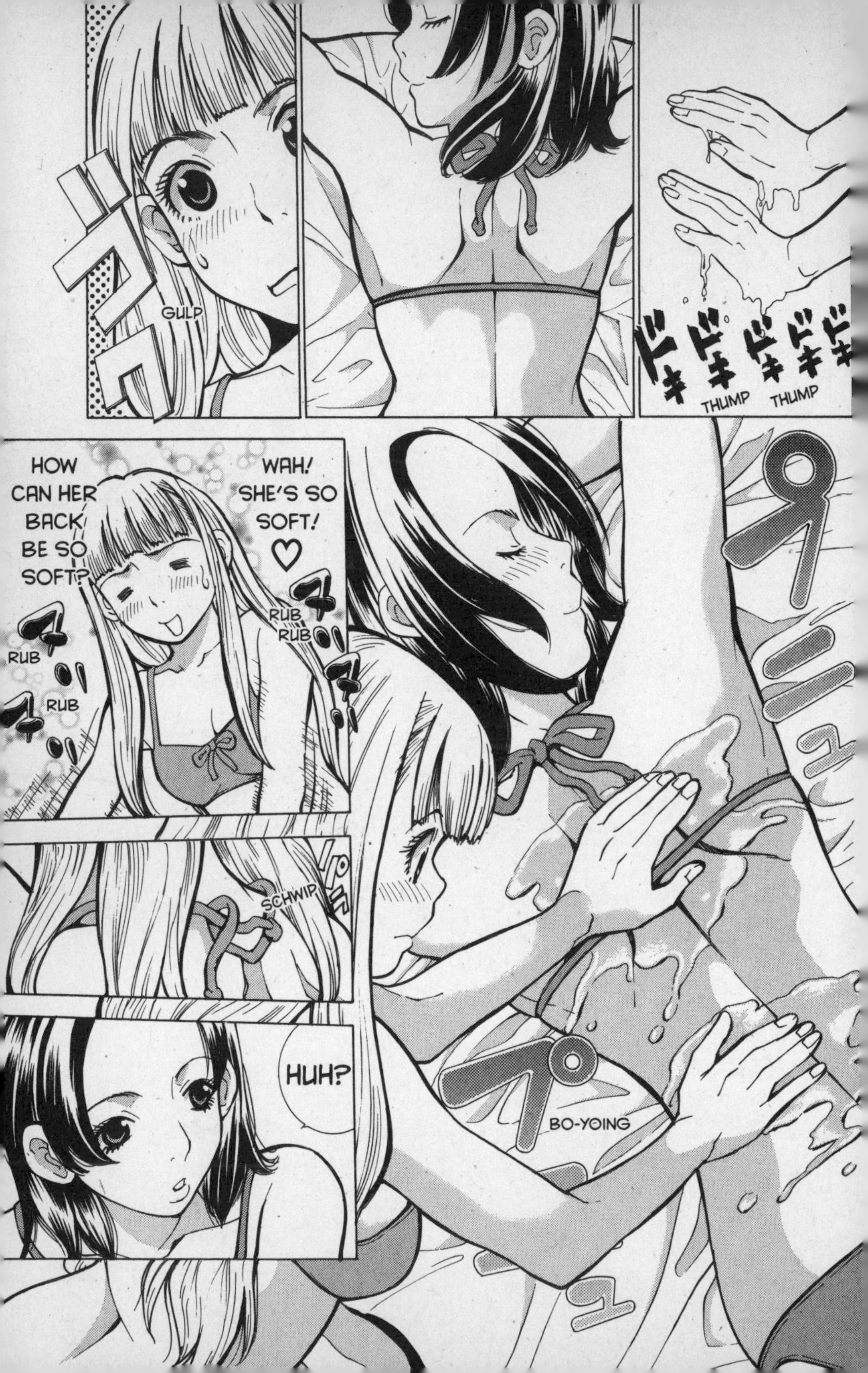
THUMP THUMP
GULP
BO-YOING
WAH! SHE'S SO SOFT! ♥
HOW CAN HER BACK BE SO SOFT?
RUB RUB
RUB
RUB
SCHWIP
HUH?

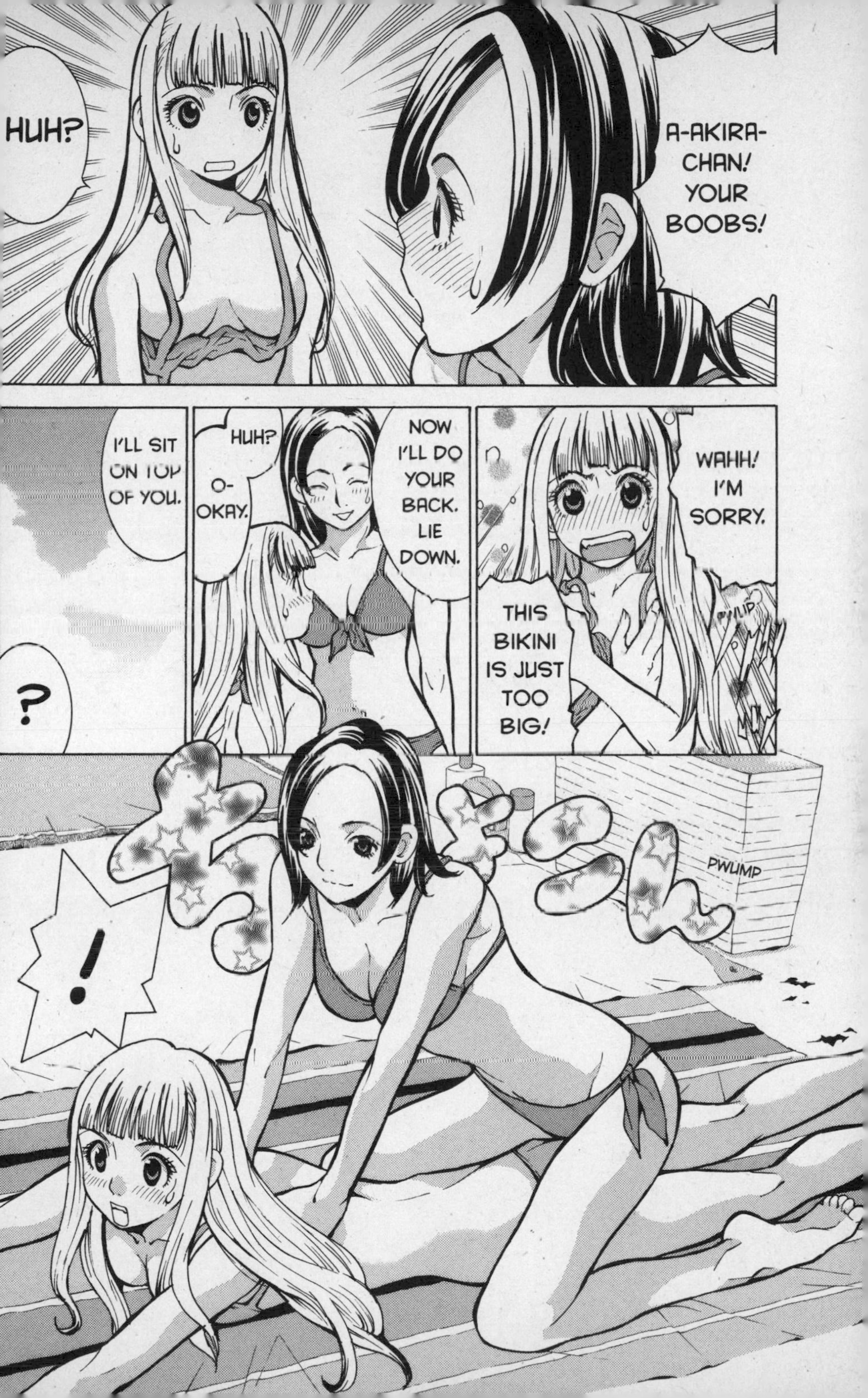
A-AKIRA-CHAN! YOUR BOOBS!
HUH?
WAHH! I'M SORRY.
THIS BIKINI IS JUST TOO BIG!
PWUP
NOW I'LL DO YOUR BACK. LIE DOWN.
HUH?
O-OKAY.
I'LL SIT ON TOP OF YOU.
?
PWUMP
!

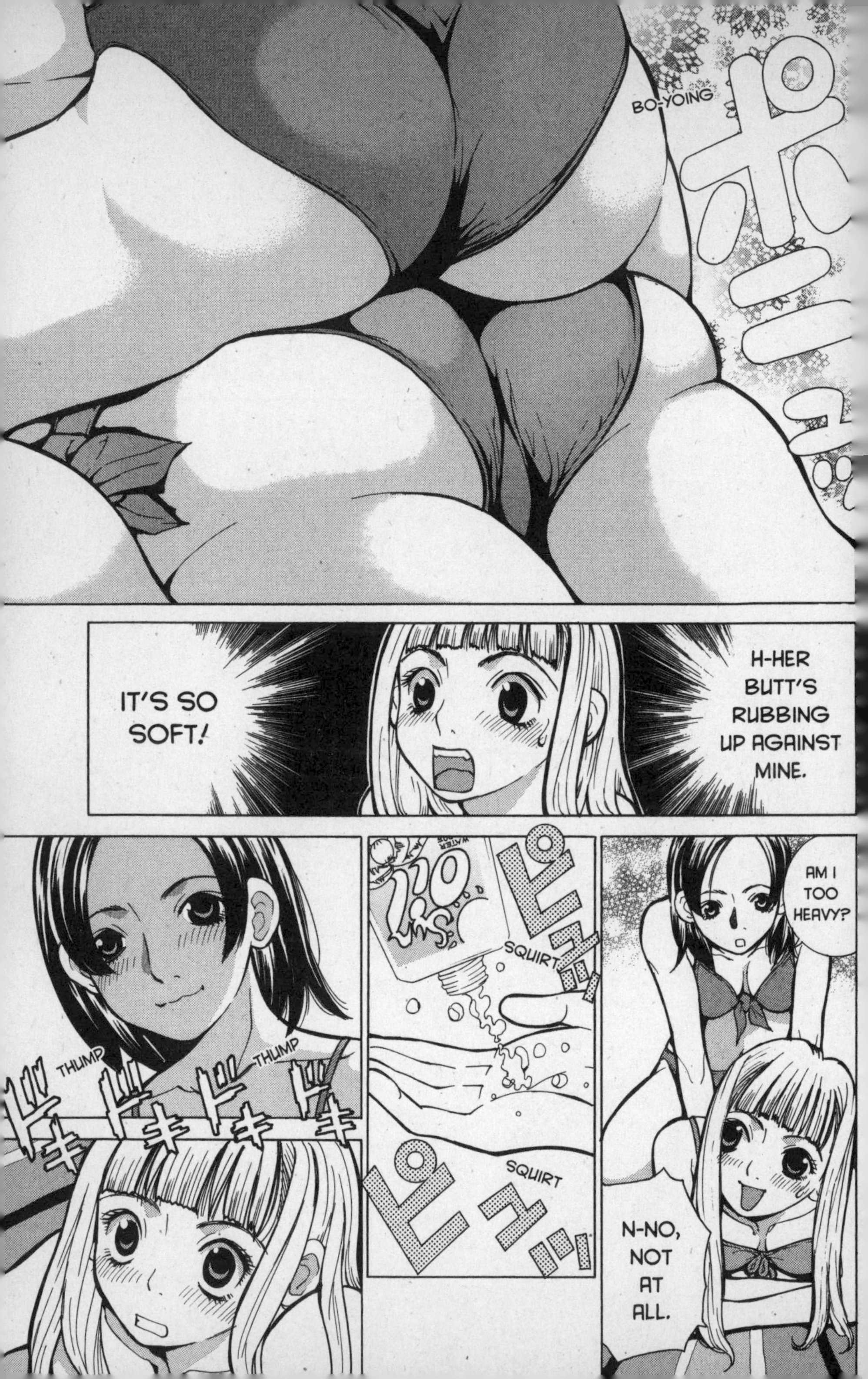
BO-YOING
H-HER BUTT'S RUBBING UP AGAINST MINE.
IT'S SO SOFT!
AM I TOO HEAVY?
N-NO, NOT AT ALL.
SQUIRT
SQUIRT
THUMP
THUMP

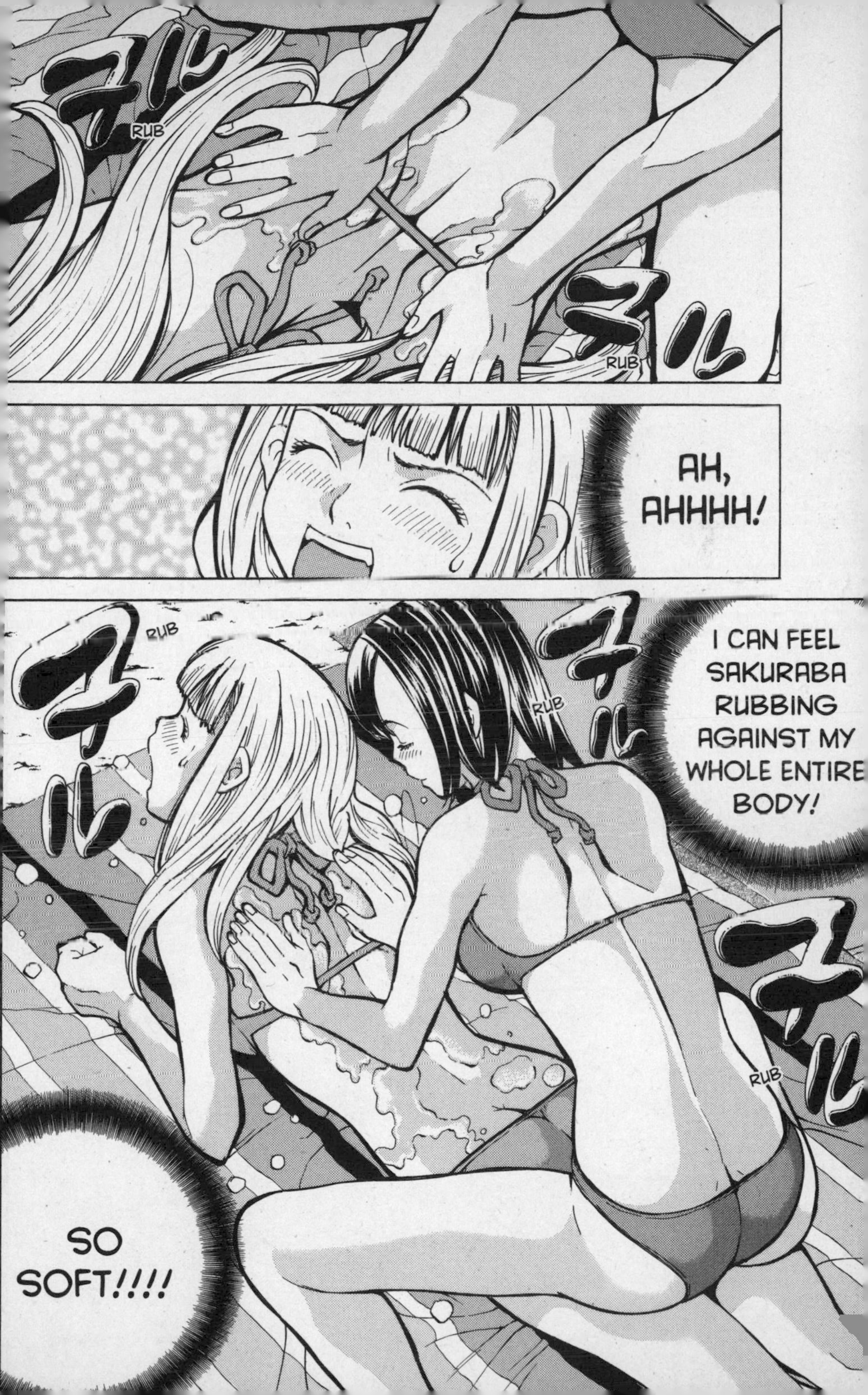
ヌル
RUB
ヌル
RUB
AH, AHHHH!
I CAN FEEL SAKURABA RUBBING AGAINST MY WHOLE ENTIRE BODY!
ヌル
RUB
ヌル
RUB
ヌル
RUB
SO SOFT!!!!

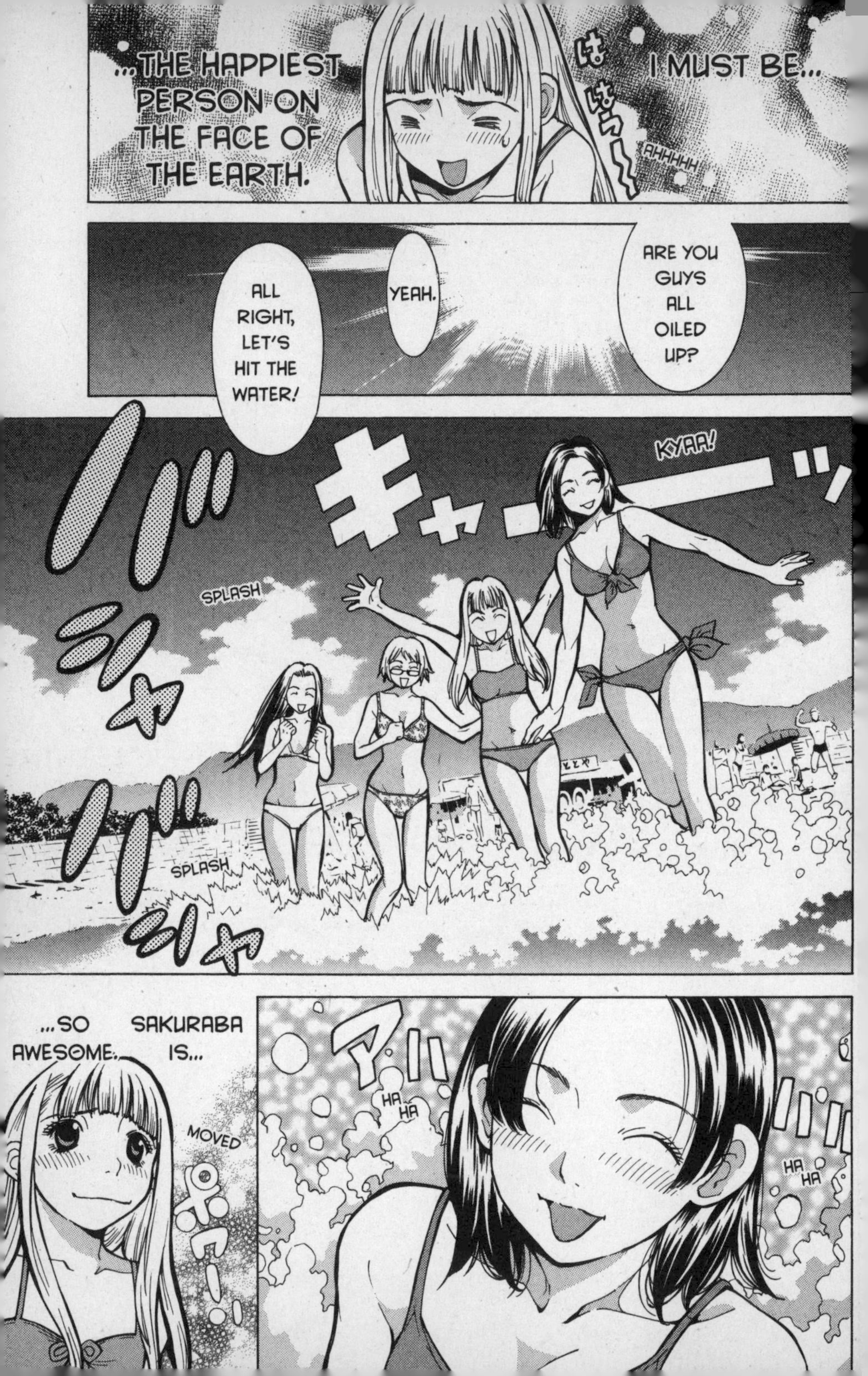
I MUST BE...
AHHHHH
...THE HAPPIEST PERSON ON THE FACE OF THE EARTH.
ARE YOU GUYS ALL OILED UP?
YEAH.
ALL RIGHT, LET'S HIT THE WATER!
KYAA!
SPLASH
SPLASH
HA HA
HA HA
SAKURABA IS...
...SO AWESOME.
MOVED

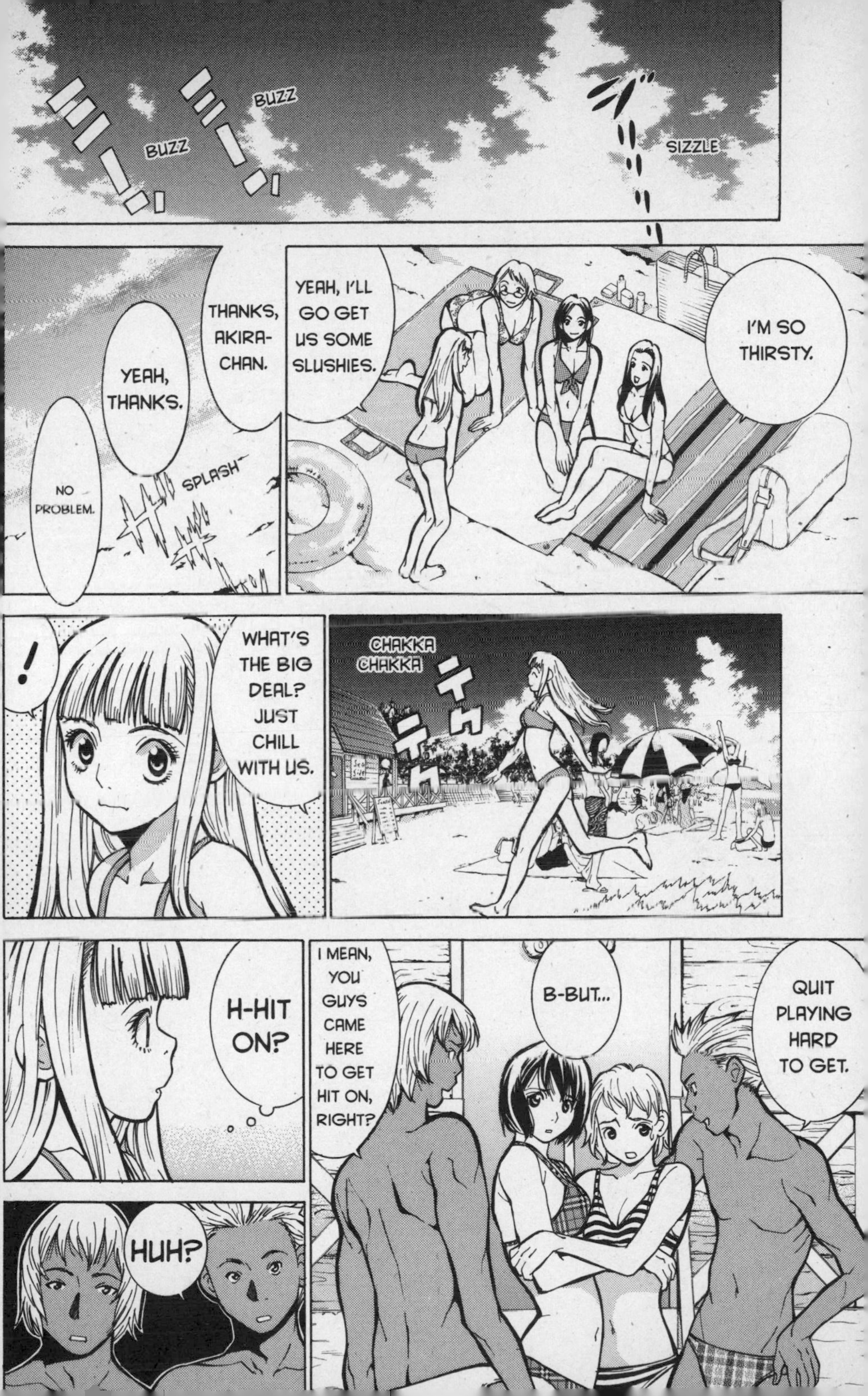
SIZZLE
BUZZ
BUZZ
I'M SO THIRSTY.
YEAH, I'LL GO GET US SOME SLUSHIES.
THANKS, AKIRA-CHAN.
YEAH, THANKS.
NO PROBLEM.
SPLASH
CHAKKA CHAKKA
WHAT'S THE BIG DEAL? JUST CHILL WITH US.
!
QUIT PLAYING HARD TO GET.
B-BUT...
I MEAN, YOU GUYS CAME HERE TO GET HIT ON, RIGHT?
H-HIT ON?
HUH?

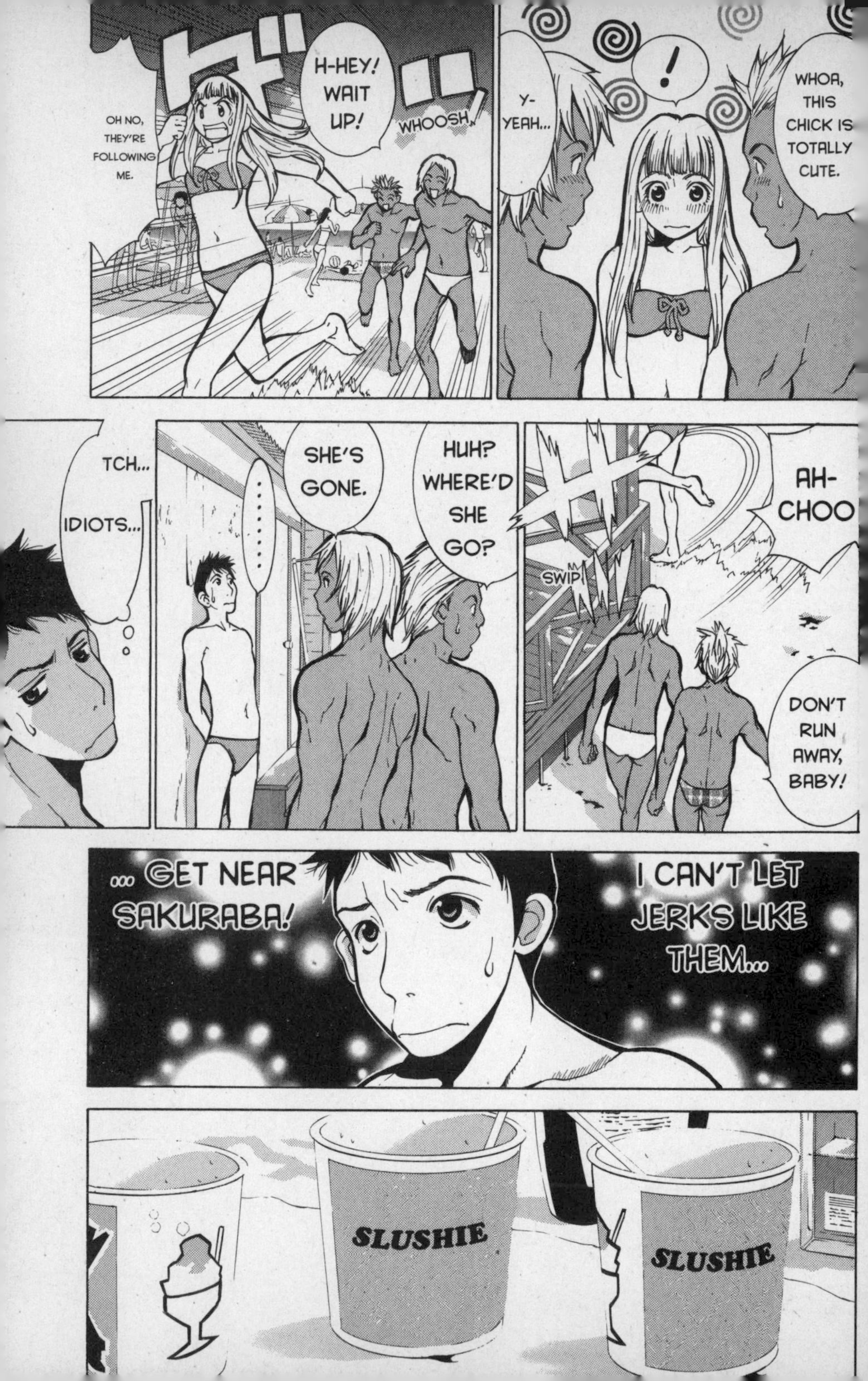
WHOA, THIS CHICK IS TOTALLY CUTE.
!
Y-YEAH...
H-HEY! WAIT UP!
WHOOSH
OH NO, THEY'RE FOLLOWING ME.
AH-CHOO
SWIP
DON'T RUN AWAY, BABY!
HUH? WHERE'D SHE GO?
SHE'S GONE.
......
TCH...
IDIOTS...
I CAN'T LET JERKS LIKE THEM...
... GET NEAR SAKURABA!
SLUSHIE
SLUSHIE

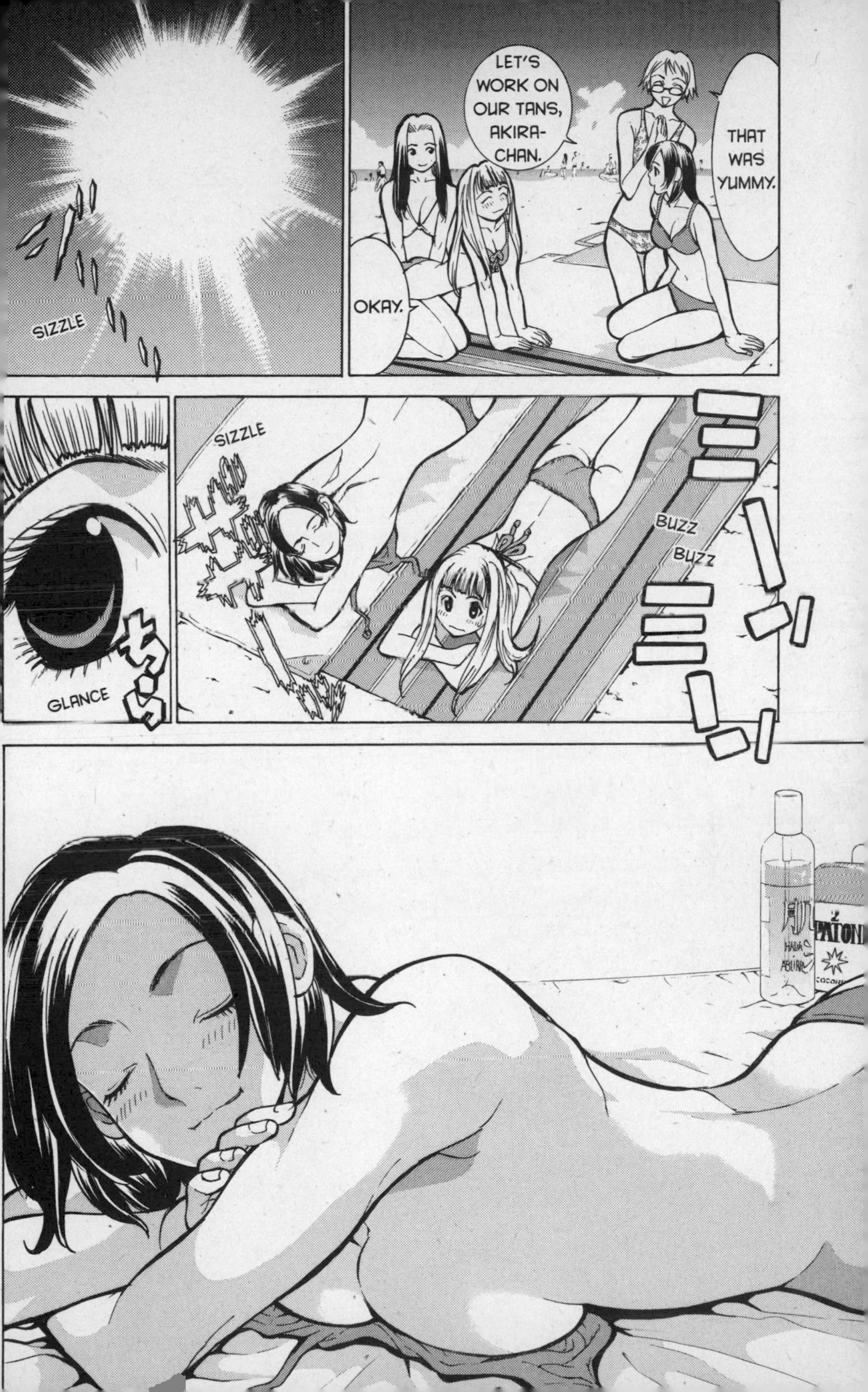
THAT WAS YUMMY.
LET'S WORK ON OUR TANS, AKIRA-CHAN.
OKAY.
SIZZLE
BUZZ
BUZZ
SIZZLE
GLANCE

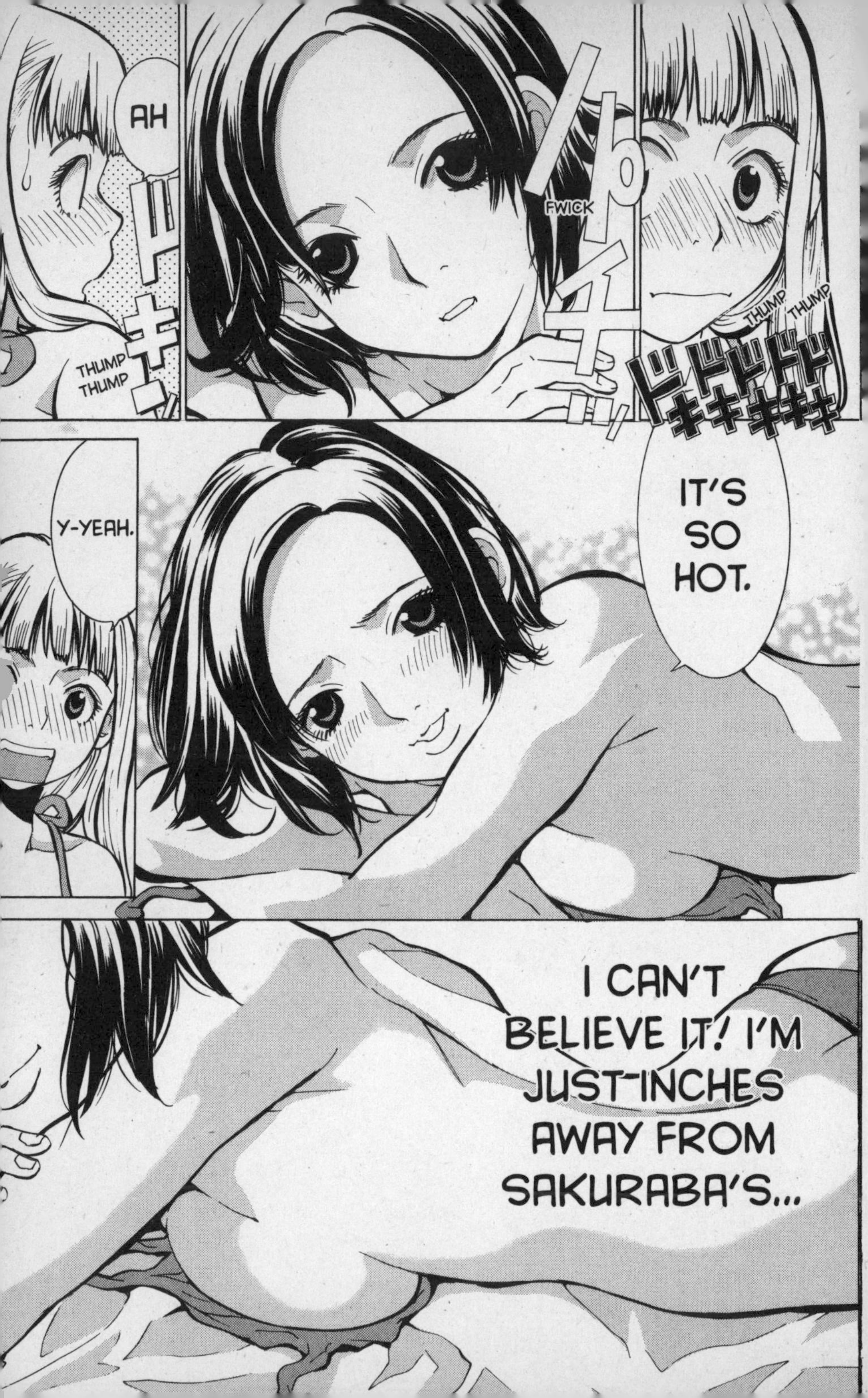
THUMP THUMP
FWICK
AH
THUMP THUMP
IT'S SO HOT.
Y-YEAH.
I CAN'T BELIEVE IT! I'M JUST INCHES AWAY FROM SAKURABA'S...

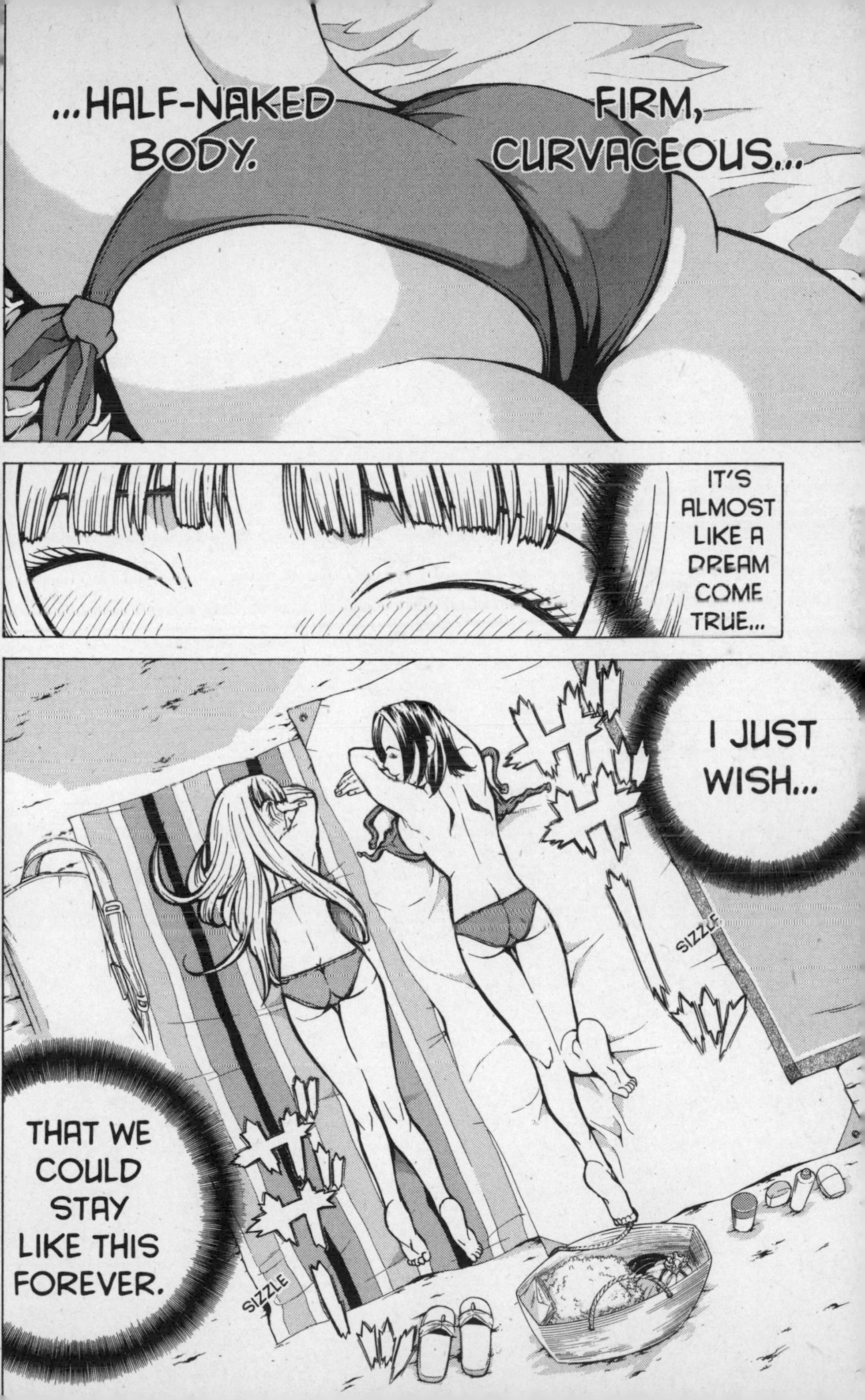
FIRM, CURVACEOUS...
...HALF-NAKED BODY.
IT'S ALMOST LIKE A DREAM COME TRUE...
I JUST WISH...
SIZZLE
THAT WE COULD STAY LIKE THIS FOREVER.
SIZZLE

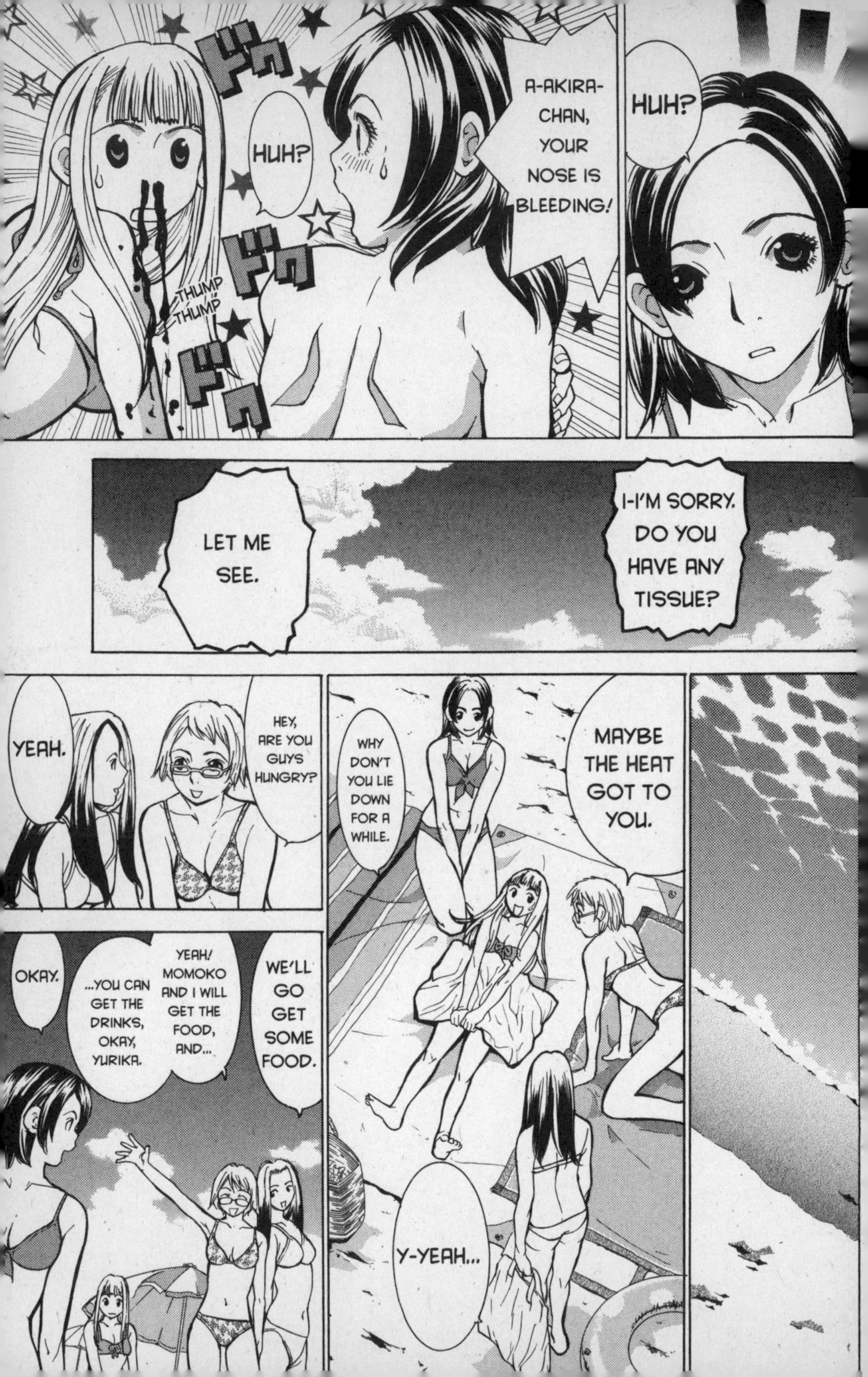
HUH?
A-AKIRA-CHAN, YOUR NOSE IS BLEEDING!
HUH?
THUMP THUMP
I-I'M SORRY. DO YOU HAVE ANY TISSUE?
LET ME SEE.
MAYBE THE HEAT GOT TO YOU.
WHY DON'T YOU LIE DOWN FOR A WHILE.
Y-YEAH...
HEY, ARE YOU GUYS HUNGRY?
YEAH.
WE'LL GO GET SOME FOOD.
YEAH! MOMOKO AND I WILL GET THE FOOD, AND...
...YOU CAN GET THE DRINKS, OKAY, YURIKA.
OKAY.

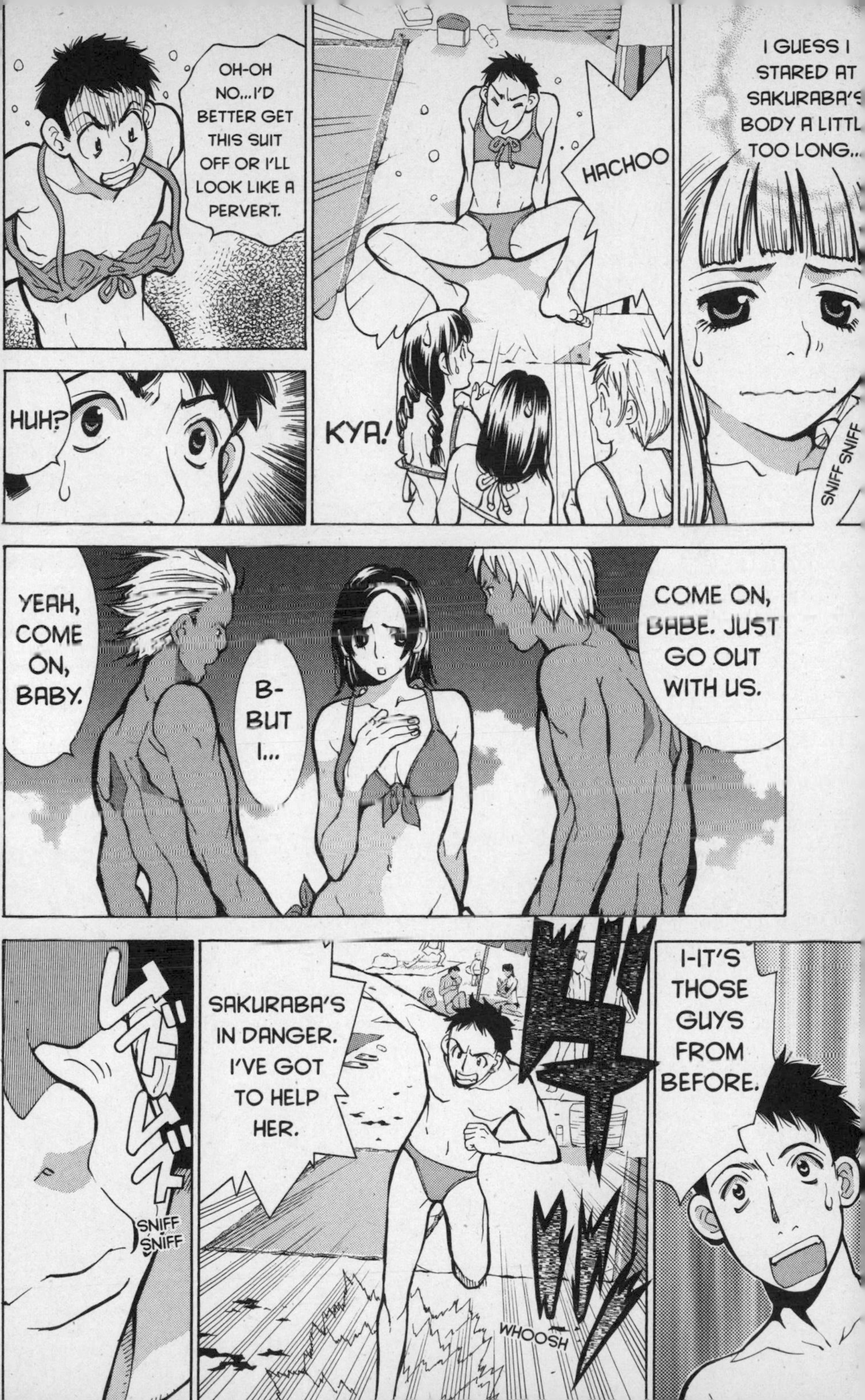

I GUESS I STARED AT SAKURABA'S BODY A LITTL TOO LONG...
SNIFF SNIFF
HACHOO
KYA!
OH-OH NO...I'D BETTER GET THIS SUIT OFF OR I'LL LOOK LIKE A PERVERT.
HUH?
COME ON, BABE. JUST GO OUT WITH US.
B-BUT I...
YEAH, COME ON, BABY.
I-IT'S THOSE GUYS FROM BEFORE.
SAKURABA'S IN DANGER. I'VE GOT TO HELP HER.
WHOOSH
SNIFF SNIFF

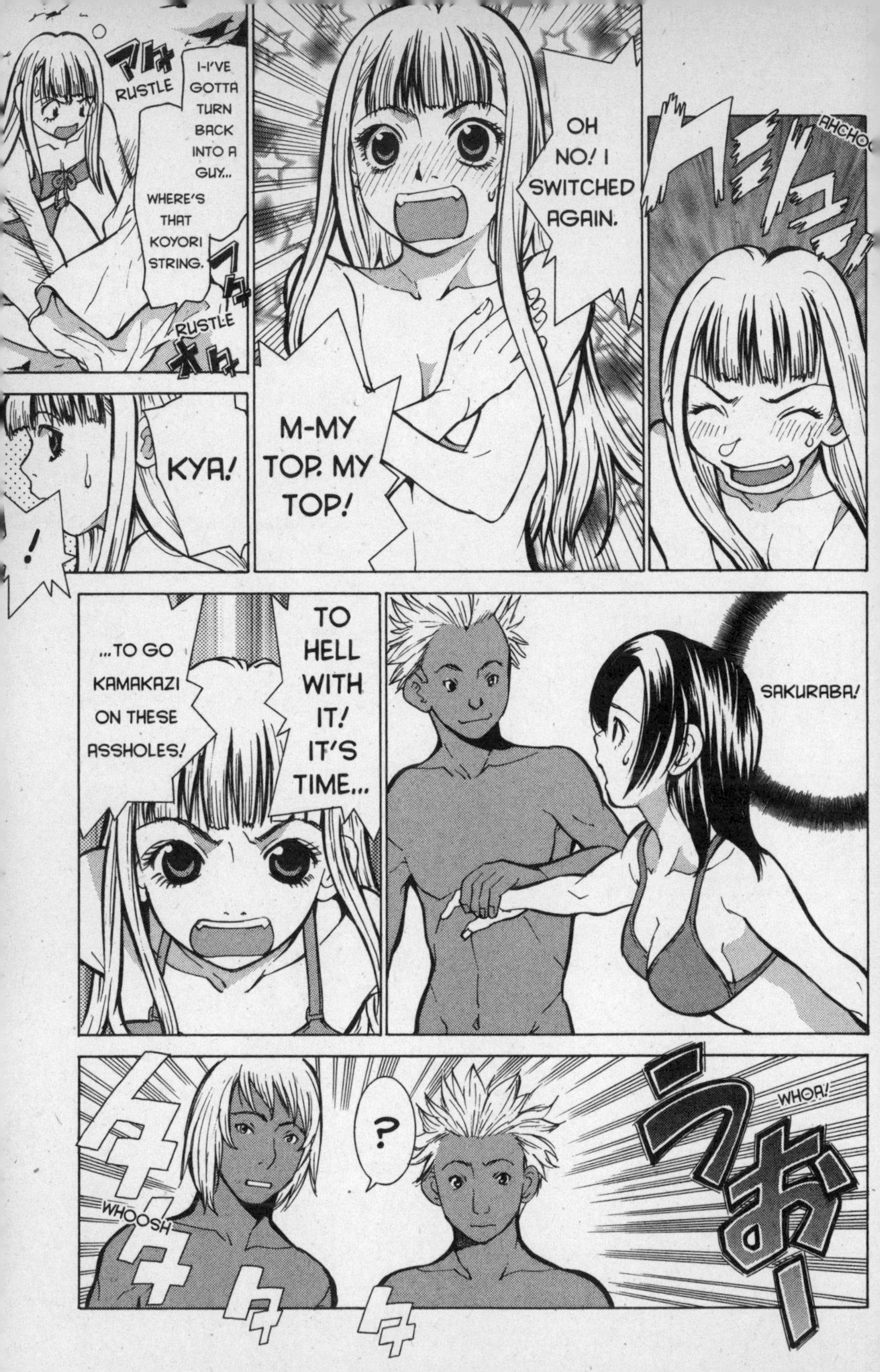
AHCHOO
OH NO! I SWITCHED AGAIN.
M-MY TOP. MY TOP!
RUSTLE
I-I'VE GOTTA TURN BACK INTO A GUY...
WHERE'S THAT KOYORI STRING.
RUSTLE
KYA!
!
SAKURABA!
TO HELL WITH IT! IT'S TIME...
...TO GO KAMAKAZI ON THESE ASSHOLES!
WHOA!
?
WHOOSH

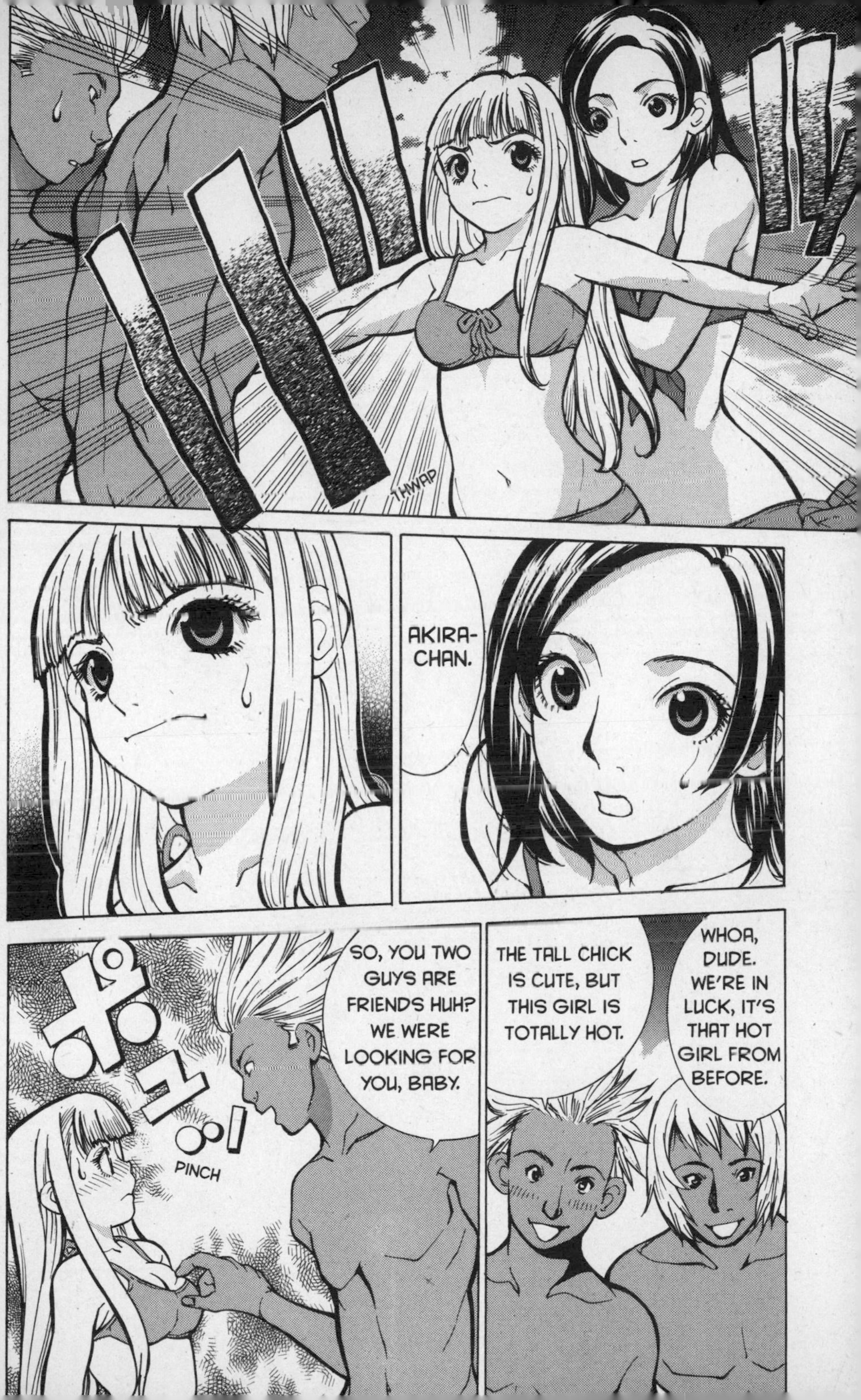
THWAP
AKIRA-CHAN.
WHOA, DUDE. WE'RE IN LUCK, IT'S THAT HOT GIRL FROM BEFORE.
THE TALL CHICK IS CUTE, BUT THIS GIRL IS TOTALLY HOT.
SO, YOU TWO GUYS ARE FRIENDS HUH? WE WERE LOOKING FOR YOU, BABY.
PINCH

PLEASE, STOP!

YOU LITTLE—!

SAKURABA IS SACRIFICING HERSELF TO PROTECT ME.

SA-SAKURABA

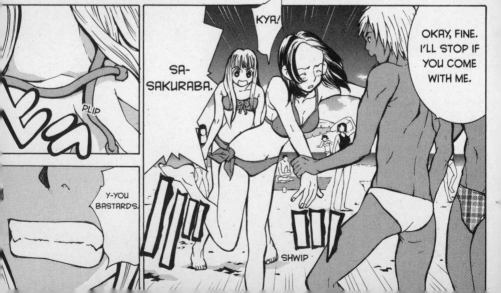

KYA!

SA-SAKURABA.

OKAY, FINE. I'LL STOP IF YOU COME WITH ME.

PLIP

Y-YOU BASTARDS.

SHWIP

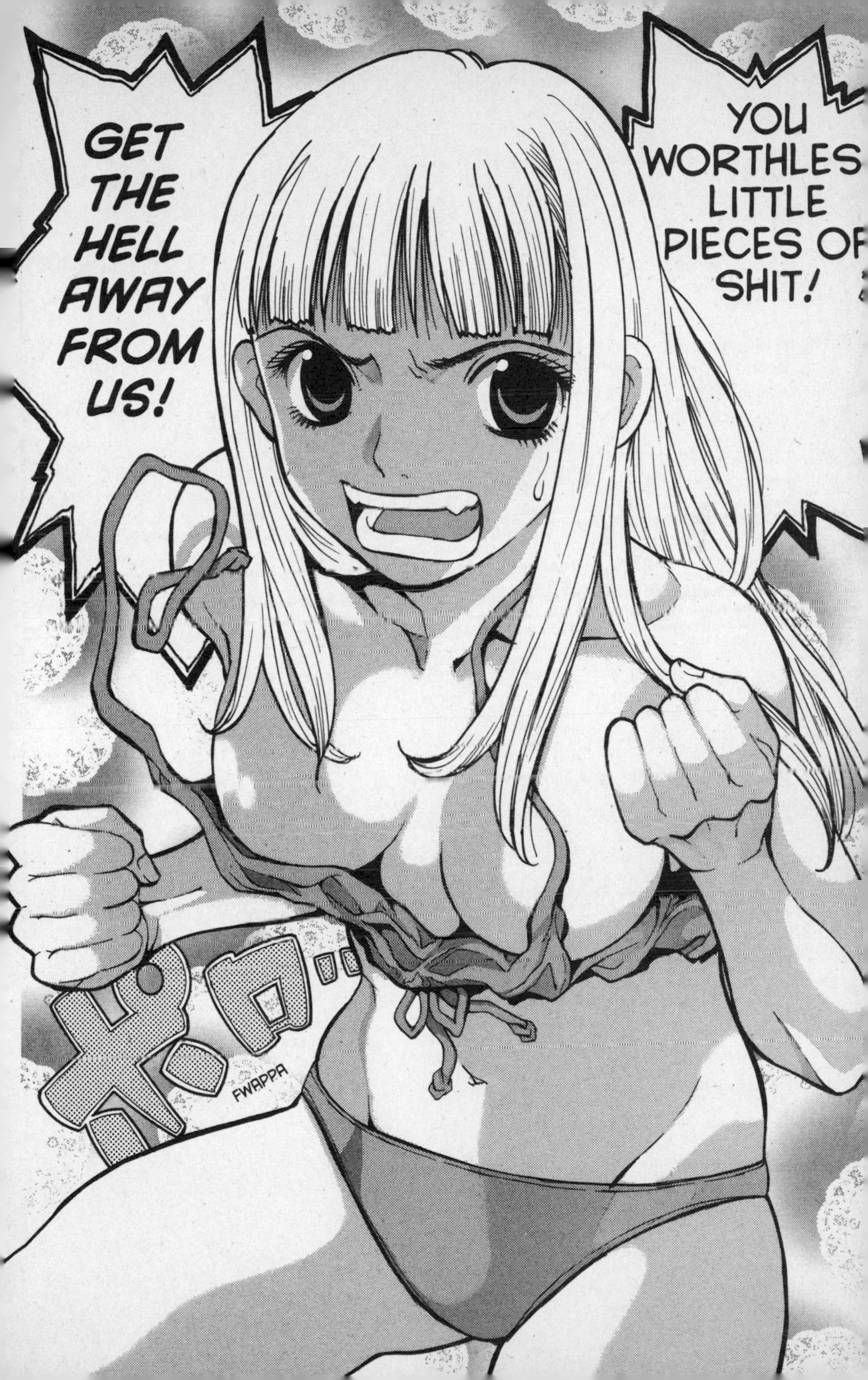
YOU WORTHLES LITTLE PIECES OF SHIT!
GET THE HELL AWAY FROM US!
FWAPPA

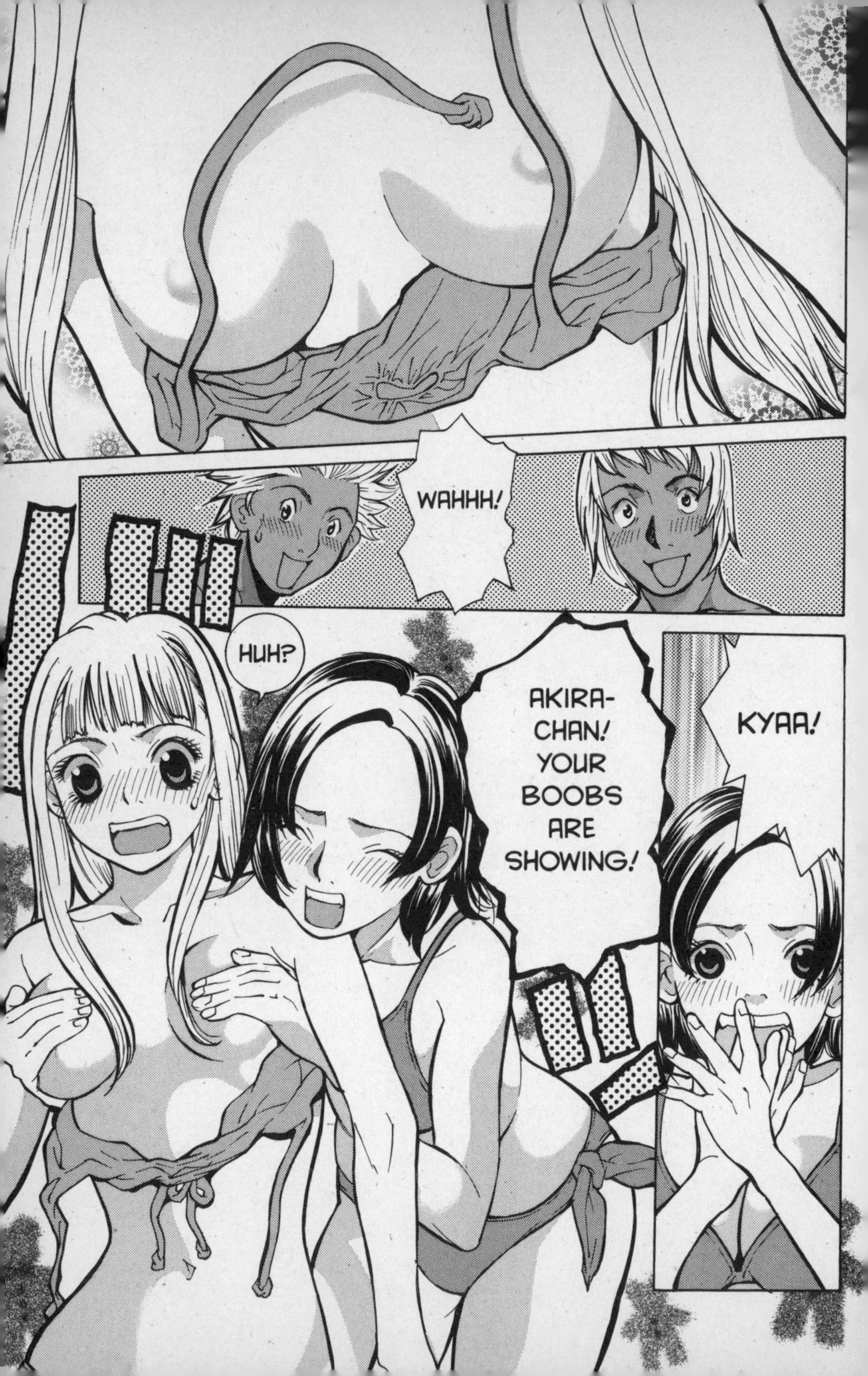
WAHHH!
KYAA!
AKIRA-CHAN! YOUR BOOBS ARE SHOWING!
HUH?

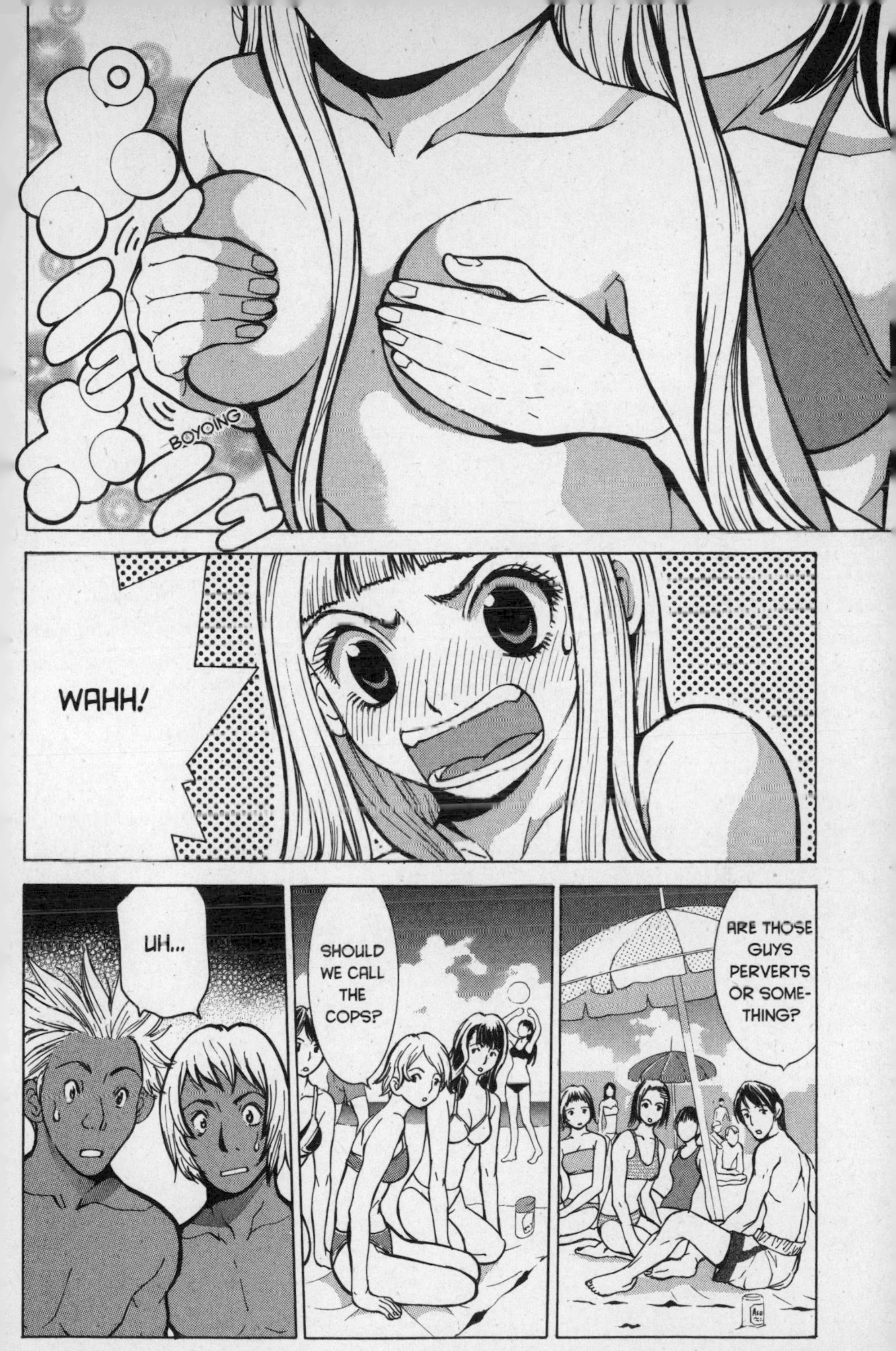
BOYOING
WAHH!
ARE THOSE GUYS PERVERTS OR SOME-THING?
SHOULD WE CALL THE COPS?
UH...

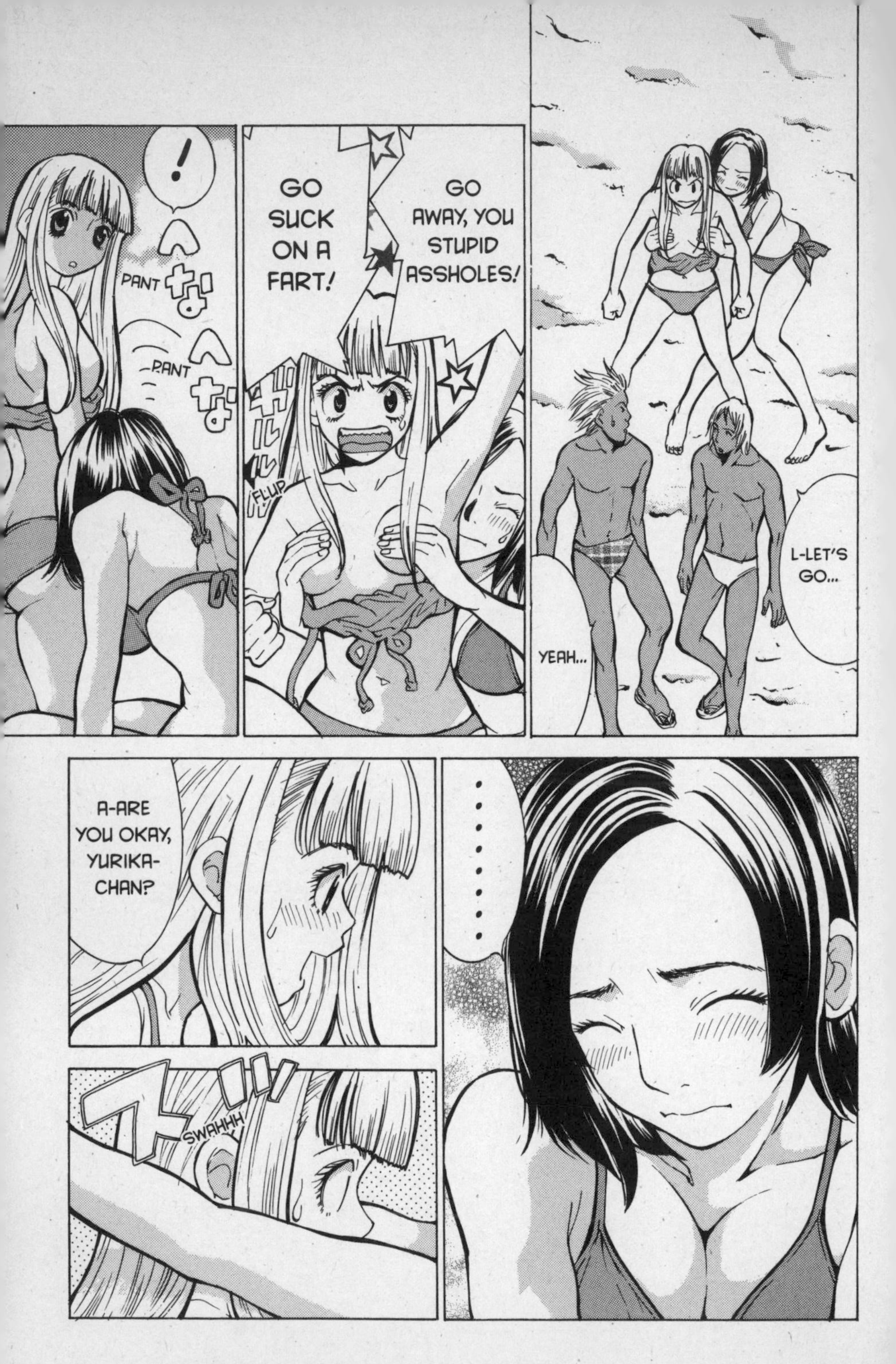
L-LET'S GO...
YEAH...
GO AWAY, YOU STUPID ASSHOLES!
GO SUCK ON A FART!
FLUP
!
PANT
PANT
....
A-ARE YOU OKAY, YURIKA-CHAN?
SWAHHH

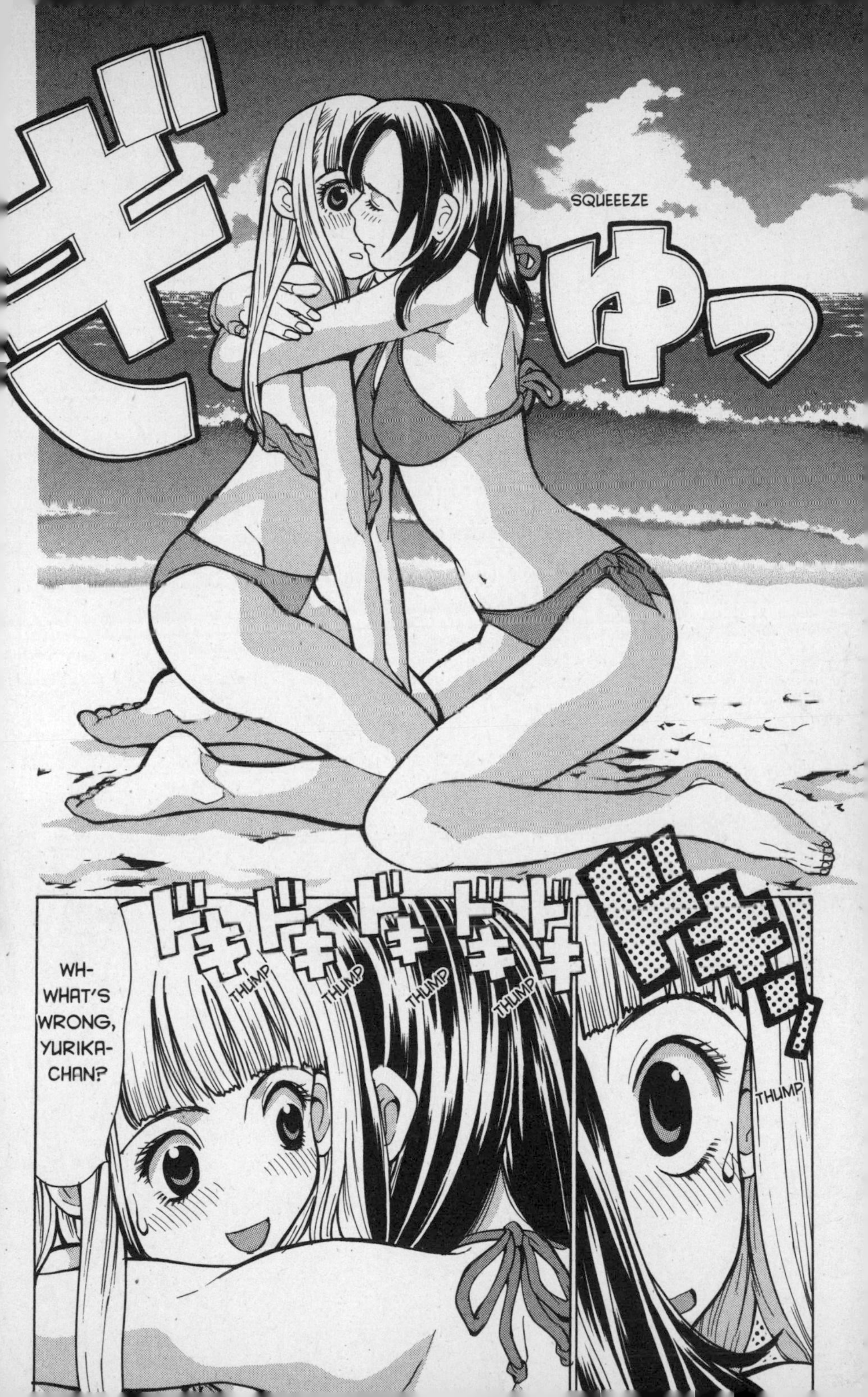
ぎゅっ
SQUEEEZE
ドキッ
THUMP
ドキドキドキドキ
THUMP
THUMP
THUMP
THUMP
WH- WHAT'S WRONG, YURIKA-CHAN?

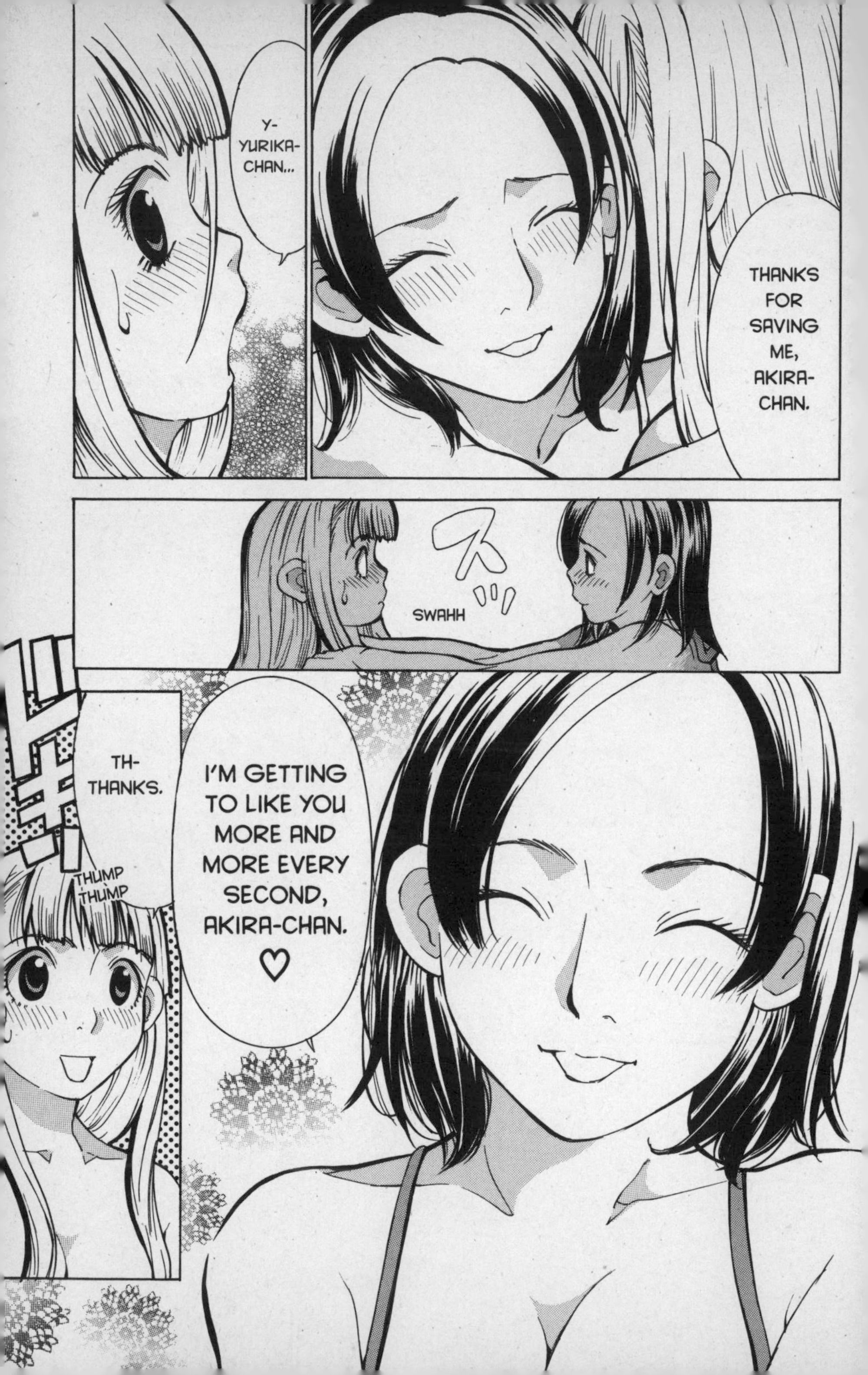
THANKS FOR SAVING ME, AKIRA-CHAN.
Y-YURIKA-CHAN...
ス
SWAHH
I'M GETTING TO LIKE YOU MORE AND MORE EVERY SECOND, AKIRA-CHAN. ♡
TH-THANKS.
THUMP THUMP

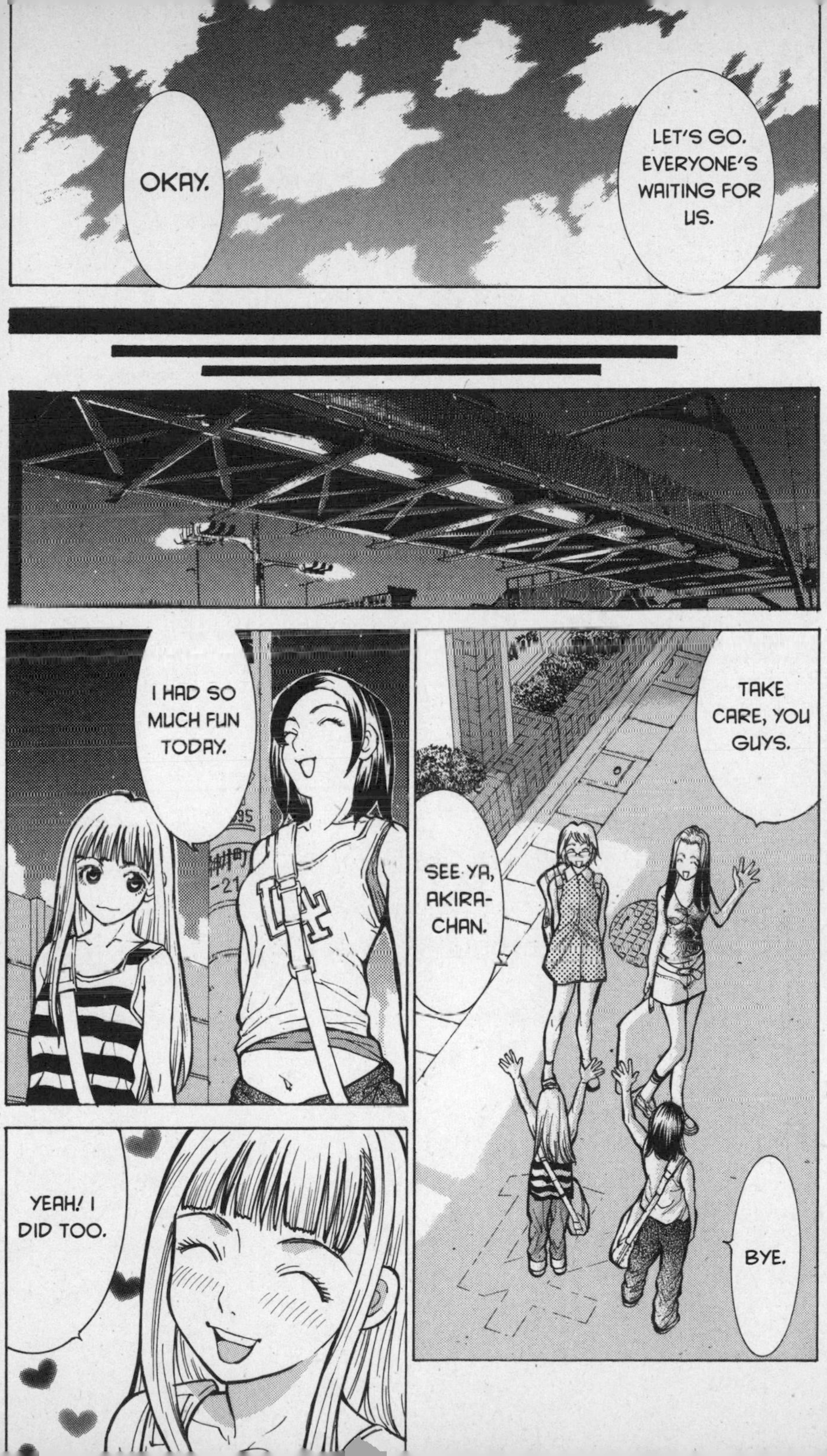
LET'S GO. EVERYONE'S WAITING FOR US.
OKAY.
TAKE CARE, YOU GUYS.
SEE YA, AKIRA-CHAN.
BYE.
I HAD SO MUCH FUN TODAY.
YEAH! I DID TOO.

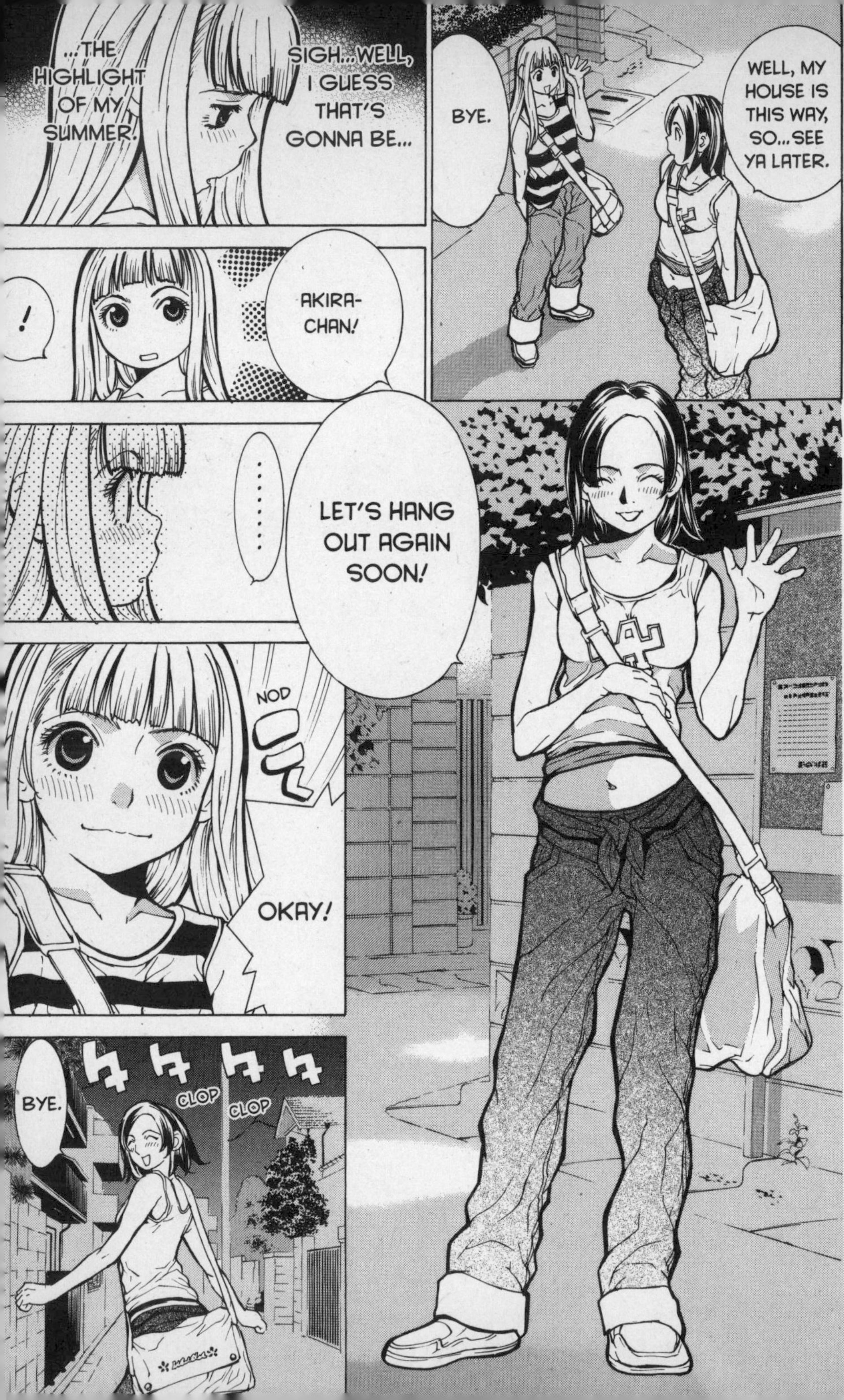
WELL, MY HOUSE IS THIS WAY, SO...SEE YA LATER.
BYE.
SIGH...WELL, I GUESS THAT'S GONNA BE...
...THE HIGHLIGHT OF MY SUMMER.
LET'S HANG OUT AGAIN SOON!
AKIRA-CHAN!
!
......
NOD
OKAY!
CLOP
CLOP
BYE.

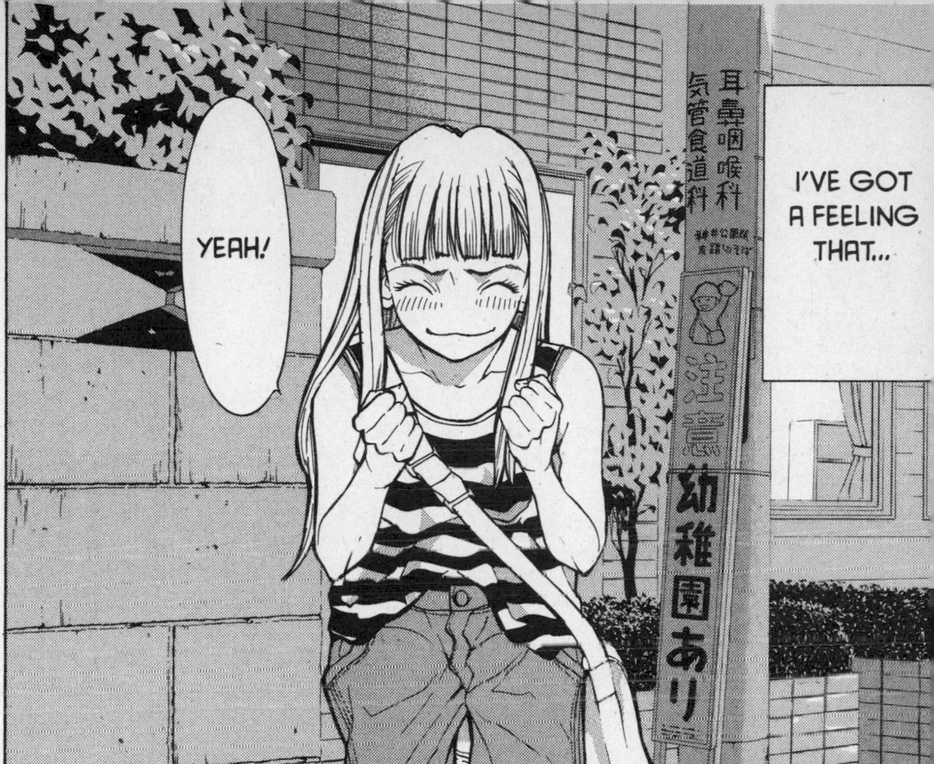
I'VE GOT A FEELING THAT...
耳鼻咽喉科
気管食道科
注意
幼稚園あり
YEAH!
THIS IS GONNA BE THE BEST SUMMER EVER!

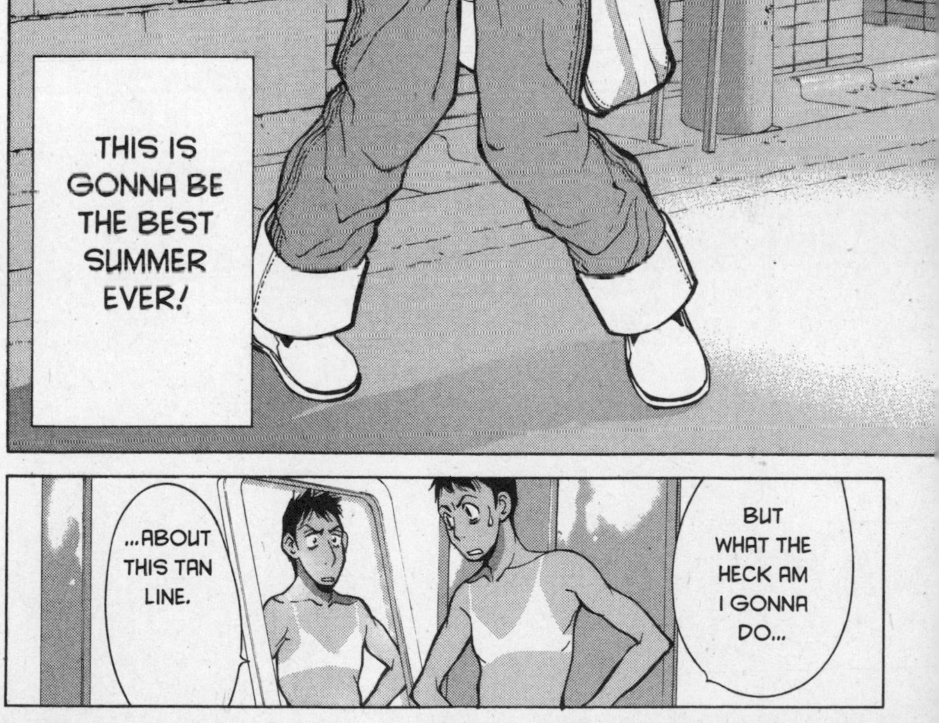
BUT WHAT THE HECK AM I GONNA DO...
...ABOUT THIS TAN LINE.

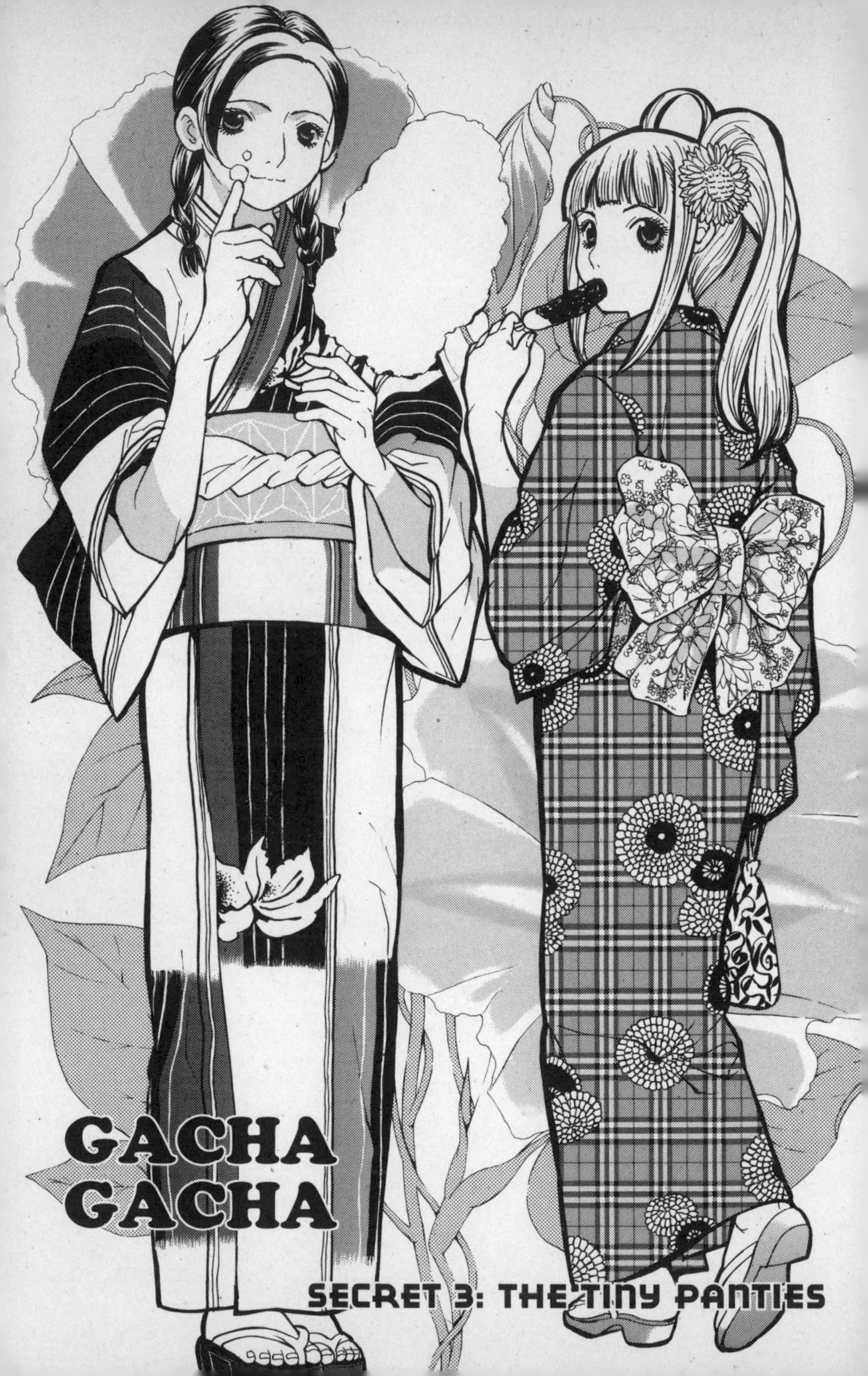
GACHA GACHA
SECRET 3: THE TINY PANTIES

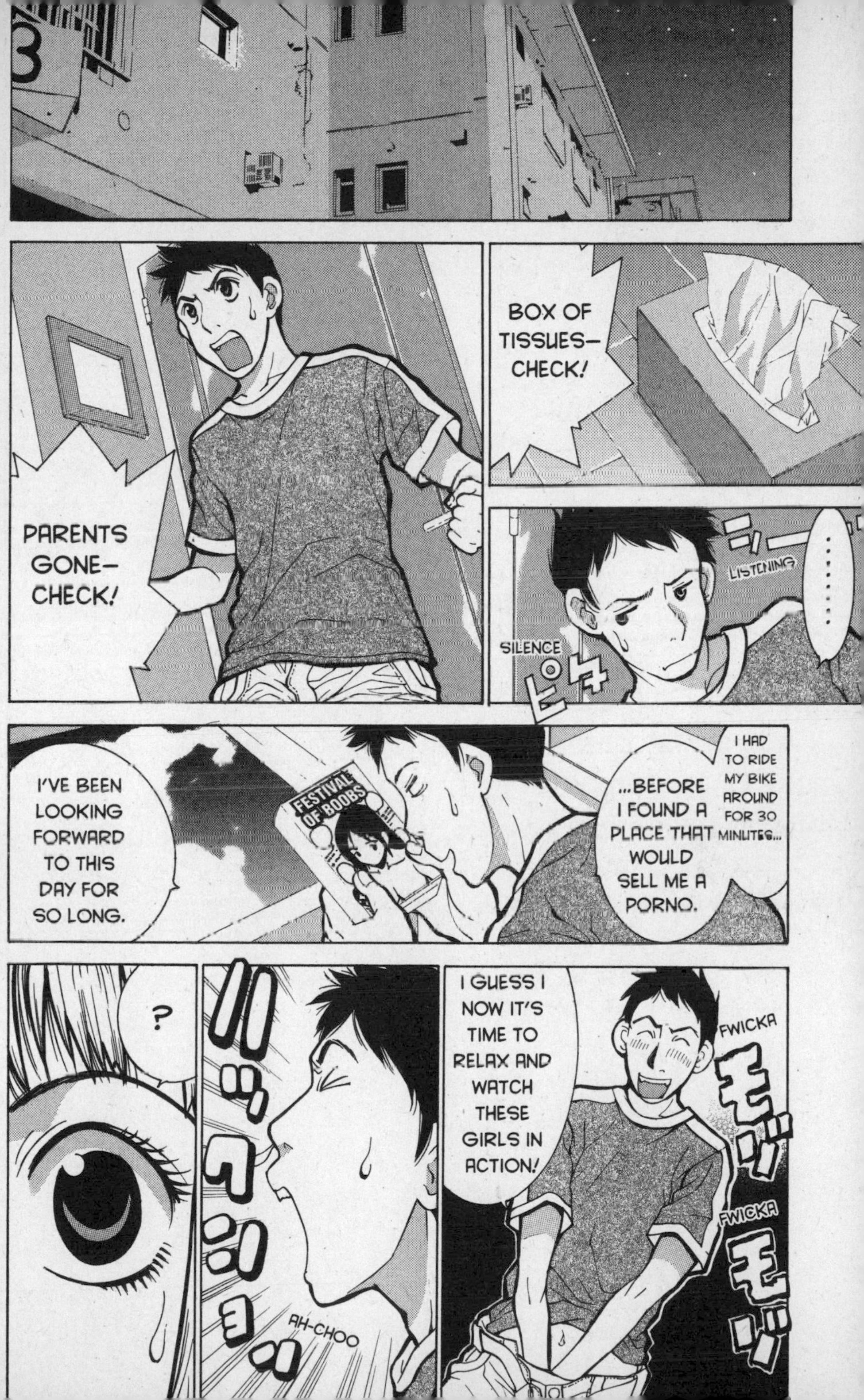
BOX OF TISSUES— CHECK!
LISTENING
......
SILENCE
PARENTS GONE— CHECK!
I HAD TO RIDE MY BIKE AROUND FOR 30 MINUTES...
...BEFORE I FOUND A PLACE THAT WOULD SELL ME A PORNO.
FESTIVAL OF BOOBS
I'VE BEEN LOOKING FORWARD TO THIS DAY FOR SO LONG.
I GUESS I NOW IT'S TIME TO RELAX AND WATCH THESE GIRLS IN ACTION!
FWICKA
FWICKA
AH-CHOO
?

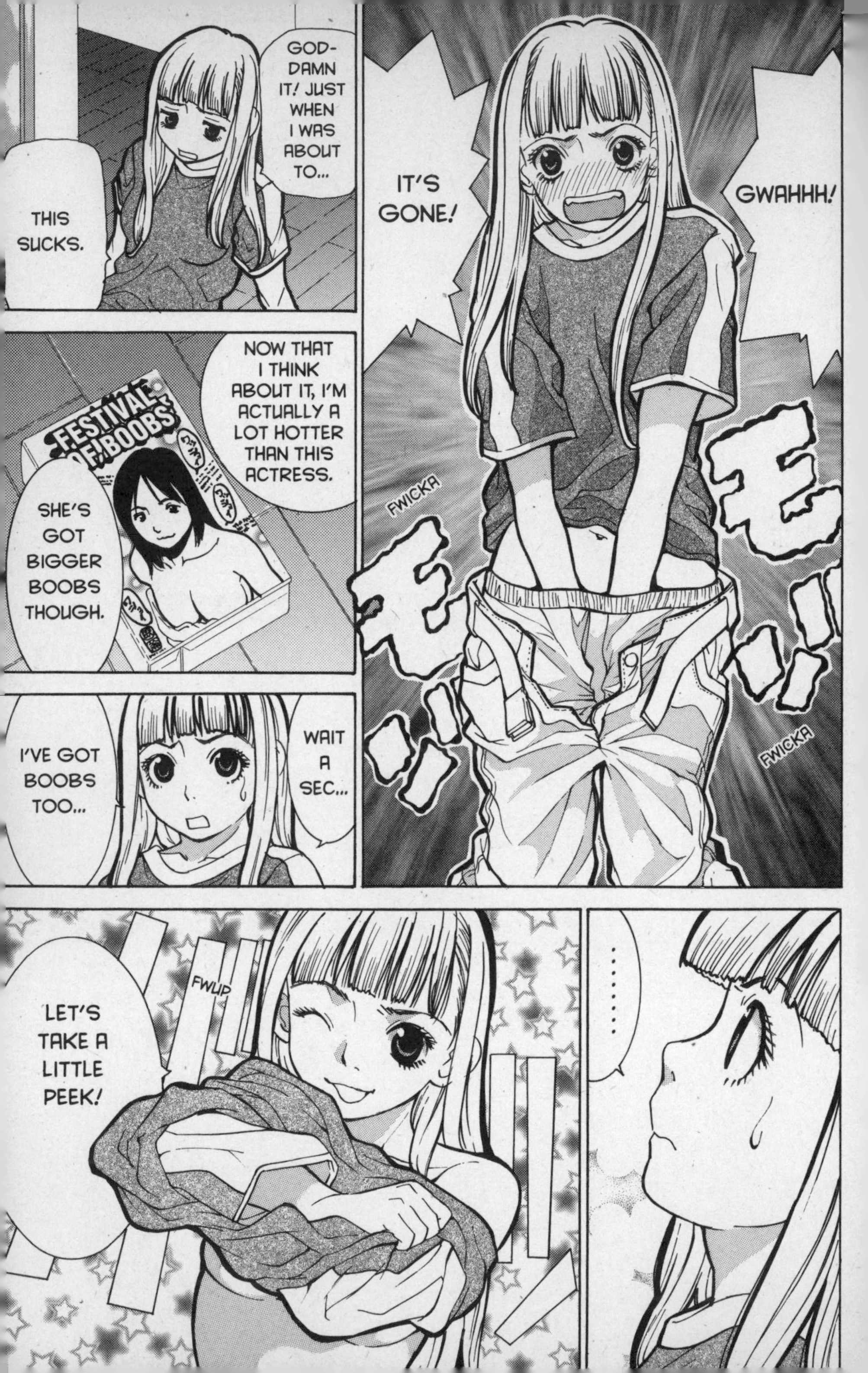
GWAHHH!
IT'S GONE!
FWICKA
FWICKA
GOD-DAMN IT! JUST WHEN I WAS ABOUT TO...
THIS SUCKS.
NOW THAT I THINK ABOUT IT, I'M ACTUALLY A LOT HOTTER THAN THIS ACTRESS.
FESTIVAL OF BOOBS
SHE'S GOT BIGGER BOOBS THOUGH.
WAIT A SEC...
I'VE GOT BOOBS TOO...
......
FWUP
LET'S TAKE A LITTLE PEEK!

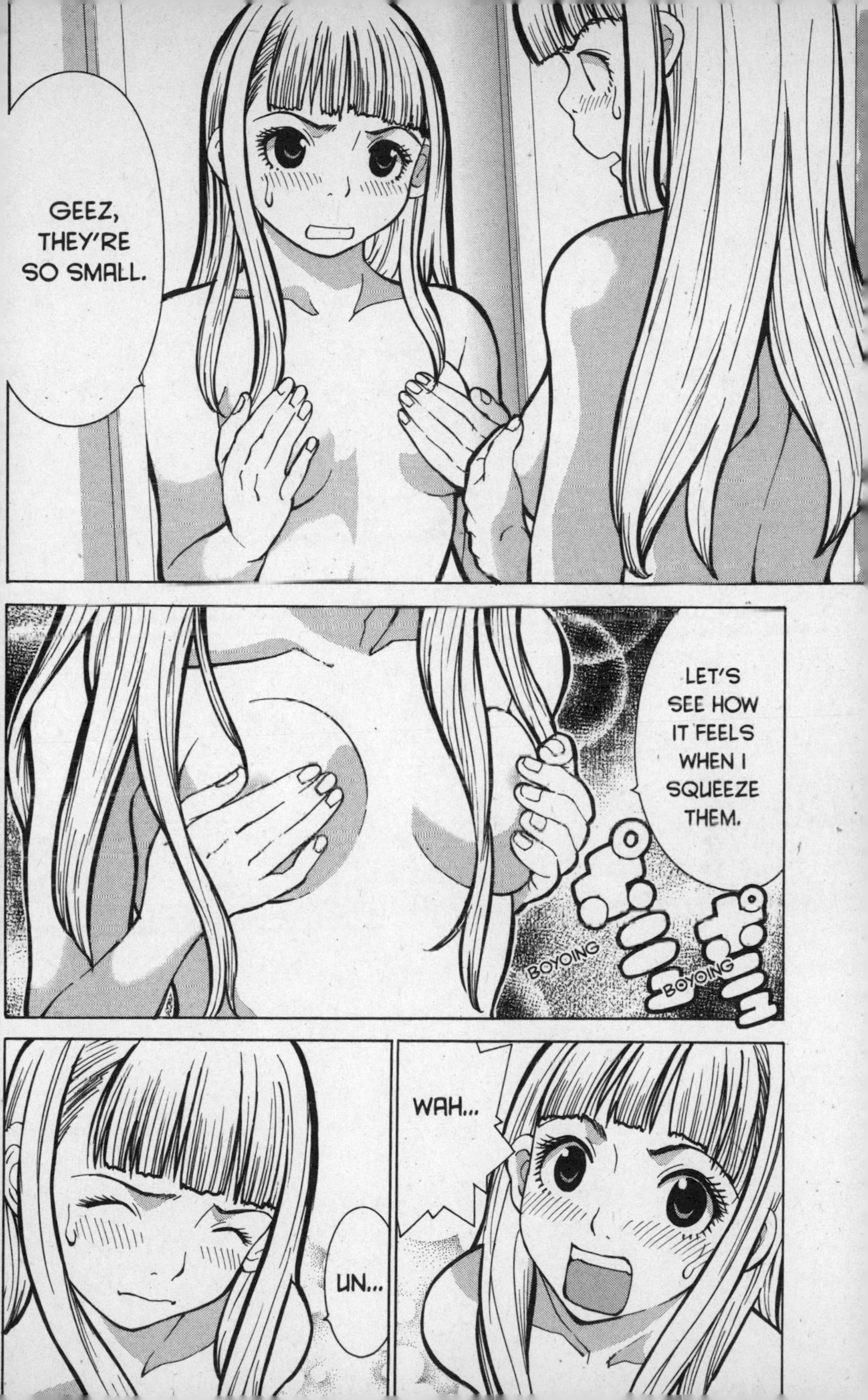
GEEZ, THEY'RE SO SMALL.
LET'S SEE HOW IT FEELS WHEN I SQUEEZE THEM.
BOYOING
BOYOING
WAH...
UN...

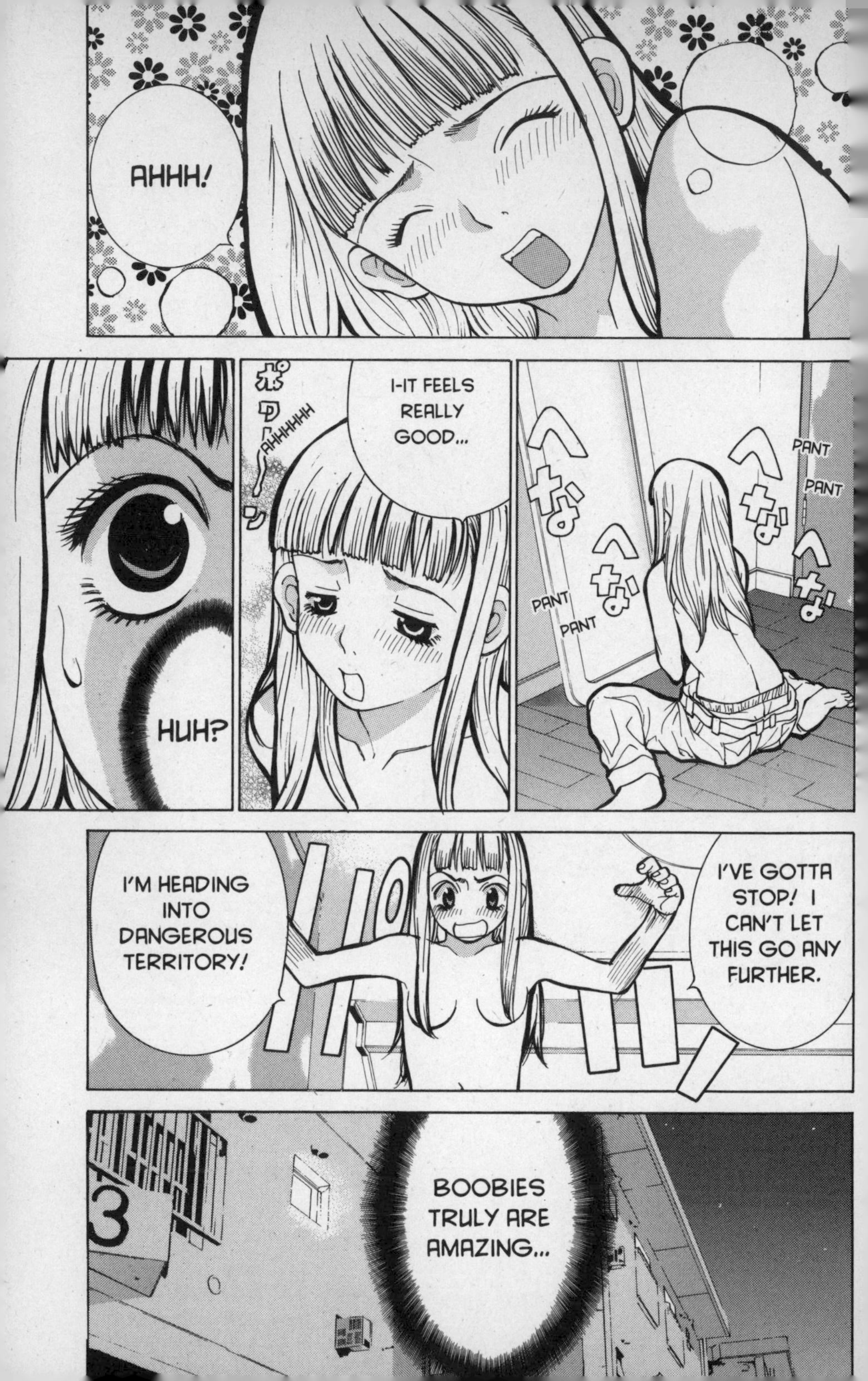

AHHH!
へな へな へな へな
PANT
PANT
PANT
PANT
AHHHHH
I-IT FEELS REALLY GOOD...
HUH?
I'VE GOTTA STOP! I CAN'T LET THIS GO ANY FURTHER.
I'M HEADING INTO DANGEROUS TERRITORY!
BOOBIES TRULY ARE AMAZING...

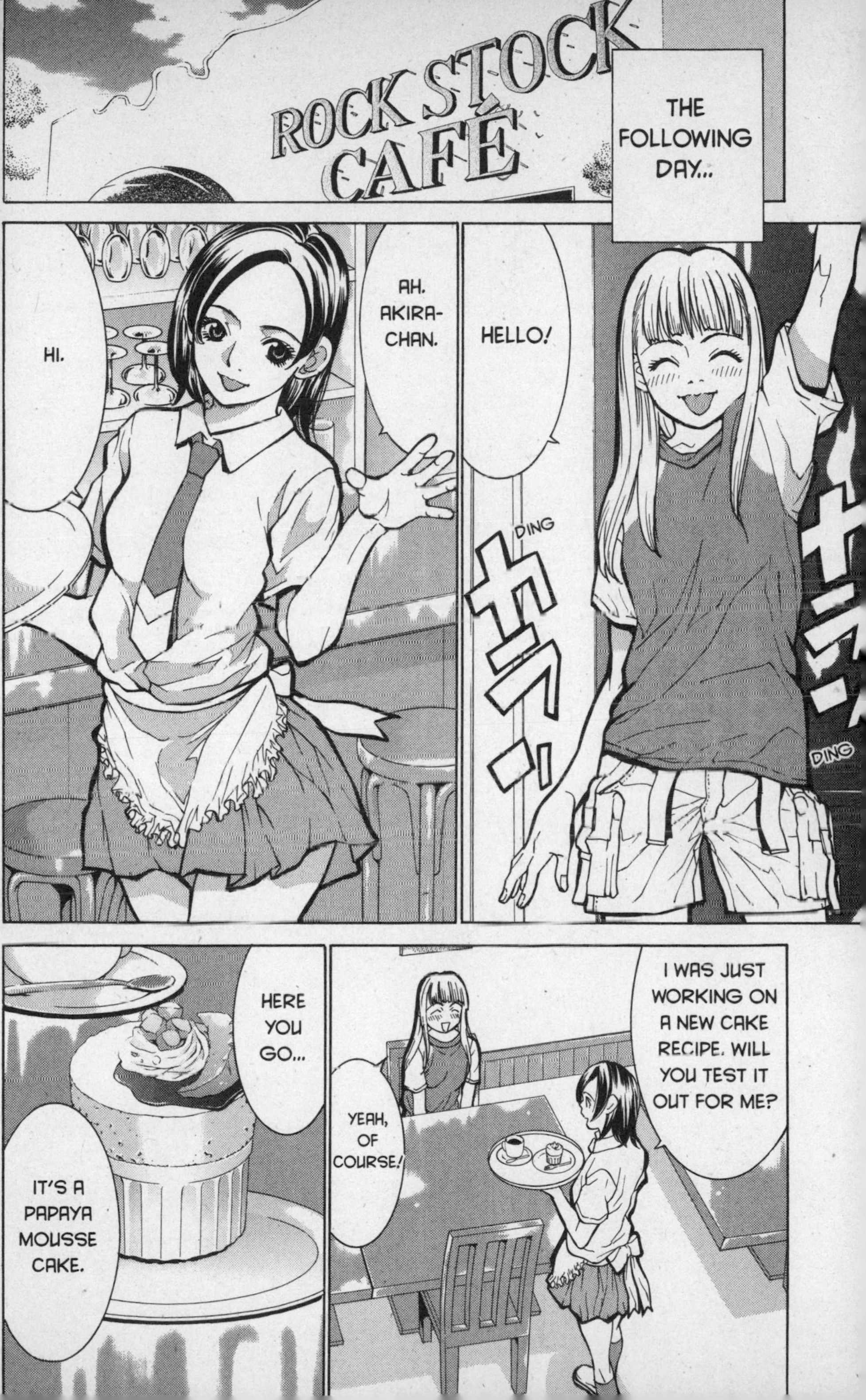
ROCK STOCK CAFÉ
THE FOLLOWING DAY...
HELLO!
DING
DING
AH. AKIRA-CHAN.
HI.
I WAS JUST WORKING ON A NEW CAKE RECIPE. WILL YOU TEST IT OUT FOR ME?
YEAH, OF COURSE!
HERE YOU GO...
IT'S A PAPAYA MOUSSE CAKE.

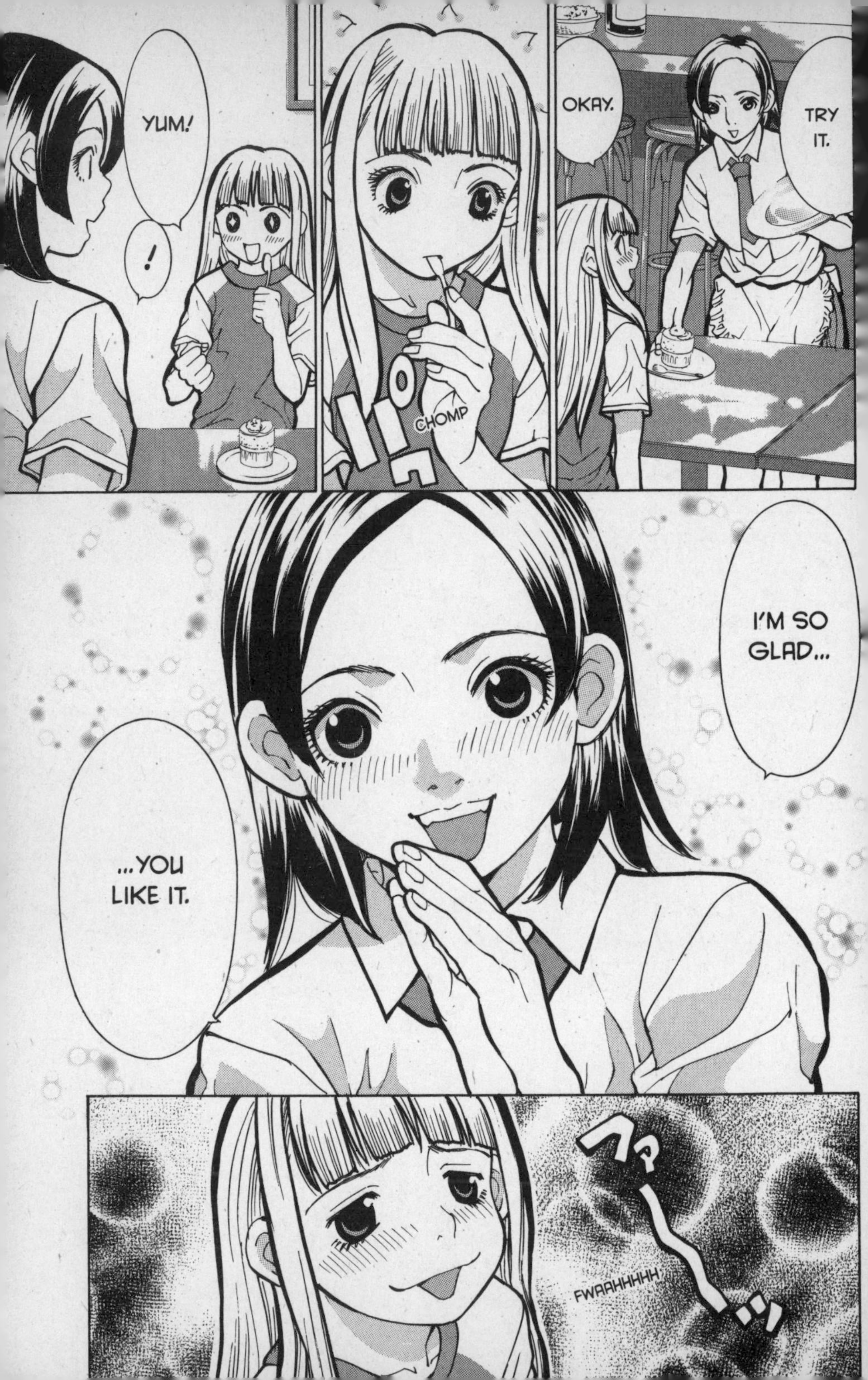
TRY IT.
OKAY.
CHOMP
YUM!
!
I'M SO GLAD...
...YOU LIKE IT.
FWAAHHHHH

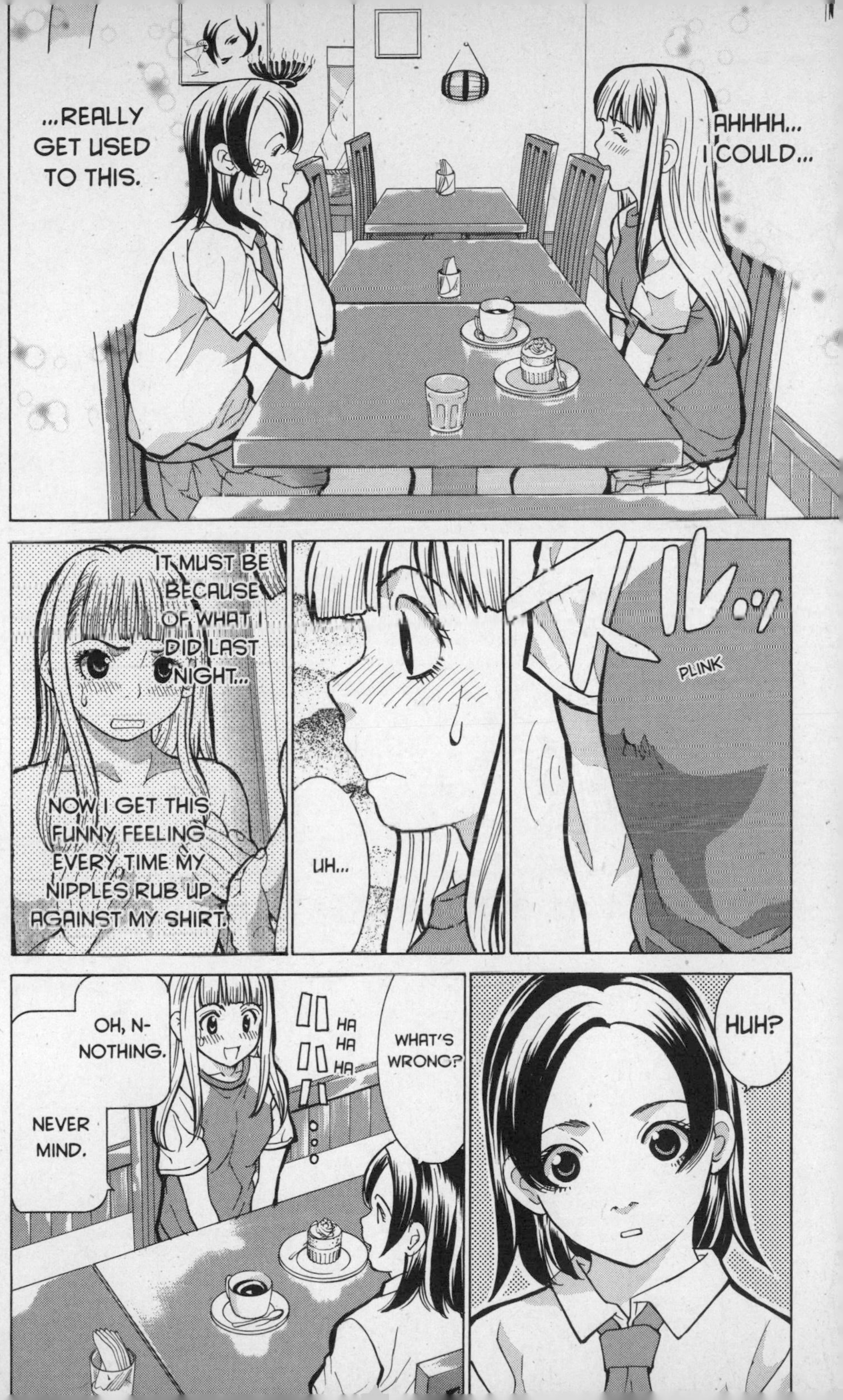
AHHHH... I COULD...
...REALLY GET USED TO THIS.
スル...
PLINK
UH...
IT MUST BE BECAUSE OF WHAT I DID LAST NIGHT...
NOW I GET THIS FUNNY FEELING EVERY TIME MY NIPPLES RUB UP AGAINST MY SHIRT.
HUH?
WHAT'S WRONG?
HA HA HA
OH, N- NOTHING.
NEVER MIND.

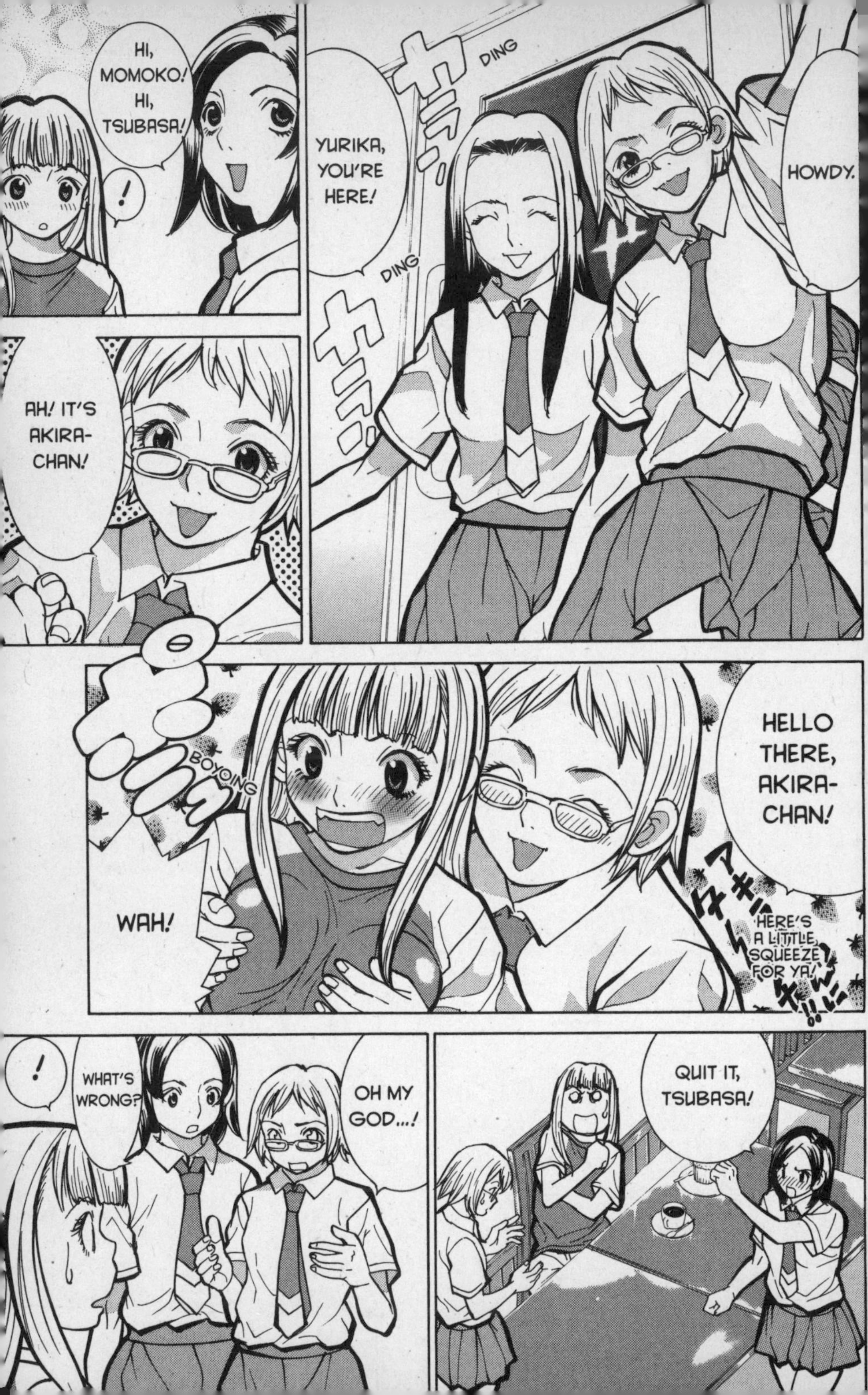
DING
HOWDY.
YURIKA, YOU'RE HERE!
DING
HI, MOMOKO! HI, TSUBASA!
!
AH! IT'S AKIRA-CHAN!
HELLO THERE, AKIRA-CHAN!
HERE'S A LITTLE SQUEEZE FOR YA!
BOYOING
WAH!
QUIT IT, TSUBASA!
OH MY GOD...!
WHAT'S WRONG?
!

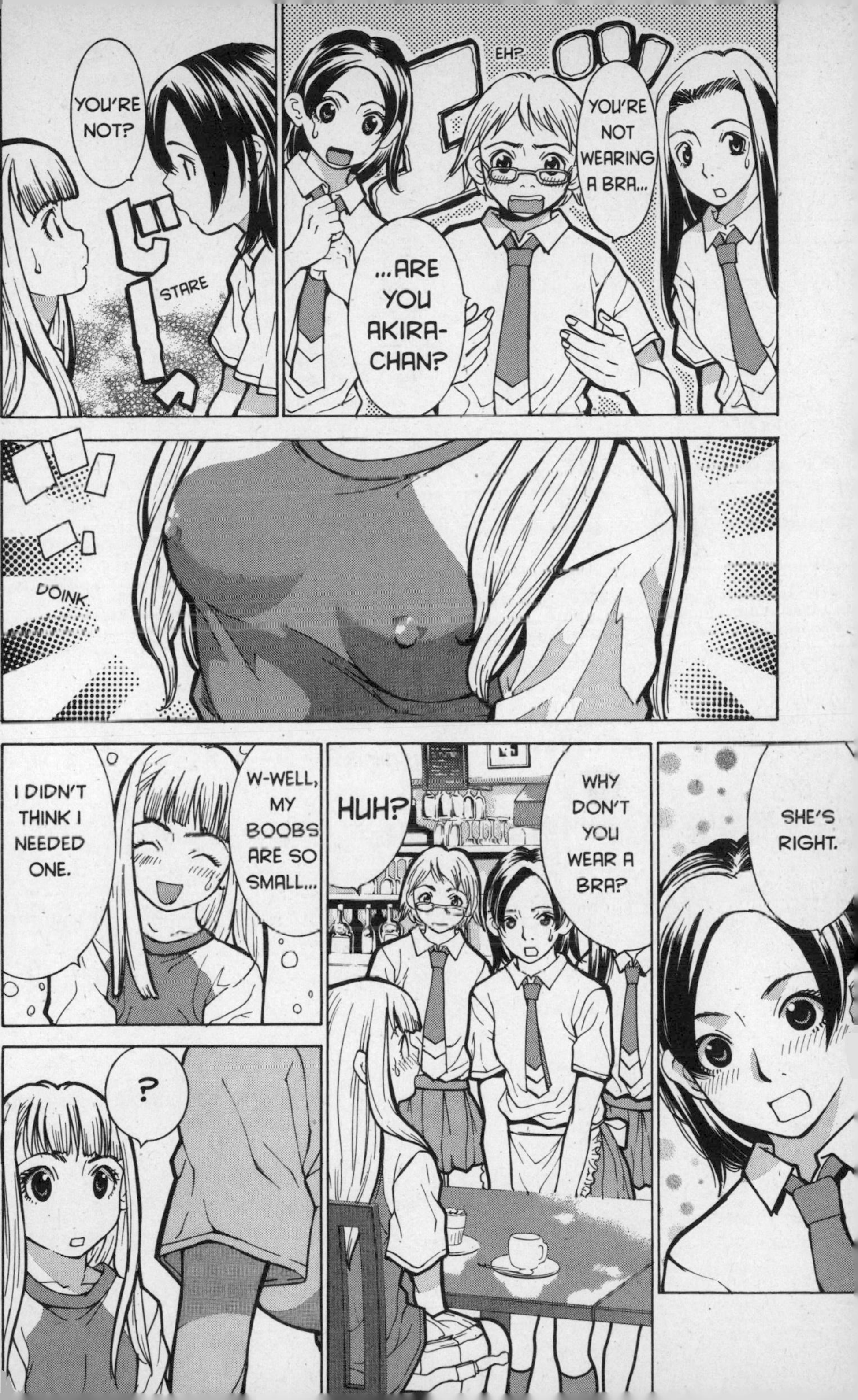
EHP
YOU'RE NOT WEARING A BRA...
...ARE YOU AKIRA-CHAN?
YOU'RE NOT?
STARE
DOINK
SHE'S RIGHT.
WHY DON'T YOU WEAR A BRA?
HUH?
W-WELL, MY BOOBS ARE SO SMALL...
I DIDN'T THINK I NEEDED ONE.
?

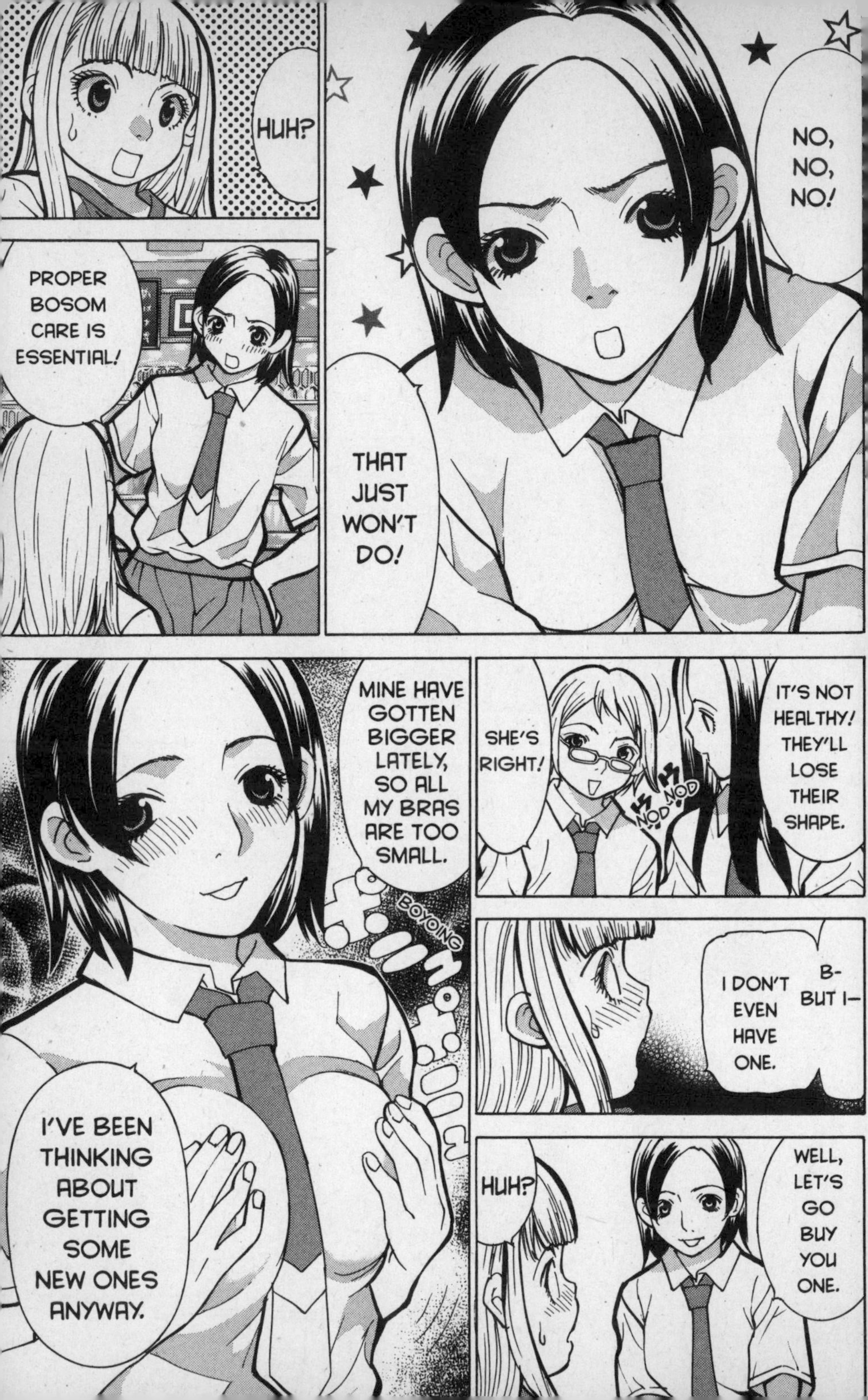
NO, NO, NO!
THAT JUST WON'T DO!
HUH?
PROPER BOSOM CARE IS ESSENTIAL!
IT'S NOT HEALTHY! THEY'LL LOSE THEIR SHAPE.
NOD NOD
SHE'S RIGHT!
B- BUT I—
I DON'T EVEN HAVE ONE.
WELL, LET'S GO BUY YOU ONE.
HUH?
MINE HAVE GOTTEN BIGGER LATELY, SO ALL MY BRAS ARE TOO SMALL.
BOYOING
I'VE BEEN THINKING ABOUT GETTING SOME NEW ONES ANYWAY.

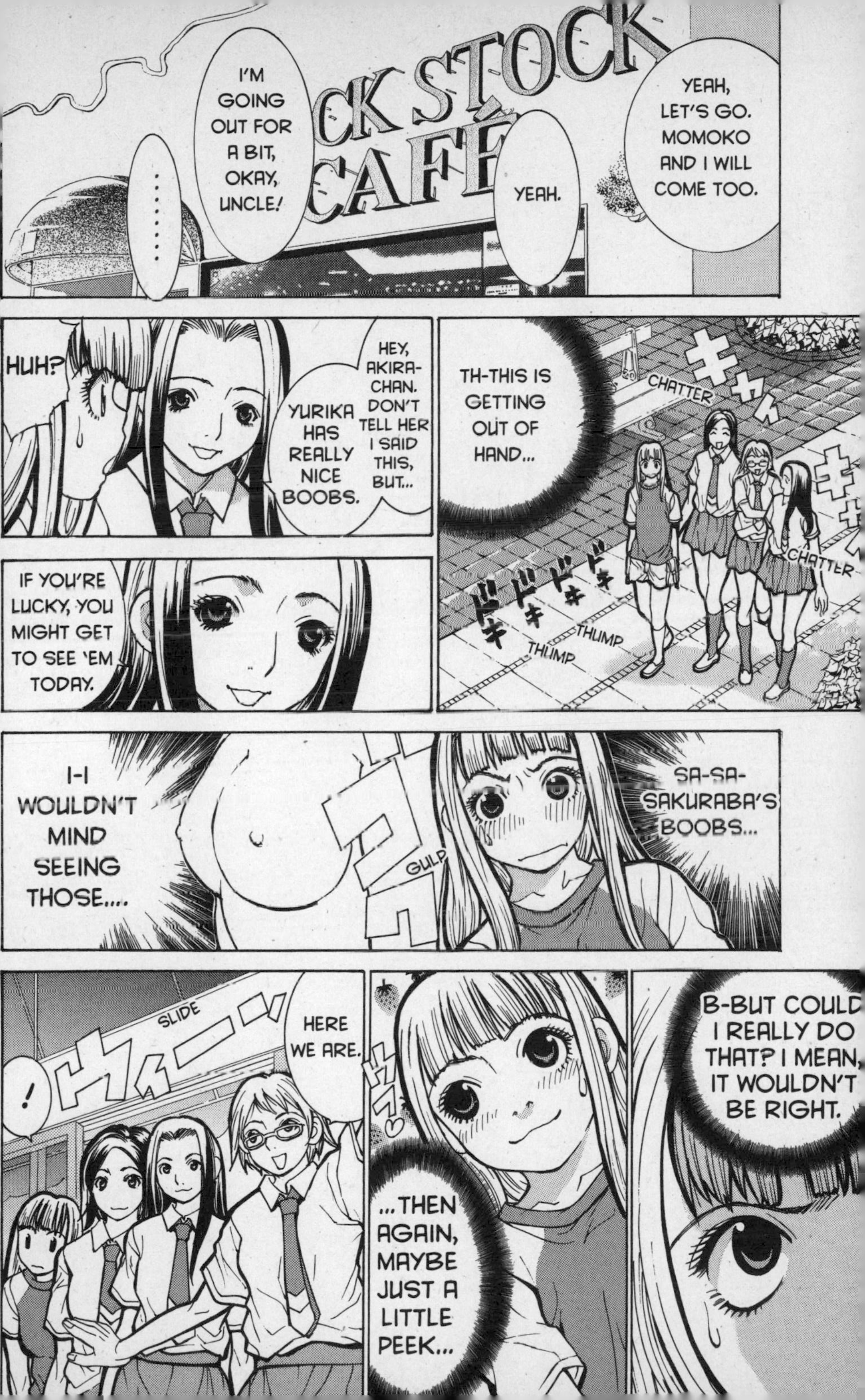
YEAH, LET'S GO. MOMOKO AND I WILL COME TOO.
YEAH.
I'M GOING OUT FOR A BIT, OKAY, UNCLE!
......
TH-THIS IS GETTING OUT OF HAND...
CHATTER
CHATTER
THUMP
THUMP
HEY, AKIRA-CHAN. DON'T TELL HER I SAID THIS, BUT...
YURIKA HAS REALLY NICE BOOBS.
HUH?
IF YOU'RE LUCKY, YOU MIGHT GET TO SEE 'EM TODAY.
SA-SA-SAKURABA'S BOOBS...
GULP
I-I WOULDN'T MIND SEEING THOSE....
B-BUT COULD I REALLY DO THAT? I MEAN, IT WOULDN'T BE RIGHT.
...THEN AGAIN, MAYBE JUST A LITTLE PEEK...
HERE WE ARE.
SLIDE
!

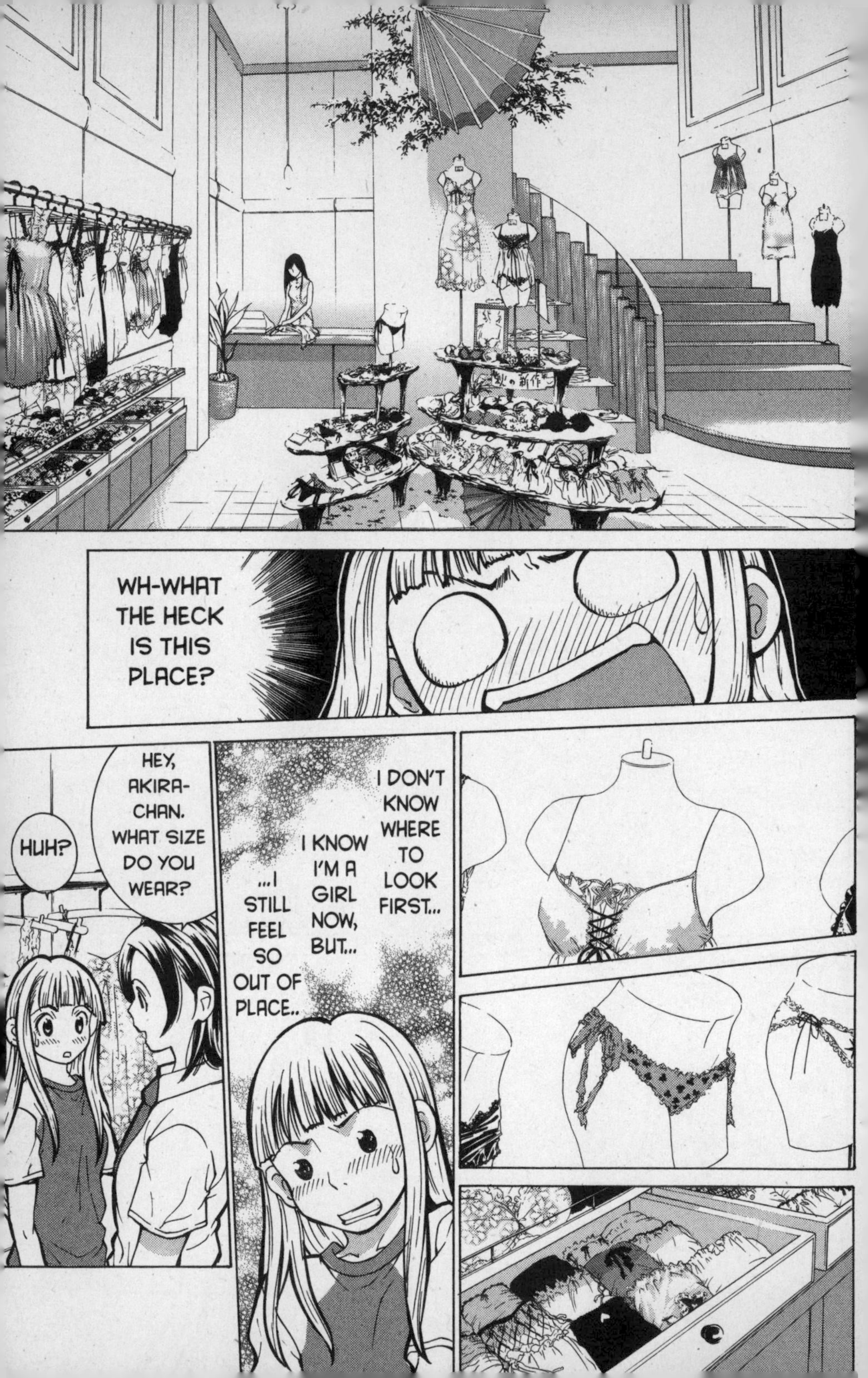
WH-WHAT THE HECK IS THIS PLACE?
I DON'T KNOW WHERE TO LOOK FIRST...
I KNOW I'M A GIRL NOW, BUT...
...I STILL FEEL SO OUT OF PLACE..
HEY, AKIRA-CHAN. WHAT SIZE DO YOU WEAR?
HUH?

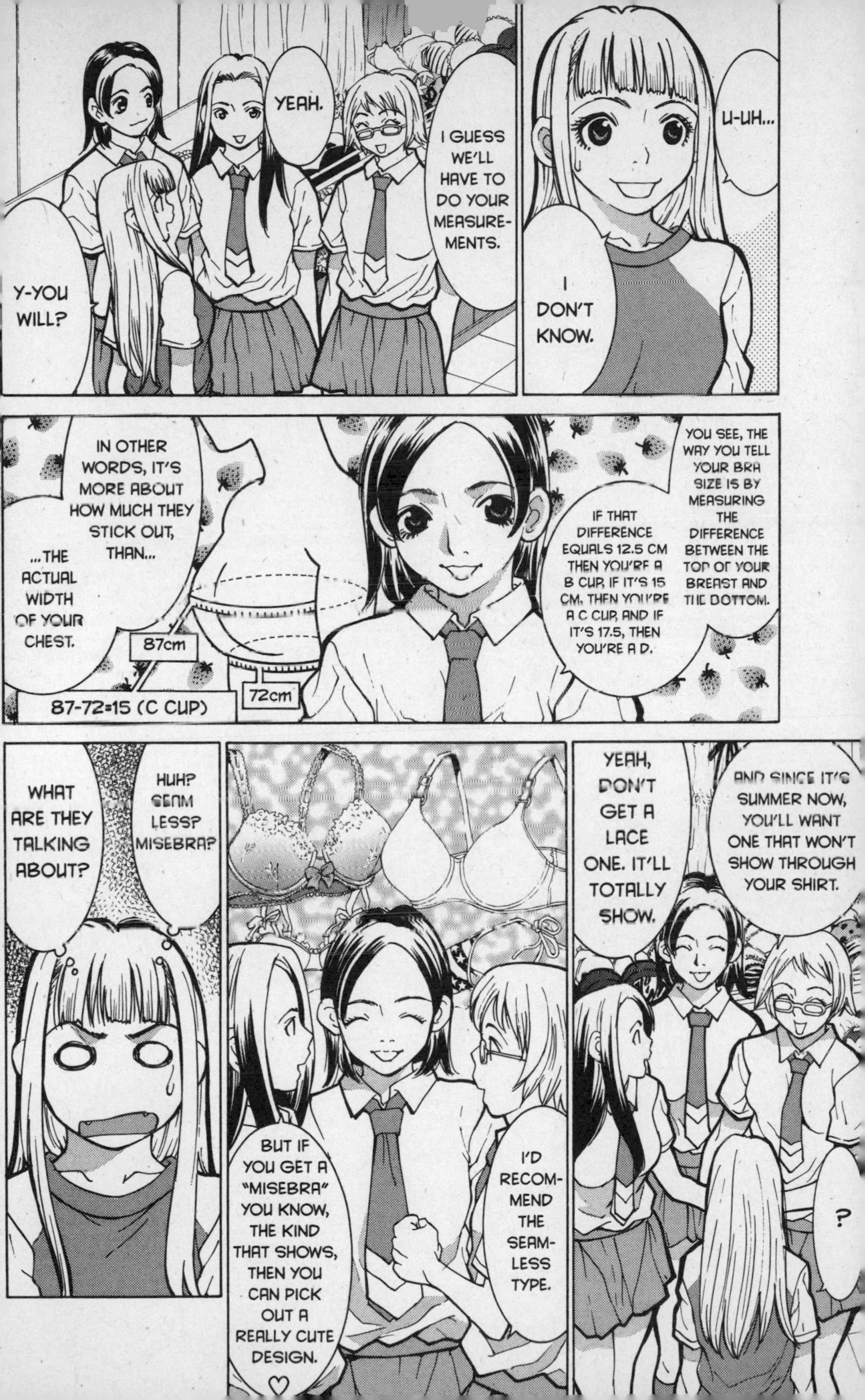
U-UH...
I DON'T KNOW.
I GUESS WE'LL HAVE TO DO YOUR MEASURE-MENTS.
YEAH.
Y-YOU WILL?
YOU SEE, THE WAY YOU TELL YOUR BRA SIZE IS BY MEASURING THE DIFFERENCE BETWEEN THE TOP OF YOUR BREAST AND THE BOTTOM.
IF THAT DIFFERENCE EQUALS 12.5 CM THEN YOU'RE A B CUP, IF IT'S 15 CM, THEN YOU'RE A C CUP, AND IF IT'S 17.5, THEN YOU'RE A D.
IN OTHER WORDS, IT'S MORE ABOUT HOW MUCH THEY STICK OUT, THAN...
...THE ACTUAL WIDTH OF YOUR CHEST.
87cm
72cm
87-72=15 (C CUP)
AND SINCE IT'S SUMMER NOW, YOU'LL WANT ONE THAT WON'T SHOW THROUGH YOUR SHIRT.
YEAH, DON'T GET A LACE ONE. IT'LL TOTALLY SHOW.
?
I'D RECOM-MEND THE SEAM-LESS TYPE.
BUT IF YOU GET A "MISEBRA" YOU KNOW, THE KIND THAT SHOWS, THEN YOU CAN PICK OUT A REALLY CUTE DESIGN. ♡
HUH? SEAM LESS? MISEBRA?
WHAT ARE THEY TALKING ABOUT?

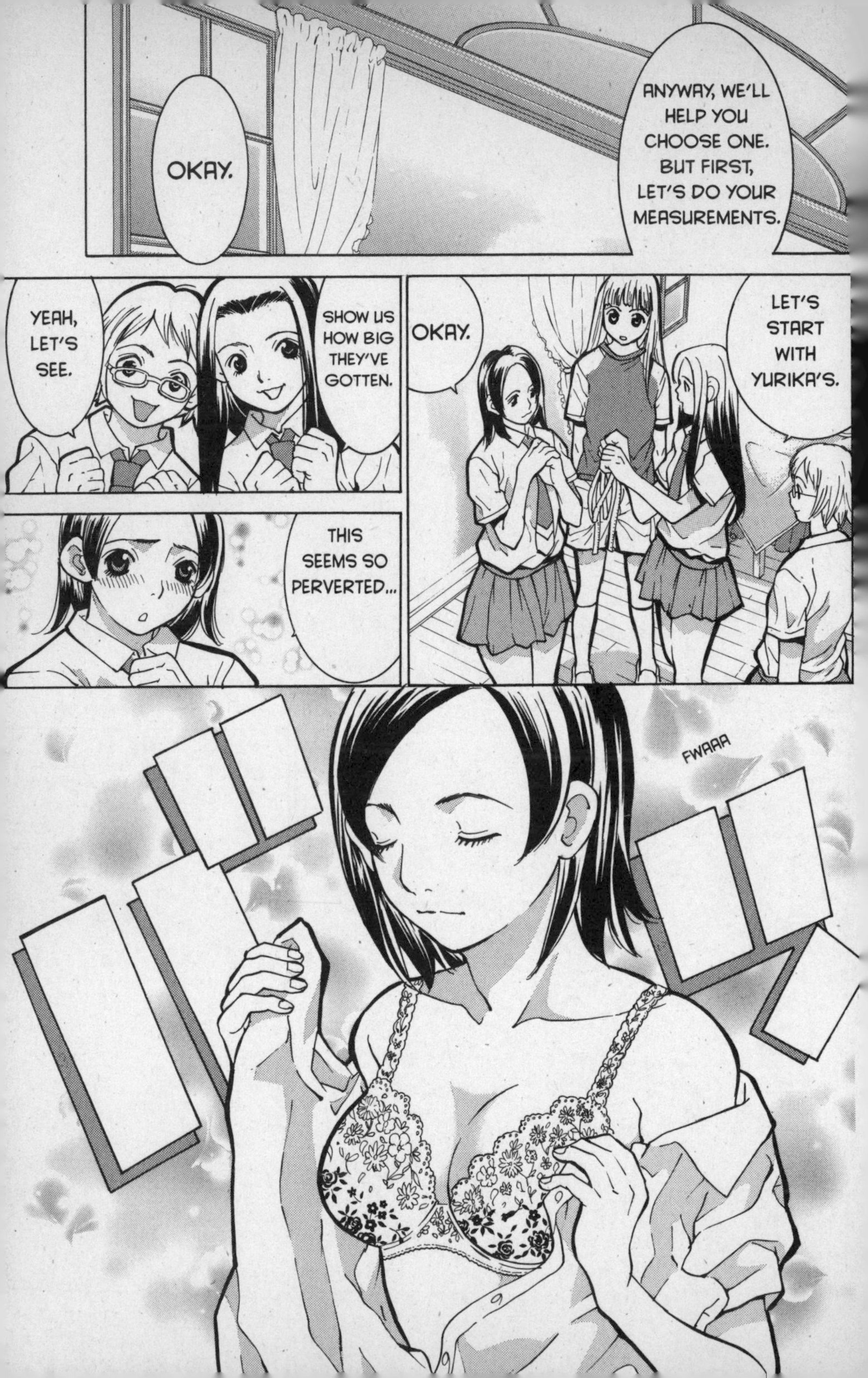
ANYWAY, WE'LL HELP YOU CHOOSE ONE. BUT FIRST, LET'S DO YOUR MEASUREMENTS.
OKAY.
LET'S START WITH YURIKA'S.
OKAY.
SHOW US HOW BIG THEY'VE GOTTEN.
YEAH, LET'S SEE.
THIS SEEMS SO PERVERTED...
FWAAA

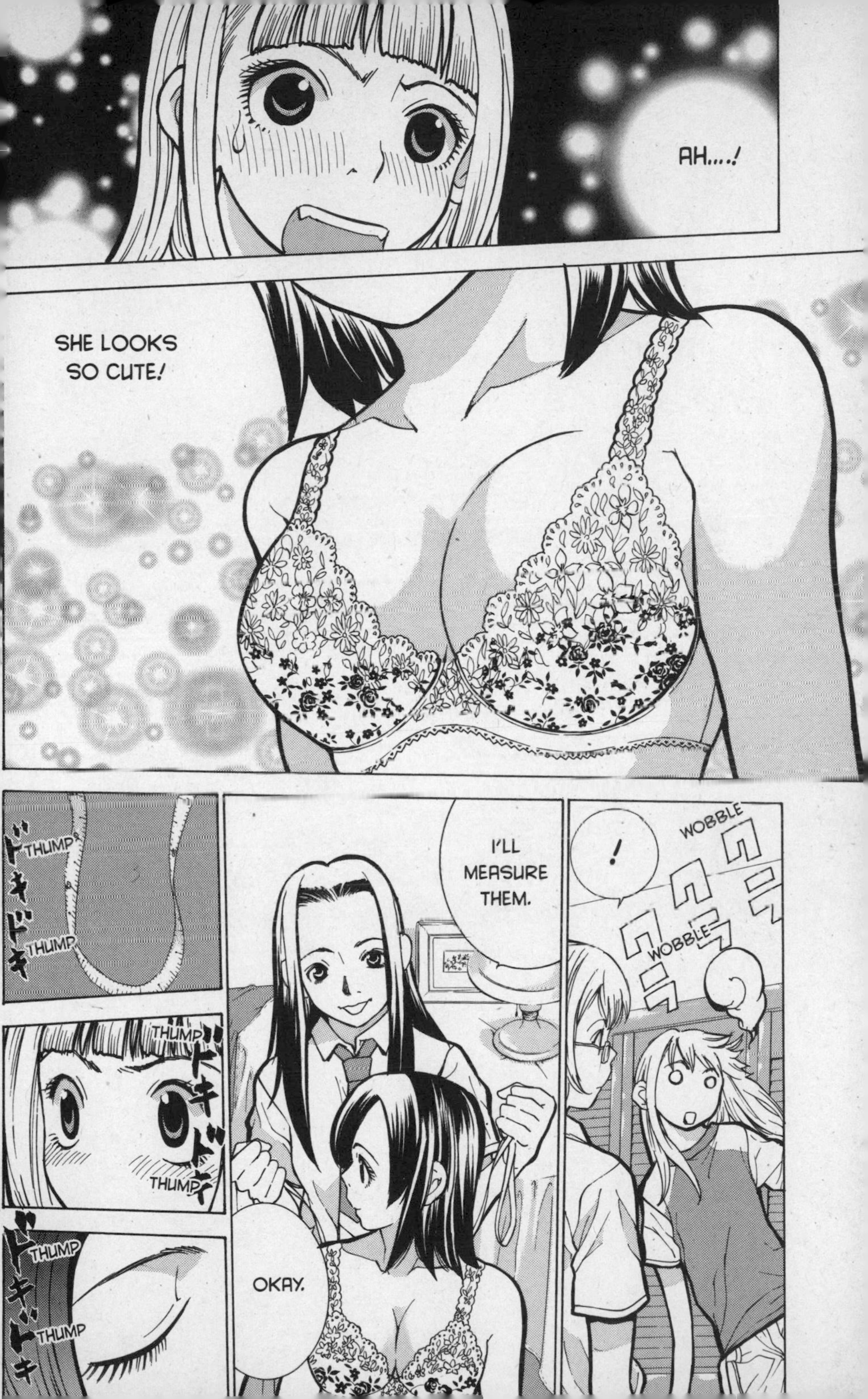
AH....!
SHE LOOKS SO CUTE!
!
WOBBLE
WOBBLE
I'LL MEASURE THEM.
OKAY.
THUMP
THUMP
ドキドキ
THUMP
THUMP
ドキドキ
THUMP
THUMP
ドキドキ

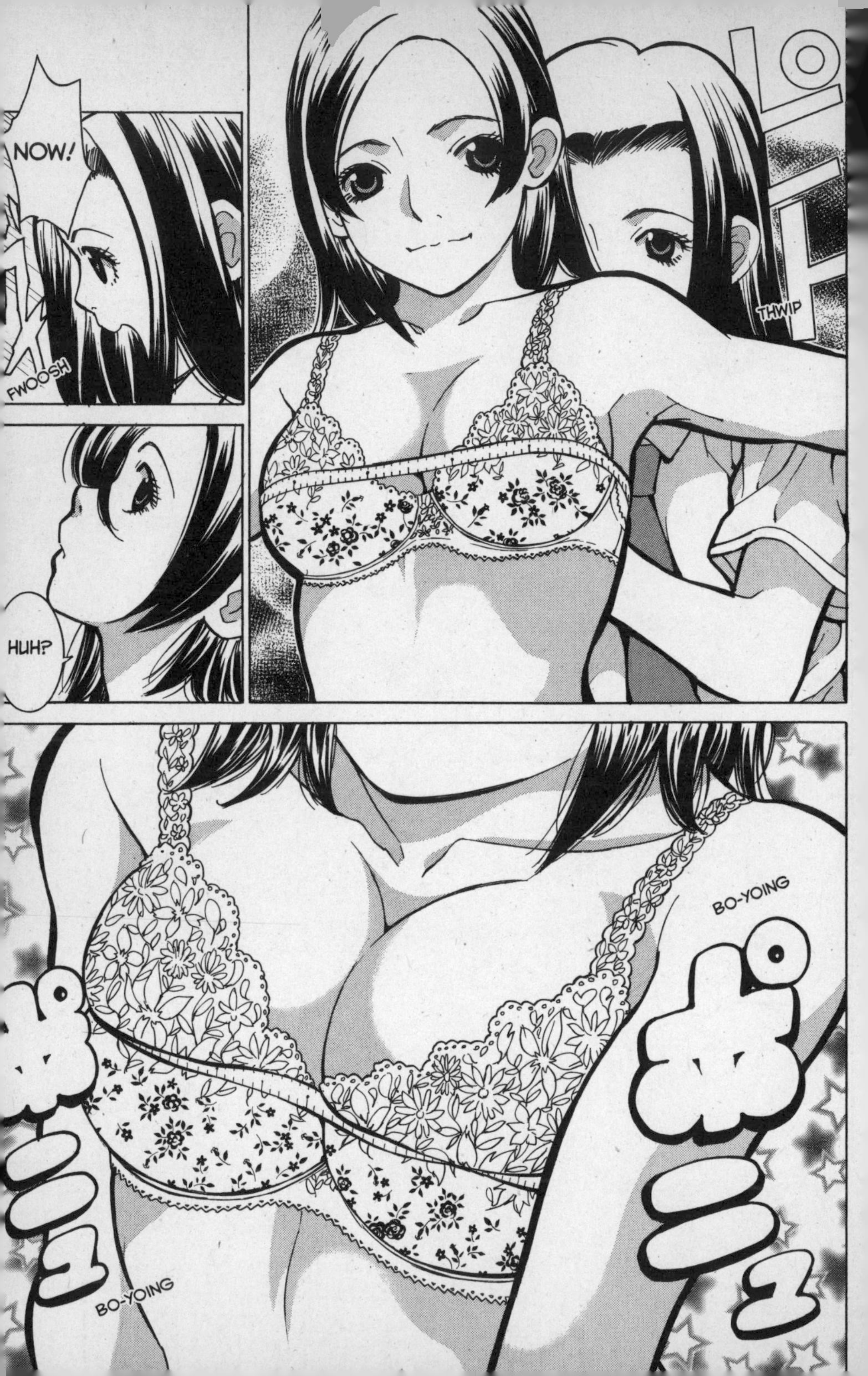
THWIP
NOW!
FWOOSH
HUH?
BO-YOING
BO-YOING

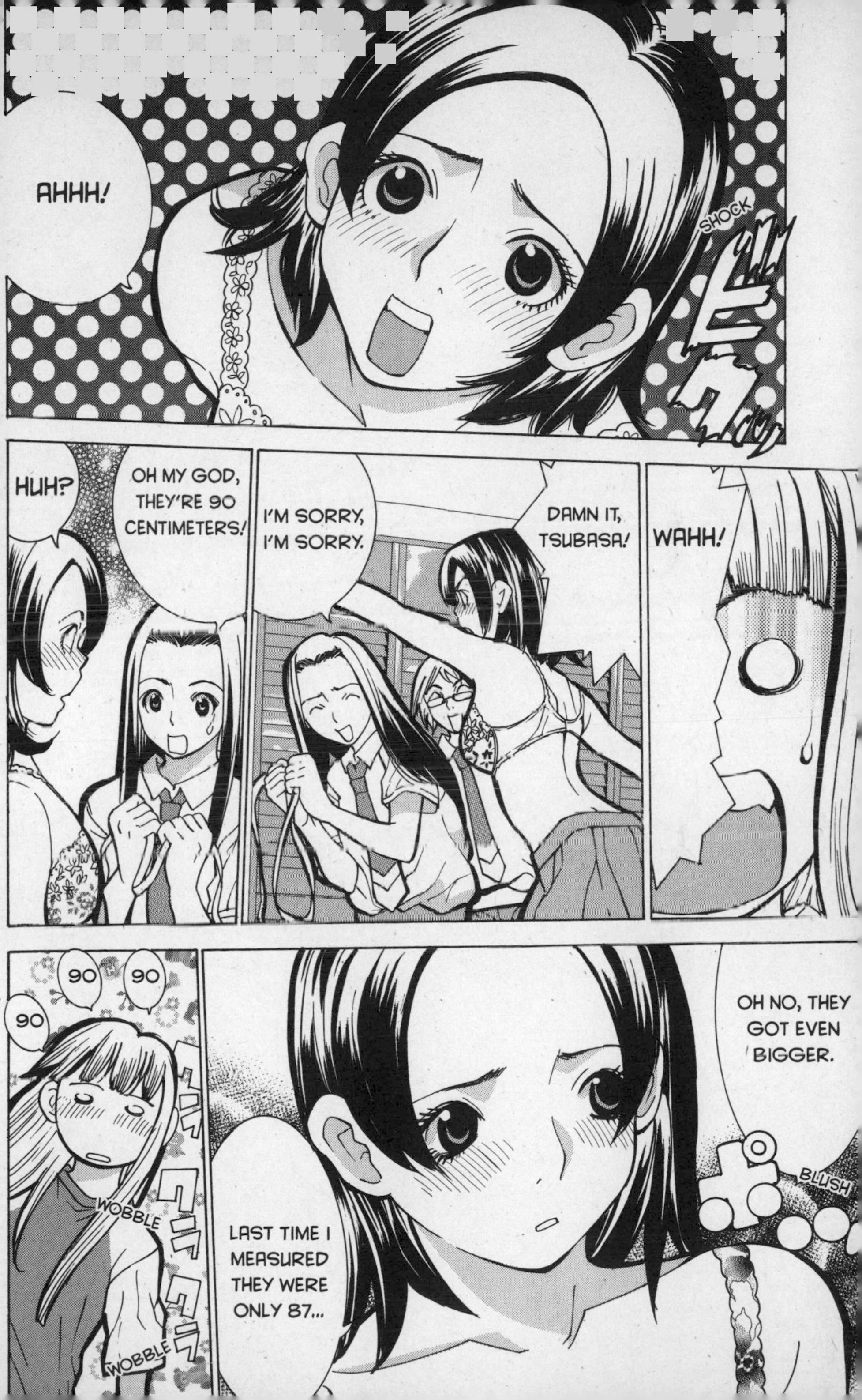
AHHH!
SHOCK
WAHH!
DAMN IT, TSUBASA!
I'M SORRY, I'M SORRY.
OH MY GOD, THEY'RE 90 CENTIMETERS!
HUH?
OH NO, THEY GOT EVEN BIGGER.
BLUSH
LAST TIME I MEASURED THEY WERE ONLY 87...
90
90
90
WOBBLE
WOBBLE

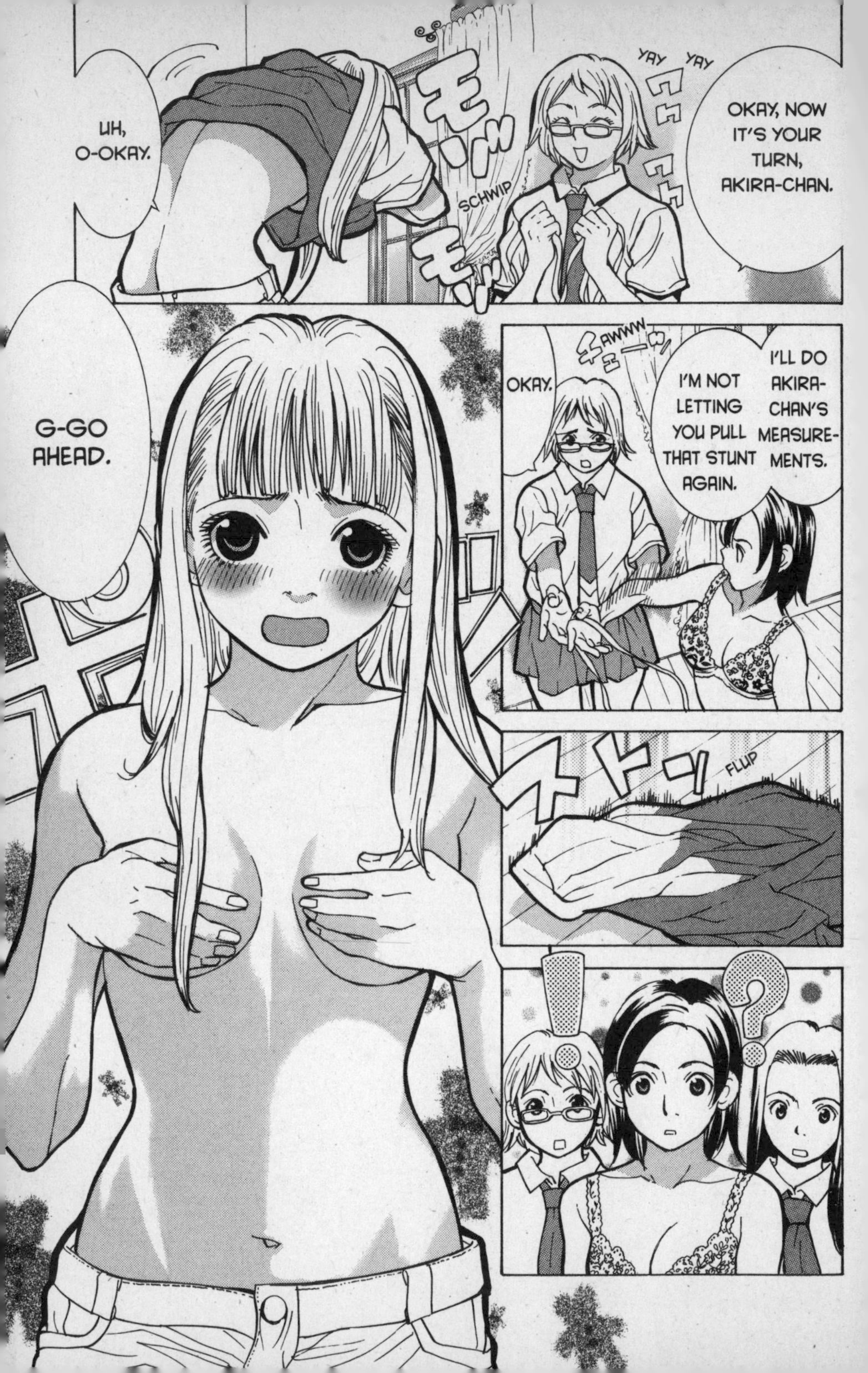
OKAY, NOW IT'S YOUR TURN, AKIRA-CHAN.
YAY YAY
SCHWIP
UH, O-OKAY.
I'LL DO AKIRA-CHAN'S MEASUREMENTS.
I'M NOT LETTING YOU PULL THAT STUNT AGAIN.
AWWWW
OKAY.
FLUP
G-GO AHEAD.

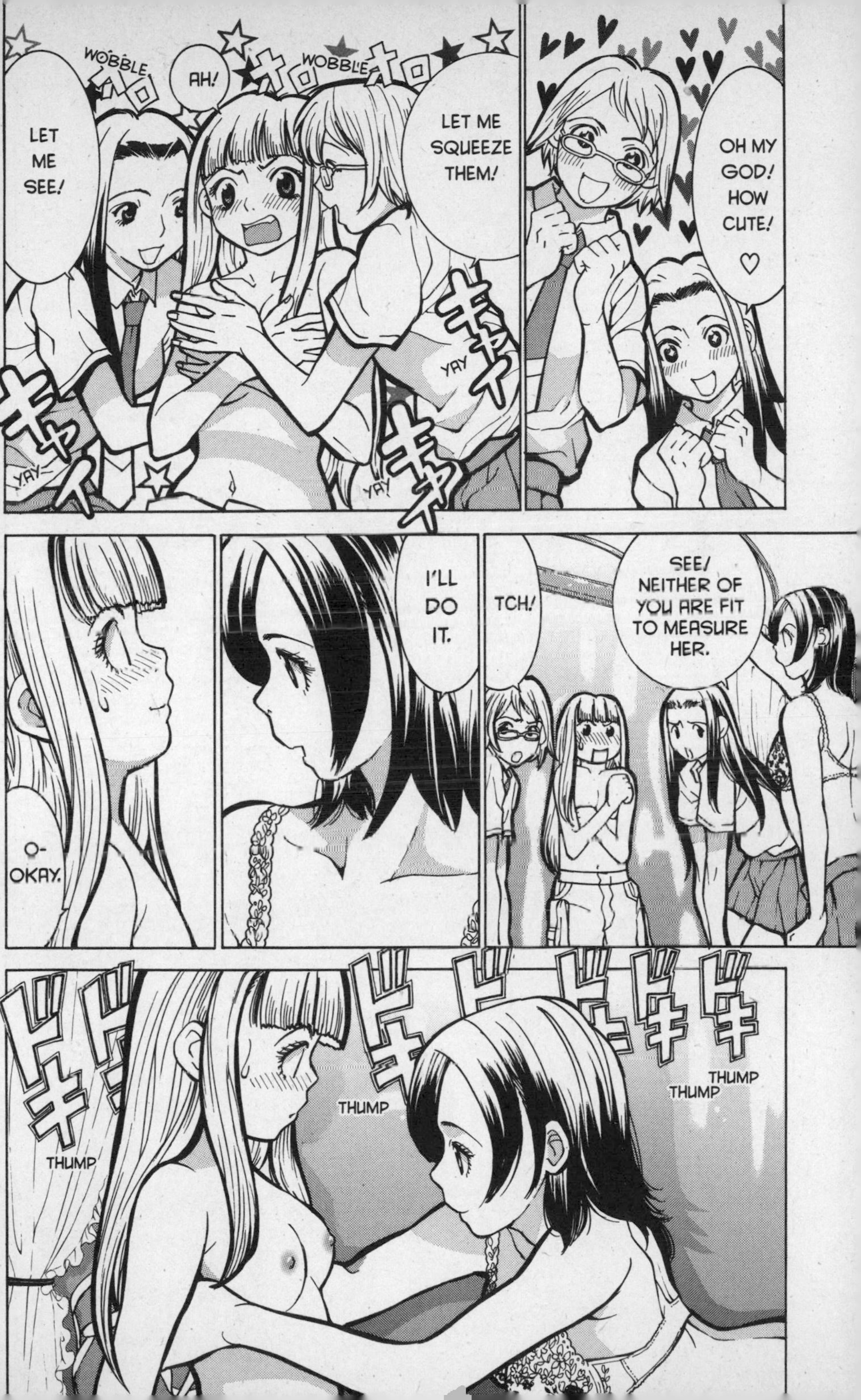
OH MY GOD! HOW CUTE! ♡
LET ME SQUEEZE THEM!
WOBBLE
AH!
WOBBLE
LET ME SEE!
YAY
YAY
YAY
SEE/ NEITHER OF YOU ARE FIT TO MEASURE HER.
TCH!
I'LL DO IT.
O-OKAY.
THUMP
THUMP
THUMP
THUMP

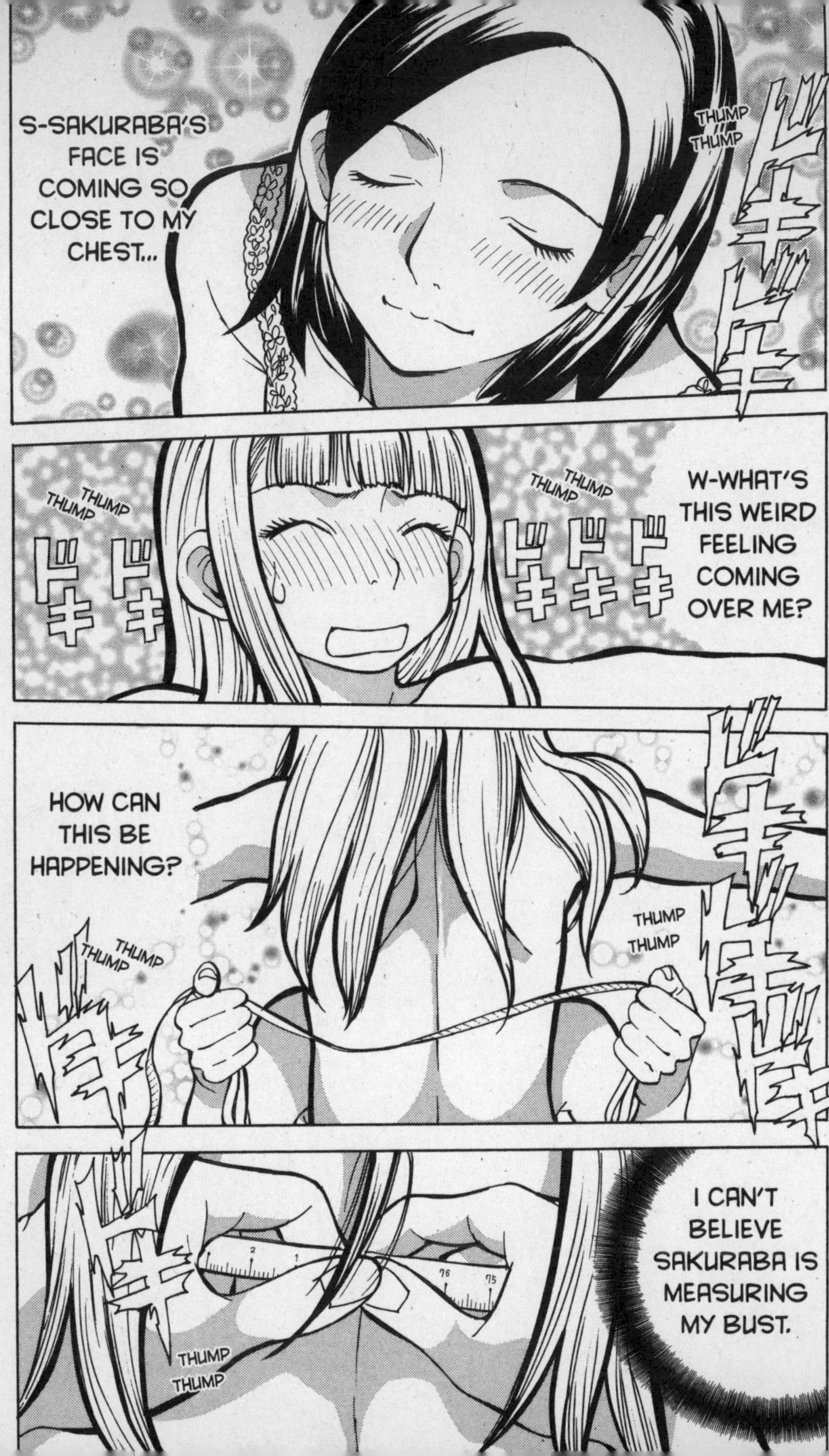
THUMP THUMP
S-SAKURABA'S FACE IS COMING SO CLOSE TO MY CHEST...
W-WHAT'S THIS WEIRD FEELING COMING OVER ME?
ドキドキドキ
THUMP THUMP
THUMP THUMP
ドキドキ
THUMP THUMP
HOW CAN THIS BE HAPPENING?
THUMP THUMP
I CAN'T BELIEVE SAKURABA IS MEASURING MY BUST.
THUMP THUMP

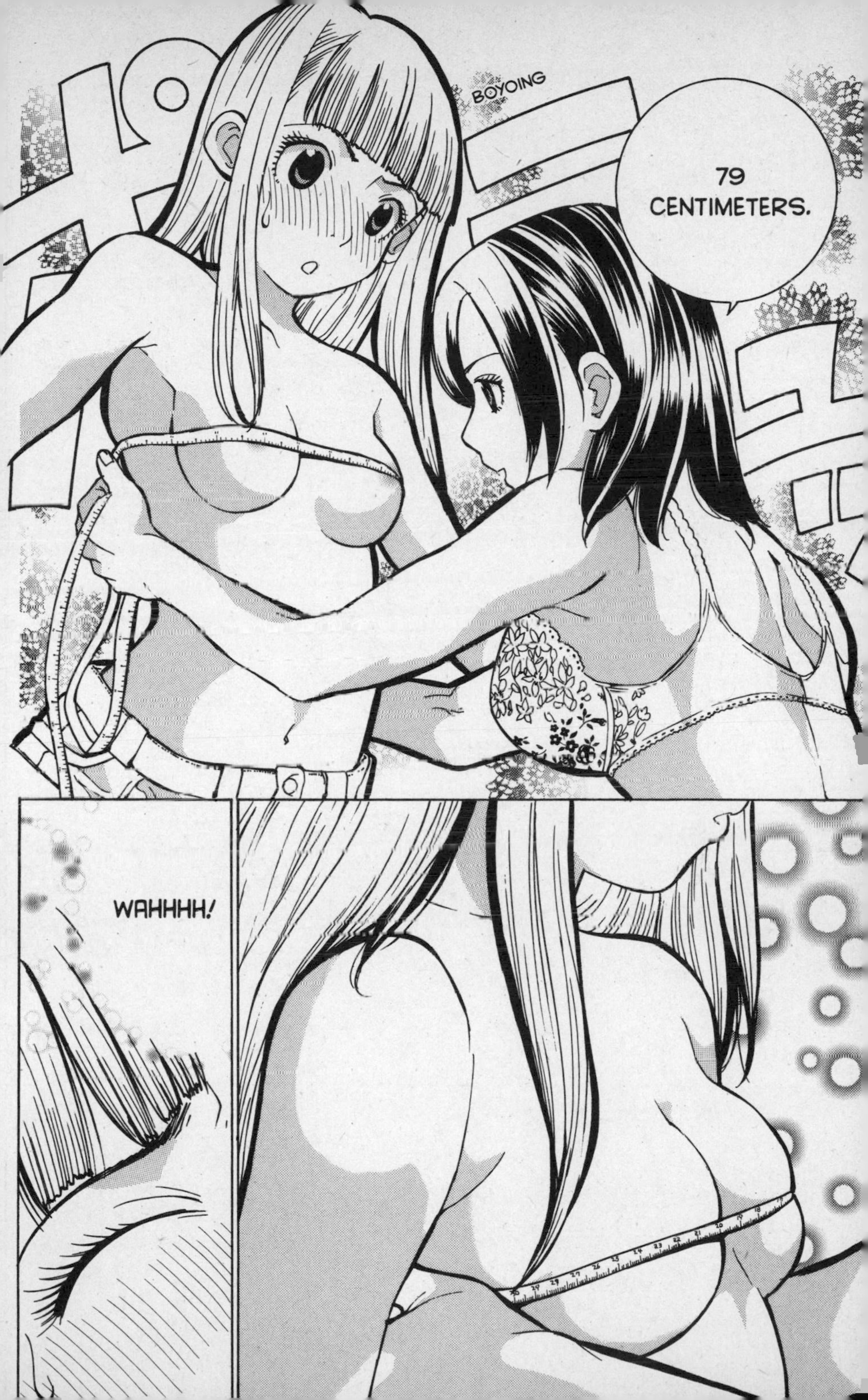
BOYOING
79 CENTIMETERS.
WAHHHH!

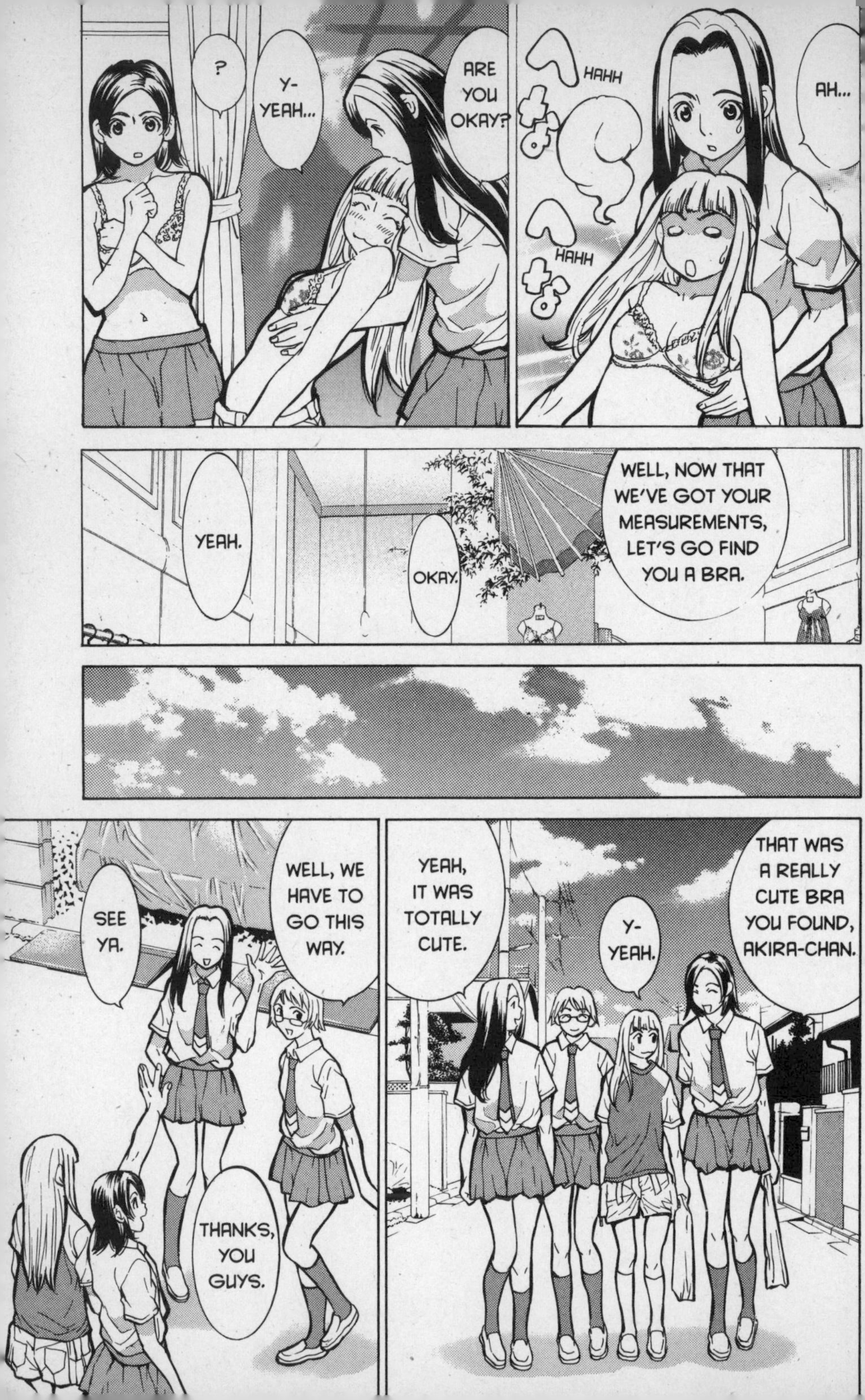
AH...
HAHH
HAHH
ARE YOU OKAY?
Y-YEAH...
?
WELL, NOW THAT WE'VE GOT YOUR MEASUREMENTS, LET'S GO FIND YOU A BRA.
OKAY.
YEAH.
THAT WAS A REALLY CUTE BRA YOU FOUND, AKIRA-CHAN.
Y-YEAH.
YEAH, IT WAS TOTALLY CUTE.
WELL, WE HAVE TO GO THIS WAY.
SEE YA.
THANKS, YOU GUYS.

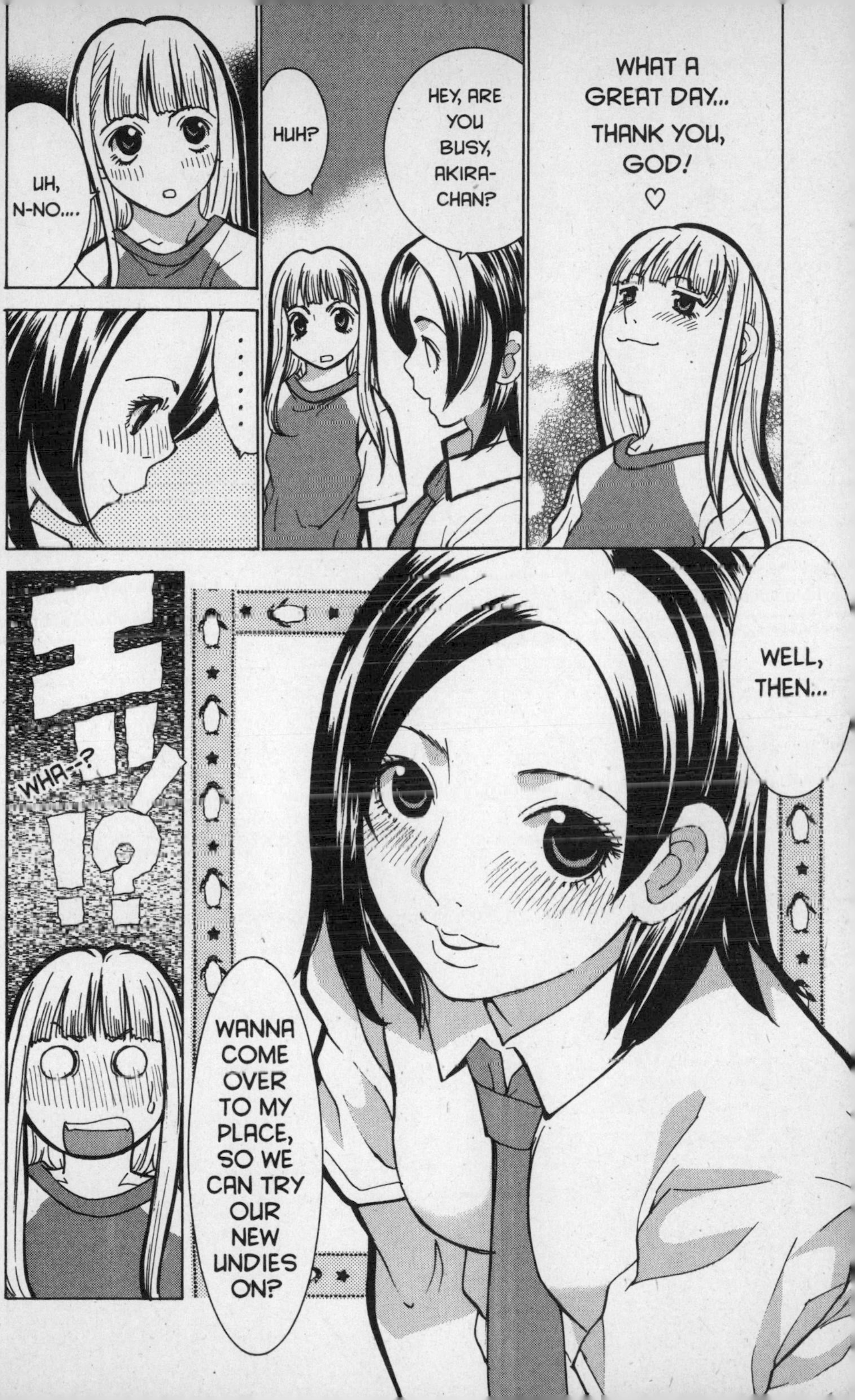
WHAT A GREAT DAY... THANK YOU, GOD! ♡
HEY, ARE YOU BUSY, AKIRA-CHAN?
HUH?
UH, N-NO....
......
WELL, THEN...
WANNA COME OVER TO MY PLACE, SO WE CAN TRY OUR NEW UNDIES ON?
WHA--?

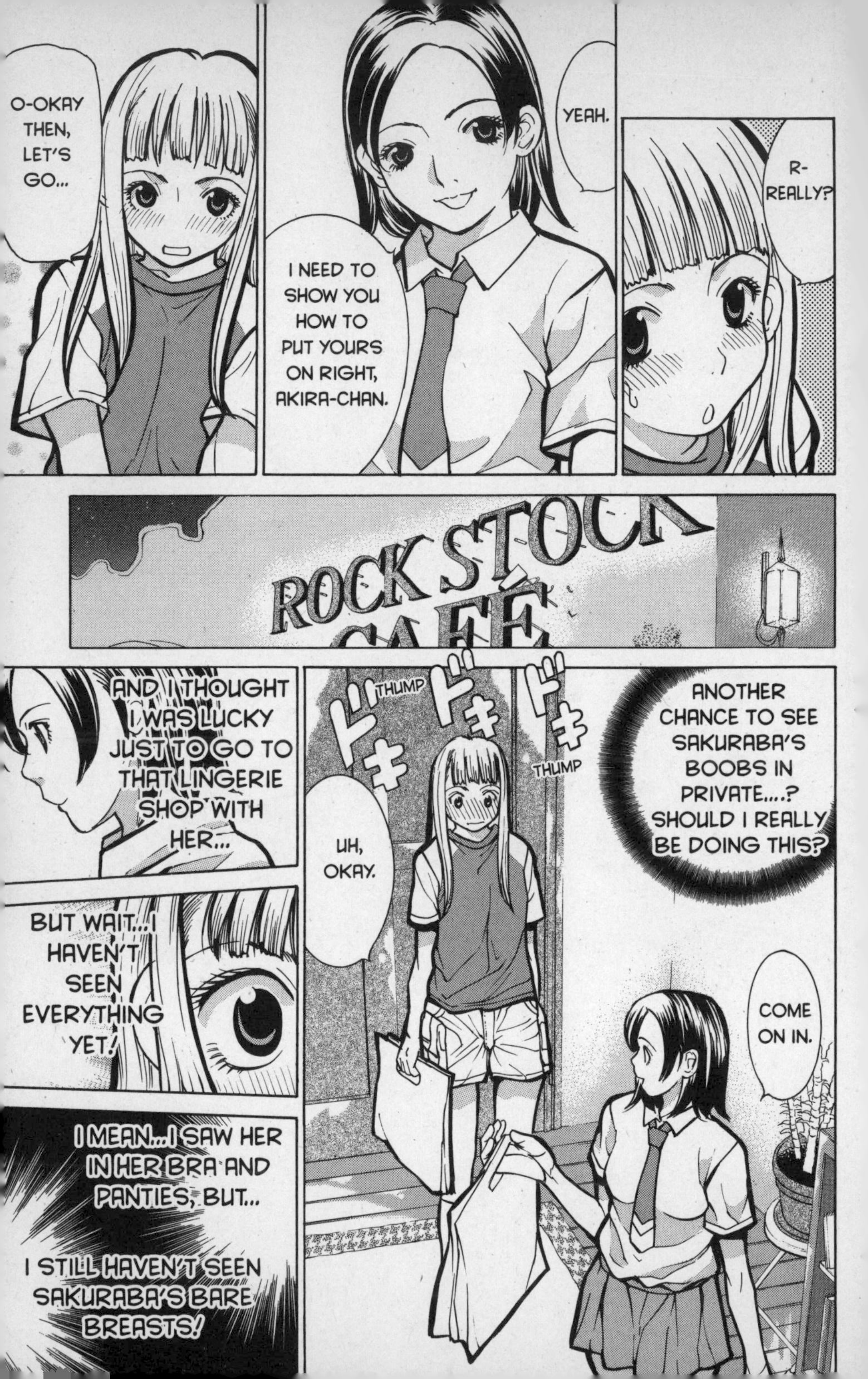
R-REALLY?
YEAH.
I NEED TO SHOW YOU HOW TO PUT YOURS ON RIGHT, AKIRA-CHAN.
O-OKAY THEN, LET'S GO...
ROCK STOCK CAFÉ
ANOTHER CHANCE TO SEE SAKURABA'S BOOBS IN PRIVATE....? SHOULD I REALLY BE DOING THIS?
ドキ THUMP
ドキ
ドキ THUMP
COME ON IN.
UH, OKAY.
AND I THOUGHT I WAS LUCKY JUST TO GO TO THAT LINGERIE SHOP WITH HER...
BUT WAIT...I HAVEN'T SEEN EVERYTHING YET!
I MEAN...I SAW HER IN HER BRA AND PANTIES, BUT...
I STILL HAVEN'T SEEN SAKURABA'S BARE BREASTS!

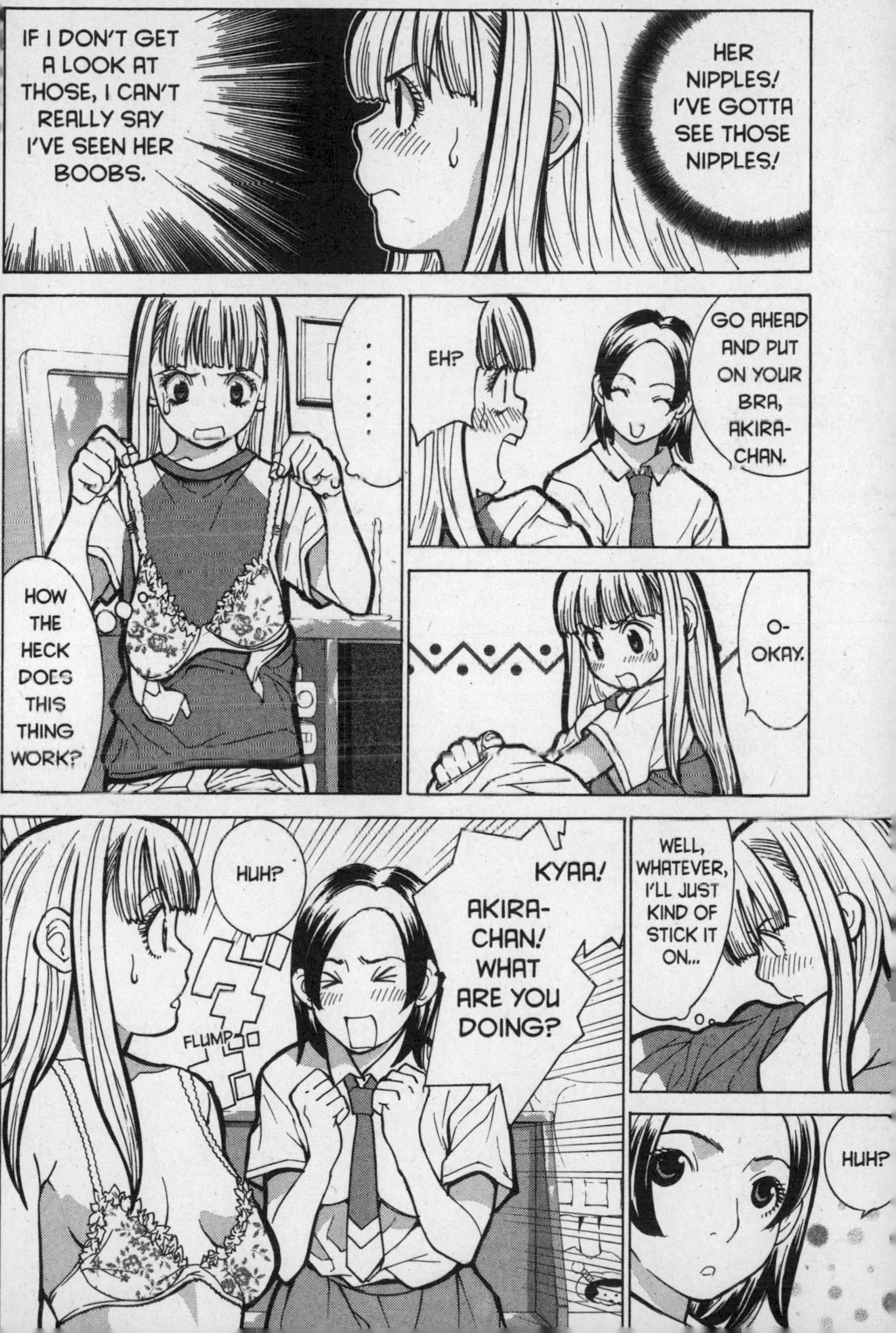
HER NIPPLES! I'VE GOTTA SEE THOSE NIPPLES!
IF I DON'T GET A LOOK AT THOSE, I CAN'T REALLY SAY I'VE SEEN HER BOOBS.
GO AHEAD AND PUT ON YOUR BRA, AKIRA-CHAN.
EH?
O-OKAY.
......
HOW THE HECK DOES THIS THING WORK?
WELL, WHATEVER, I'LL JUST KIND OF STICK IT ON...
HUH?
KYAA! AKIRA-CHAN! WHAT ARE YOU DOING?
HUH?
FLUMP

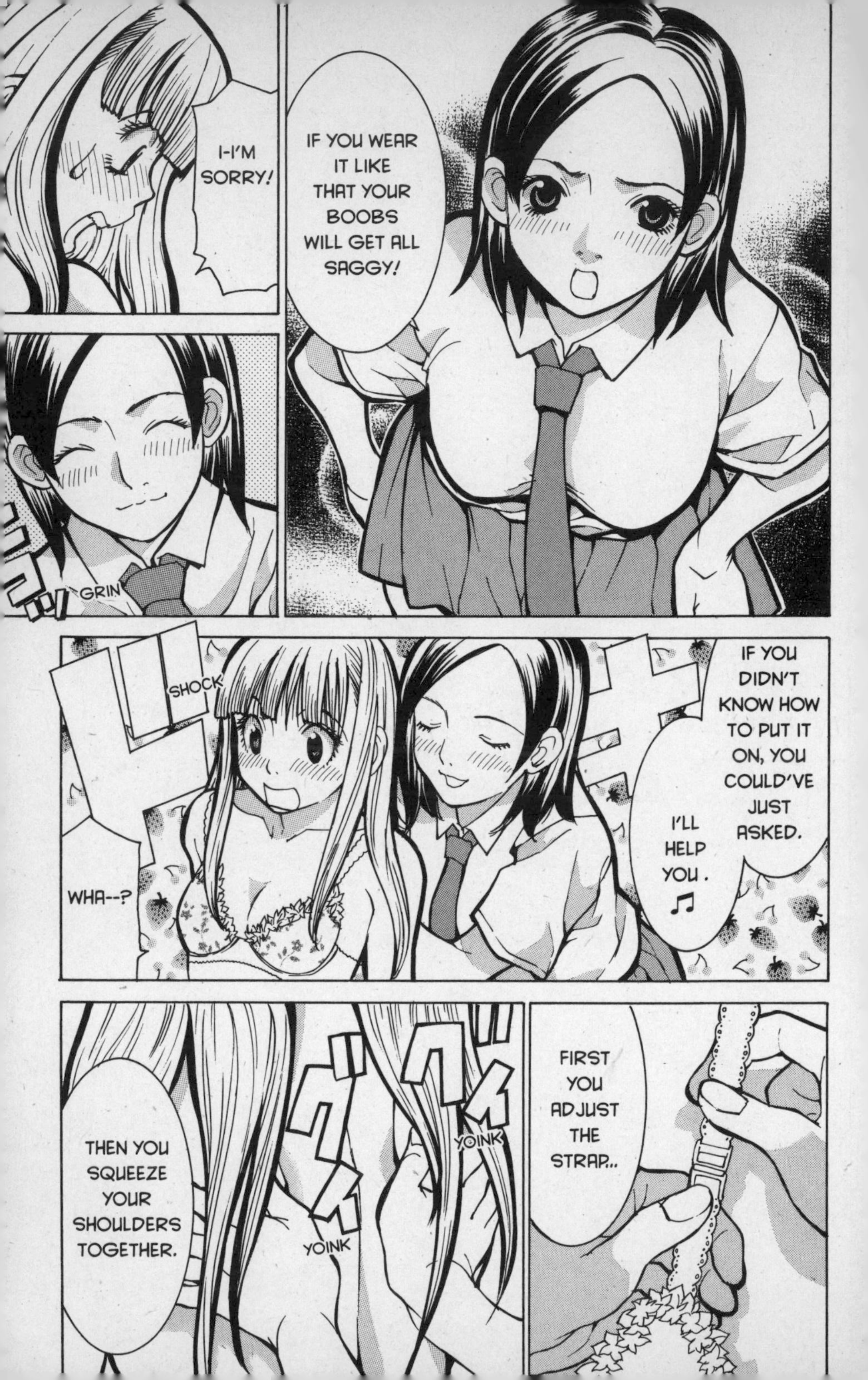
IF YOU WEAR IT LIKE THAT YOUR BOOBS WILL GET ALL SAGGY!
I-I'M SORRY!
GRIN
IF YOU DIDN'T KNOW HOW TO PUT IT ON, YOU COULD'VE JUST ASKED.
I'LL HELP YOU. ♫
SHOCK
WHA--?
FIRST YOU ADJUST THE STRAP...
YOINK
THEN YOU SQUEEZE YOUR SHOULDERS TOGETHER.
YOINK

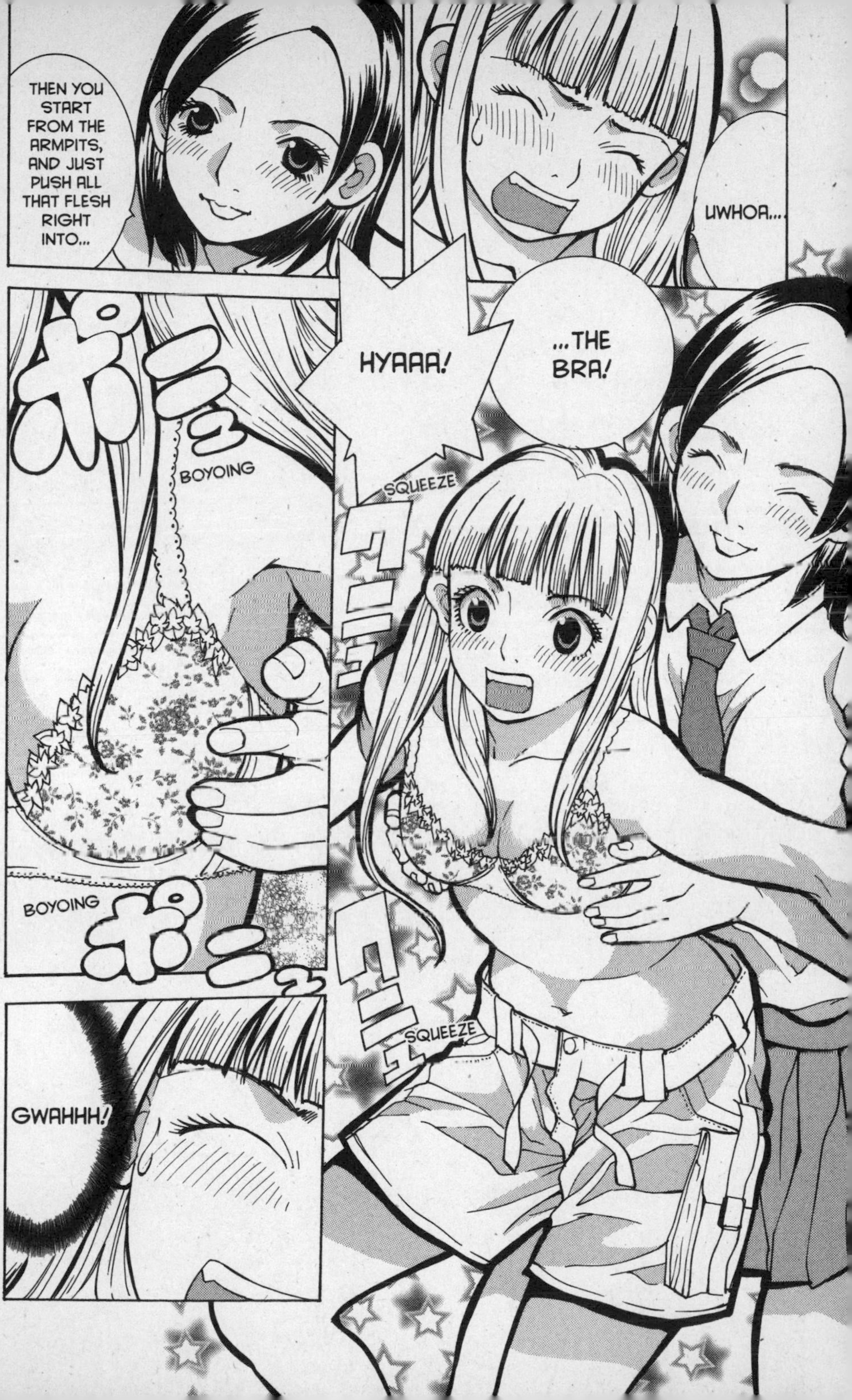
UWHOA...
THEN YOU START FROM THE ARMPITS, AND JUST PUSH ALL THAT FLESH RIGHT INTO...
...THE BRA!
HYAAA!
SQUEEZE
SQUEEZE
BOYOING
BOYOING
GWAHHH!

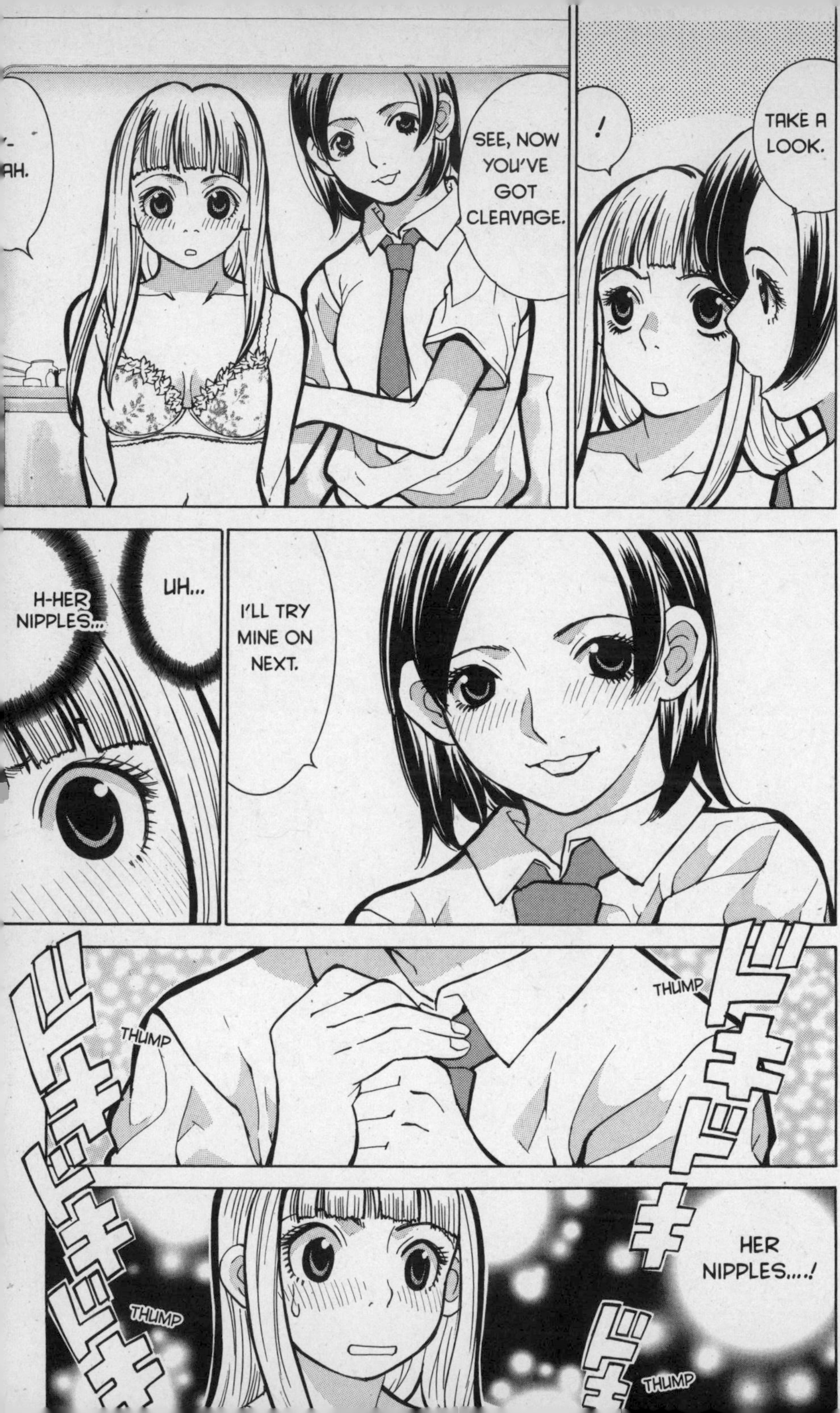
TAKE A LOOK.
!
SEE, NOW YOU'VE GOT CLEAVAGE.
AH.
I'LL TRY MINE ON NEXT.
UH...
H-HER NIPPLES...
THUMP
THUMP
HER NIPPLES....!
THUMP
THUMP

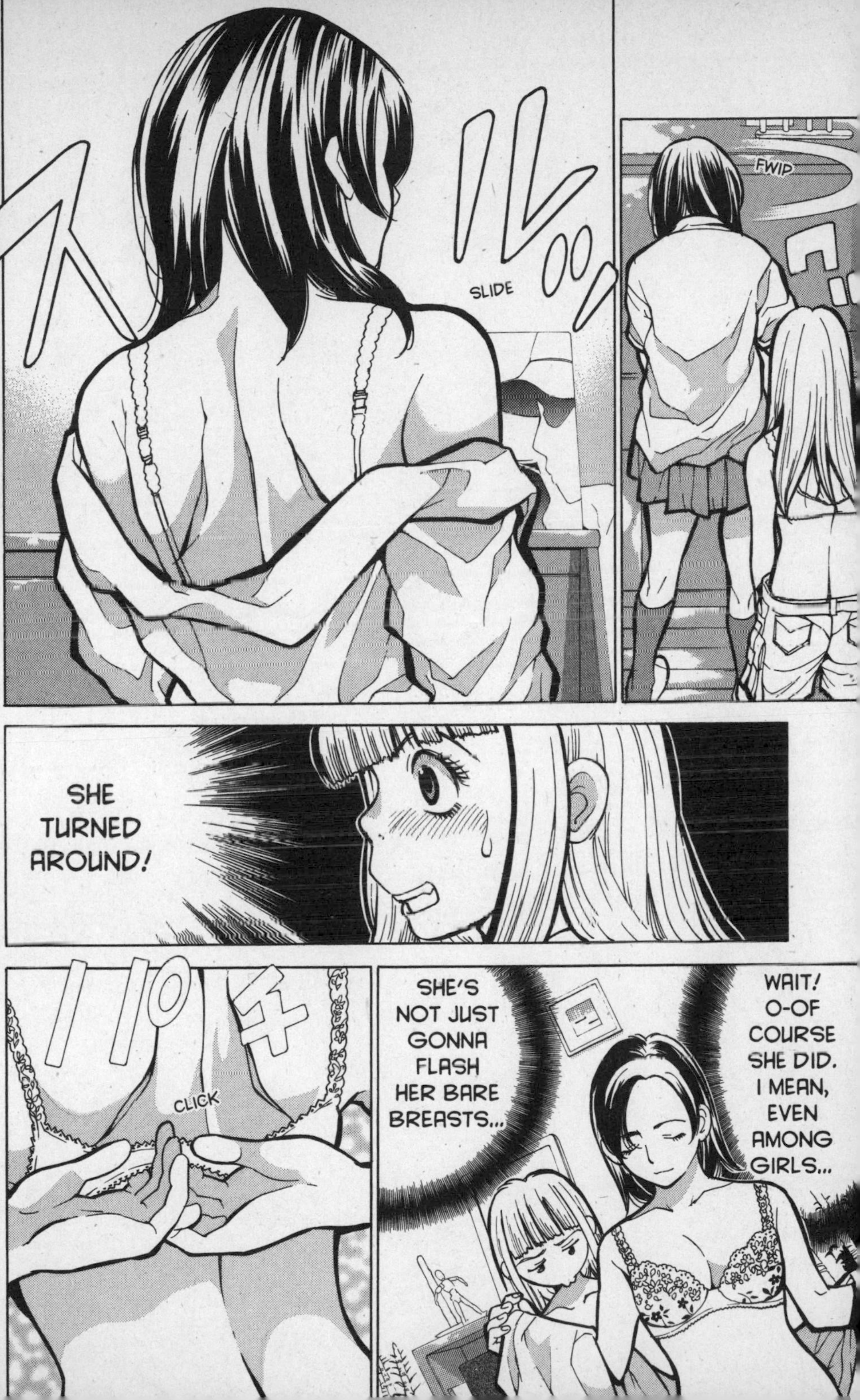
FWIP
SLIDE
SHE TURNED AROUND!
WAIT! O-OF COURSE SHE DID. I MEAN, EVEN AMONG GIRLS...
SHE'S NOT JUST GONNA FLASH HER BARE BREASTS...
CLICK

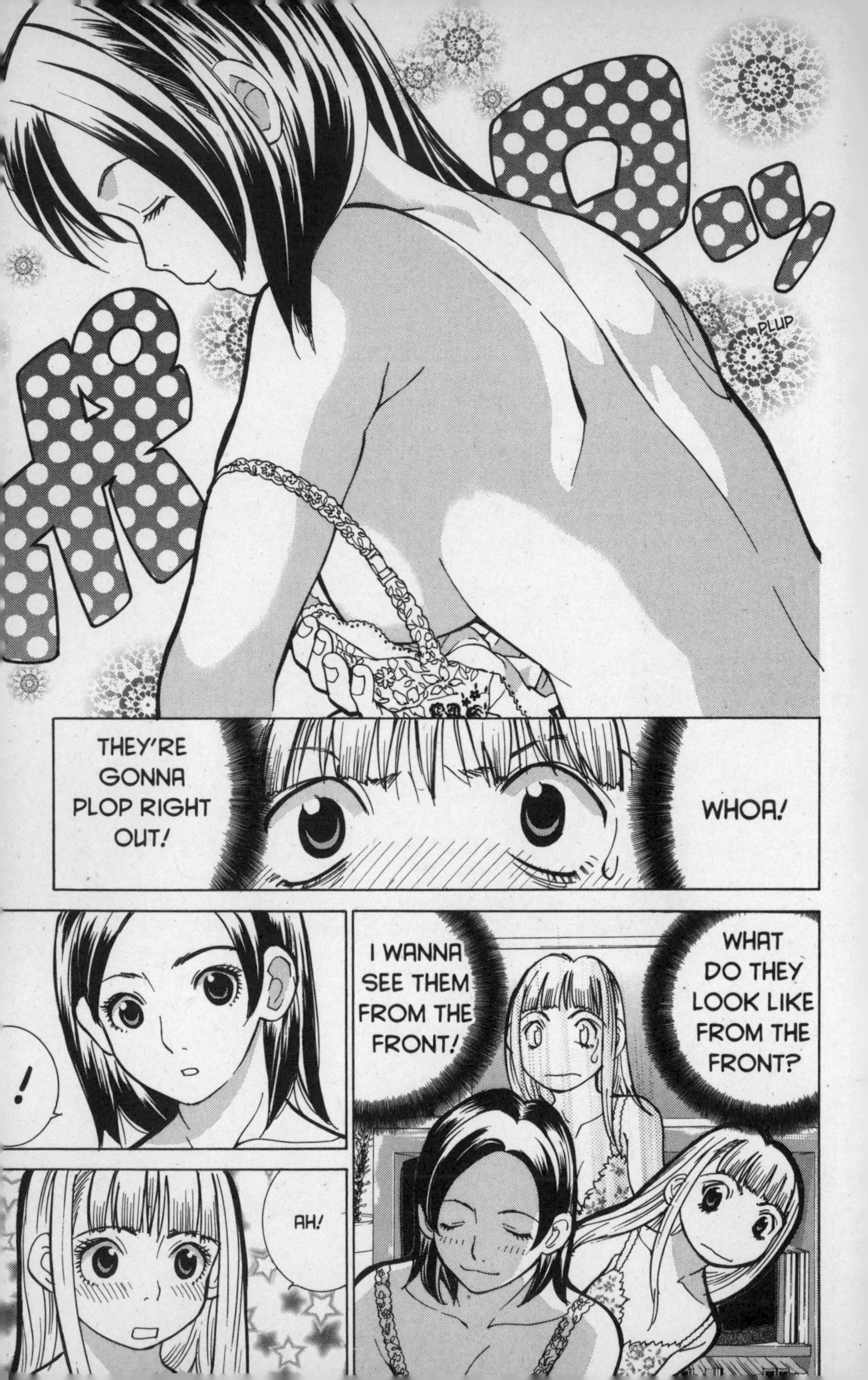
PLUP
WHOA!
THEY'RE GONNA PLOP RIGHT OUT!
WHAT DO THEY LOOK LIKE FROM THE FRONT?
I WANNA SEE THEM FROM THE FRONT!
!
AH!

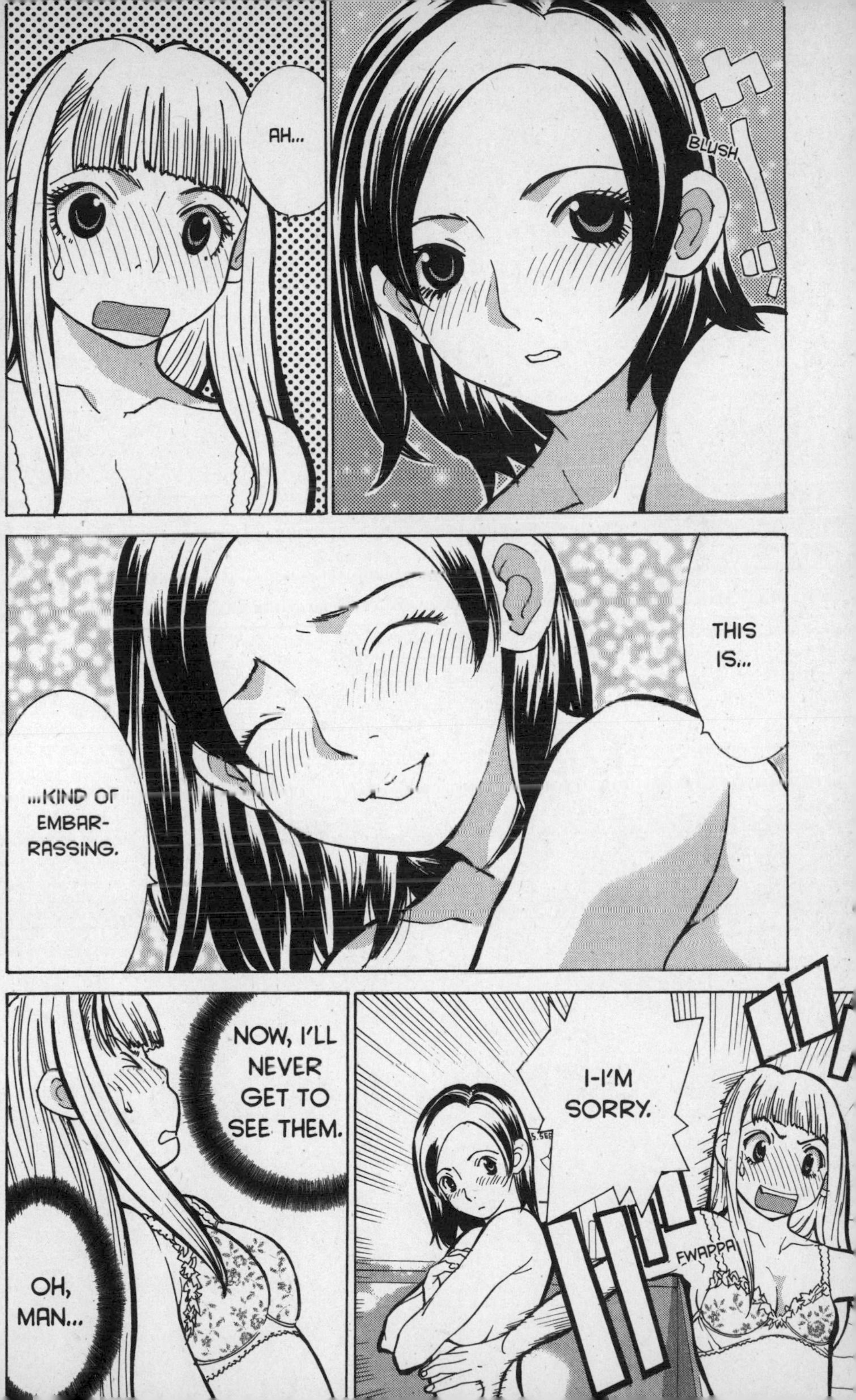
BLUSH
AH...
THIS IS...
...KIND OF EMBARRASSING.
I-I'M SORRY.
FWAPPA
NOW, I'LL NEVER GET TO SEE THEM.
OH, MAN...

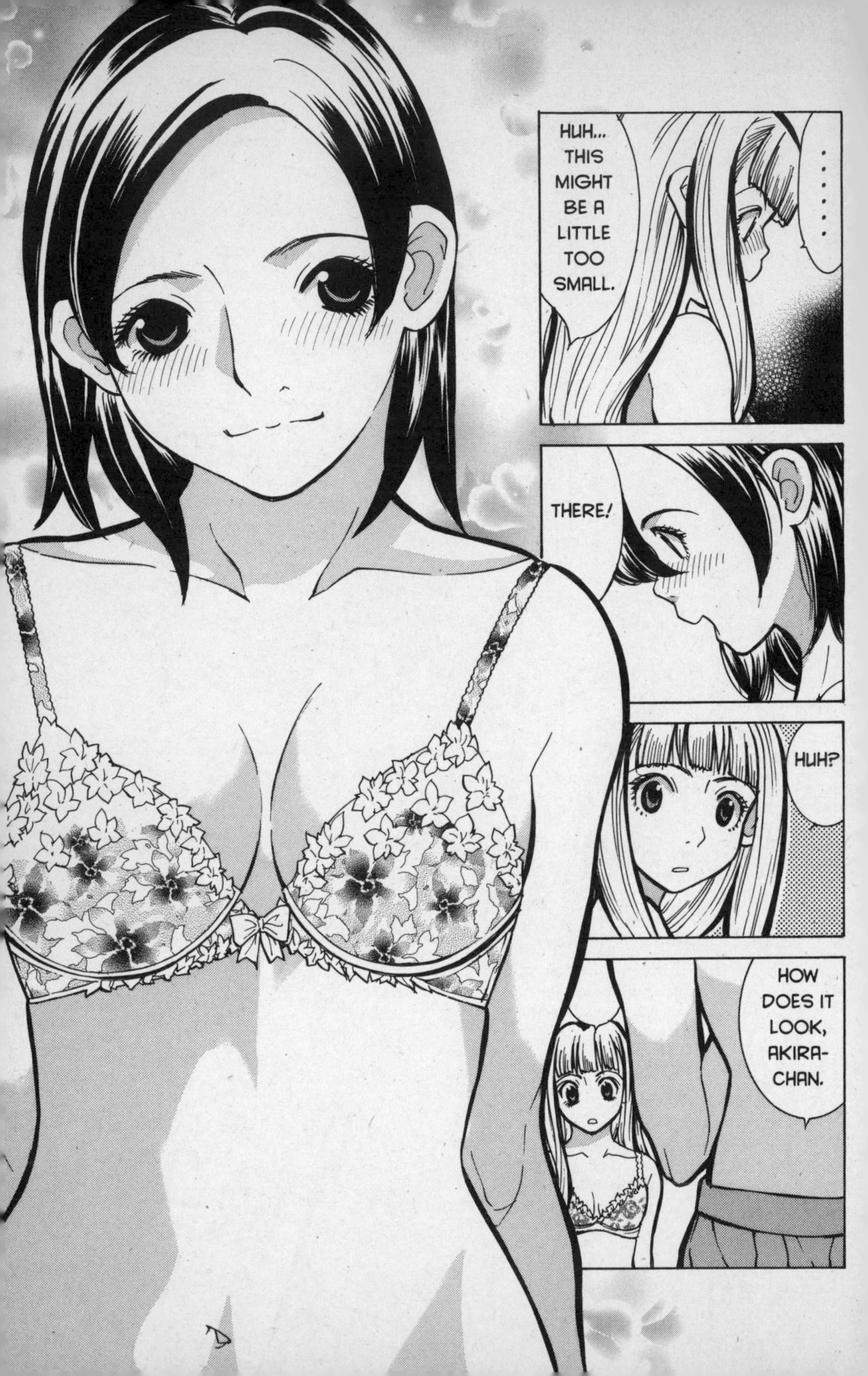
......
HUH... THIS MIGHT BE A LITTLE TOO SMALL.
THERE!
HUH?
HOW DOES IT LOOK, AKIRA-CHAN.

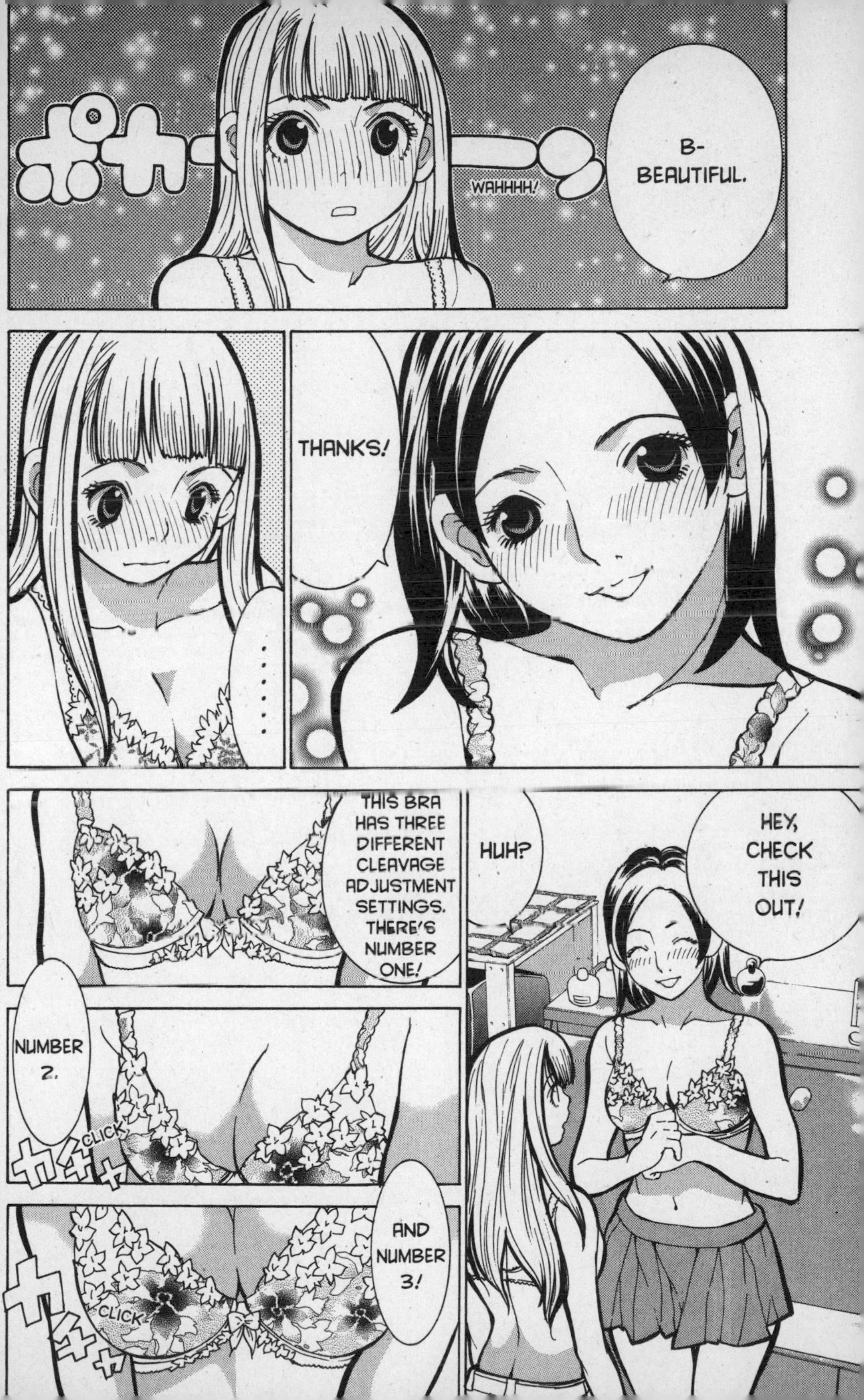
B-
BEAUTIFUL.
WAHHHH!
ポカーン
THANKS!
......
HEY, CHECK THIS OUT!
HUH?
THIS BRA HAS THREE DIFFERENT CLEAVAGE ADJUSTMENT SETTINGS. THERE'S NUMBER ONE!
NUMBER 2.
CLICK
カチャ
AND NUMBER 3!
CLICK
カチャ

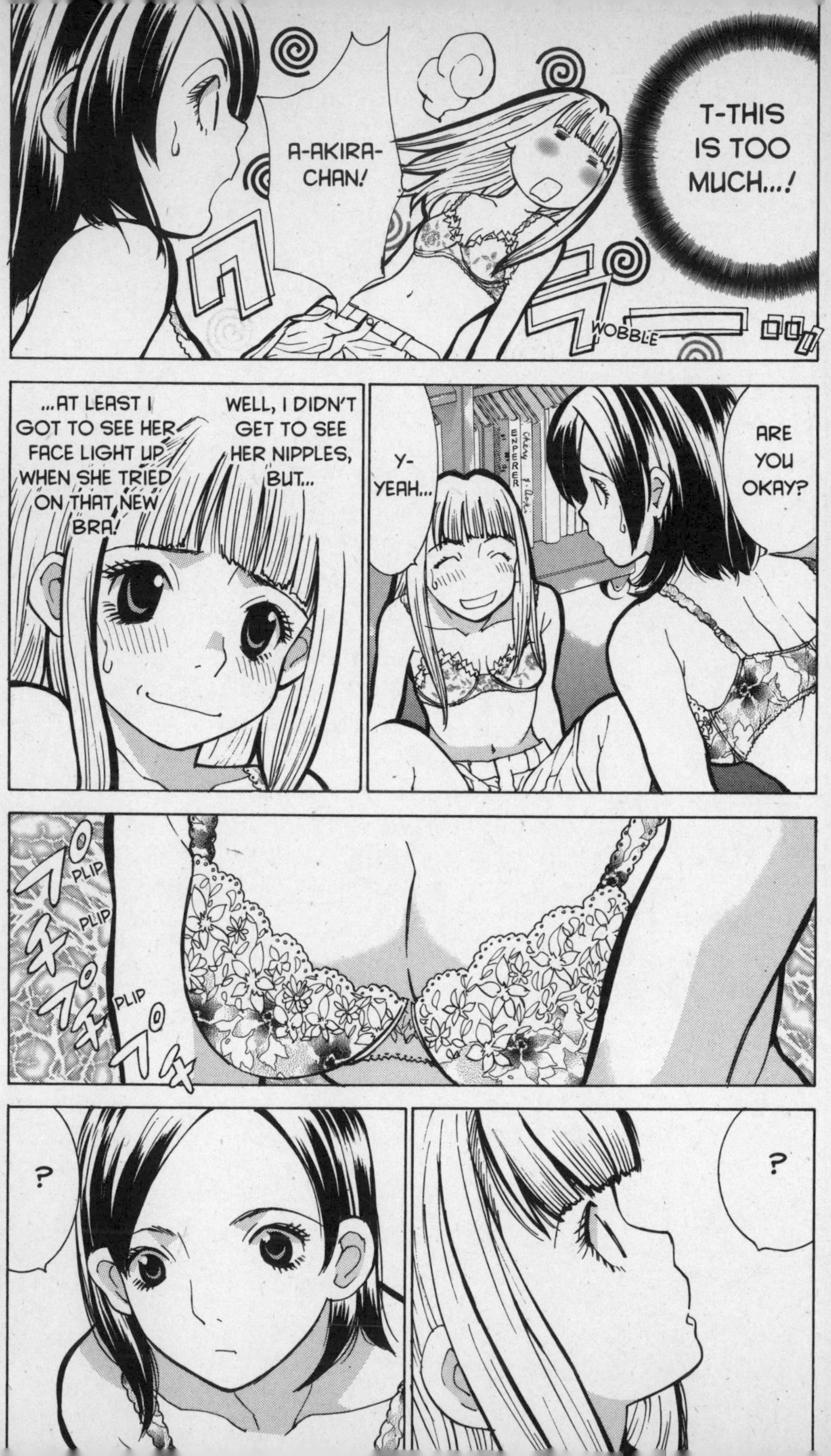
T-THIS IS TOO MUCH...!
A-AKIRA-CHAN!
WOBBLE
ARE YOU OKAY?
Y-YEAH...
WELL, I DIDN'T GET TO SEE HER NIPPLES, BUT...
...AT LEAST I GOT TO SEE HER FACE LIGHT UP WHEN SHE TRIED ON THAT NEW BRA!
PLIP
PLIP
PLIP
?
?

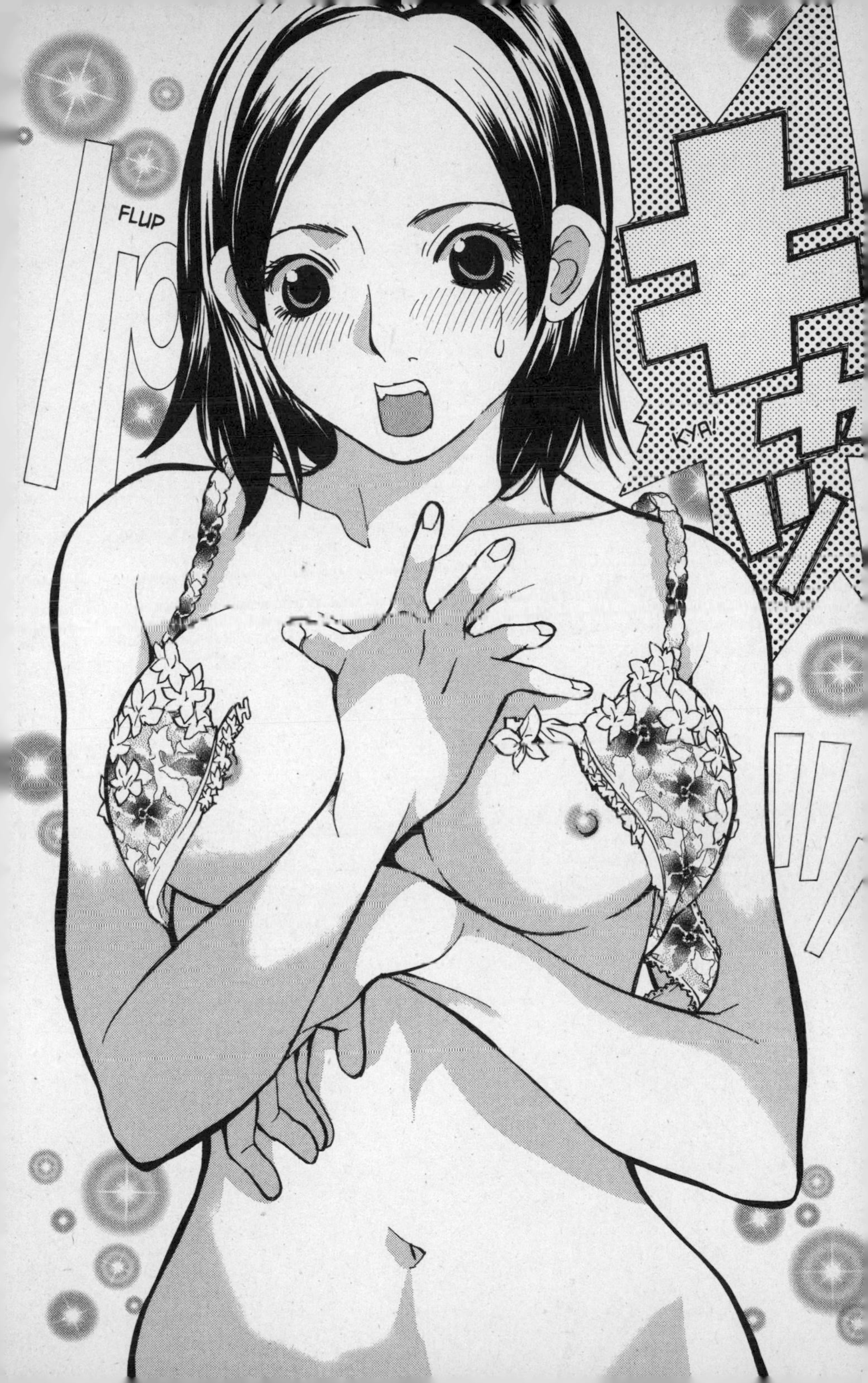
KYA!
FLUP

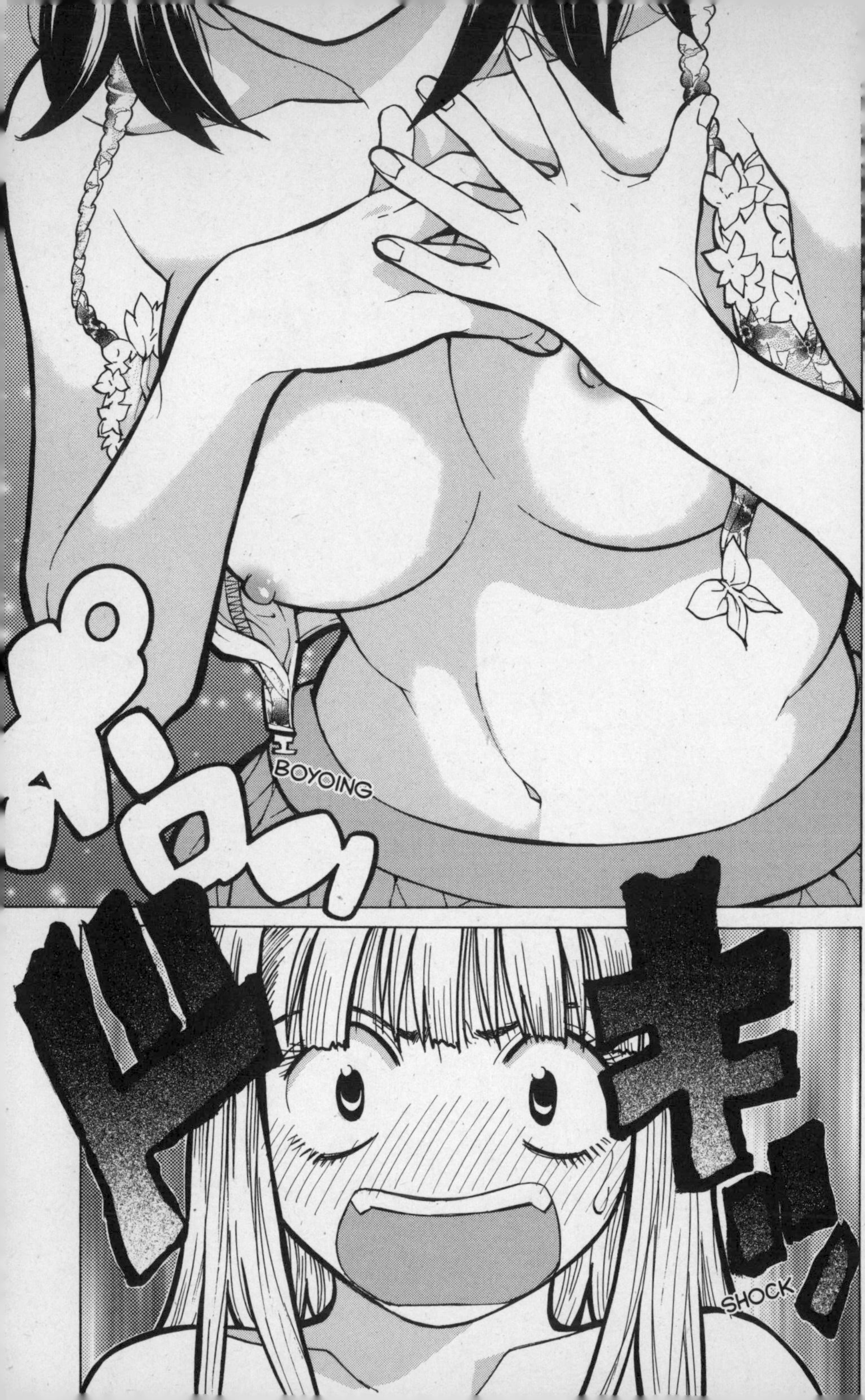
BOYOING
SHOCK

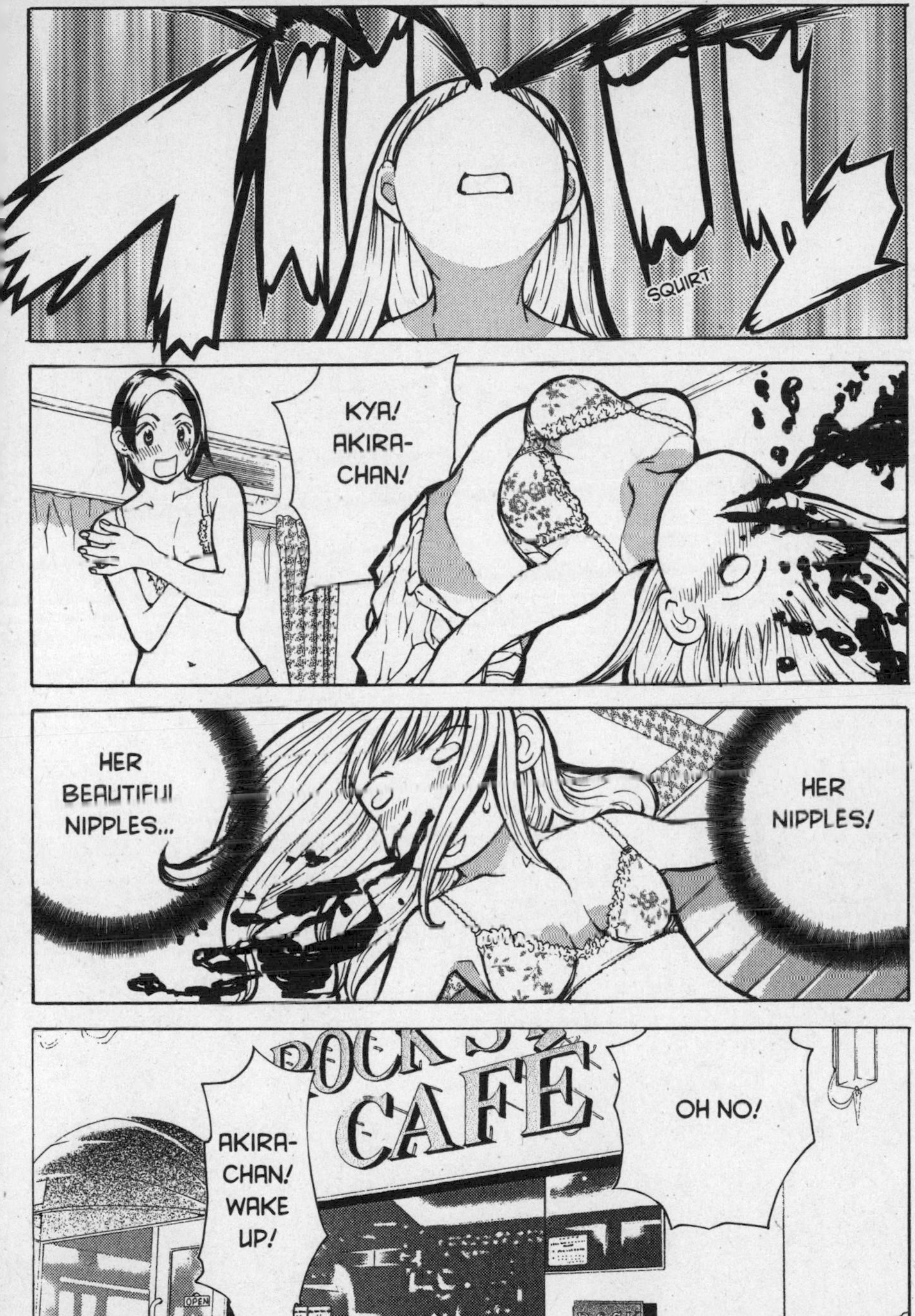
SQUIRT
KYA! AKIRA-CHAN!
HER NIPPLES!
HER BEAUTIFUL NIPPLES...
ROCK
CAFÉ
OH NO!
AKIRA-CHAN! WAKE UP!
OPEN
ROCK

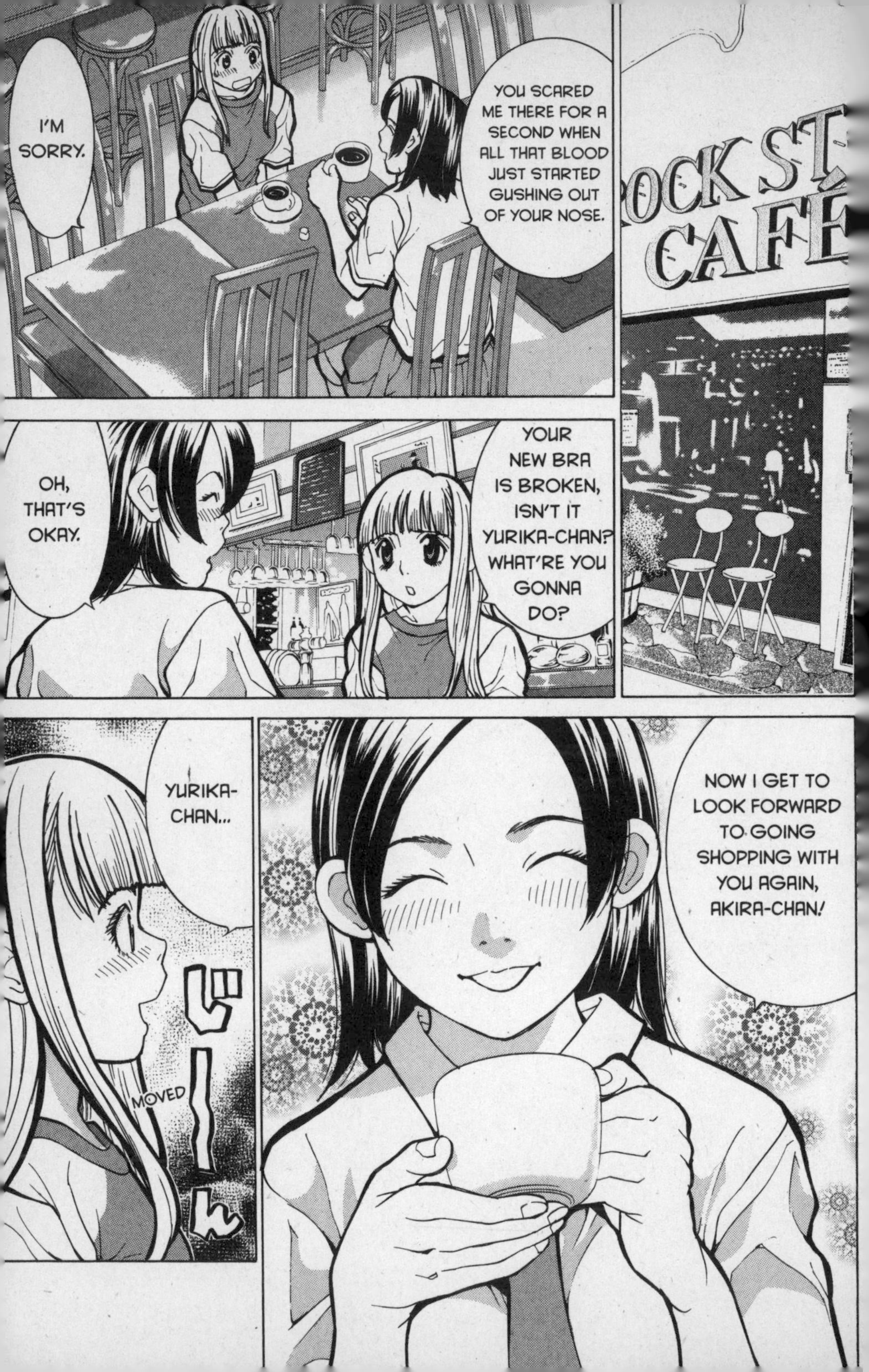
OCK ST
CAFÉ
YOU SCARED ME THERE FOR A SECOND WHEN ALL THAT BLOOD JUST STARTED GUSHING OUT OF YOUR NOSE.
I'M SORRY.
YOUR NEW BRA IS BROKEN, ISN'T IT YURIKA-CHAN? WHAT'RE YOU GONNA DO?
OH, THAT'S OKAY.
NOW I GET TO LOOK FORWARD TO GOING SHOPPING WITH YOU AGAIN, AKIRA-CHAN!
YURIKA-CHAN...
じーん
MOVED

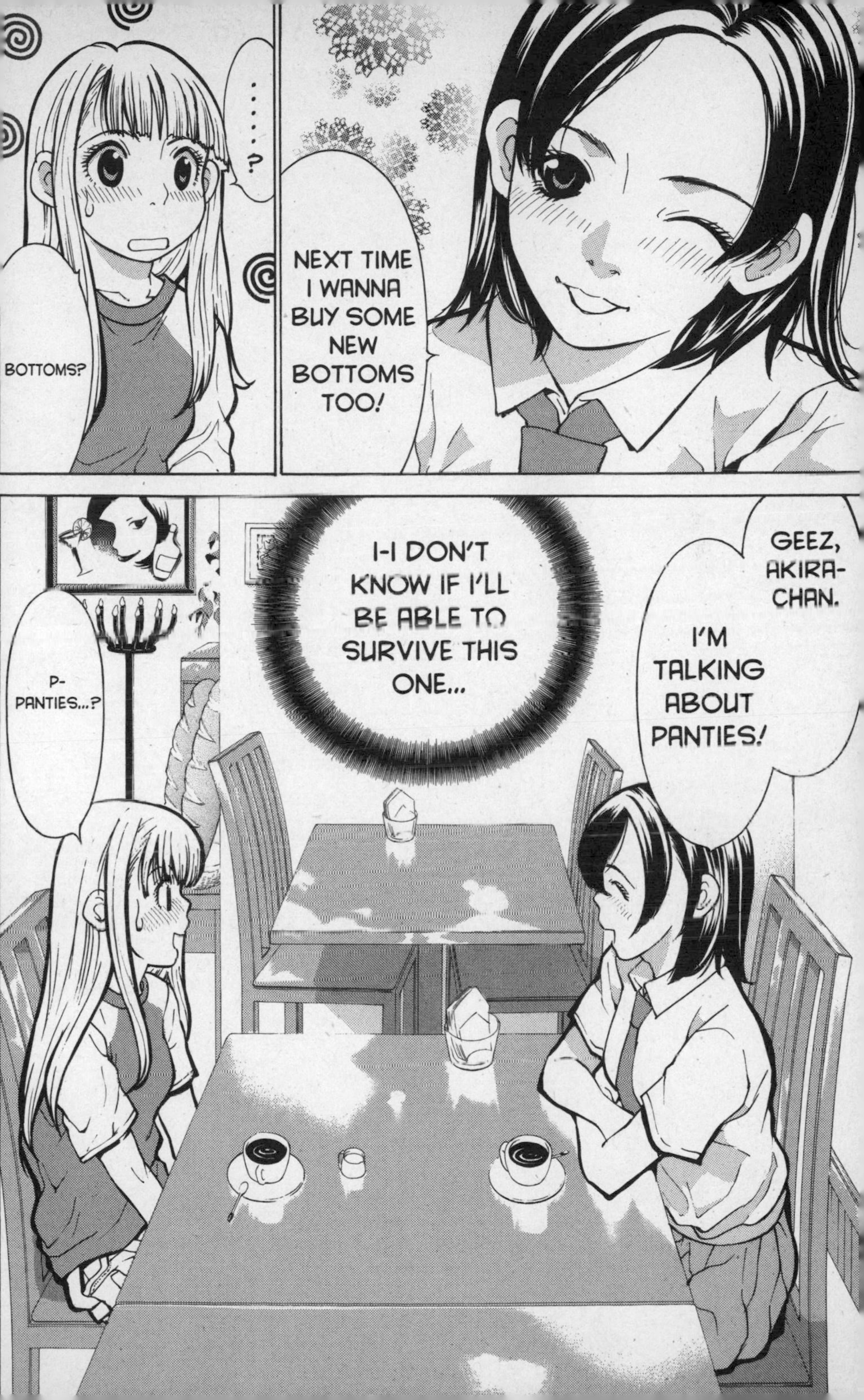
NEXT TIME I WANNA BUY SOME NEW BOTTOMS TOO!
......?
BOTTOMS?
GEEZ, AKIRA-CHAN.
I'M TALKING ABOUT PANTIES!
I-I DON'T KNOW IF I'LL BE ABLE TO SURVIVE THIS ONE...
P-PANTIES...?

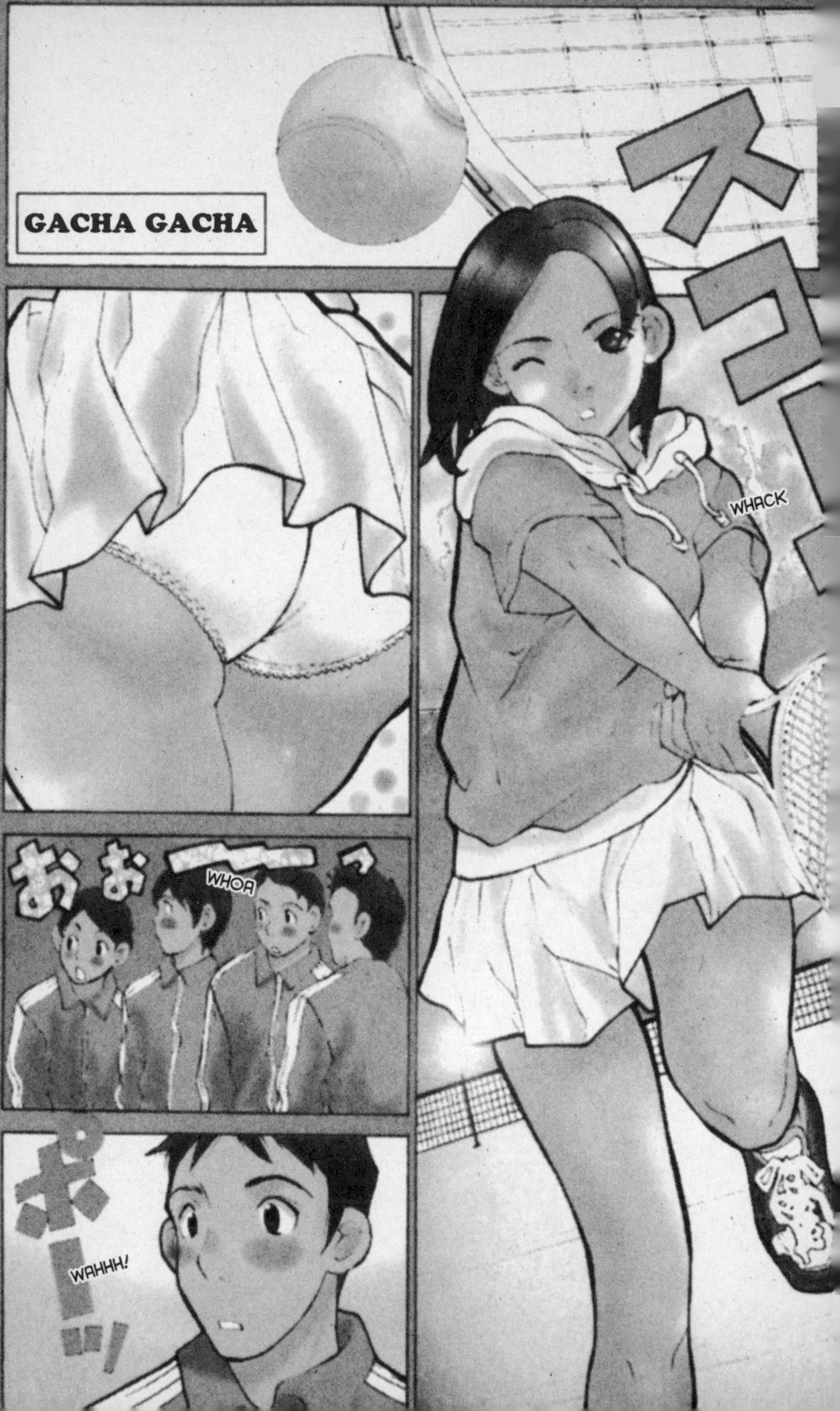

WHACK
GACHA GACHA
WHOA
WAHHH!

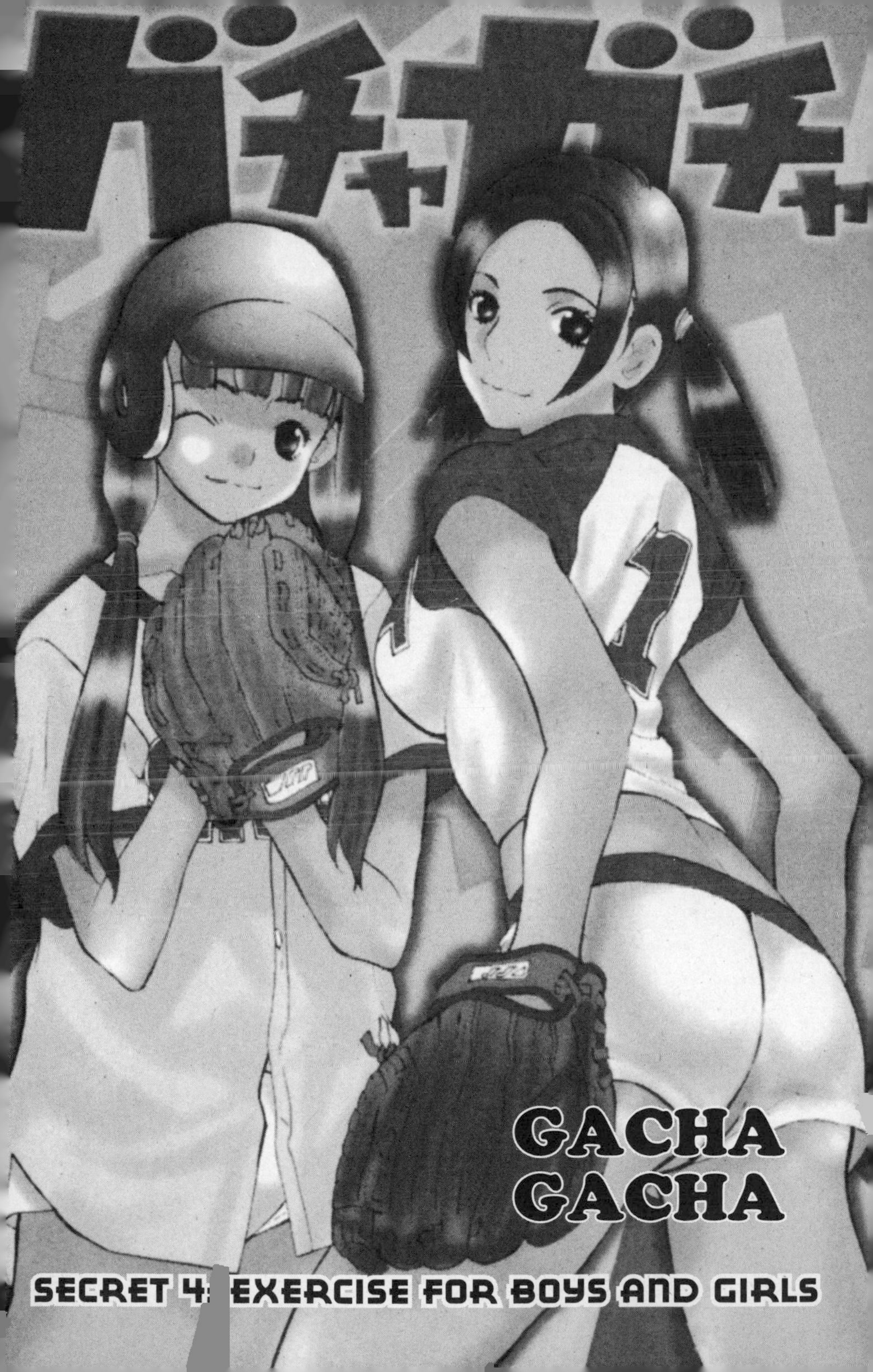
ガチャガチャ
GACHA GACHA
SECRET 4: EXERCISE FOR BOYS AND GIRLS

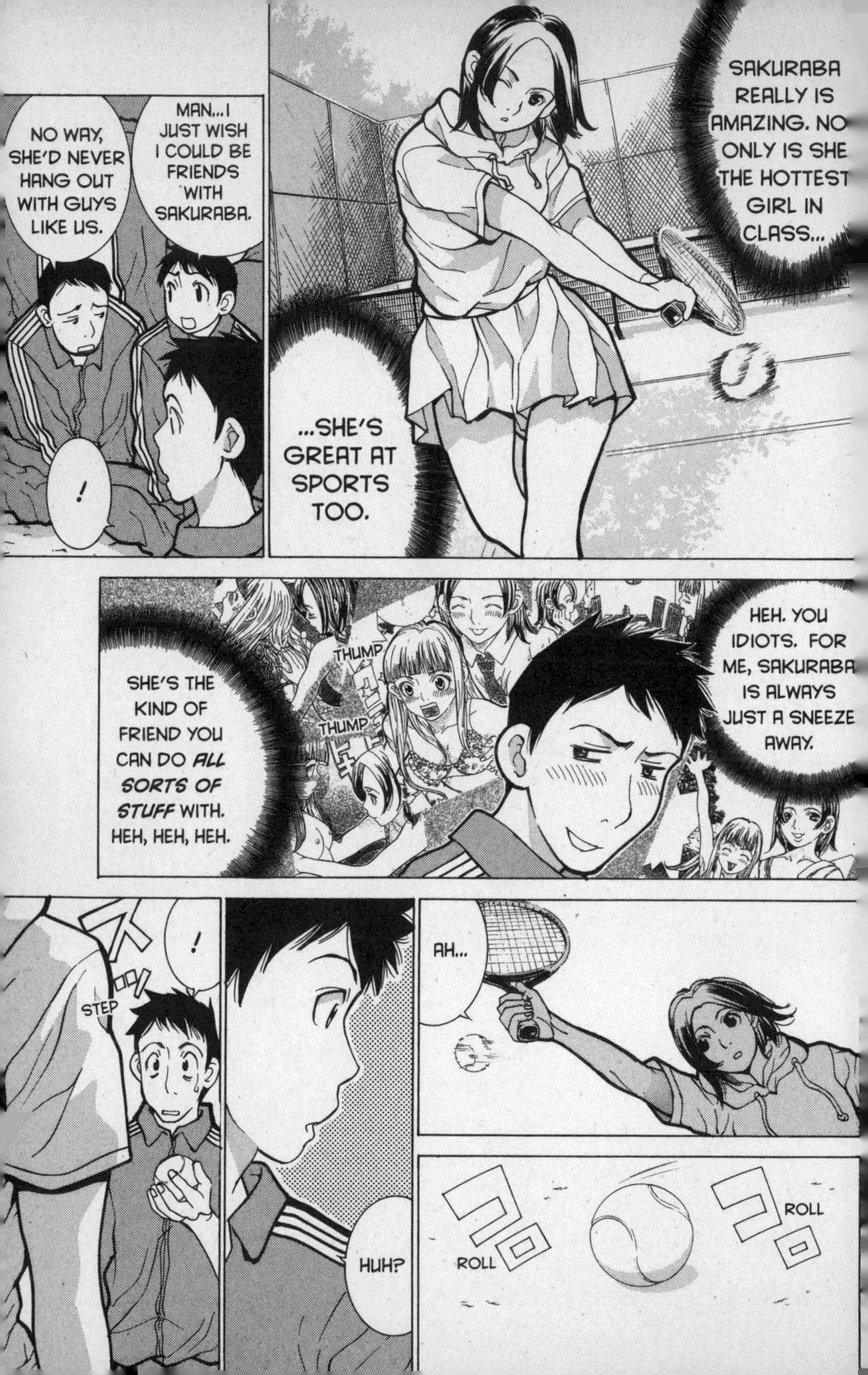
SAKURABA REALLY IS AMAZING. NO ONLY IS SHE THE HOTTEST GIRL IN CLASS...
...SHE'S GREAT AT SPORTS TOO.
MAN...I JUST WISH I COULD BE FRIENDS WITH SAKURABA.
NO WAY, SHE'D NEVER HANG OUT WITH GUYS LIKE US.
!
HEH. YOU IDIOTS. FOR ME, SAKURABA IS ALWAYS JUST A SNEEZE AWAY.
THUMP
THUMP
SHE'S THE KIND OF FRIEND YOU CAN DO ALL SORTS OF STUFF WITH. HEH, HEH, HEH.
AH...
ROLL
ROLL
HUH?
!
STEP

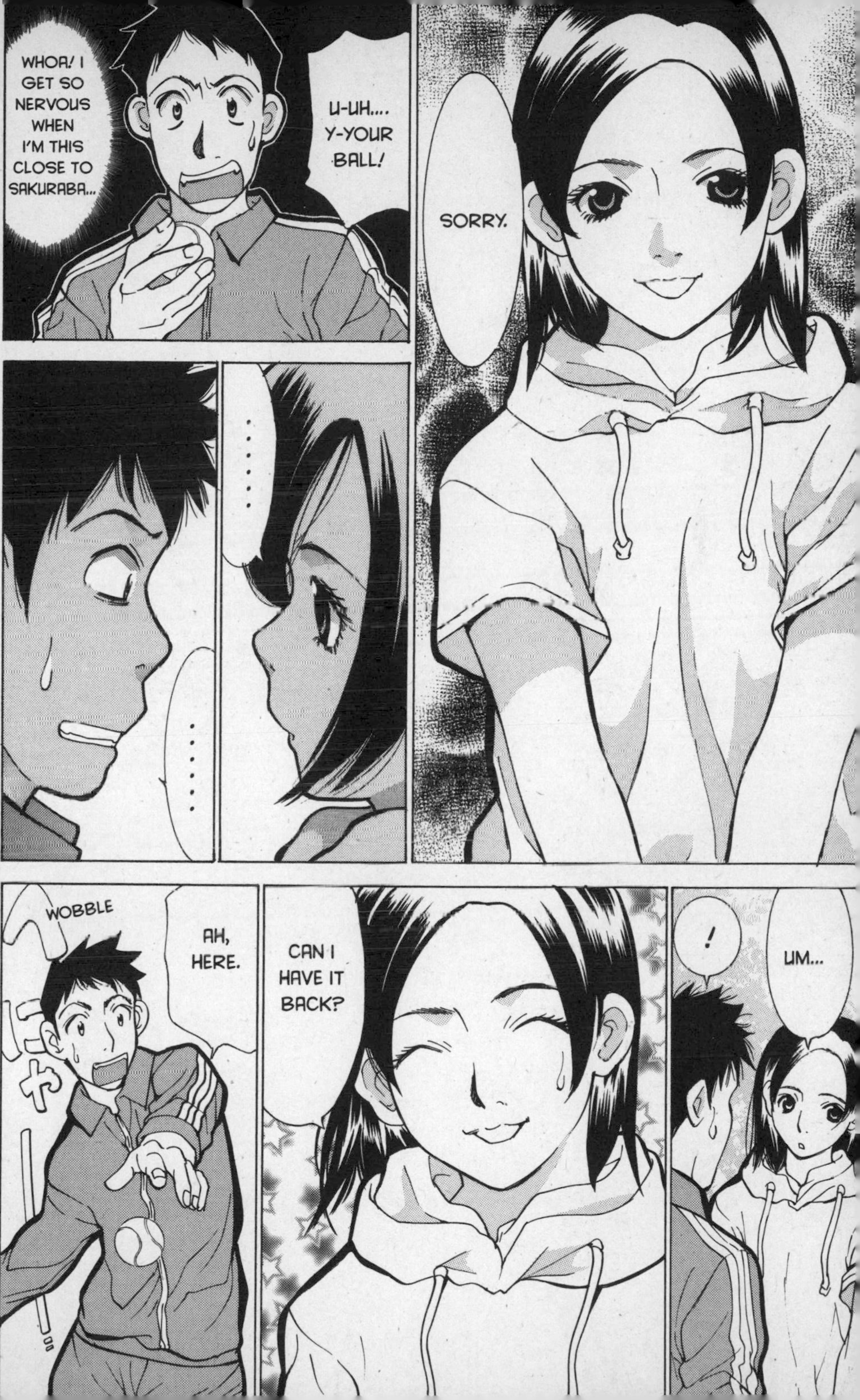
SORRY.
U-UH.... Y-YOUR BALL!
WHOA! I GET SO NERVOUS WHEN I'M THIS CLOSE TO SAKURABA...
......
......
UM...
!
CAN I HAVE IT BACK?
AH, HERE.
WOBBLE
にや

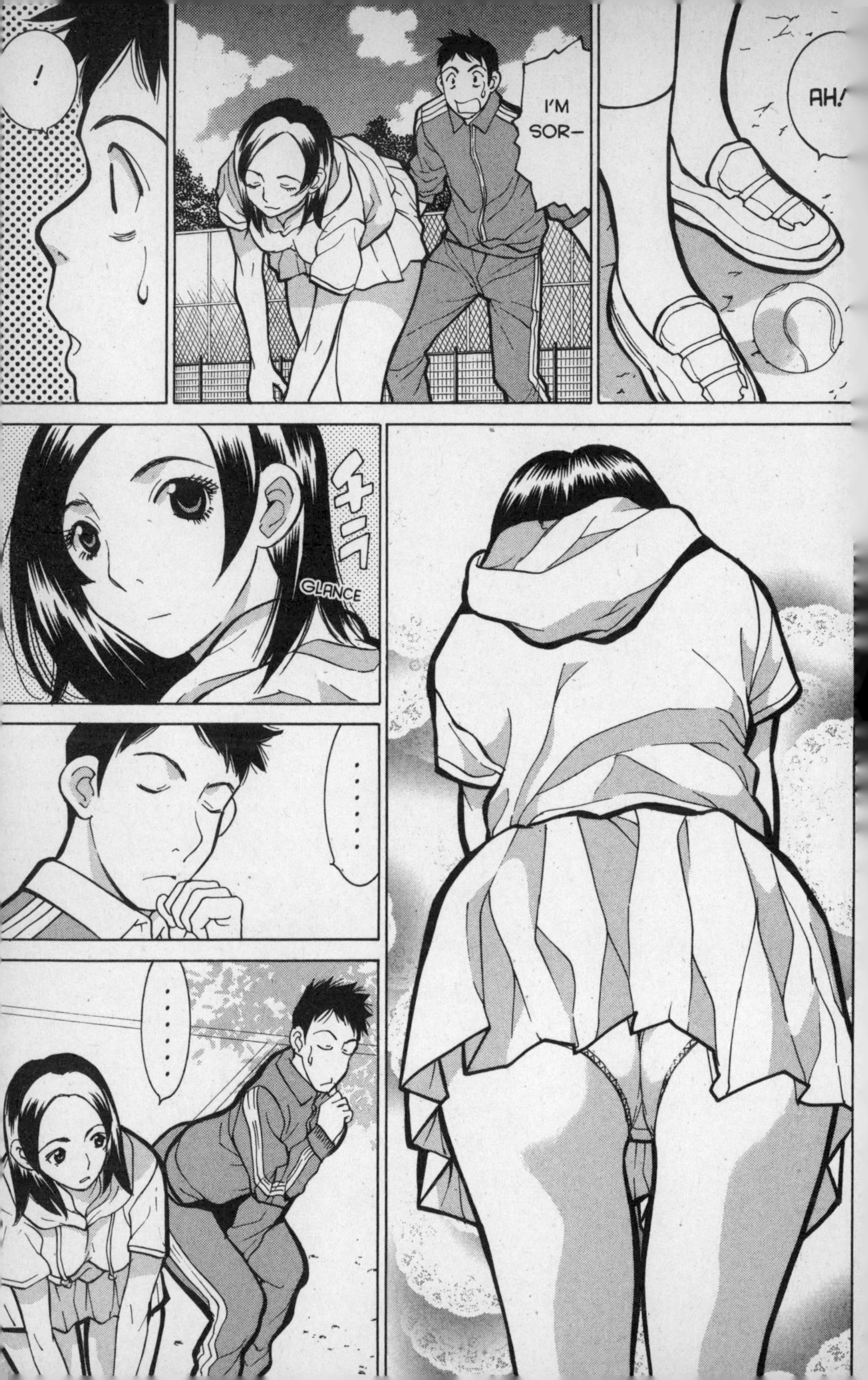
AH!
I'M SOR—
!
チラ
GLANCE
......
......

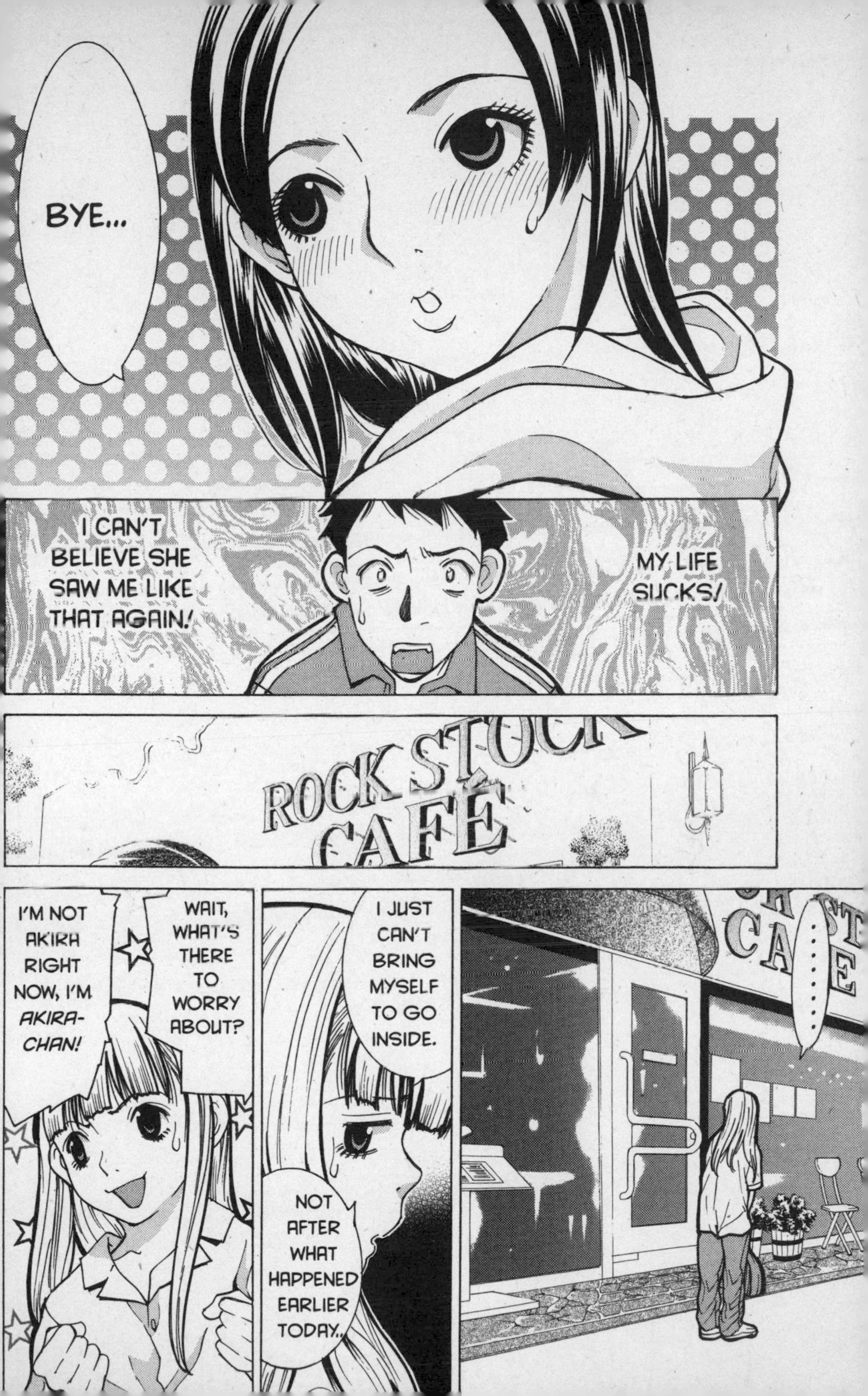
BYE...
I CAN'T BELIEVE SHE SAW ME LIKE THAT AGAIN!
MY LIFE SUCKS!
ROCK STOCK CAFÉ
......
I JUST CAN'T BRING MYSELF TO GO INSIDE.
NOT AFTER WHAT HAPPENED EARLIER TODAY..
WAIT, WHAT'S THERE TO WORRY ABOUT?
I'M NOT AKIRA RIGHT NOW, I'M *AKIRA-CHAN!*

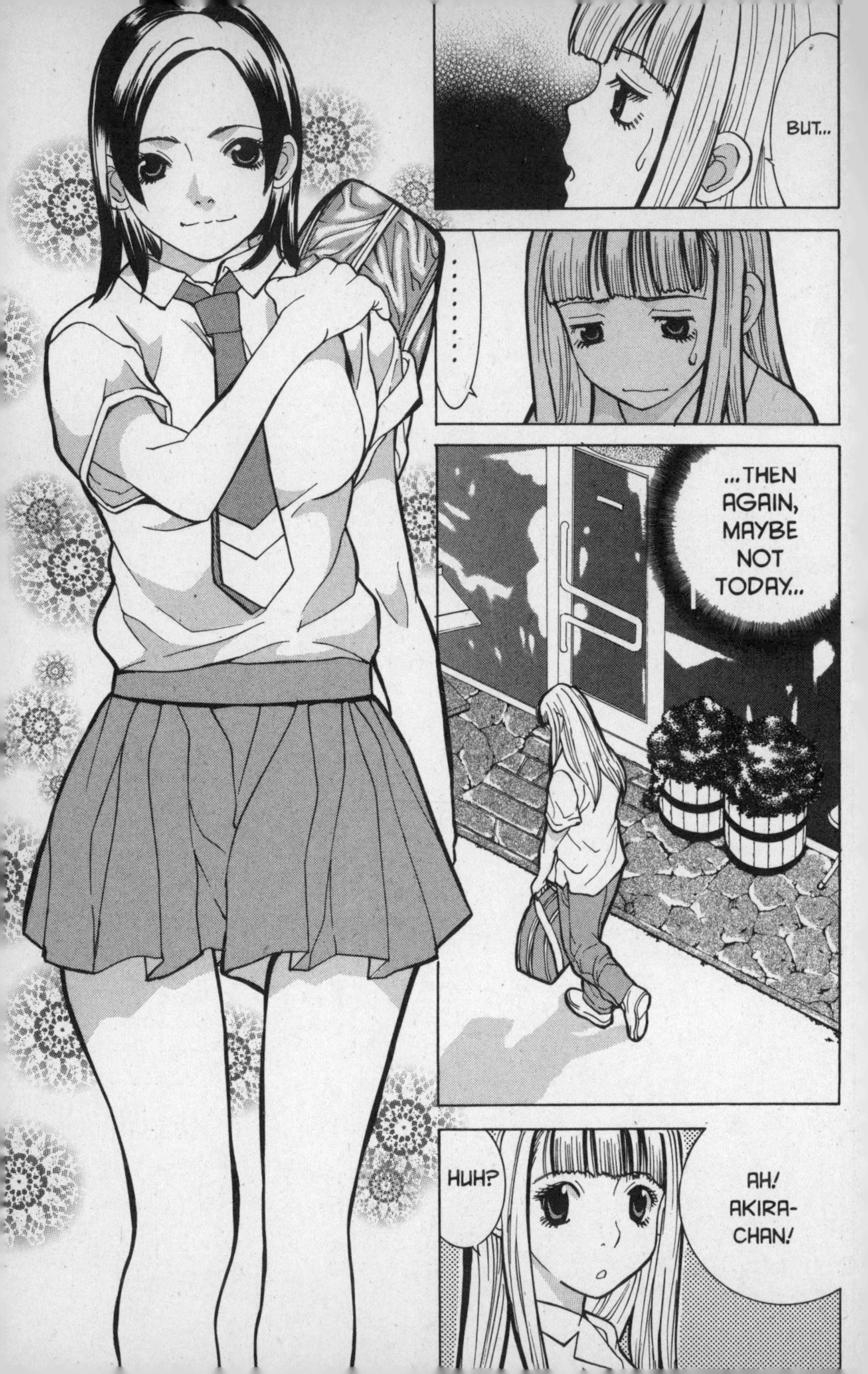
BUT...
......
...THEN AGAIN, MAYBE NOT TODAY...
AH! AKIRA-CHAN!
HUH?

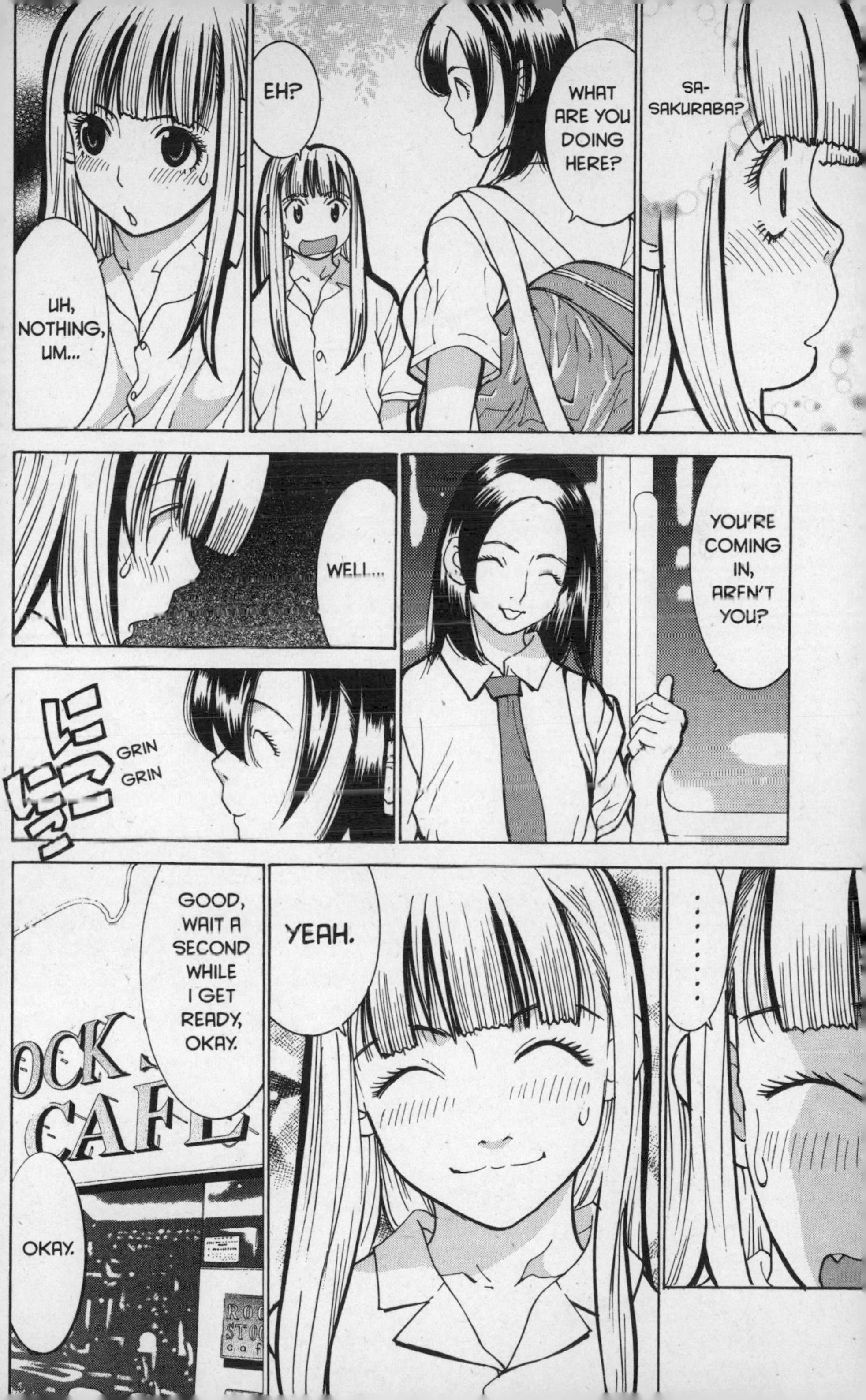
SA-SAKURABA?
WHAT ARE YOU DOING HERE?
EH?
UH, NOTHING, UM...
YOU'RE COMING IN, AREN'T YOU?
WELL...
GRIN GRIN
......
YEAH.
GOOD, WAIT A SECOND WHILE I GET READY, OKAY.
OKAY.

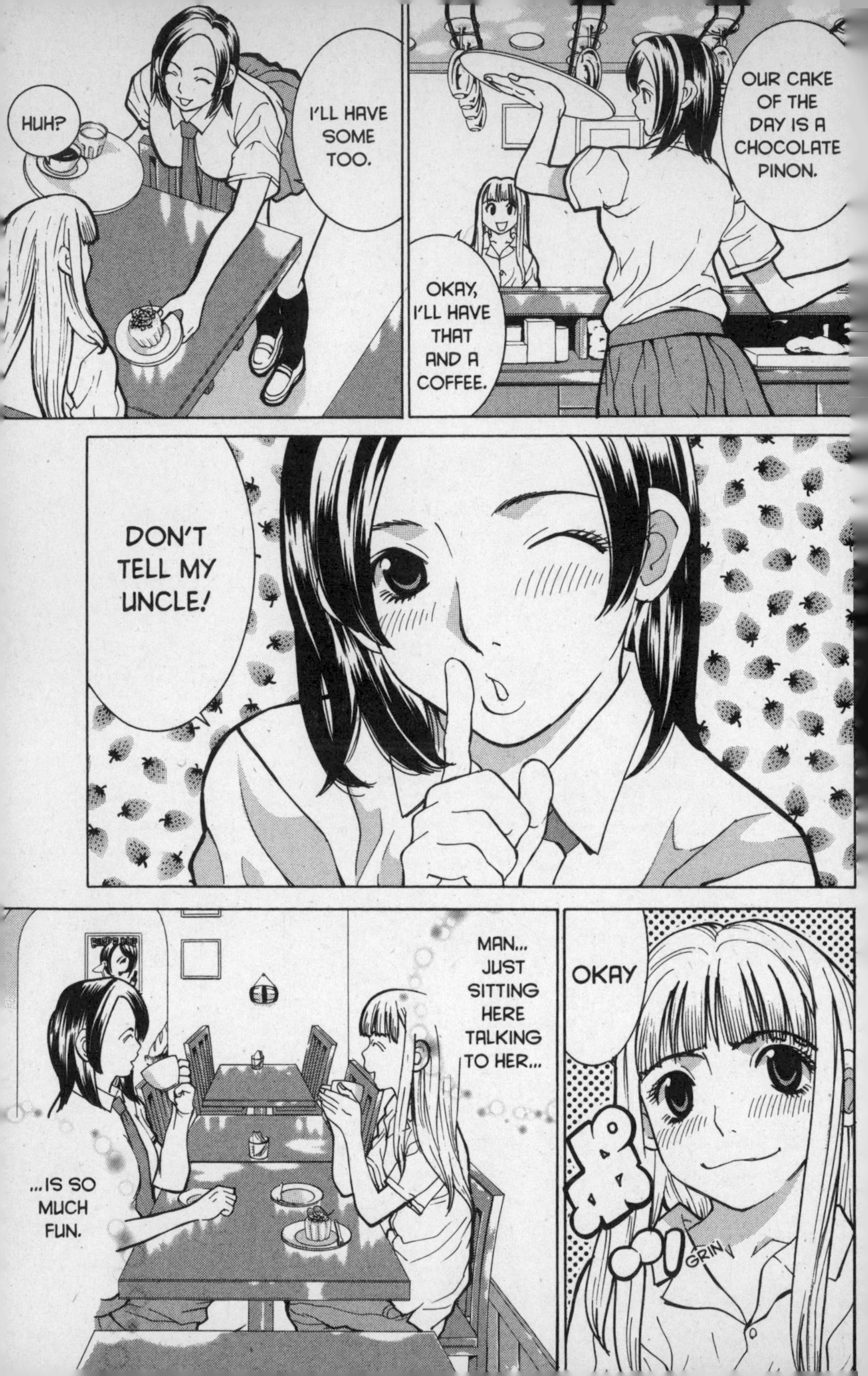
OUR CAKE OF THE DAY IS A CHOCOLATE PINON.
OKAY, I'LL HAVE THAT AND A COFFEE.
I'LL HAVE SOME TOO.
HUH?
DON'T TELL MY UNCLE!
OKAY
GRIN
MAN... JUST SITTING HERE TALKING TO HER...
...IS SO MUCH FUN.

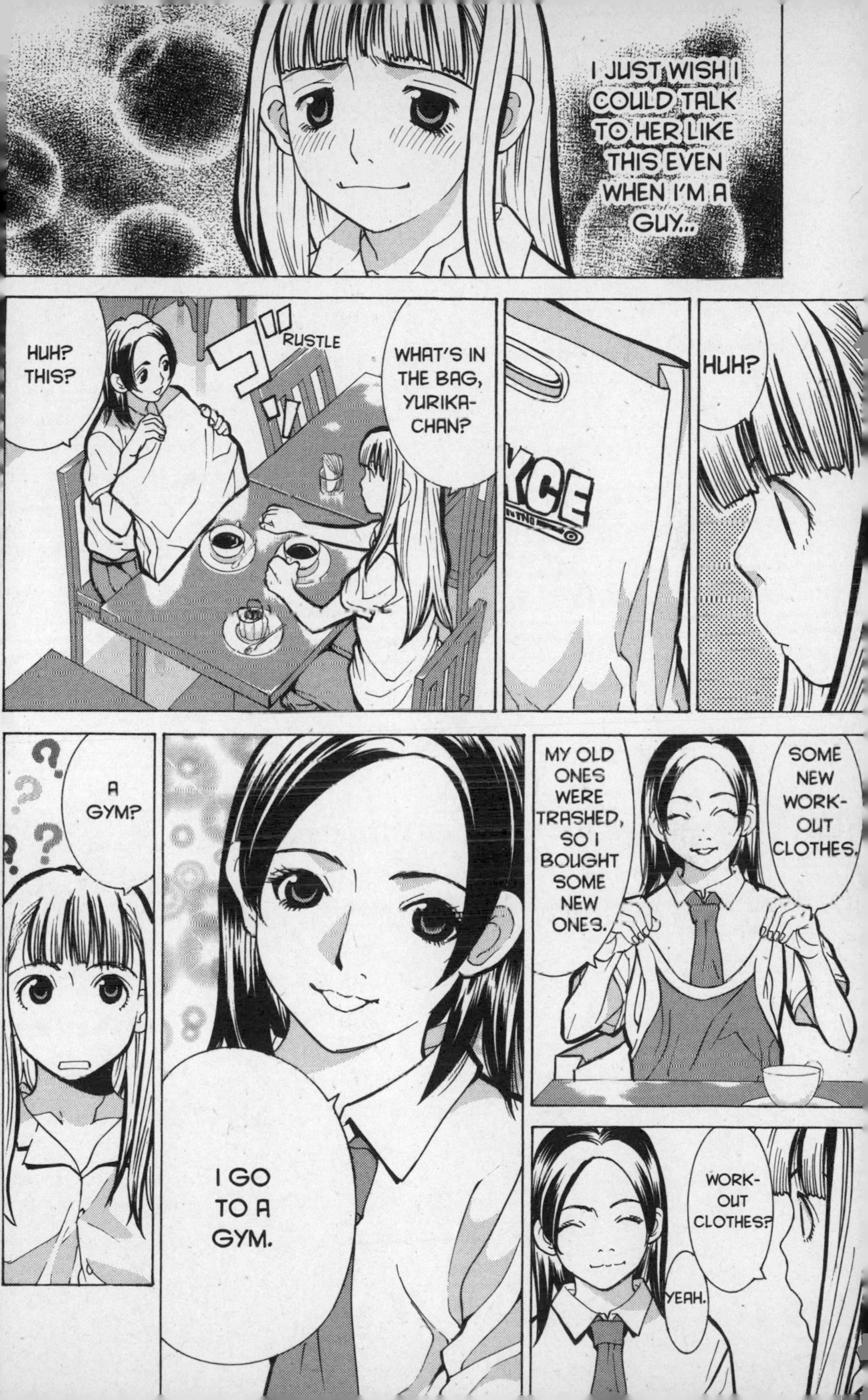
I JUST WISH I COULD TALK TO HER LIKE THIS EVEN WHEN I'M A GUY...
HUH?
WHAT'S IN THE BAG, YURIKA-CHAN?
RUSTLE
HUH? THIS?
SOME NEW WORK-OUT CLOTHES.
MY OLD ONES WERE TRASHED, SO I BOUGHT SOME NEW ONES.
WORK-OUT CLOTHES?
YEAH.
I GO TO A GYM.
A GYM?

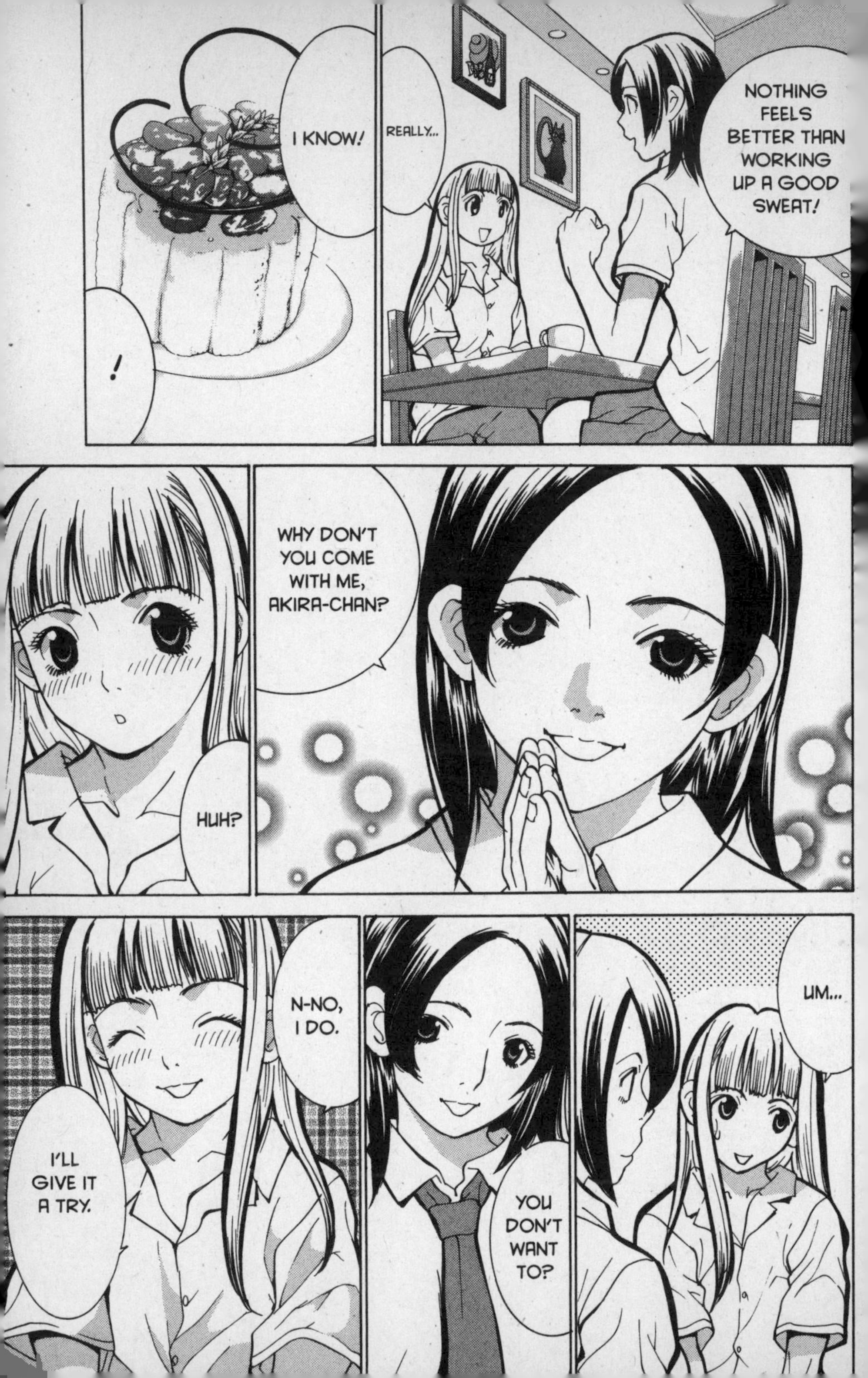
NOTHING FEELS BETTER THAN WORKING UP A GOOD SWEAT!
REALLY...
I KNOW!
!
WHY DON'T YOU COME WITH ME, AKIRA-CHAN?
HUH?
UM...
YOU DON'T WANT TO?
N-NO, I DO.
I'LL GIVE IT A TRY.

OKAY.

ROCK STOCK CAFÉ

I'LL MEET YOU AT THE GYM.

OKAY.

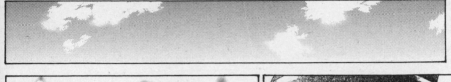

THE GYM...

WHAT IF I WERE TO GO THERE AS A GUY AND JUST HAPPEN TO BUMP INTO SAKURABA...

BYE.

BYE.

OKAY, THAT'S IT! TOMORROW, I'M GOING TO THE GYM AS A GUY.

AND I'LL GET JUST A LITTLE CLOSER TO BECOMING FRIENDS WITH SAKURABA.

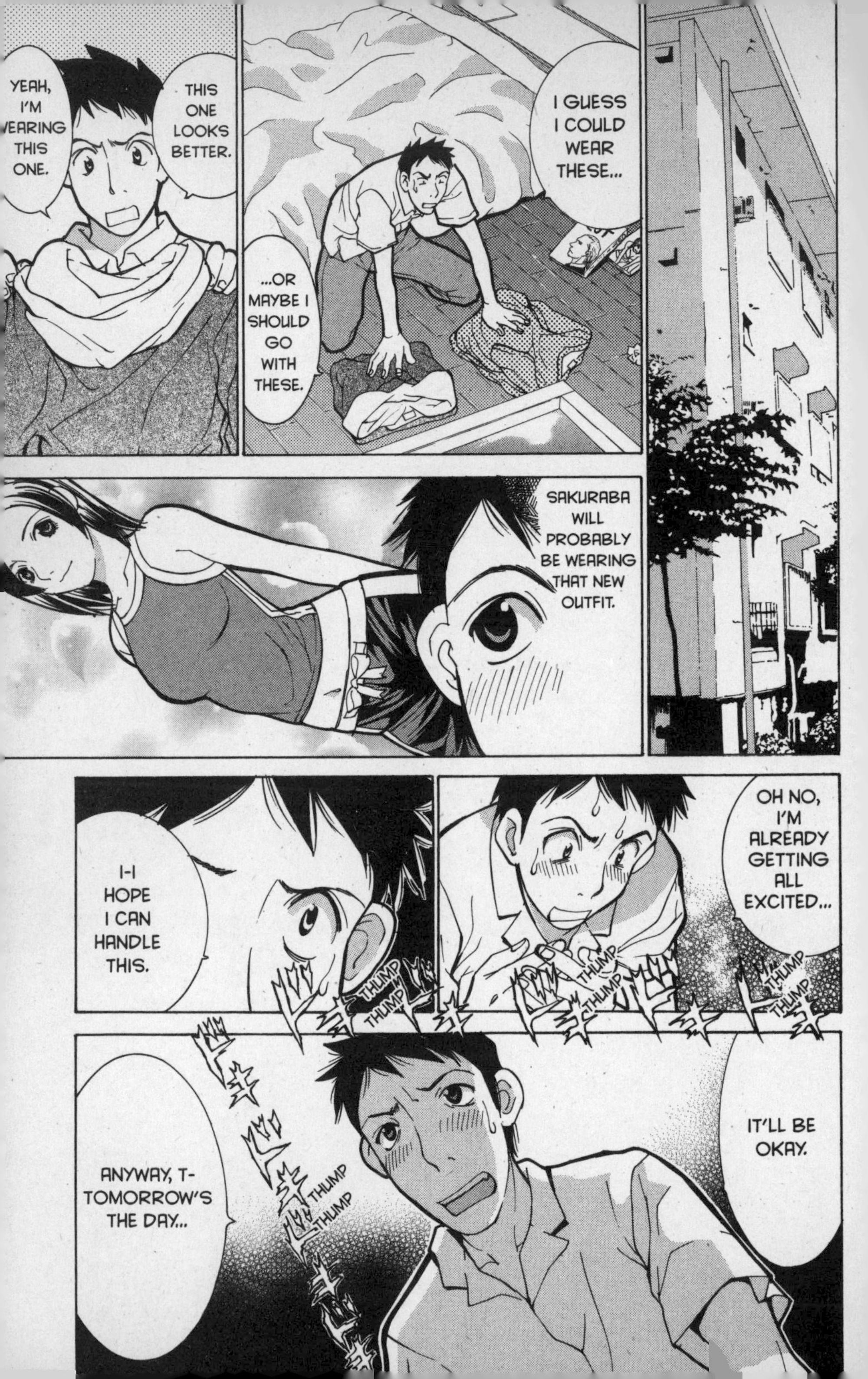
I GUESS I COULD WEAR THESE...
...OR MAYBE I SHOULD GO WITH THESE.
THIS ONE LOOKS BETTER.
YEAH, I'M WEARING THIS ONE.
SAKURABA WILL PROBABLY BE WEARING THAT NEW OUTFIT.
OH NO, I'M ALREADY GETTING ALL EXCITED...
THUMP THUMP
THUMP THUMP
I-I HOPE I CAN HANDLE THIS.
THUMP THUMP
IT'LL BE OKAY.
ANYWAY, T-TOMORROW'S THE DAY...
THUMP THUMP

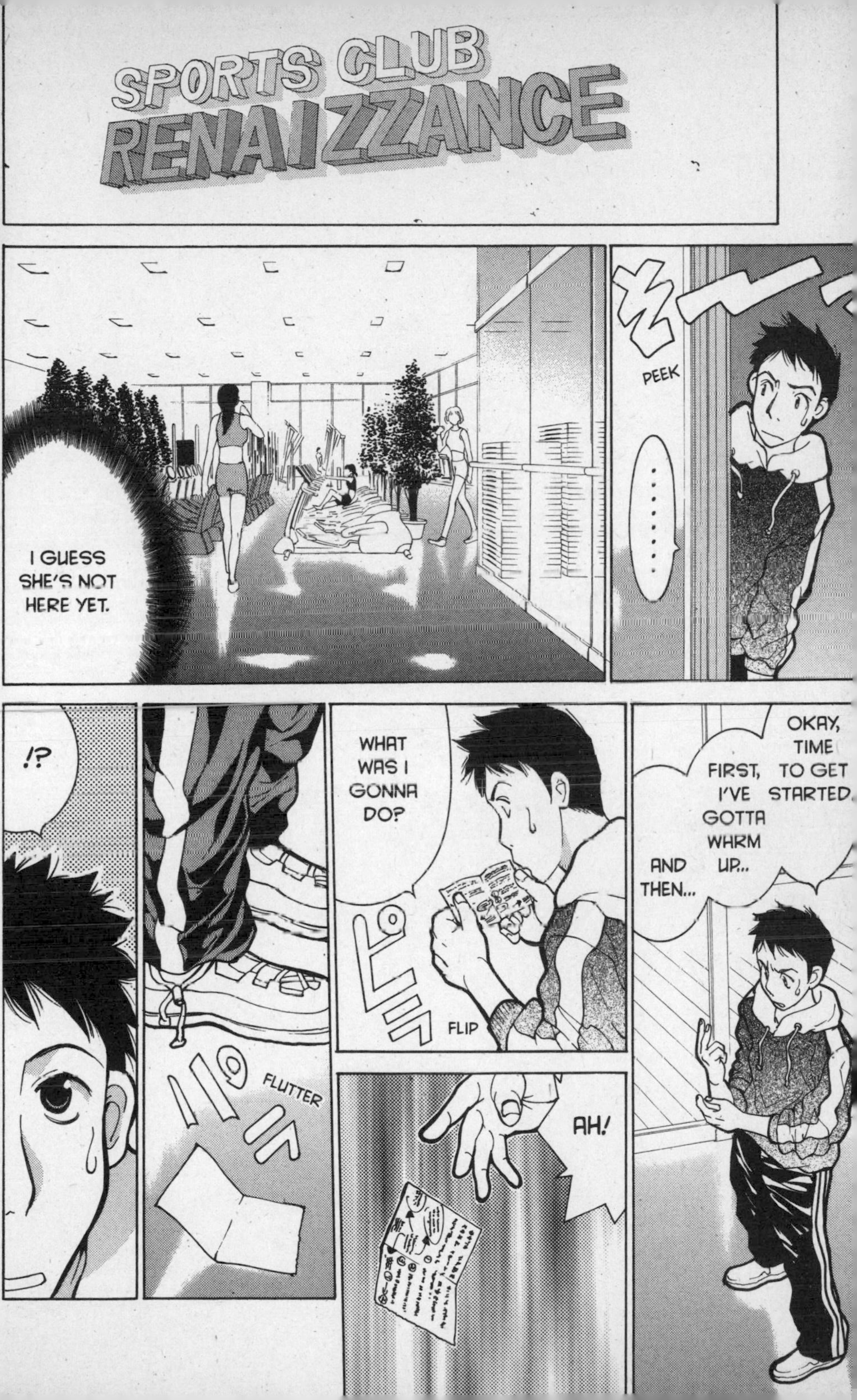
SPORTS CLUB RENAIZZANCE
そーーっ
PEEK
......
I GUESS SHE'S NOT HERE YET.
OKAY, TIME TO GET STARTED.
FIRST, I'VE GOTTA WARM UP... AND THEN...
WHAT WAS I GONNA DO?
FLIP
AH!
FLUTTER
!?

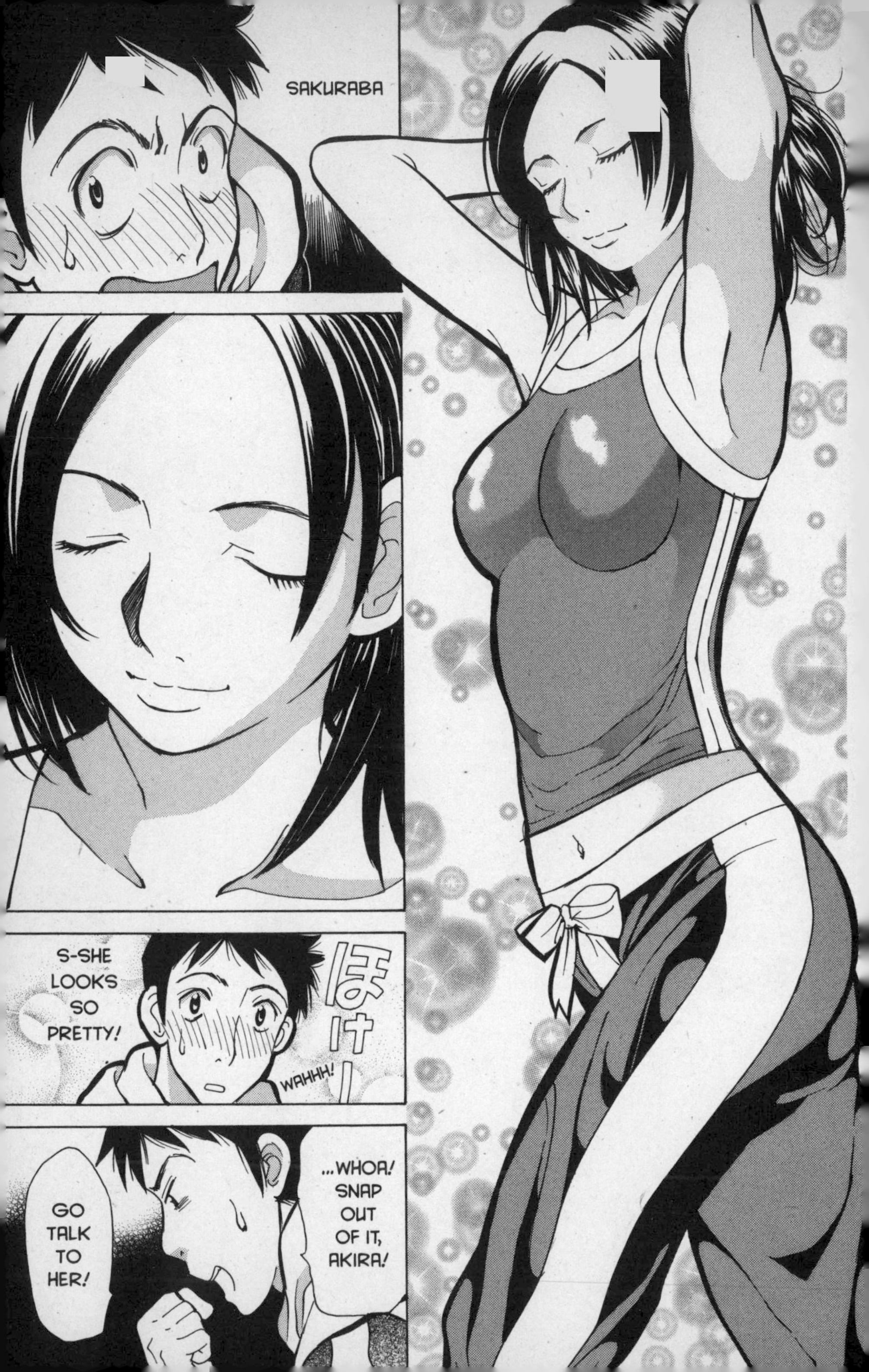
SAKURABA
S-SHE LOOKS SO PRETTY!
ほけー
WAHHH!
...WHOA! SNAP OUT OF IT, AKIRA!
GO TALK TO HER!

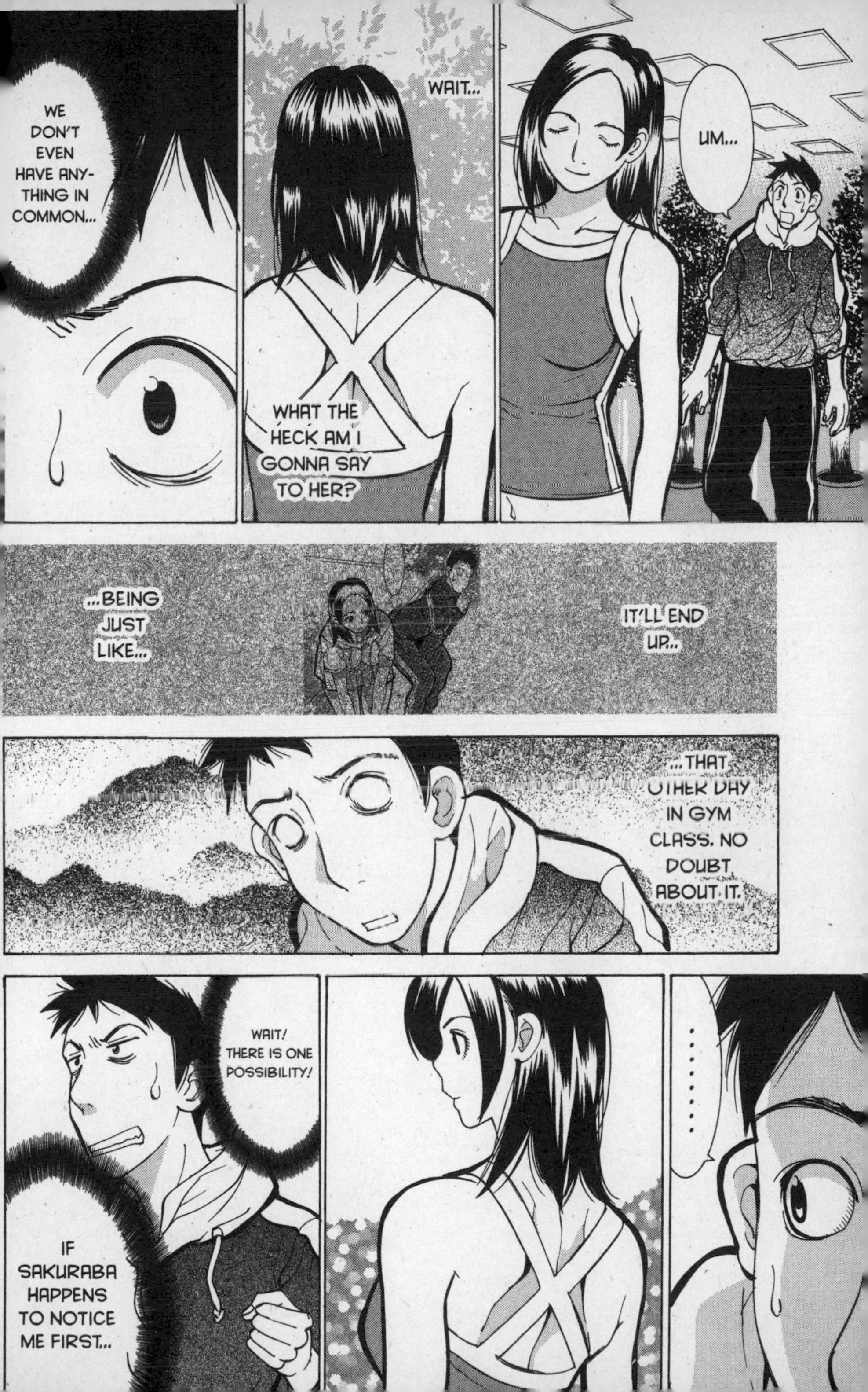
UM...
WAIT...
WHAT THE HECK AM I GONNA SAY TO HER?
WE DON'T EVEN HAVE ANY-THING IN COMMON...
IT'LL END UP...
...BEING JUST LIKE...
...THAT OTHER DAY IN GYM CLASS. NO DOUBT ABOUT IT.
......
WAIT! THERE IS ONE POSSIBILITY!
IF SAKURABA HAPPENS TO NOTICE ME FIRST...

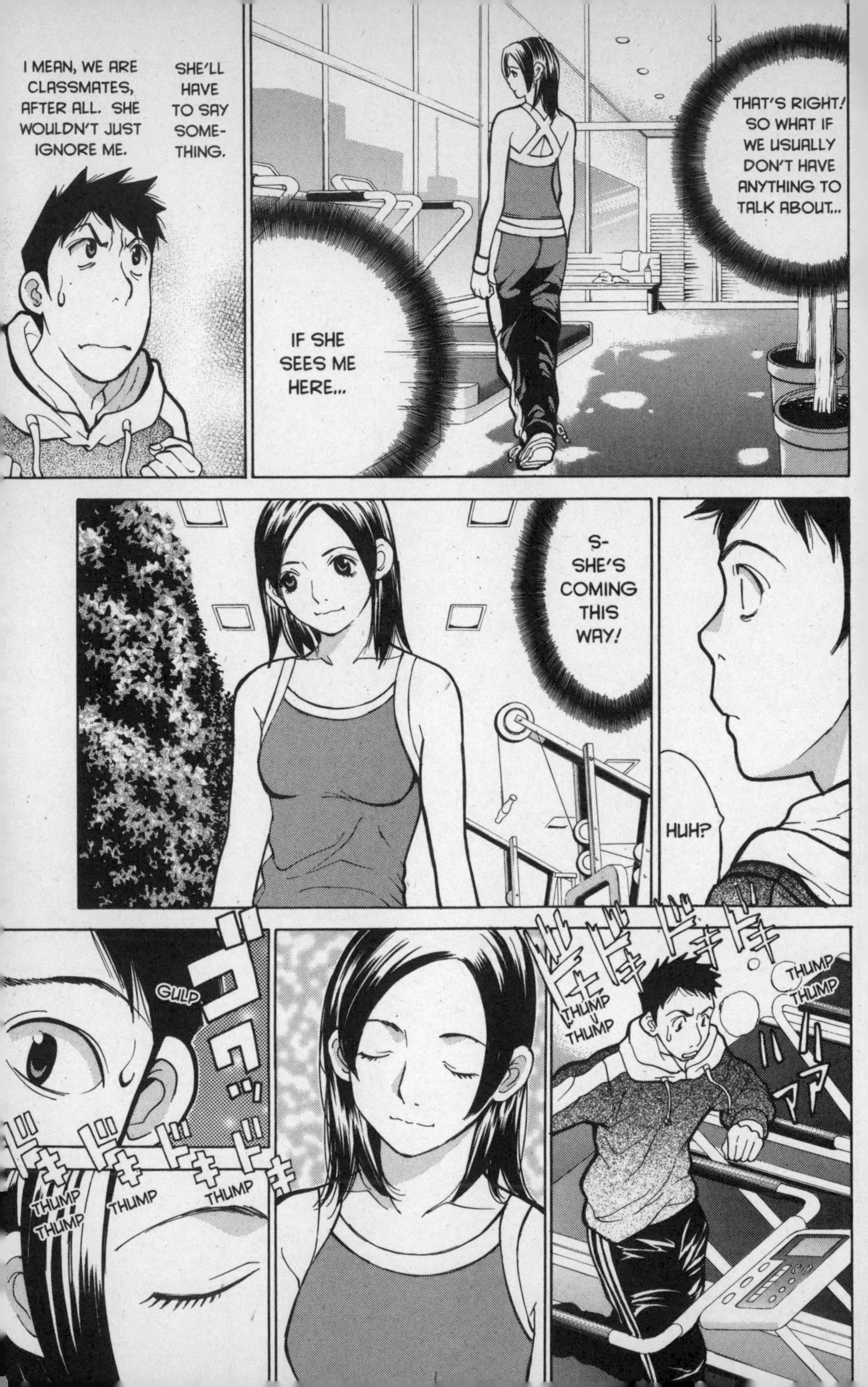
THAT'S RIGHT! SO WHAT IF WE USUALLY DON'T HAVE ANYTHING TO TALK ABOUT...
IF SHE SEES ME HERE...
SHE'LL HAVE TO SAY SOME-THING.
I MEAN, WE ARE CLASSMATES, AFTER ALL. SHE WOULDN'T JUST IGNORE ME.
HUH?
S-SHE'S COMING THIS WAY!
THUMP THUMP
THUMP THUMP
ハア
GULP
THUMP
THUMP
THUMP THUMP

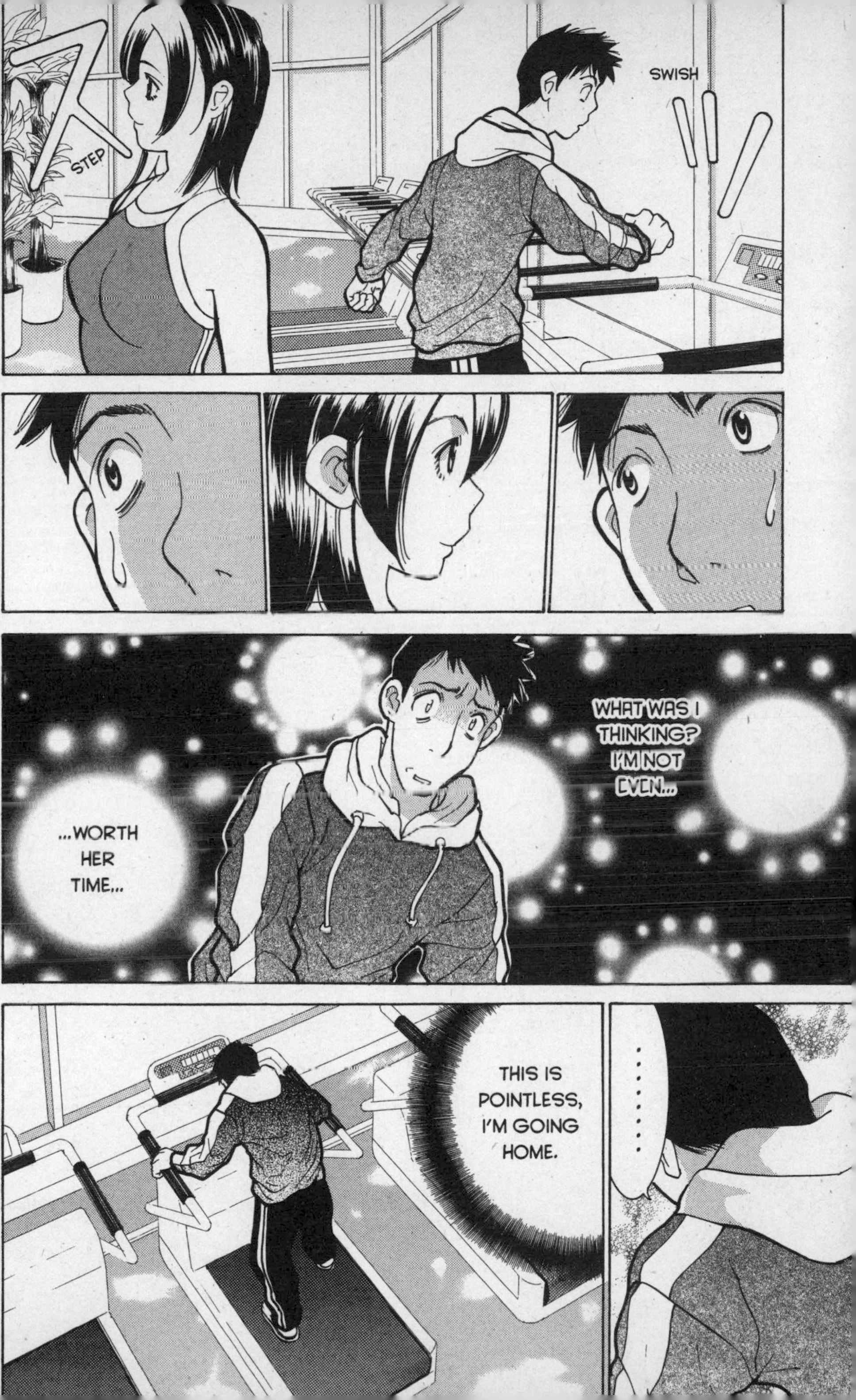
SWISH
STEP
WHAT WAS I THINKING? I'M NOT EVEN...
...WORTH HER TIME...
......
THIS IS POINTLESS, I'M GOING HOME.

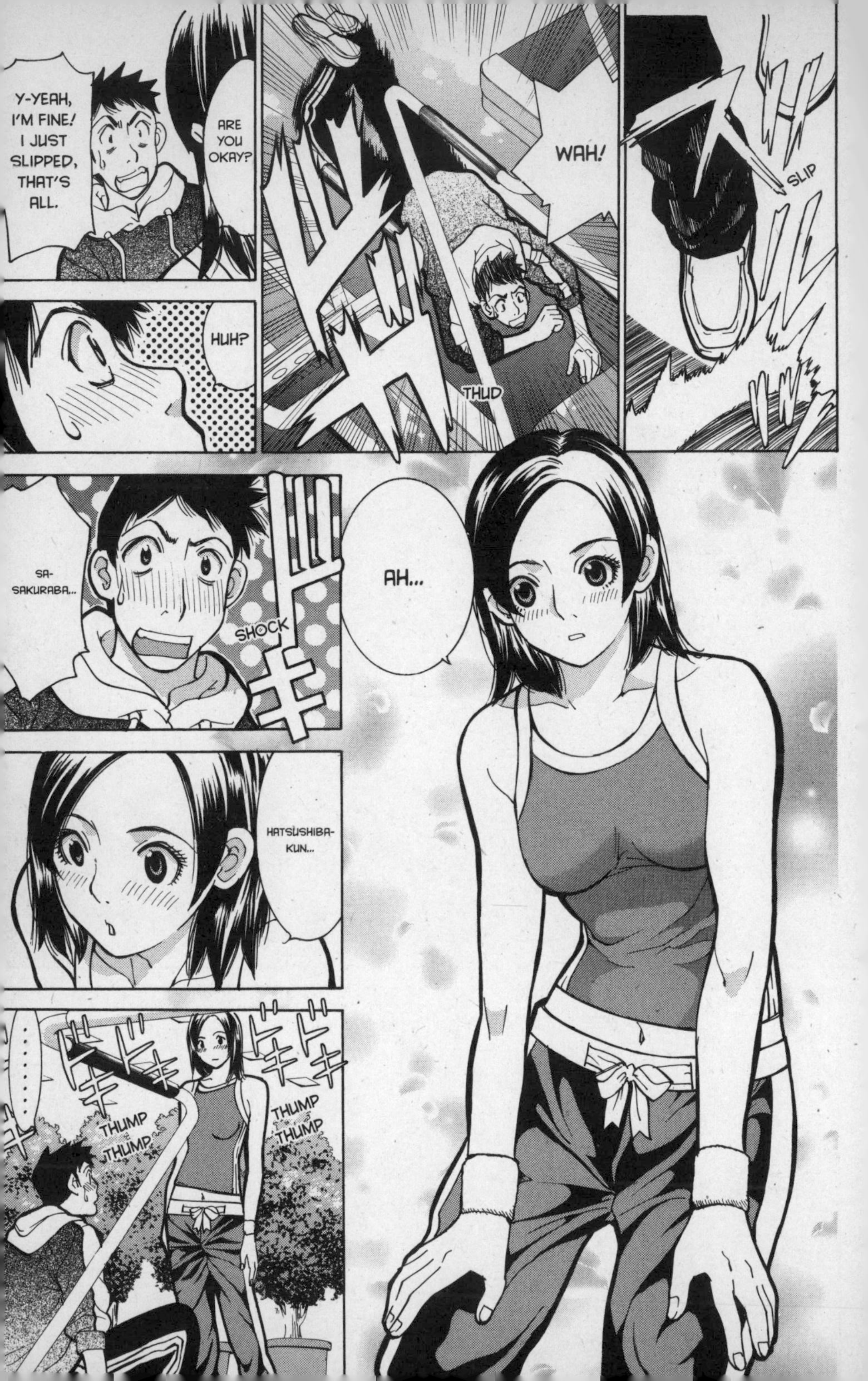
SLIP
WAH!
THUD
ARE YOU OKAY?
Y-YEAH, I'M FINE! I JUST SLIPPED, THAT'S ALL.
HUH?
AH...
SHOCK
SA-SAKURABA...
HATSUSHIBA-KUN...
THUMP THUMP
THUMP THUMP
...

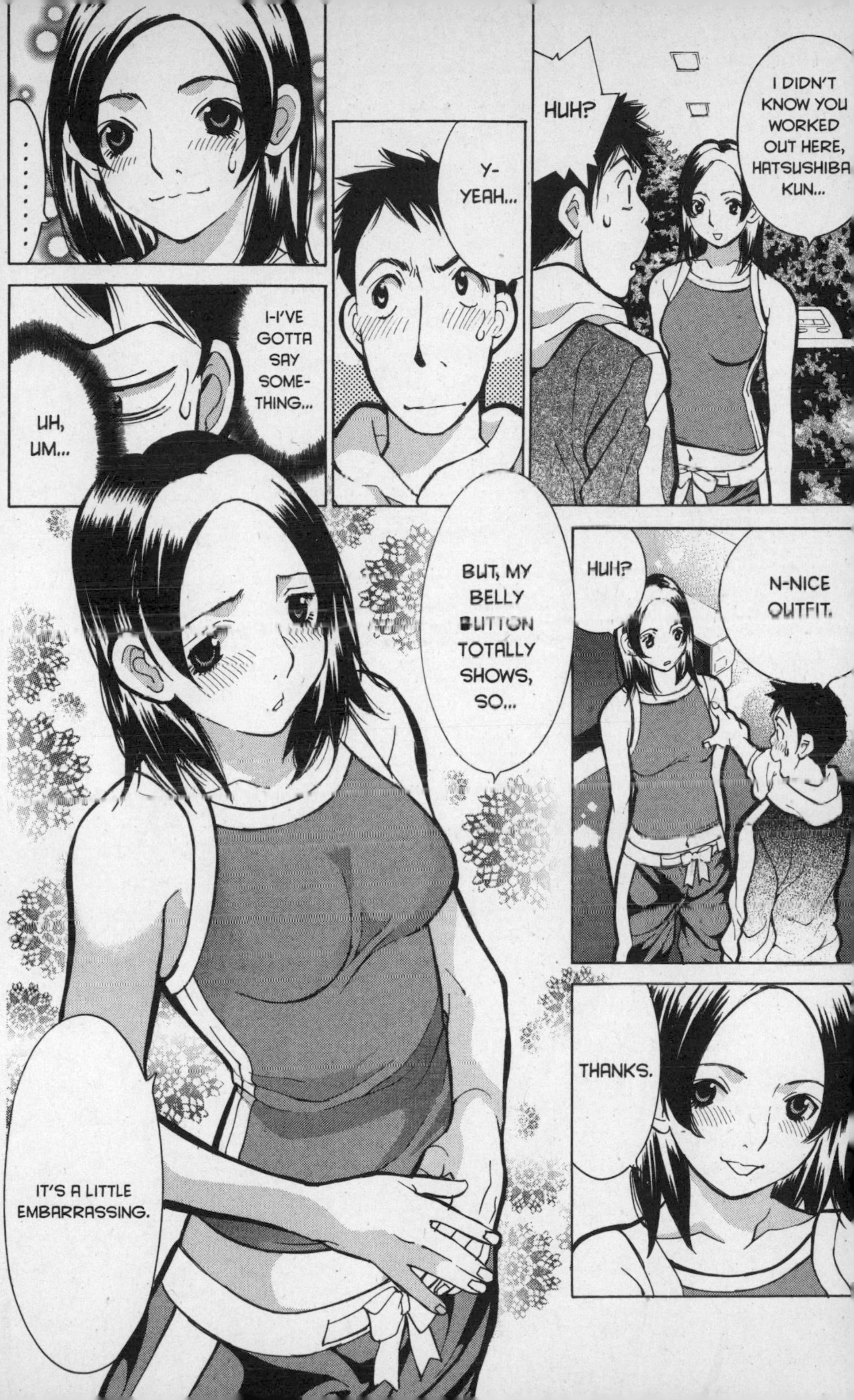
I DIDN'T KNOW YOU WORKED OUT HERE, HATSUSHIBA KUN...
HUH?
Y-YEAH...
......
I-I'VE GOTTA SAY SOME-THING...
UH, UM...
N-NICE OUTFIT.
HUH?
THANKS.
BUT, MY BELLY BUTTON TOTALLY SHOWS, SO...
IT'S A LITTLE EMBARRASSING.

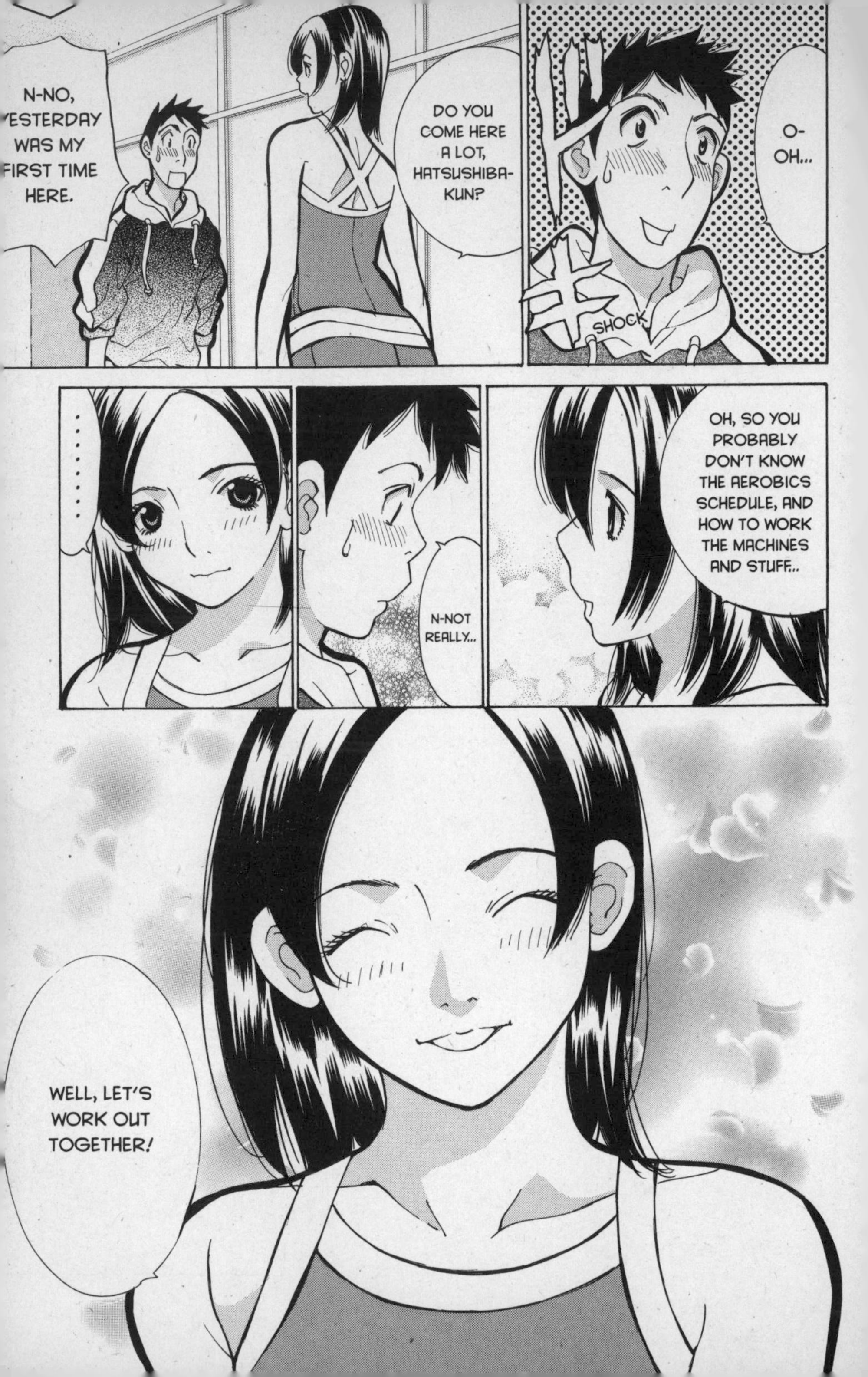
O-OH...
SHOCK
DO YOU COME HERE A LOT, HATSUSHIBA-KUN?
N-NO, YESTERDAY WAS MY FIRST TIME HERE.
OH, SO YOU PROBABLY DON'T KNOW THE AEROBICS SCHEDULE, AND HOW TO WORK THE MACHINES AND STUFF...
N-NOT REALLY...
......
WELL, LET'S WORK OUT TOGETHER!

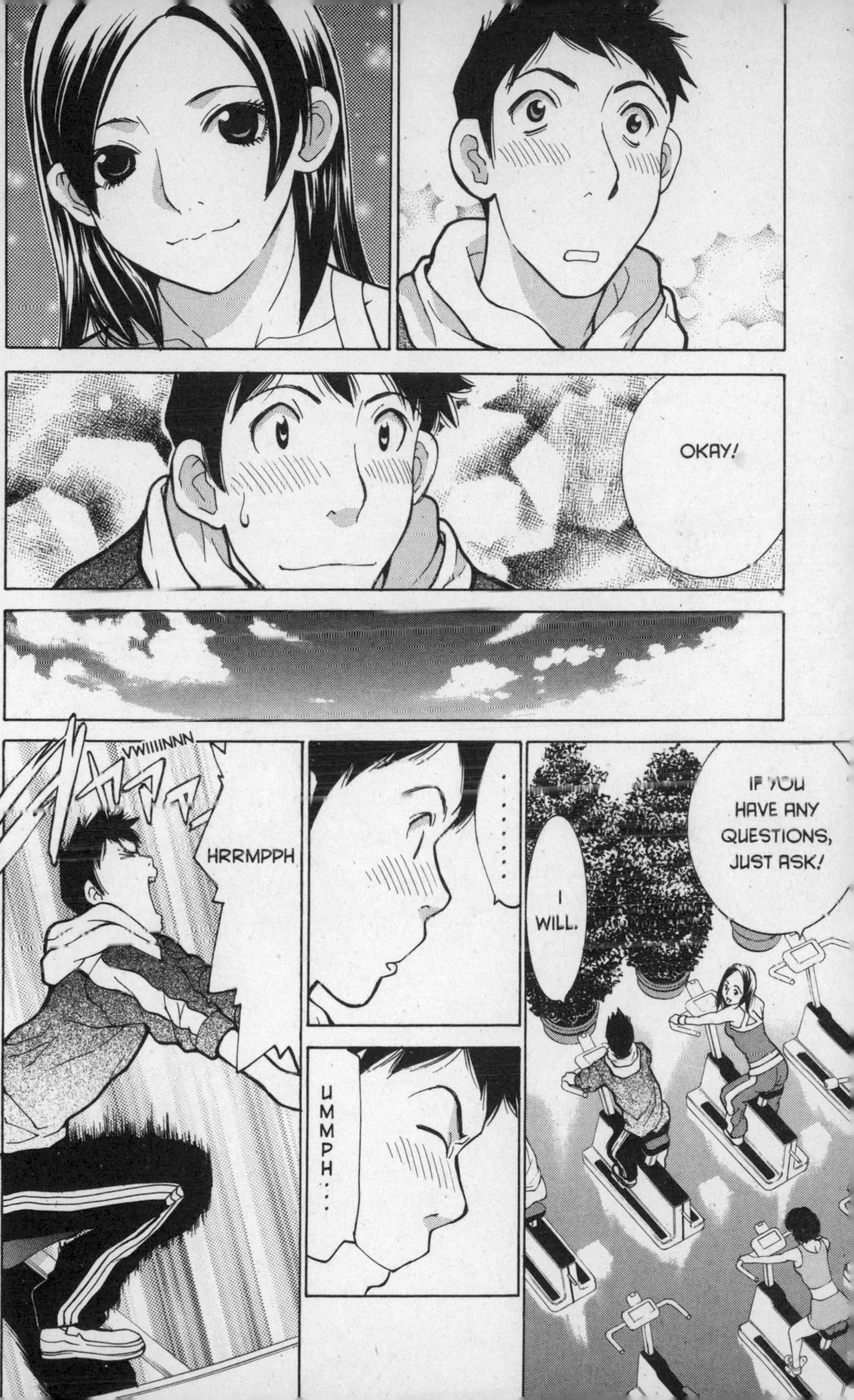
OKAY!
IF YOU HAVE ANY QUESTIONS, JUST ASK!
I WILL.
......
UMMPH...
VWIIIINNN
HRRMPPH

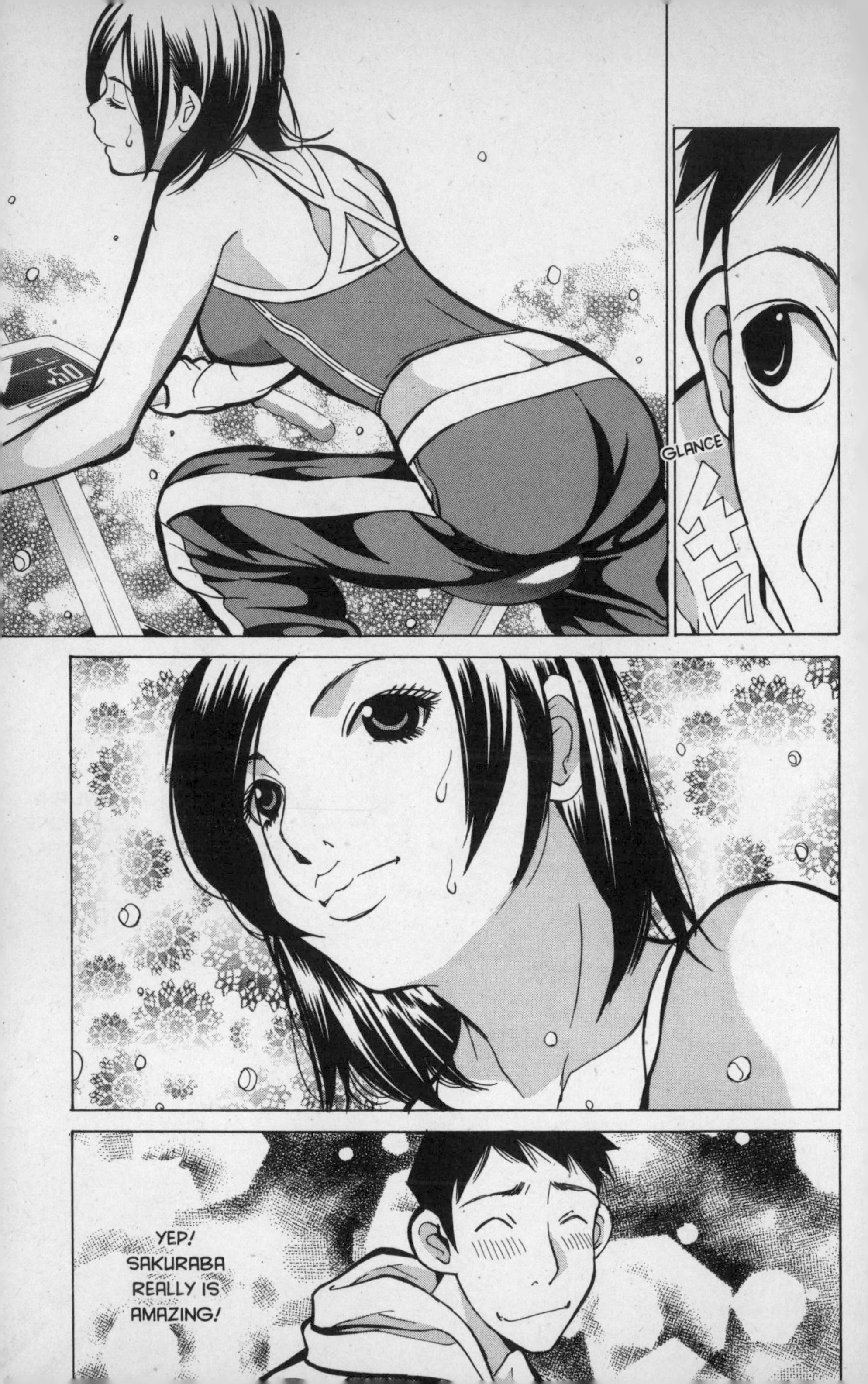
GLANCE
YEP! SAKURABA REALLY IS AMAZING!

I CAN'T BELIEVE I'M RIGHT NEXT TO SAKURABA!

IT'S ALMOST LIKE A DREAM.

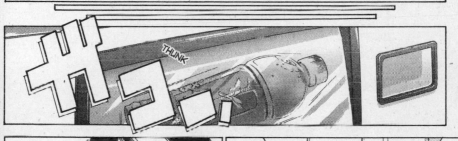

THUNK

MY TREAT.... FOR SHOWING ME AROUND AND EVERYTHING.

THANKS.

HUH?

H-HERE.

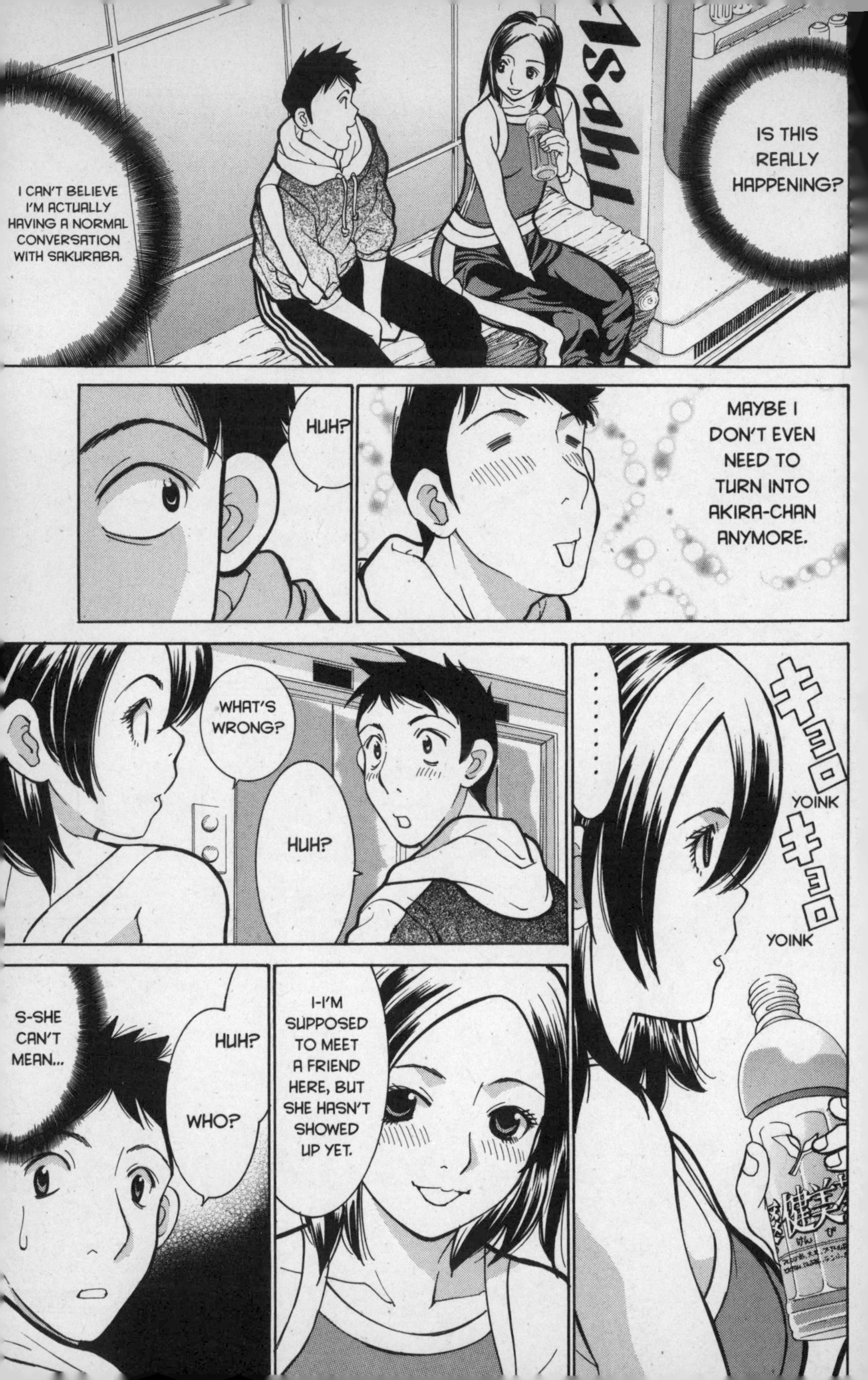
IS THIS REALLY HAPPENING?
I CAN'T BELIEVE I'M ACTUALLY HAVING A NORMAL CONVERSATION WITH SAKURABA.
MAYBE I DON'T EVEN NEED TO TURN INTO AKIRA-CHAN ANYMORE.
HUH?
......
キョロ
YOINK
キョロ
YOINK
WHAT'S WRONG?
HUH?
I-I'M SUPPOSED TO MEET A FRIEND HERE, BUT SHE HASN'T SHOWED UP YET.
HUH?
WHO?
S-SHE CAN'T MEAN...

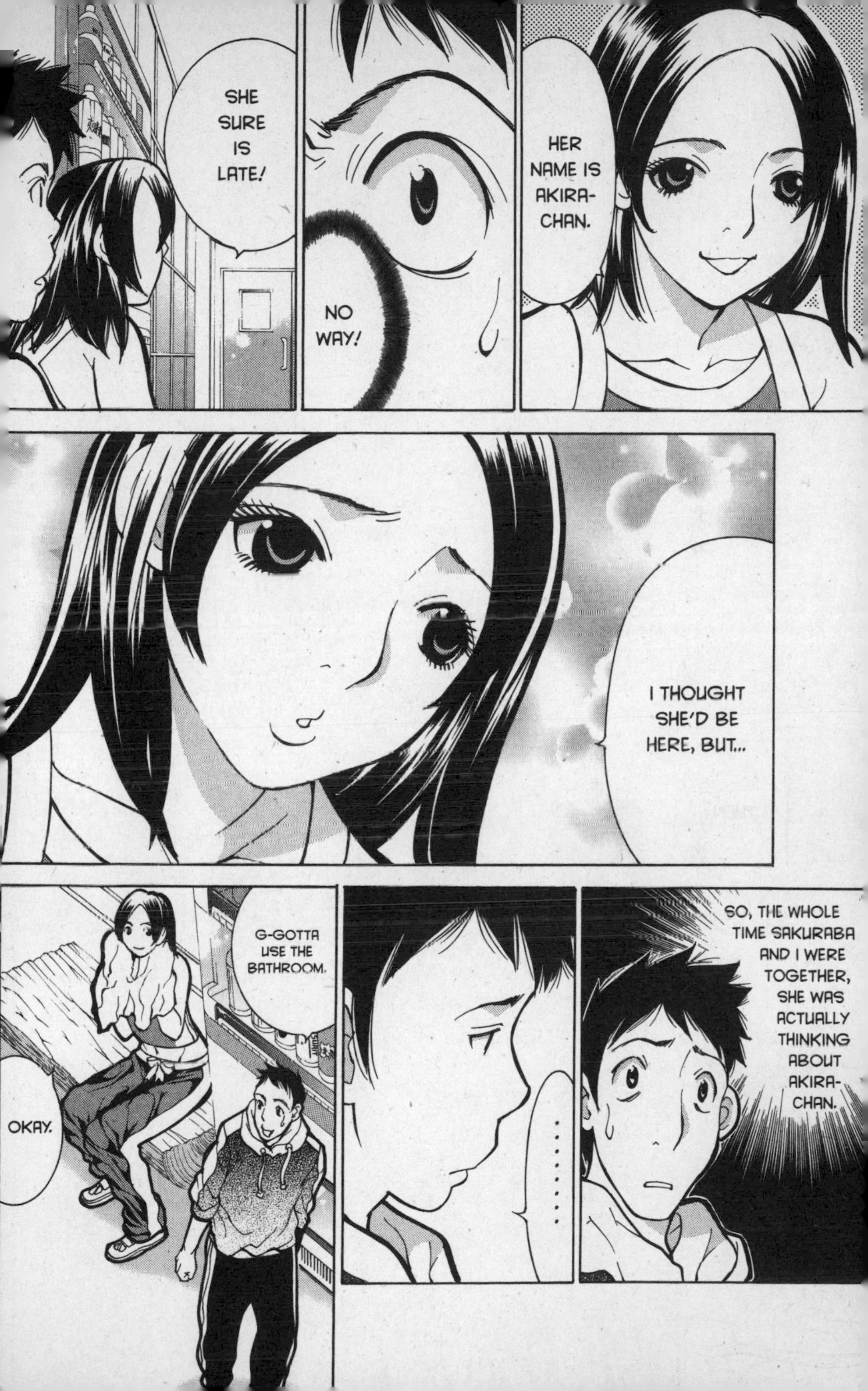
HER NAME IS AKIRA-CHAN.
NO WAY!
SHE SURE IS LATE!
I THOUGHT SHE'D BE HERE, BUT...
SO, THE WHOLE TIME SAKURABA AND I WERE TOGETHER, SHE WAS ACTUALLY THINKING ABOUT AKIRA-CHAN.
......
G-GOTTA USE THE BATHROOM.
OKAY.

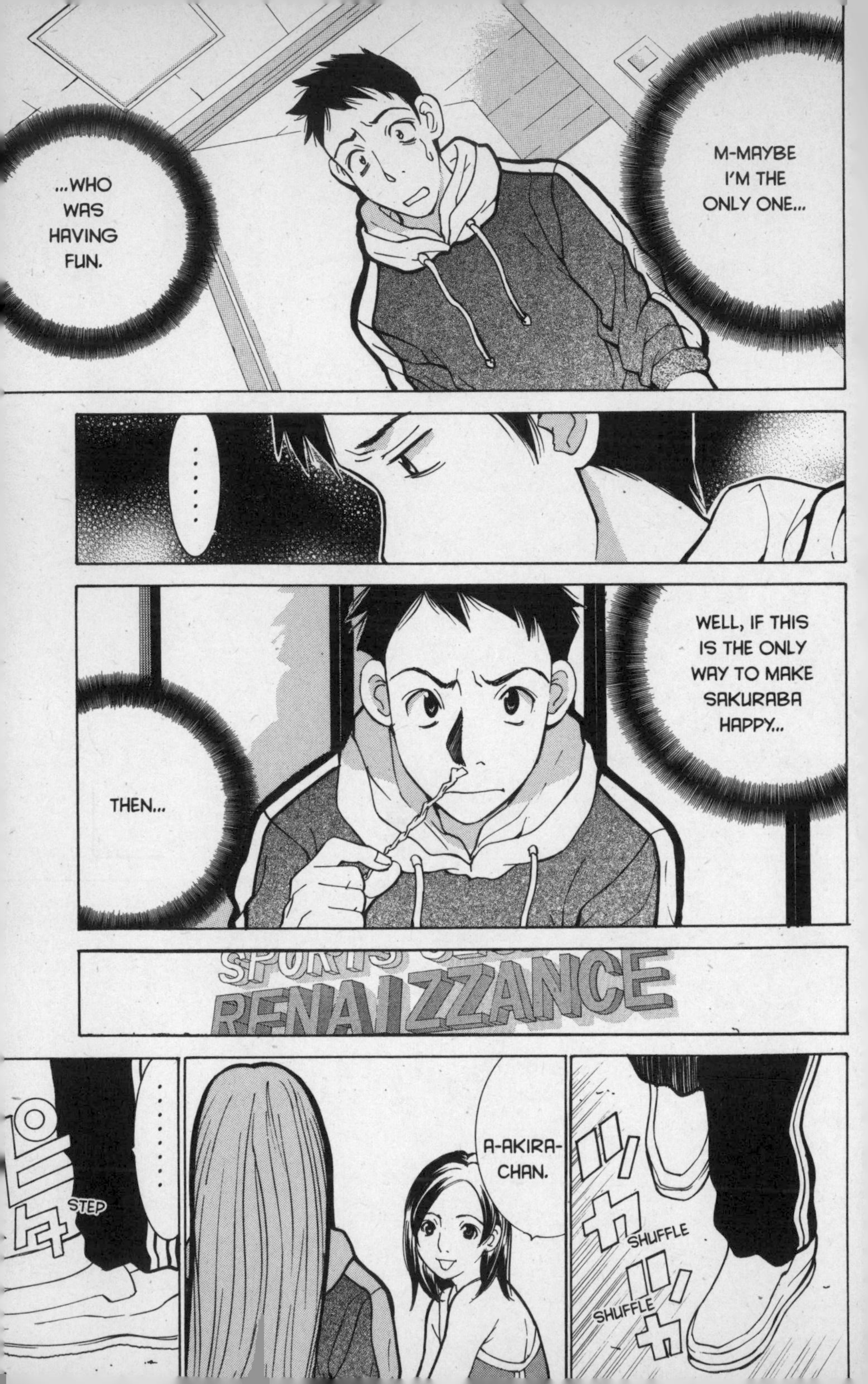
M-MAYBE I'M THE ONLY ONE...
...WHO WAS HAVING FUN.
......
WELL, IF THIS IS THE ONLY WAY TO MAKE SAKURABA HAPPY...
THEN...
SPORTS
RENAIZZANCE
SHUFFLE
SHUFFLE
A-AKIRA-CHAN.
......
STEP

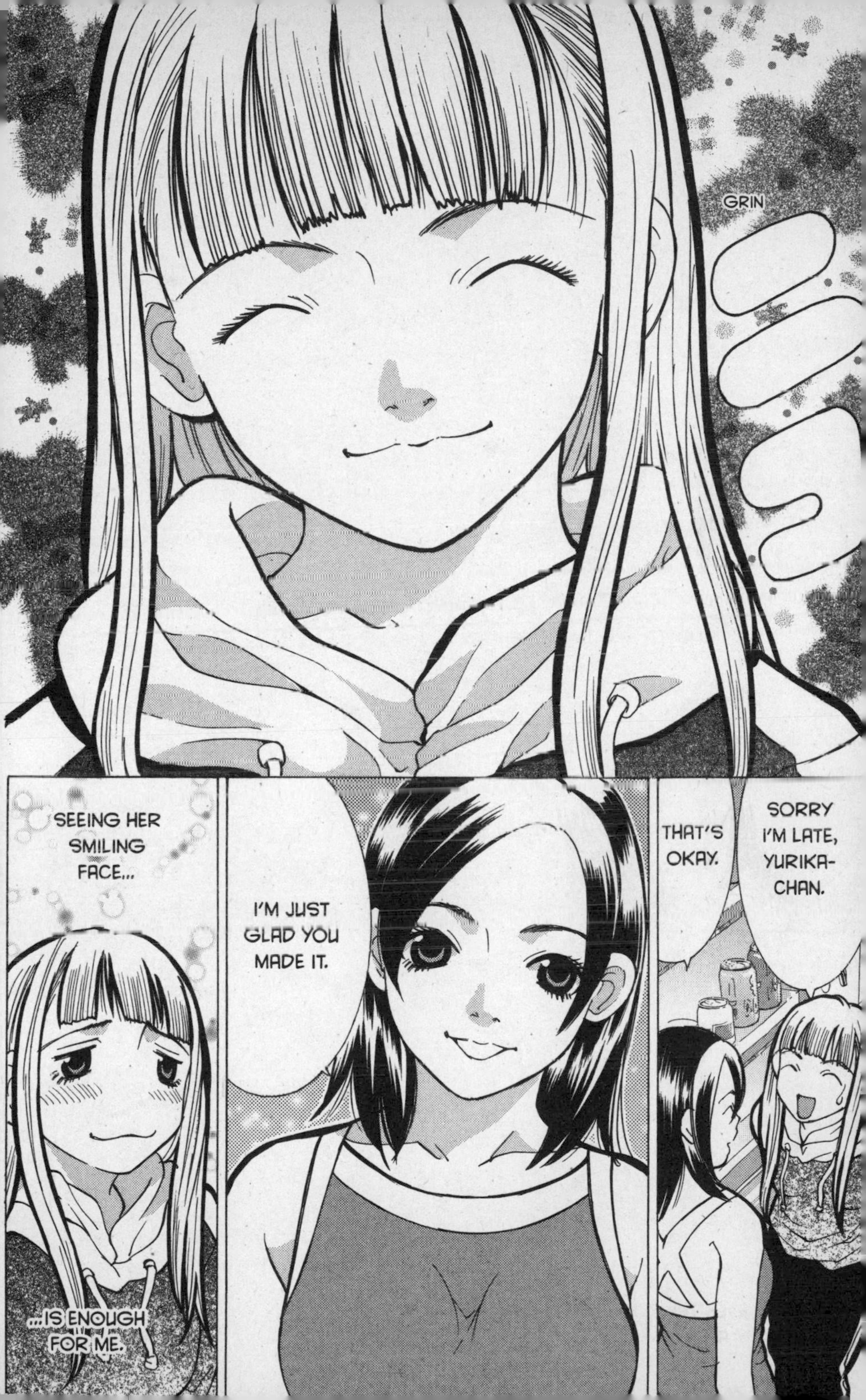
GRIN
SORRY I'M LATE, YURIKA-CHAN.
THAT'S OKAY.
I'M JUST GLAD YOU MADE IT.
SEEING HER SMILING FACE...
...IS ENOUGH FOR ME.

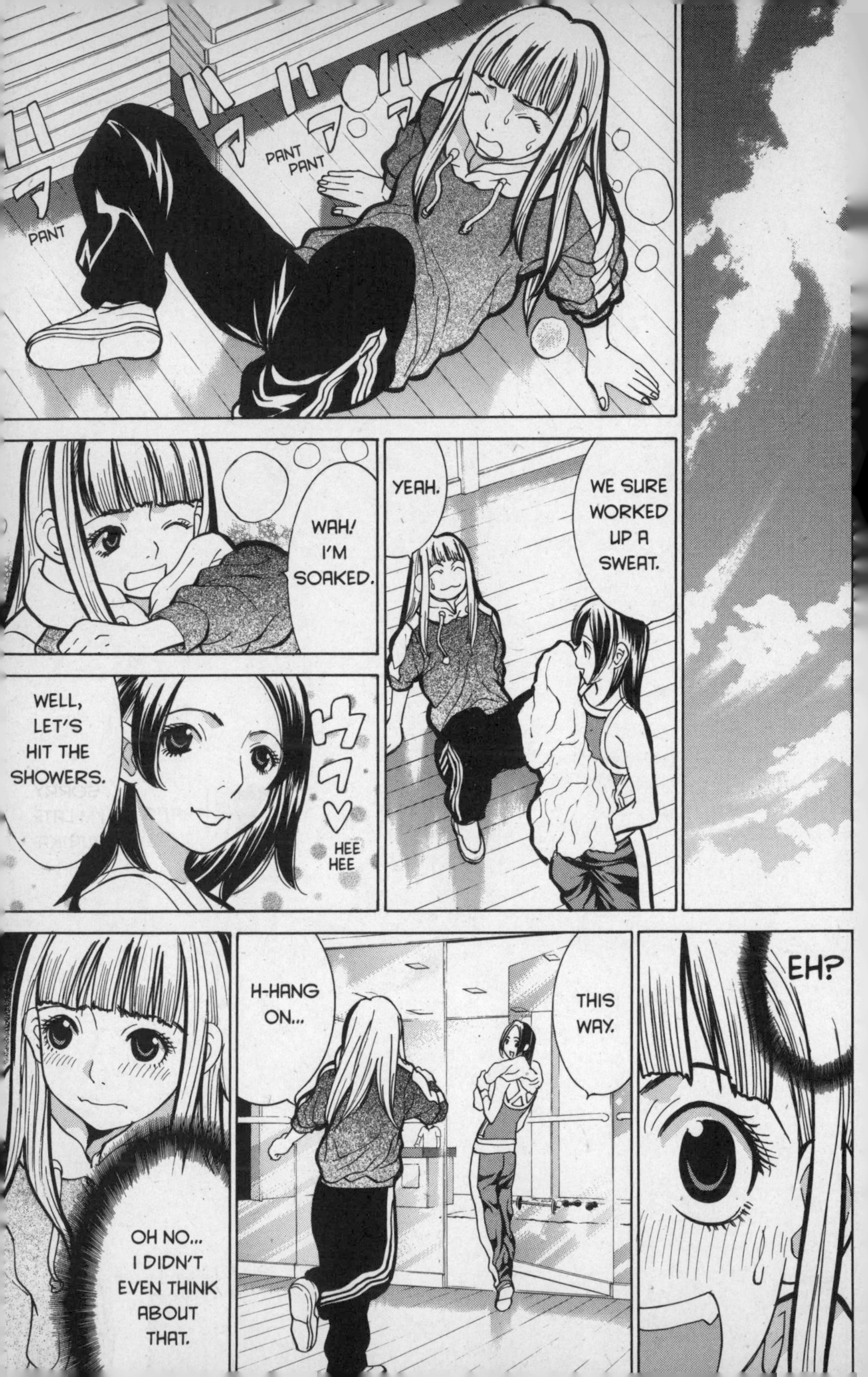
PANT PANT
PANT
WE SURE WORKED UP A SWEAT.
YEAH.
WAH! I'M SOAKED.
WELL, LET'S HIT THE SHOWERS.
HEE HEE
EH?
THIS WAY.
H-HANG ON...
OH NO... I DIDN'T EVEN THINK ABOUT THAT.

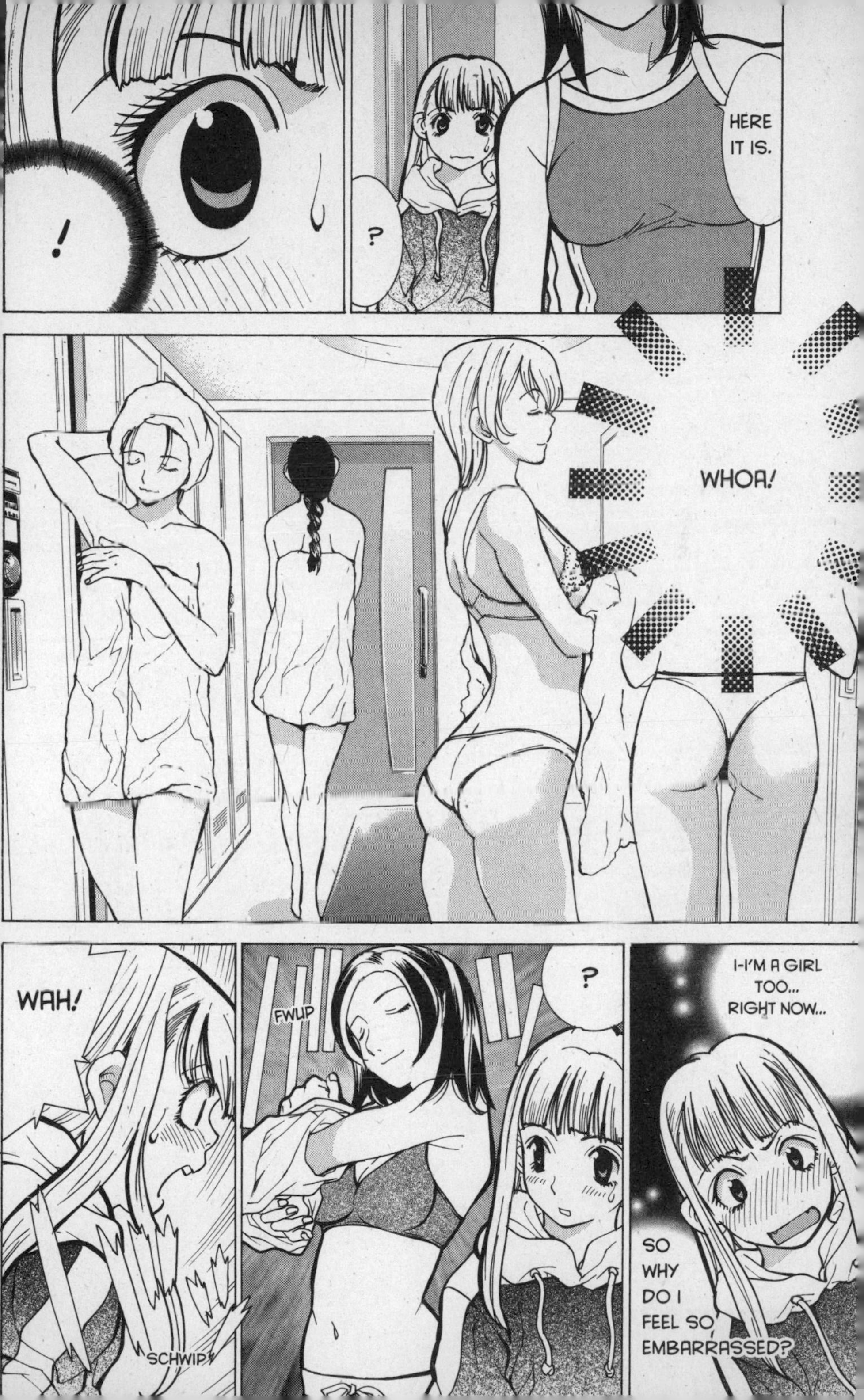
HERE IT IS.
?
!
WHOA!
I-I'M A GIRL TOO... RIGHT NOW...
SO WHY DO I FEEL SO EMBARRASSED?
?
FWUP
WAH!
SCHWIP

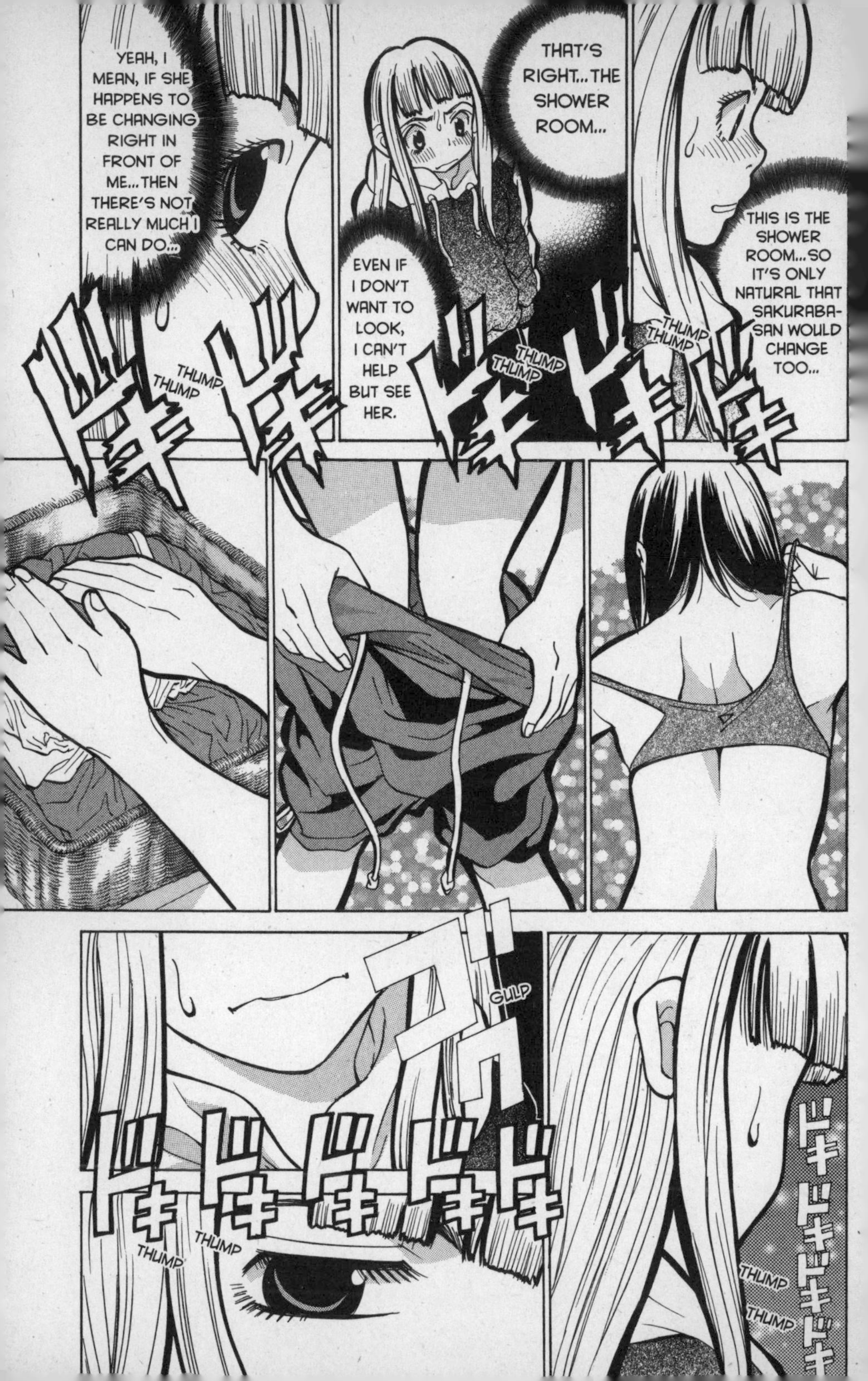
THIS IS THE SHOWER ROOM...SO IT'S ONLY NATURAL THAT SAKURABA-SAN WOULD CHANGE TOO...
THUMP THUMP
THAT'S RIGHT...THE SHOWER ROOM...
EVEN IF I DON'T WANT TO LOOK, I CAN'T HELP BUT SEE HER.
THUMP THUMP
YEAH, I MEAN, IF SHE HAPPENS TO BE CHANGING RIGHT IN FRONT OF ME...THEN THERE'S NOT REALLY MUCH I CAN DO...
THUMP THUMP
THUMP THUMP
GULP
THUMP THUMP

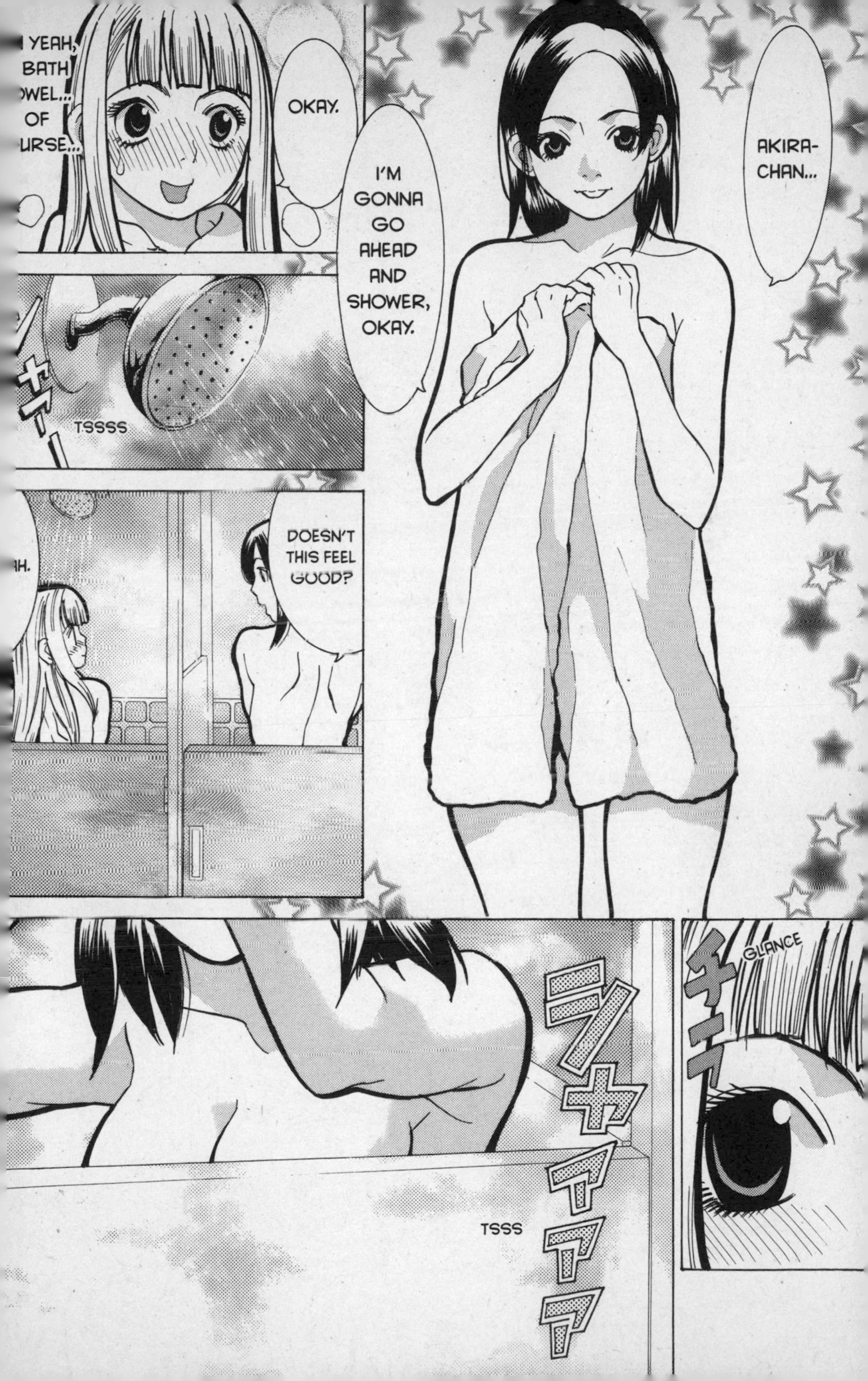
AKIRA-CHAN...
YEAH, BATH OWEL... OF URSE...
OKAY.
I'M GONNA GO AHEAD AND SHOWER, OKAY.
TSSSS
DOESN'T THIS FEEL GOOD?
AH.
GLANCE
TSSS

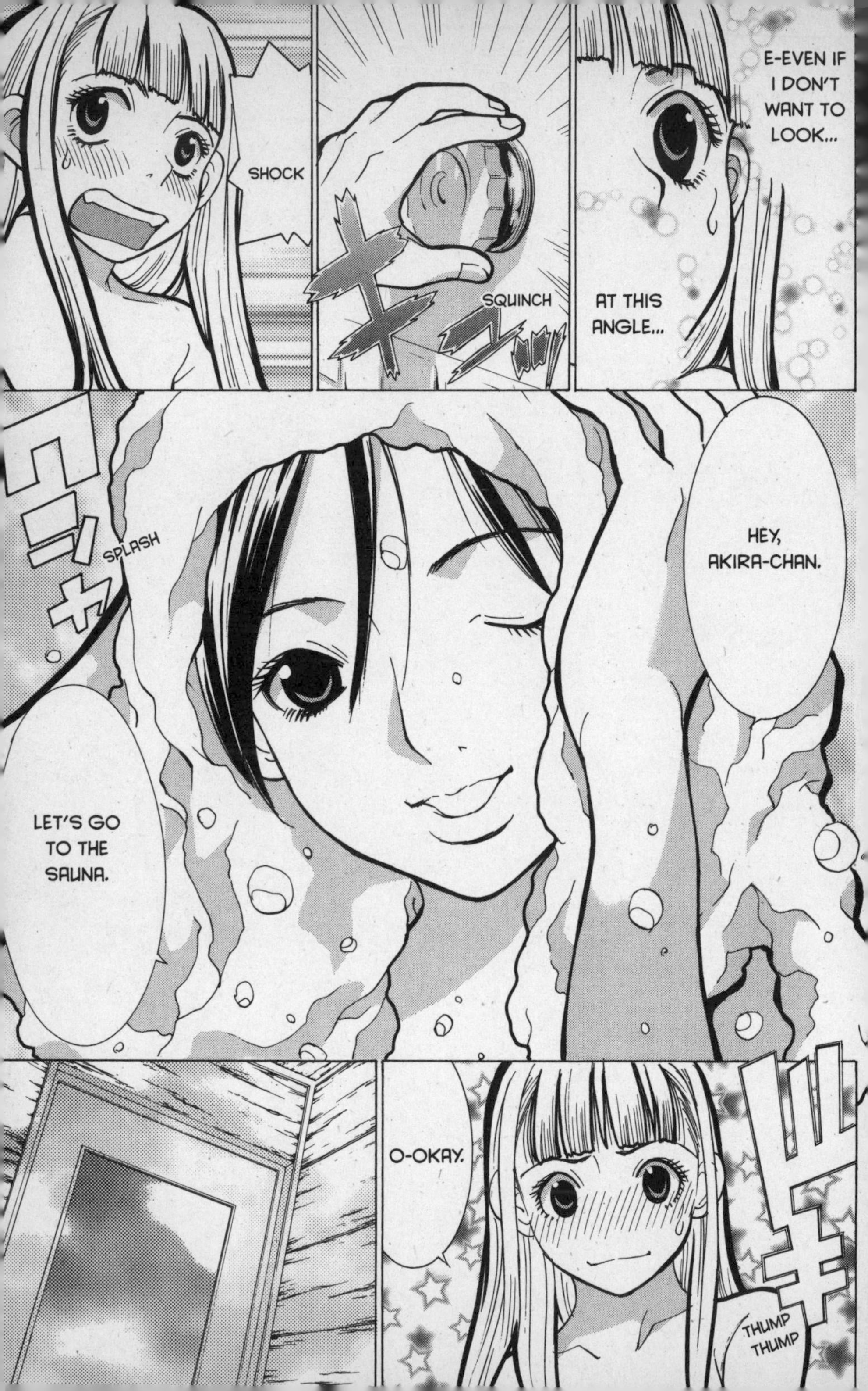
E-EVEN IF I DON'T WANT TO LOOK...
AT THIS ANGLE...
SQUINCH
SHOCK
HEY, AKIRA-CHAN.
SPLASH
LET'S GO TO THE SAUNA.
O-OKAY.
THUMP THUMP

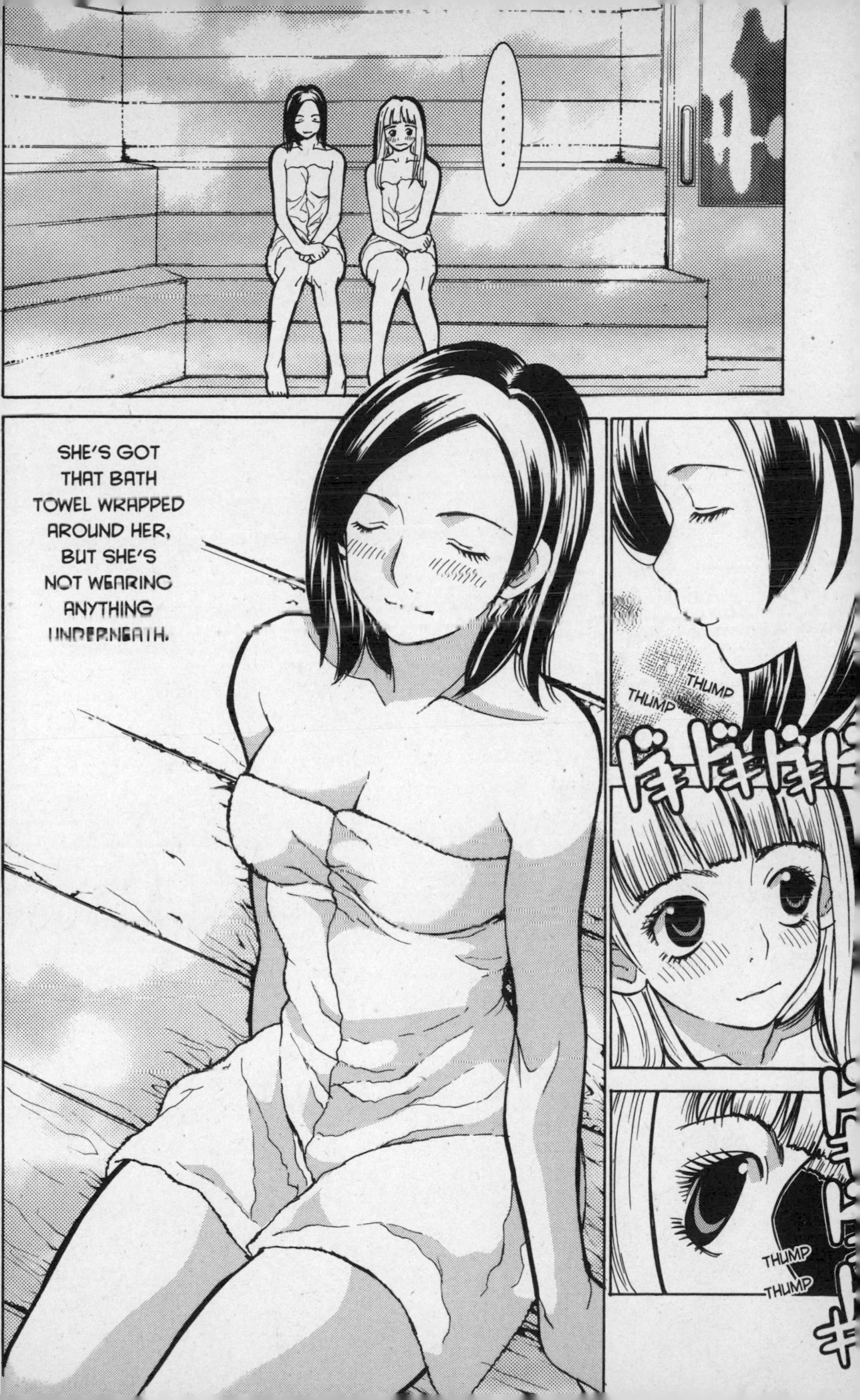
......
THUMP THUMP
THUMP THUMP
SHE'S GOT THAT BATH TOWEL WRAPPED AROUND HER, BUT SHE'S NOT WEARING ANYTHING UNDERNEATH.

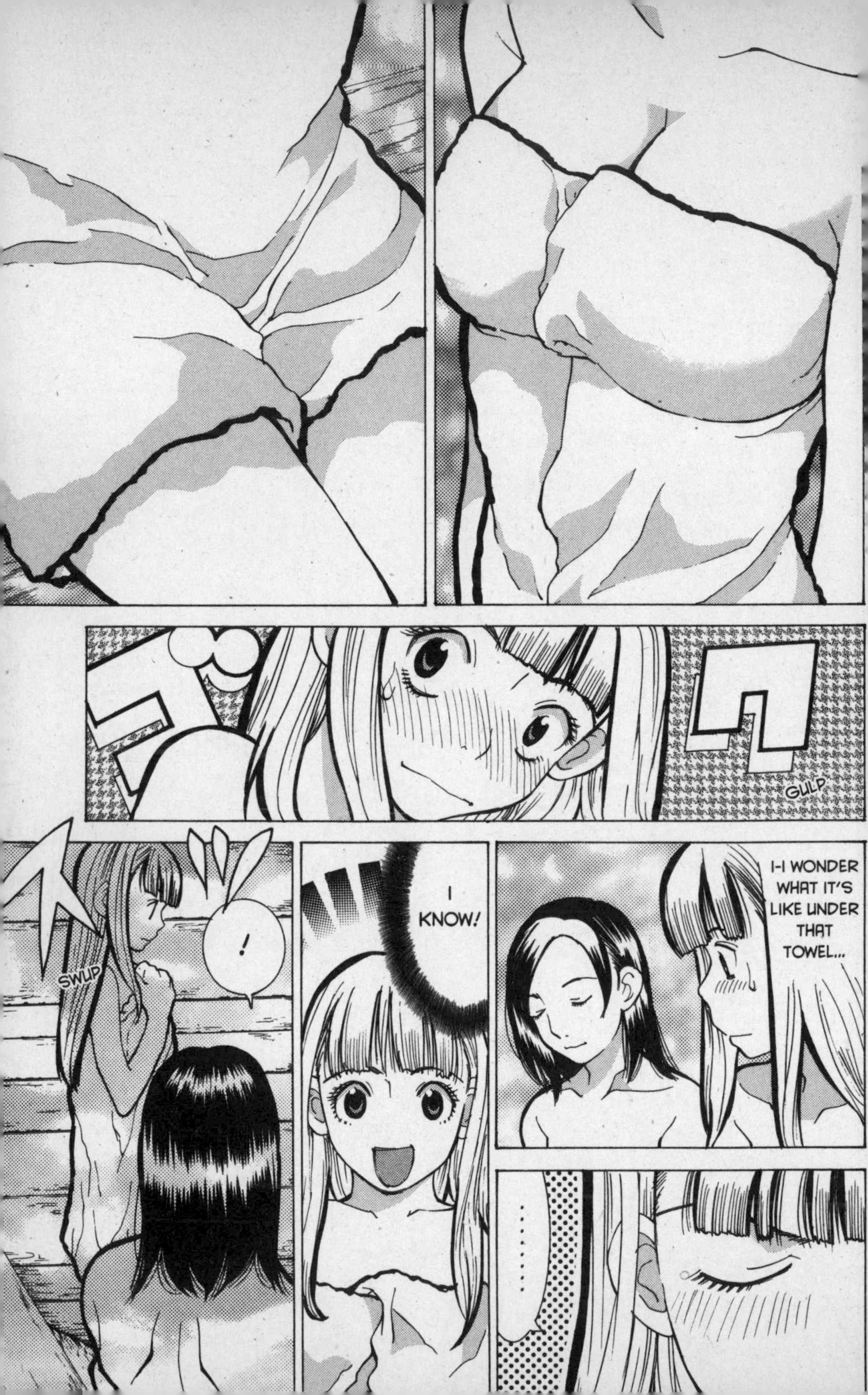
GULP
I-I WONDER WHAT IT'S LIKE UNDER THAT TOWEL...
......
I KNOW!
!
SWUP

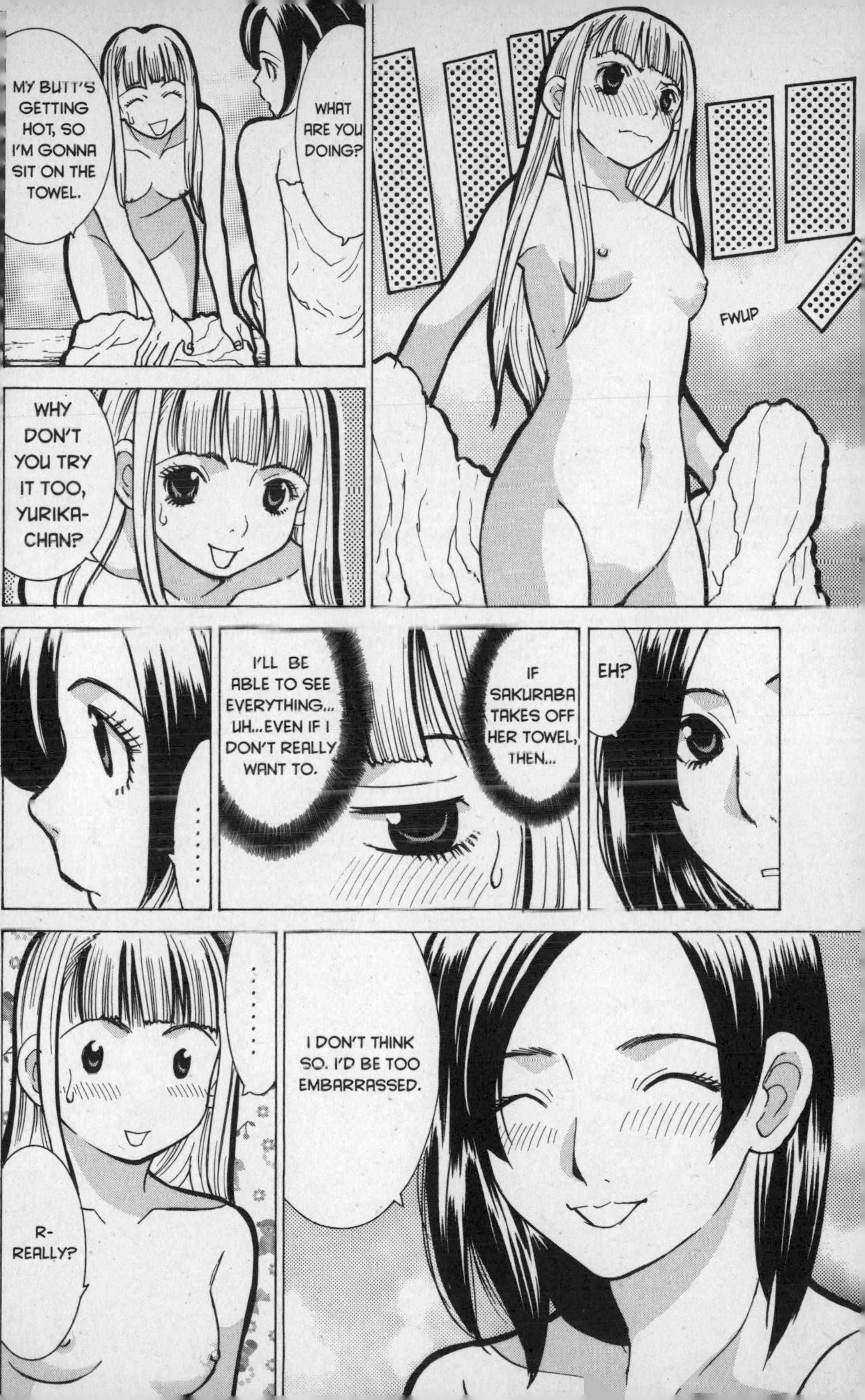
FWUP
WHAT ARE YOU DOING?
MY BUTT'S GETTING HOT, SO I'M GONNA SIT ON THE TOWEL.
WHY DON'T YOU TRY IT TOO, YURIKA-CHAN?
EH?
IF SAKURABA TAKES OFF HER TOWEL, THEN...
I'LL BE ABLE TO SEE EVERYTHING... UH...EVEN IF I DON'T REALLY WANT TO.
....
I DON'T THINK SO. I'D BE TOO EMBARRASSED.
....
R-REALLY?

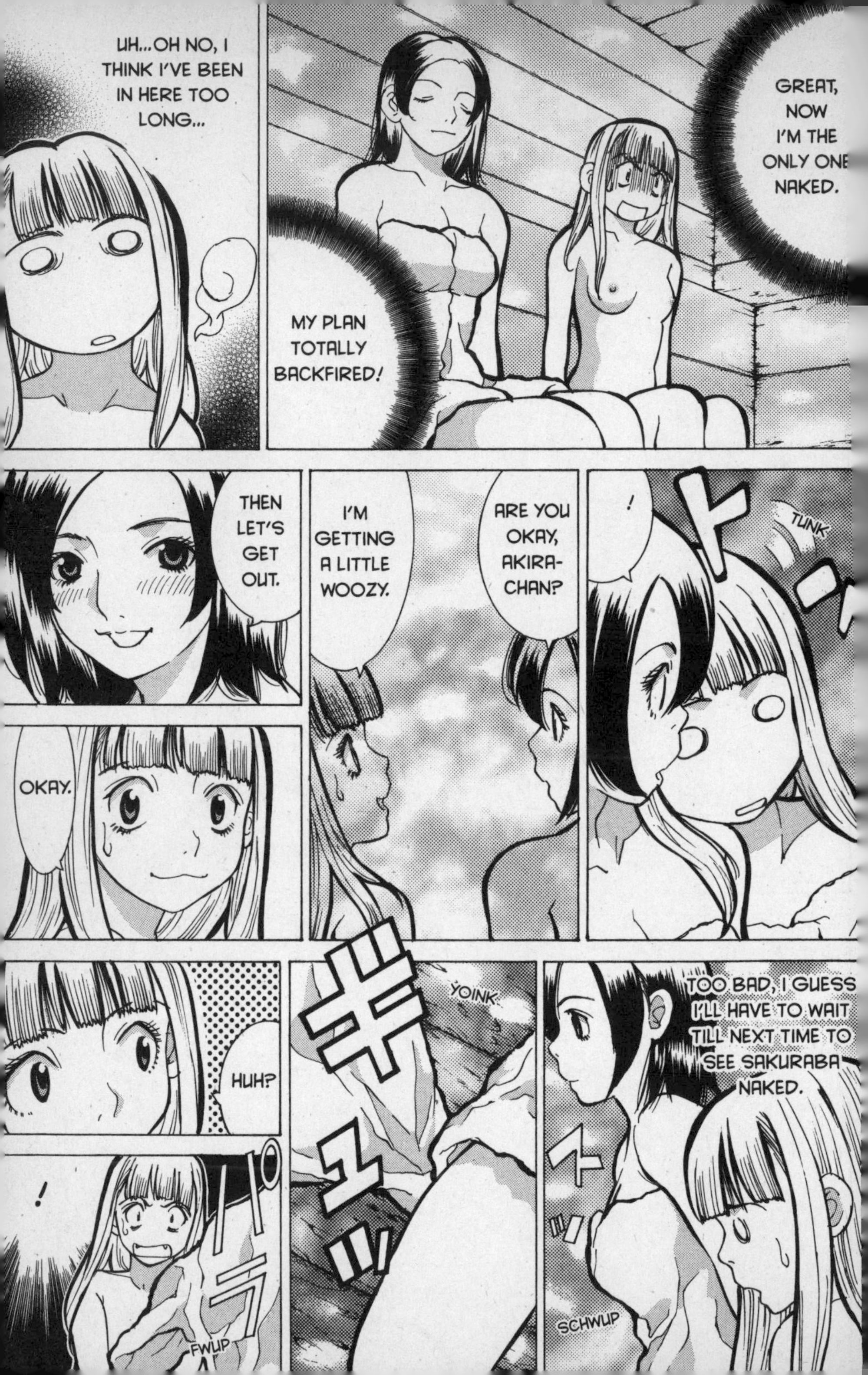
GREAT, NOW I'M THE ONLY ONE NAKED.
MY PLAN TOTALLY BACKFIRED!
UH...OH NO, I THINK I'VE BEEN IN HERE TOO LONG...
!
TUNK
ARE YOU OKAY, AKIRA-CHAN?
I'M GETTING A LITTLE WOOZY.
THEN LET'S GET OUT.
OKAY.
TOO BAD, I GUESS I'LL HAVE TO WAIT TILL NEXT TIME TO SEE SAKURABA NAKED.
SCHWUP
YOINK
HUH?
!
FWUP

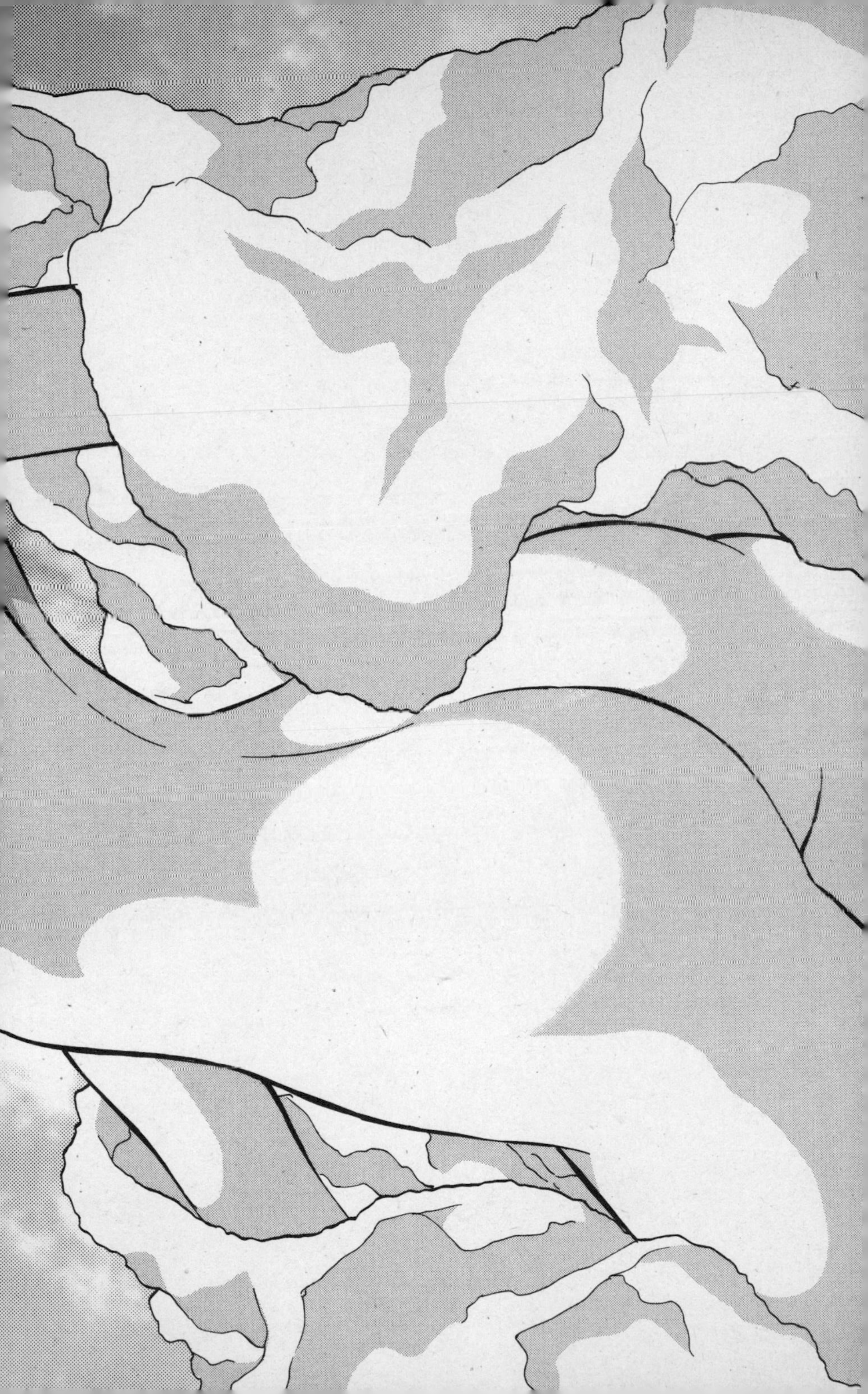

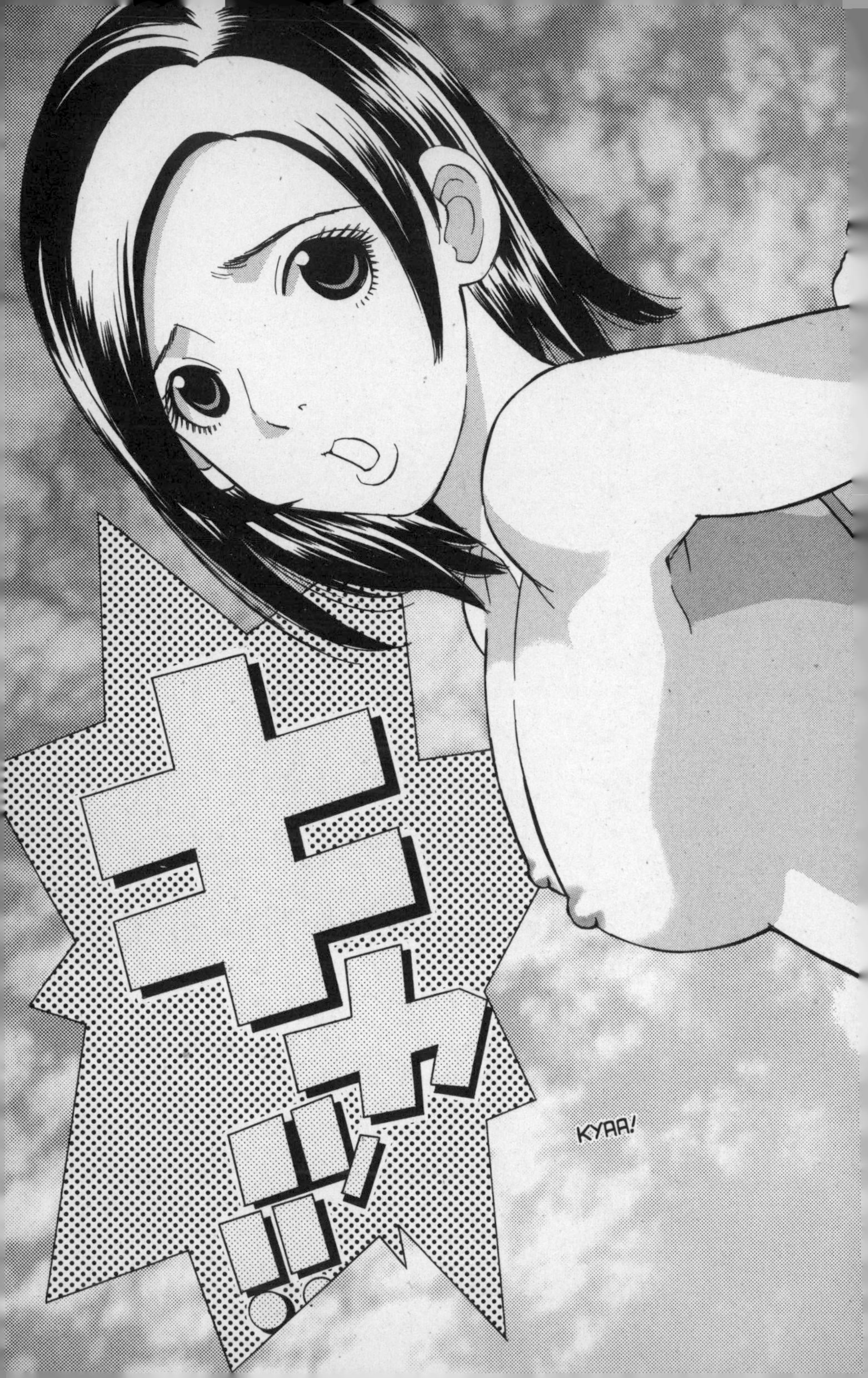

KYAA!

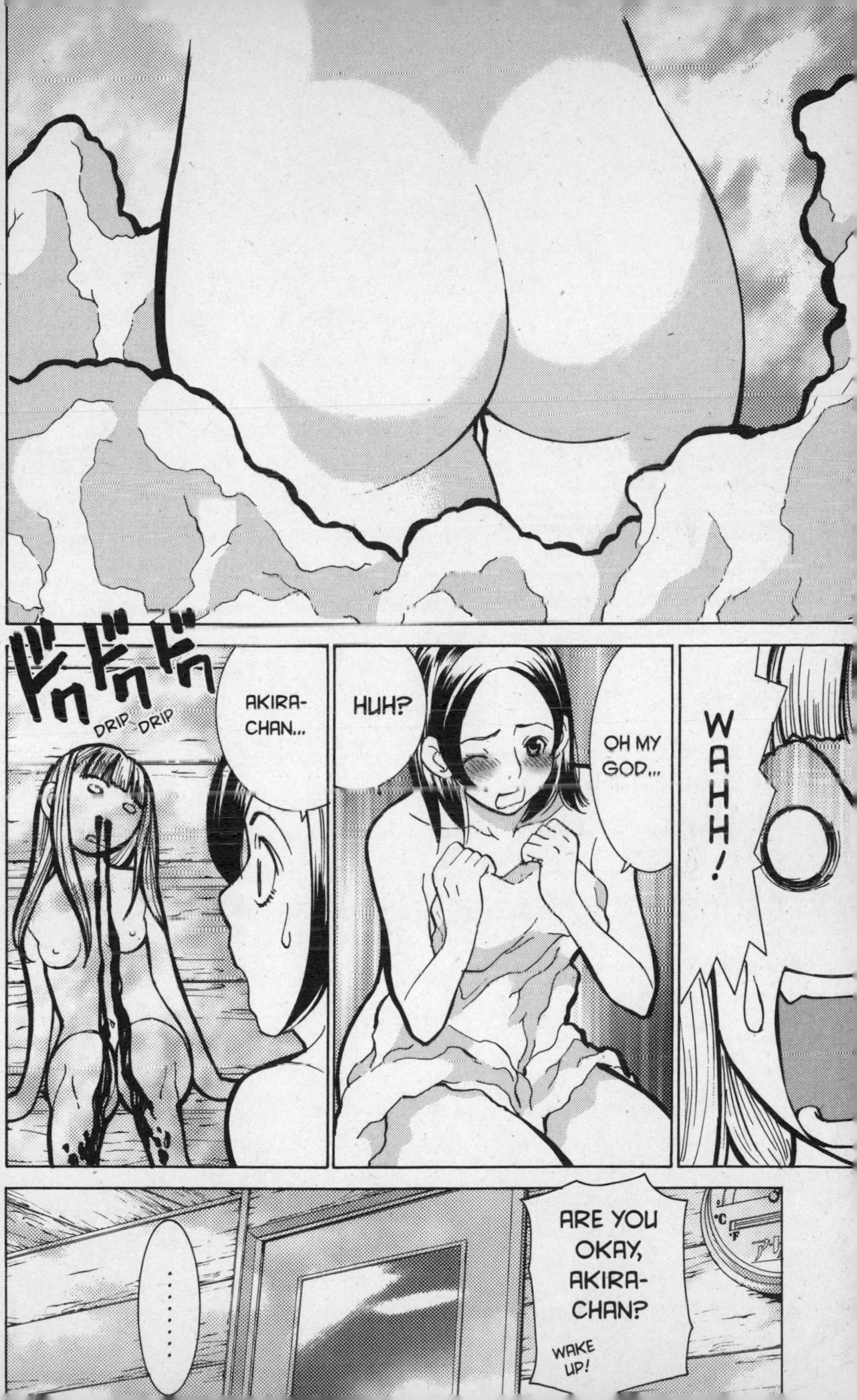
WAHH!
HUH?
OH MY GOD...
AKIRA-CHAN...
ドクドクドク
DRIP DRIP
ARE YOU OKAY, AKIRA-CHAN?
WAKE UP!
......

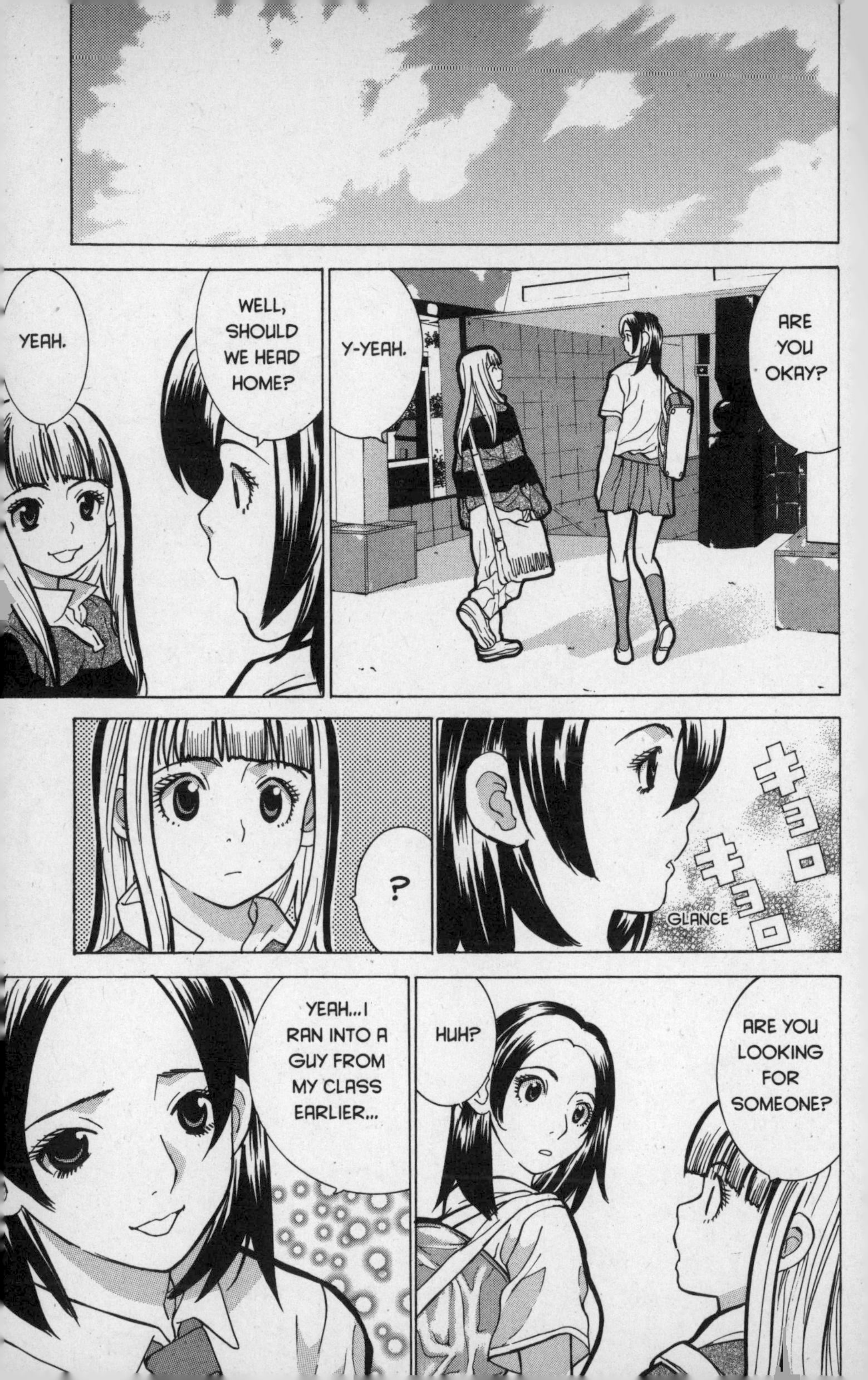
ARE YOU OKAY?
Y-YEAH.
WELL, SHOULD WE HEAD HOME?
YEAH.
キョロキョロ
GLANCE
?
ARE YOU LOOKING FOR SOMEONE?
HUH?
YEAH...I RAN INTO A GUY FROM MY CLASS EARLIER...

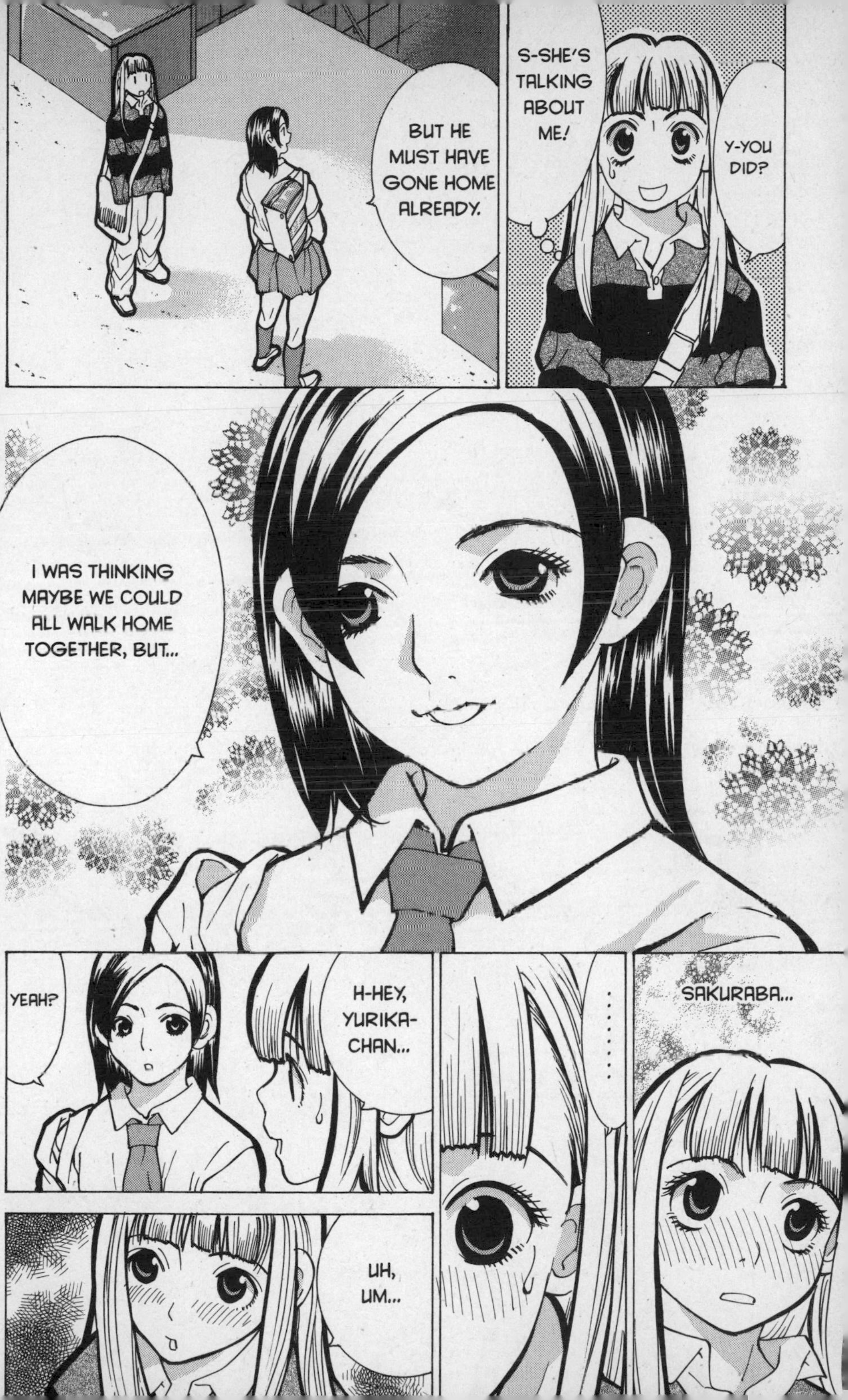
Y-YOU DID?
S-SHE'S TALKING ABOUT ME!
BUT HE MUST HAVE GONE HOME ALREADY.
I WAS THINKING MAYBE WE COULD ALL WALK HOME TOGETHER, BUT...
SAKURABA...
......
H-HEY, YURIKA-CHAN...
YEAH?
UH, UM...

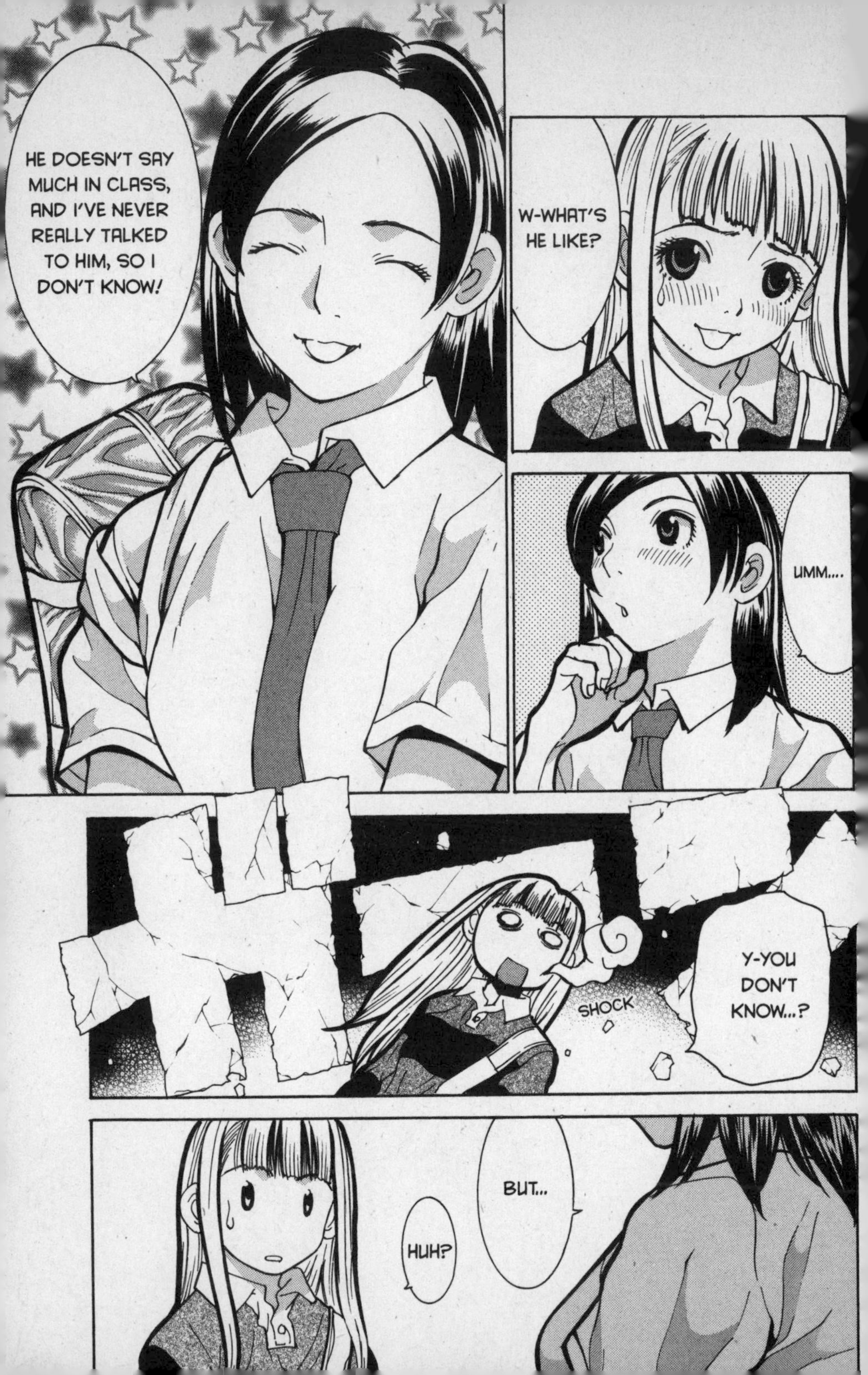
W-WHAT'S HE LIKE?
UMM....
HE DOESN'T SAY MUCH IN CLASS, AND I'VE NEVER REALLY TALKED TO HIM, SO I DON'T KNOW!
Y-YOU DON'T KNOW...?
SHOCK
BUT...
HUH?

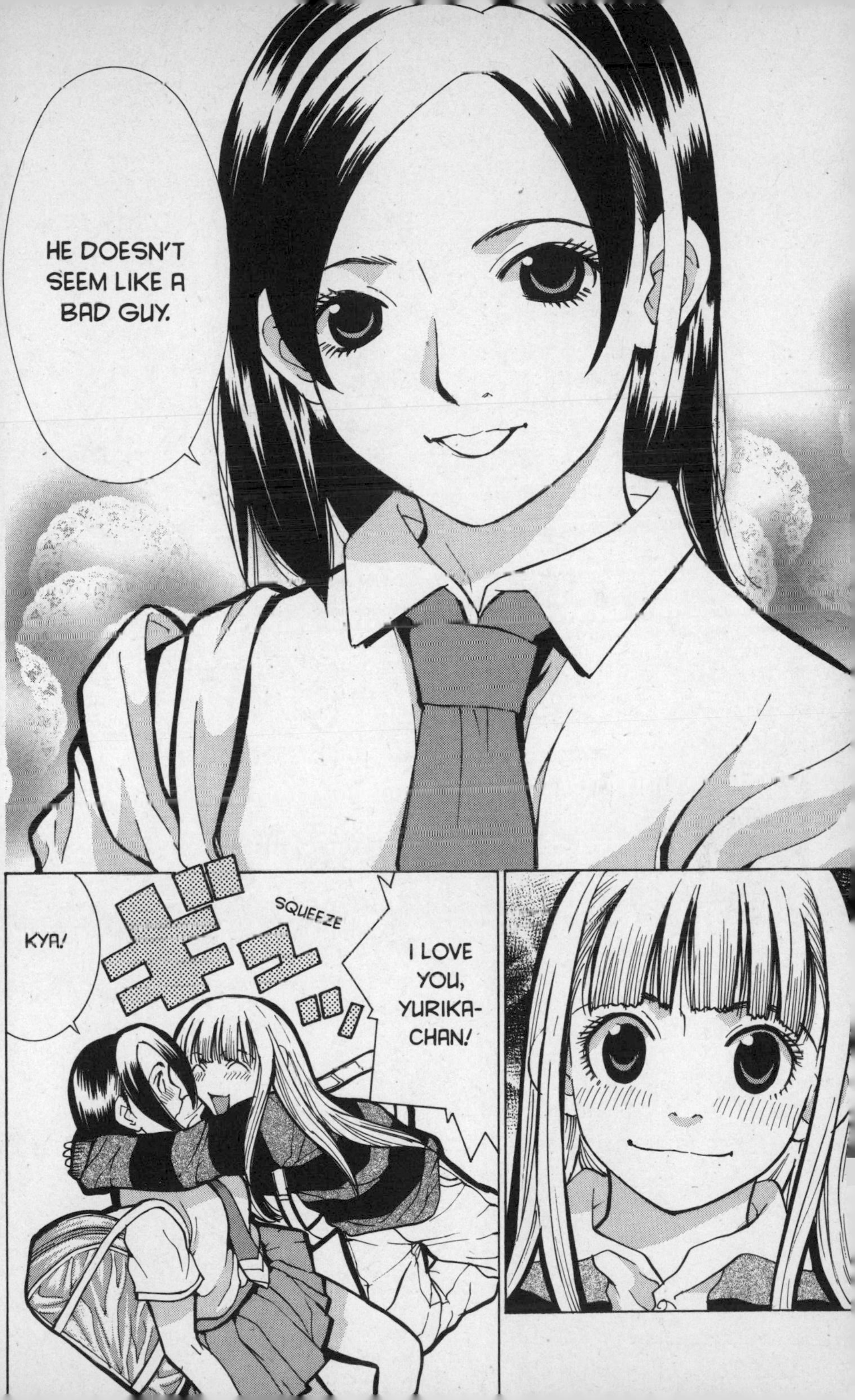
HE DOESN'T SEEM LIKE A BAD GUY.
SQUEEZE
I LOVE YOU, YURIKA-CHAN!
KYA!

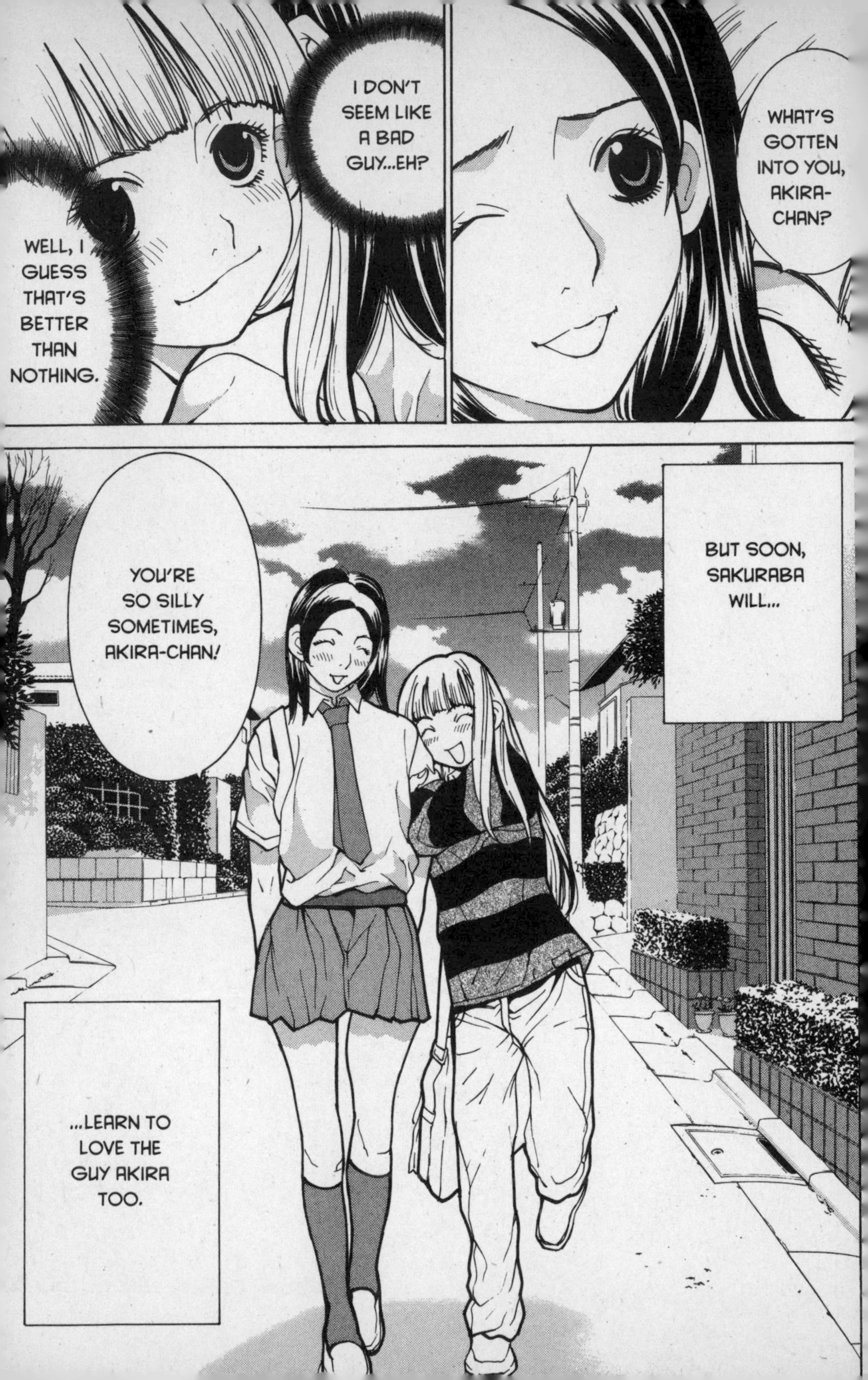
WHAT'S GOTTEN INTO YOU, AKIRA-CHAN?
I DON'T SEEM LIKE A BAD GUY...EH?
WELL, I GUESS THAT'S BETTER THAN NOTHING.
BUT SOON, SAKURABA WILL...
YOU'RE SO SILLY SOMETIMES, AKIRA-CHAN!
...LEARN TO LOVE THE GUY AKIRA TOO.

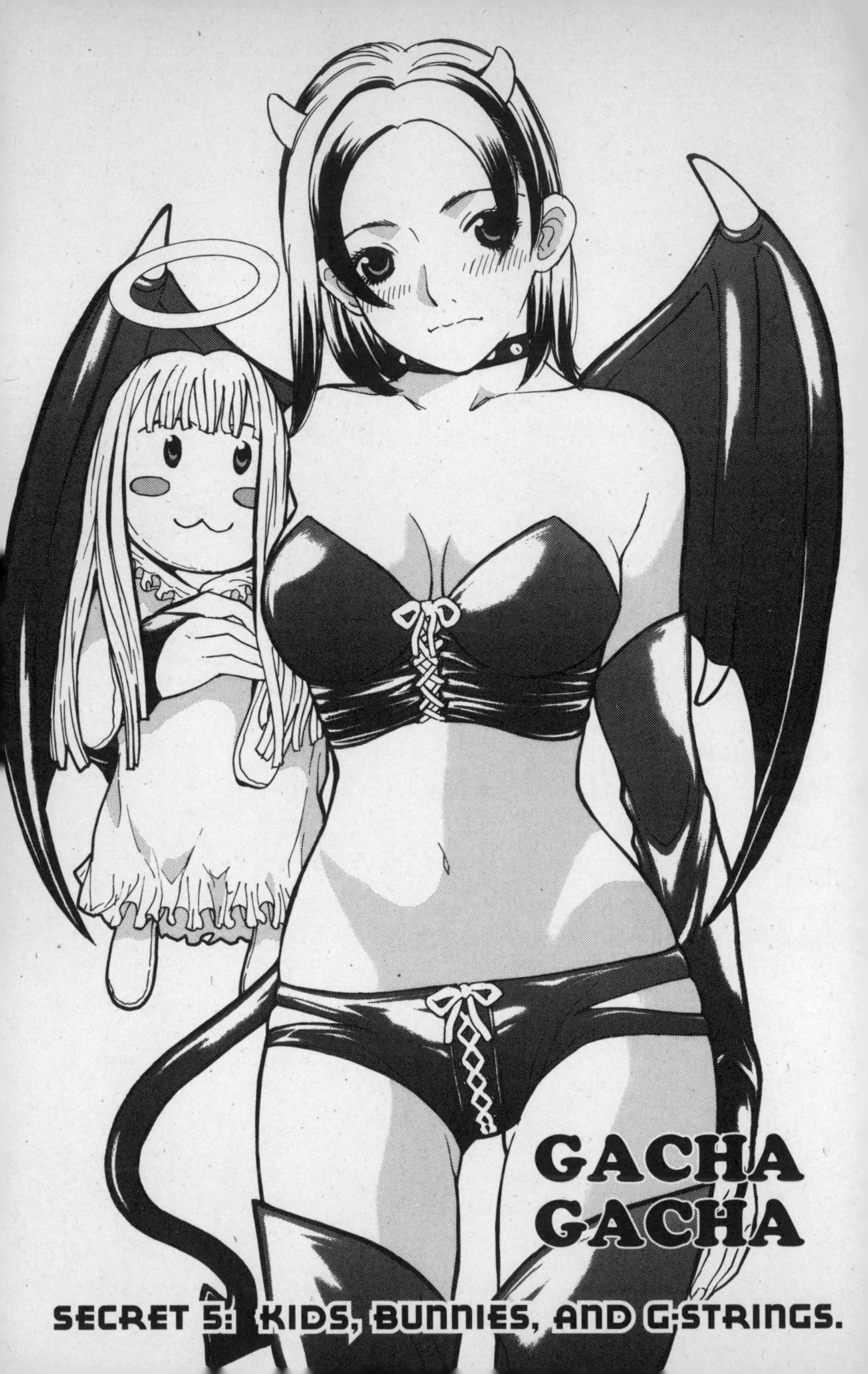
GACHA GACHA
SECRET 5: KIDS, BUNNIES, AND G-STRINGS.

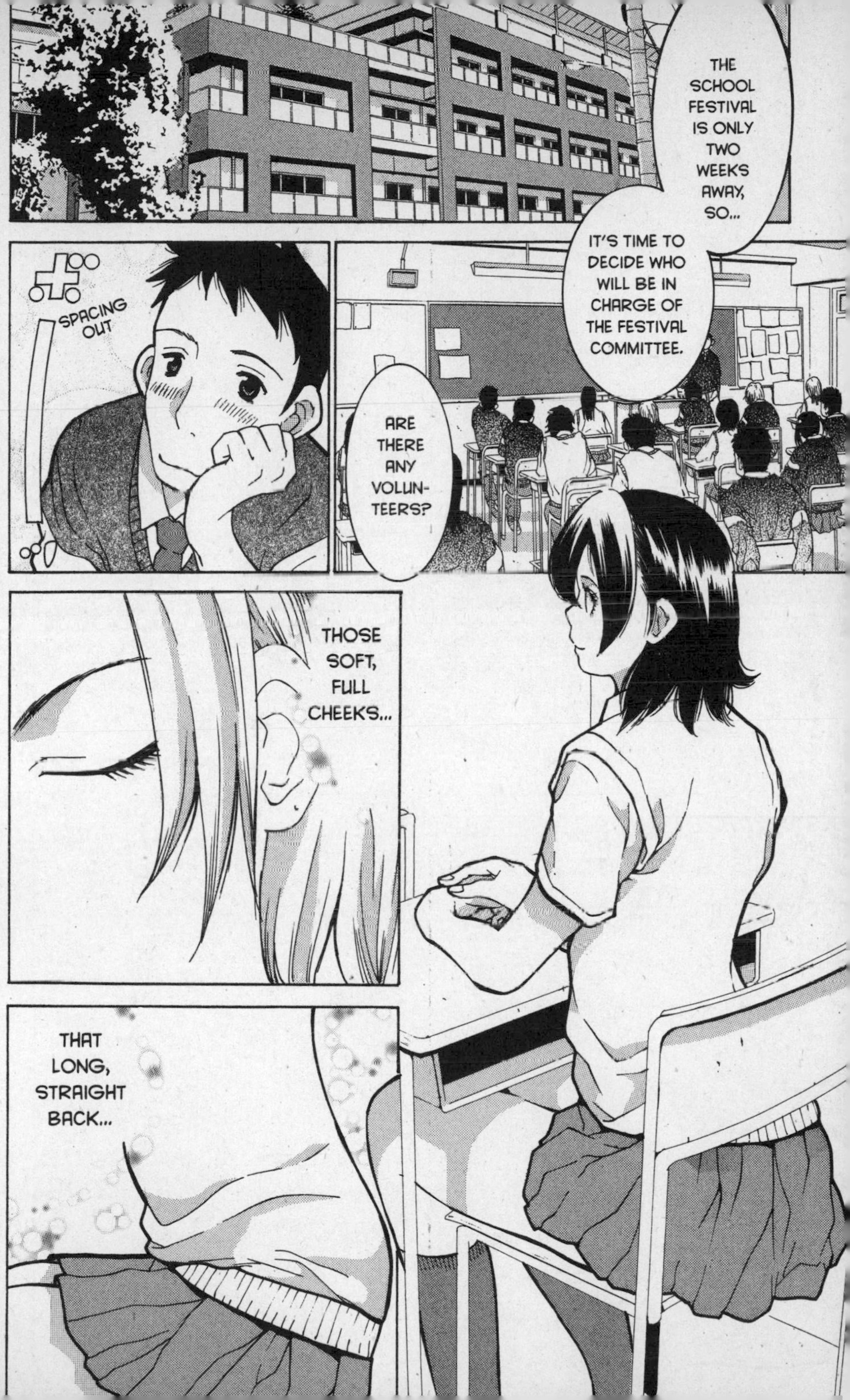
THE SCHOOL FESTIVAL IS ONLY TWO WEEKS AWAY, SO...
IT'S TIME TO DECIDE WHO WILL BE IN CHARGE OF THE FESTIVAL COMMITTEE.
ARE THERE ANY VOLUN-TEERS?
SPACING OUT
THOSE SOFT, FULL CHEEKS...
THAT LONG, STRAIGHT BACK...

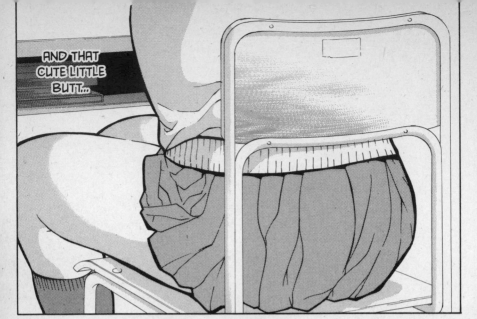

AND THAT CUTE LITTLE BUTT...

SHE'S PERFECT. SAKURABA ALWAYS LOOKS HOT NO MATTER WHAT.

FWIP

HUH?

THOINK

HUH? BUT...

NUDGE

NUDGE

HEY, YURIKA! WHY DON'T YOU VOLUNTEER?

SCHWIP

AH!

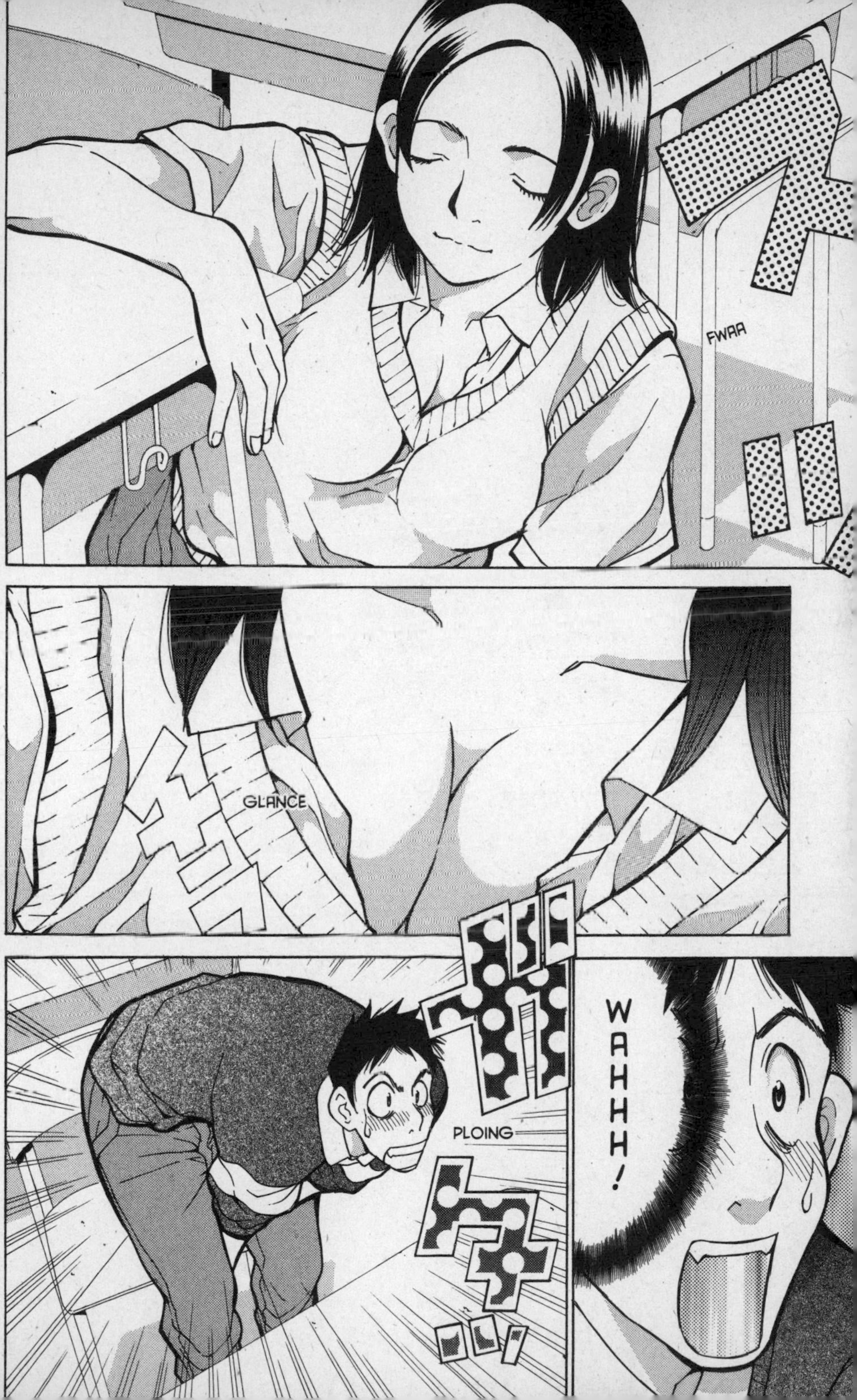
FWAA
GLANCE
WAHHH!
PLOING

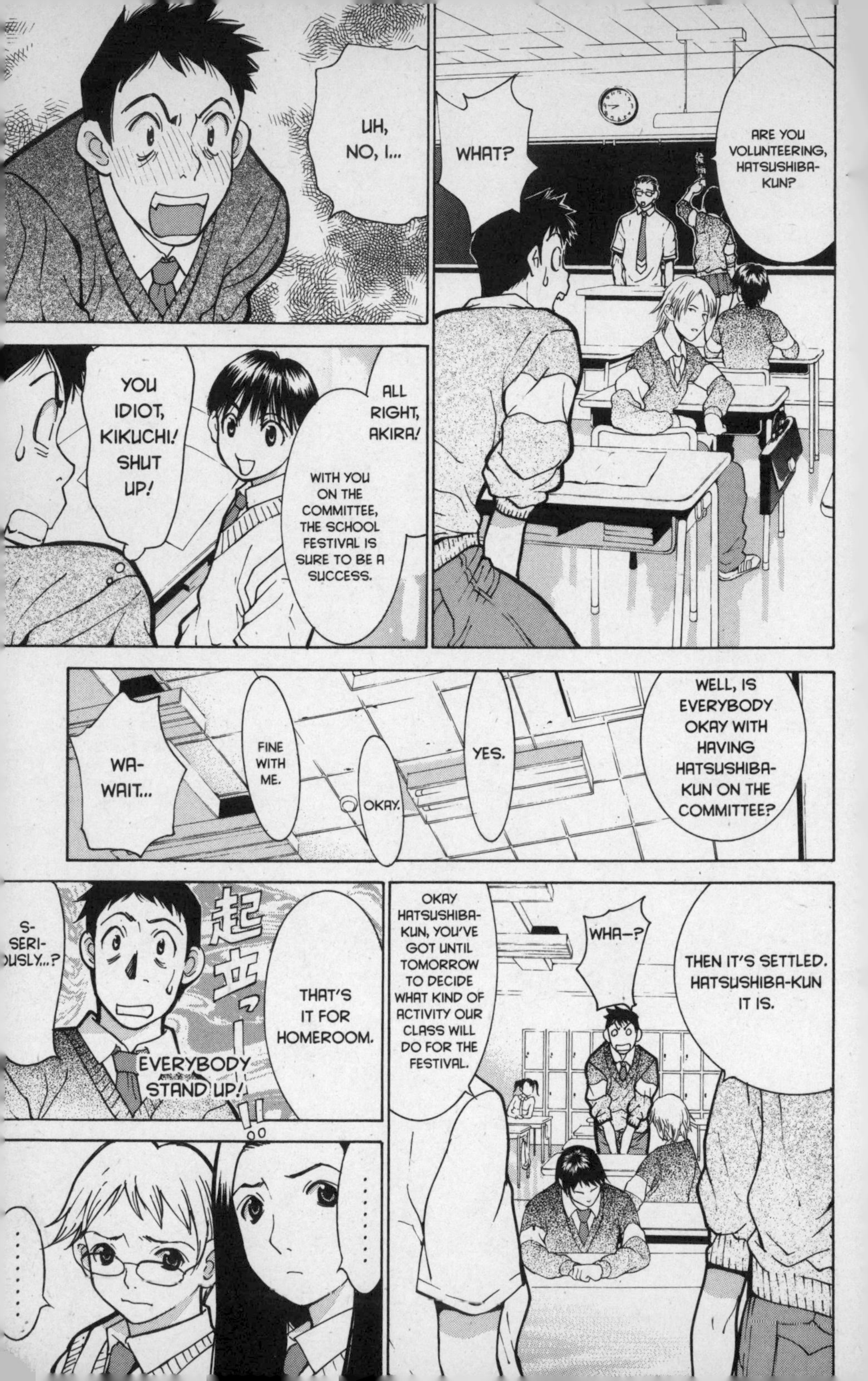
ARE YOU VOLUNTEERING, HATSUSHIBA-KUN?
WHAT?
UH, NO, I...
ALL RIGHT, AKIRA!
WITH YOU ON THE COMMITTEE, THE SCHOOL FESTIVAL IS SURE TO BE A SUCCESS.
YOU IDIOT, KIKUCHI! SHUT UP!
WELL, IS EVERYBODY OKAY WITH HAVING HATSUSHIBA-KUN ON THE COMMITTEE?
YES.
OKAY.
FINE WITH ME.
WA-WAIT...
THEN IT'S SETTLED. HATSUSHIBA-KUN IT IS.
WHA-?
OKAY HATSUSHIBA-KUN, YOU'VE GOT UNTIL TOMORROW TO DECIDE WHAT KIND OF ACTIVITY OUR CLASS WILL DO FOR THE FESTIVAL.
THAT'S IT FOR HOMEROOM.
起立っ
EVERYBODY STAND UP!
!!
S-SERIOUSLY...?
......
......

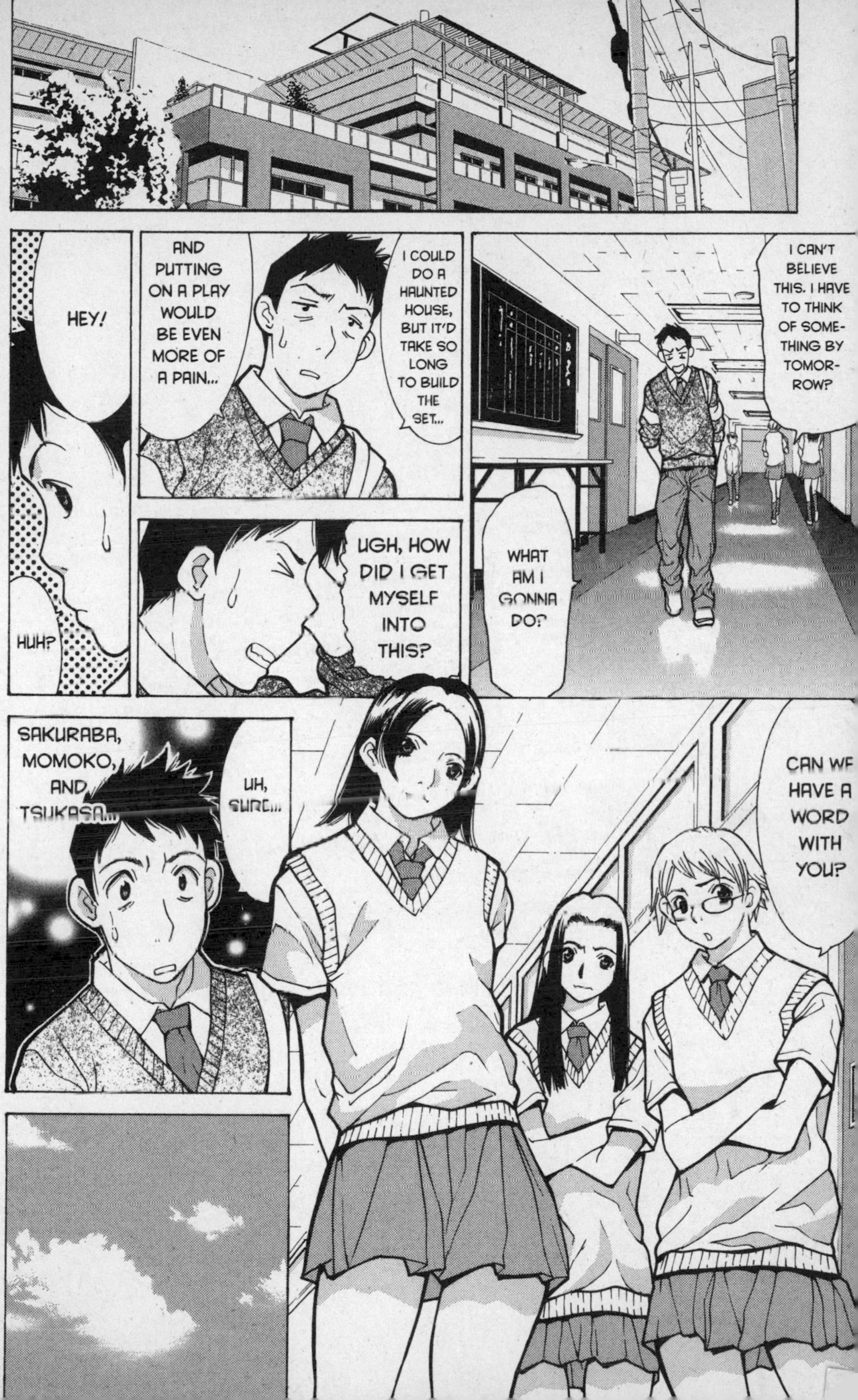
I CAN'T BELIEVE THIS. I HAVE TO THINK OF SOMETHING BY TOMORROW?
WHAT AM I GONNA DO?
I COULD DO A HAUNTED HOUSE, BUT IT'D TAKE SO LONG TO BUILD THE SET...
AND PUTTING ON A PLAY WOULD BE EVEN MORE OF A PAIN...
UGH, HOW DID I GET MYSELF INTO THIS?
HEY!
HUH?
CAN WE HAVE A WORD WITH YOU?
SAKURABA, MOMOKO, AND TSUKASA...
UH, SURE...

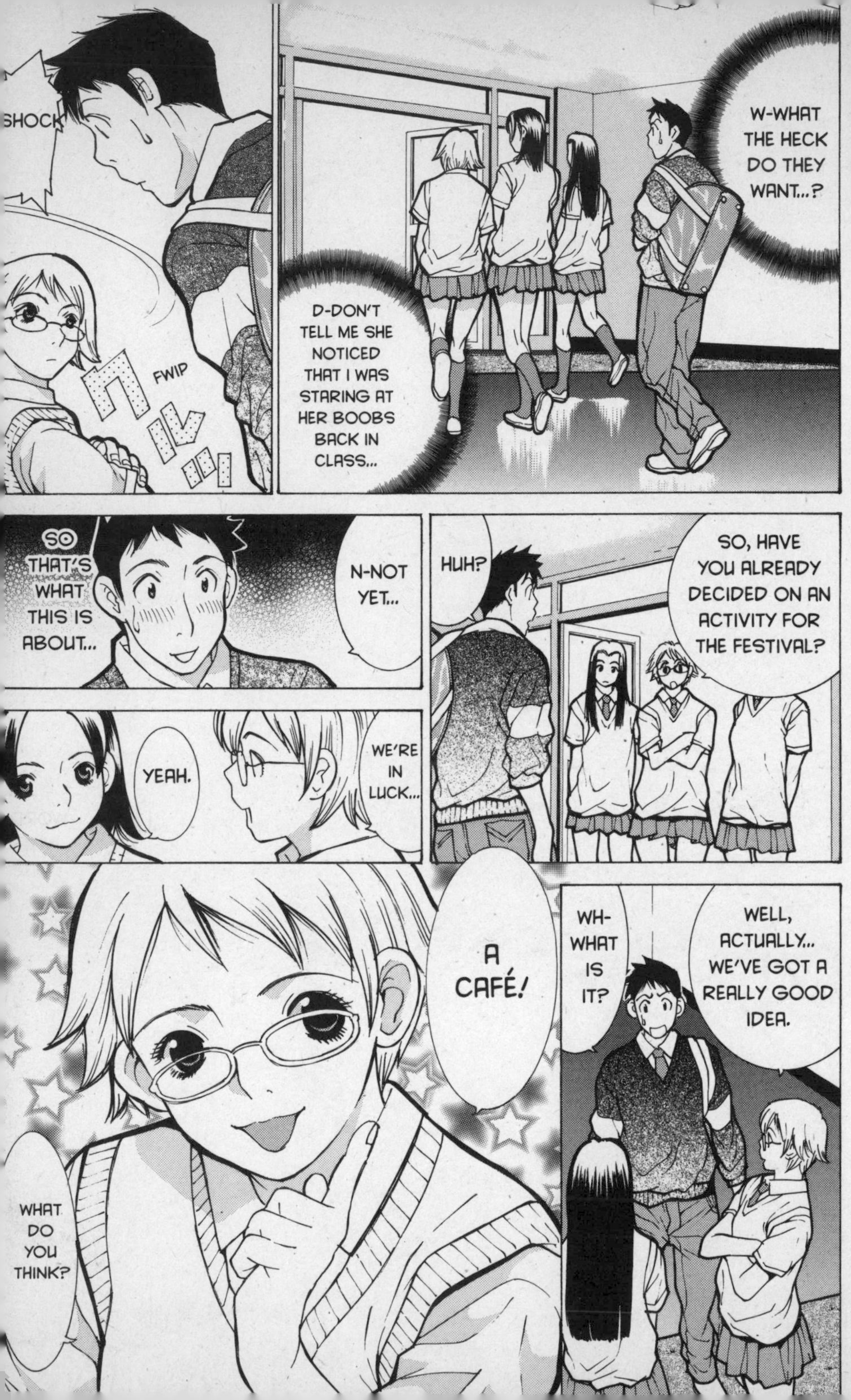

W-WHAT THE HECK DO THEY WANT...?
D-DON'T TELL ME SHE NOTICED THAT I WAS STARING AT HER BOOBS BACK IN CLASS...
SHOCK
FWIP
SO, HAVE YOU ALREADY DECIDED ON AN ACTIVITY FOR THE FESTIVAL?
HUH?
N-NOT YET...
SO THAT'S WHAT THIS IS ABOUT...
WE'RE IN LUCK...
YEAH.
WELL, ACTUALLY... WE'VE GOT A REALLY GOOD IDEA.
WH-WHAT IS IT?
A CAFÉ!
WHAT DO YOU THINK?

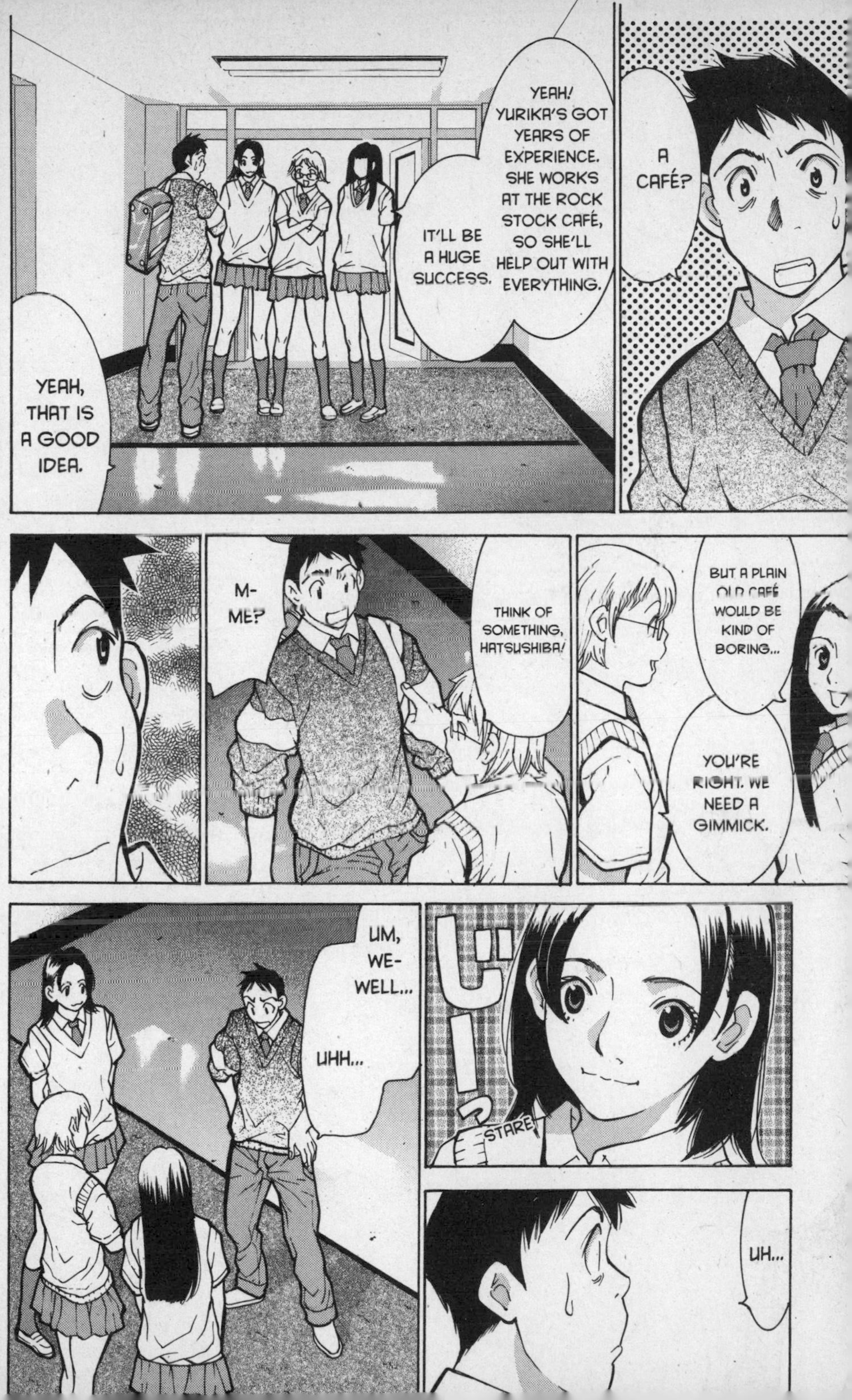
A CAFÉ?
YEAH! YURIKA'S GOT YEARS OF EXPERIENCE. SHE WORKS AT THE ROCK STOCK CAFÉ, SO SHE'LL HELP OUT WITH EVERYTHING.
IT'LL BE A HUGE SUCCESS.
YEAH, THAT IS A GOOD IDEA.
BUT A PLAIN OLD CAFÉ WOULD BE KIND OF BORING...
YOU'RE RIGHT. WE NEED A GIMMICK.
THINK OF SOMETHING, HATSUSHIBA!
M- ME?
STARE
UH...
UM, WE- WELL...
UHH...

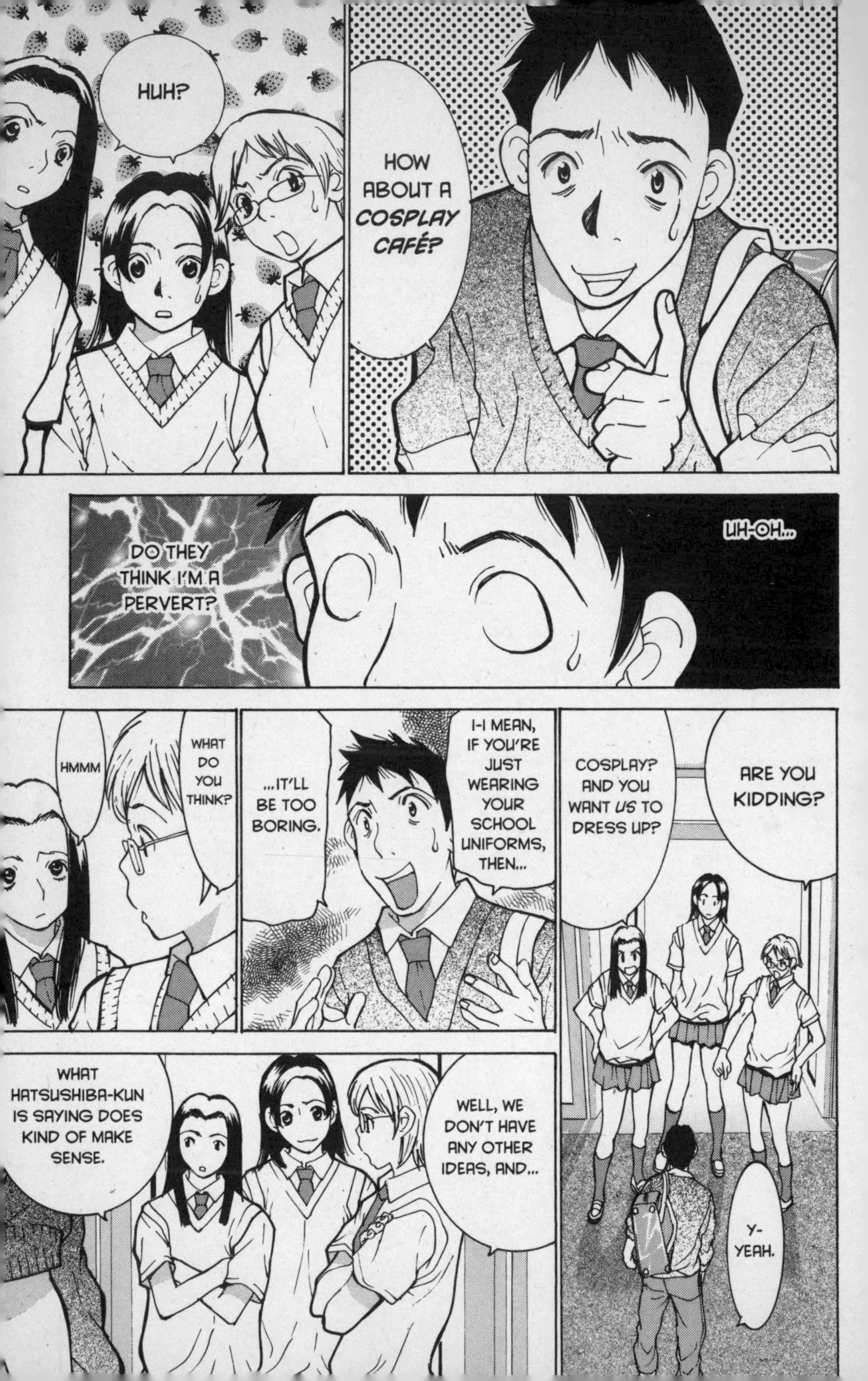
HOW ABOUT A *COSPLAY CAFÉ?*
HUH?
UH-OH...
DO THEY THINK I'M A PERVERT?
ARE YOU KIDDING?
COSPLAY? AND YOU WANT *US* TO DRESS UP?
Y-YEAH.
I-I MEAN, IF YOU'RE JUST WEARING YOUR SCHOOL UNIFORMS, THEN...
...IT'LL BE TOO BORING.
WHAT DO YOU THINK?
HMMM
WELL, WE DON'T HAVE ANY OTHER IDEAS, AND...
WHAT HATSUSHIBA-KUN IS SAYING DOES KIND OF MAKE SENSE.

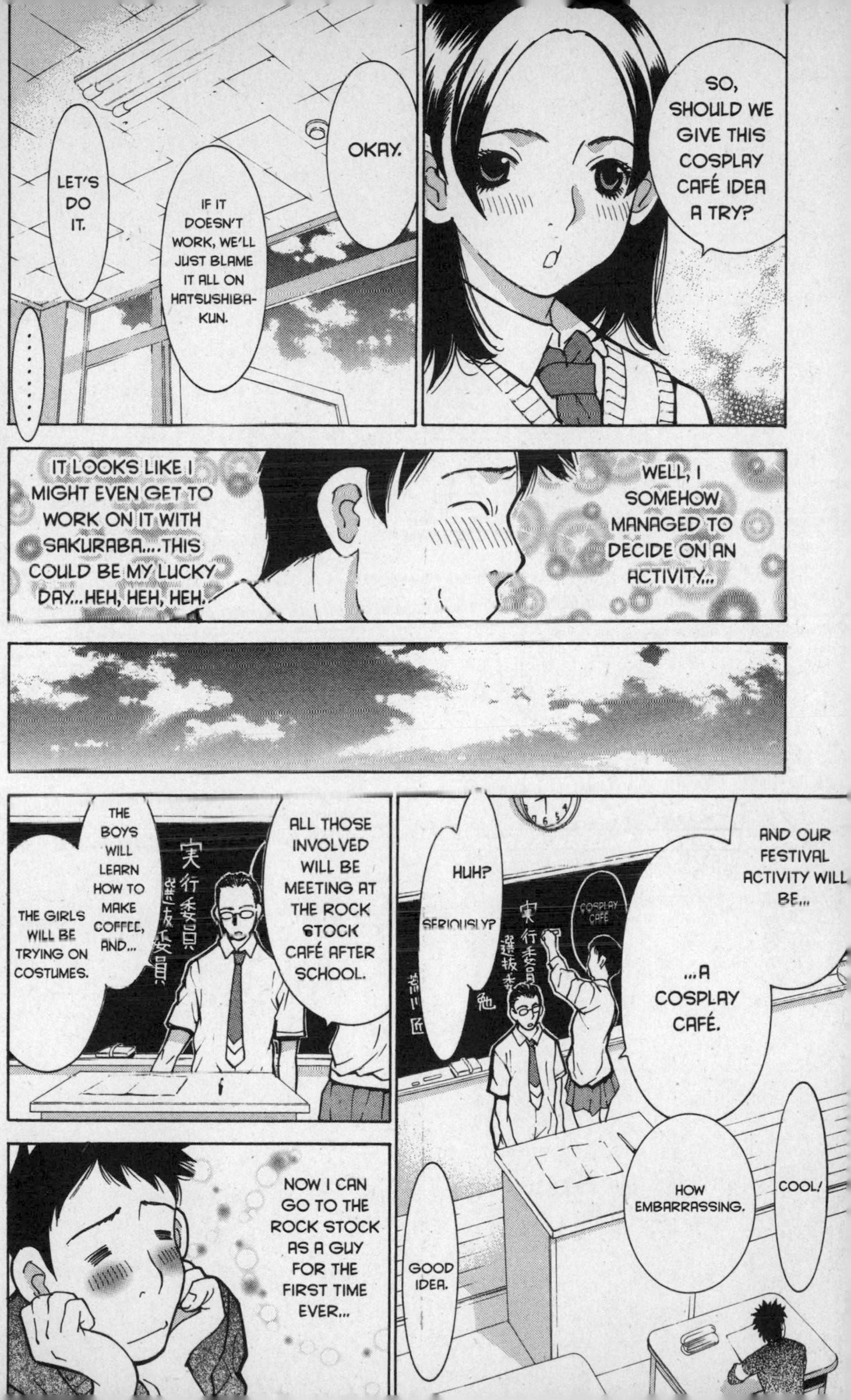
SO, SHOULD WE GIVE THIS COSPLAY CAFÉ IDEA A TRY?
OKAY.
IF IT DOESN'T WORK, WE'LL JUST BLAME IT ALL ON HATSUSHIBA-KUN.
LET'S DO IT.
......
WELL, I SOMEHOW MANAGED TO DECIDE ON AN ACTIVITY...
IT LOOKS LIKE I MIGHT EVEN GET TO WORK ON IT WITH SAKURABA.... THIS COULD BE MY LUCKY DAY...HEH, HEH, HEH.
AND OUR FESTIVAL ACTIVITY WILL BE...
...A COSPLAY CAFÉ.
COSPLAY CAFE
HUH?
SERIOUSLY?
COOL!
HOW EMBARRASSING.
GOOD IDEA.
ALL THOSE INVOLVED WILL BE MEETING AT THE ROCK STOCK CAFÉ AFTER SCHOOL.
THE BOYS WILL LEARN HOW TO MAKE COFFEE, AND...
THE GIRLS WILL BE TRYING ON COSTUMES.
NOW I CAN GO TO THE ROCK STOCK AS A GUY FOR THE FIRST TIME EVER...

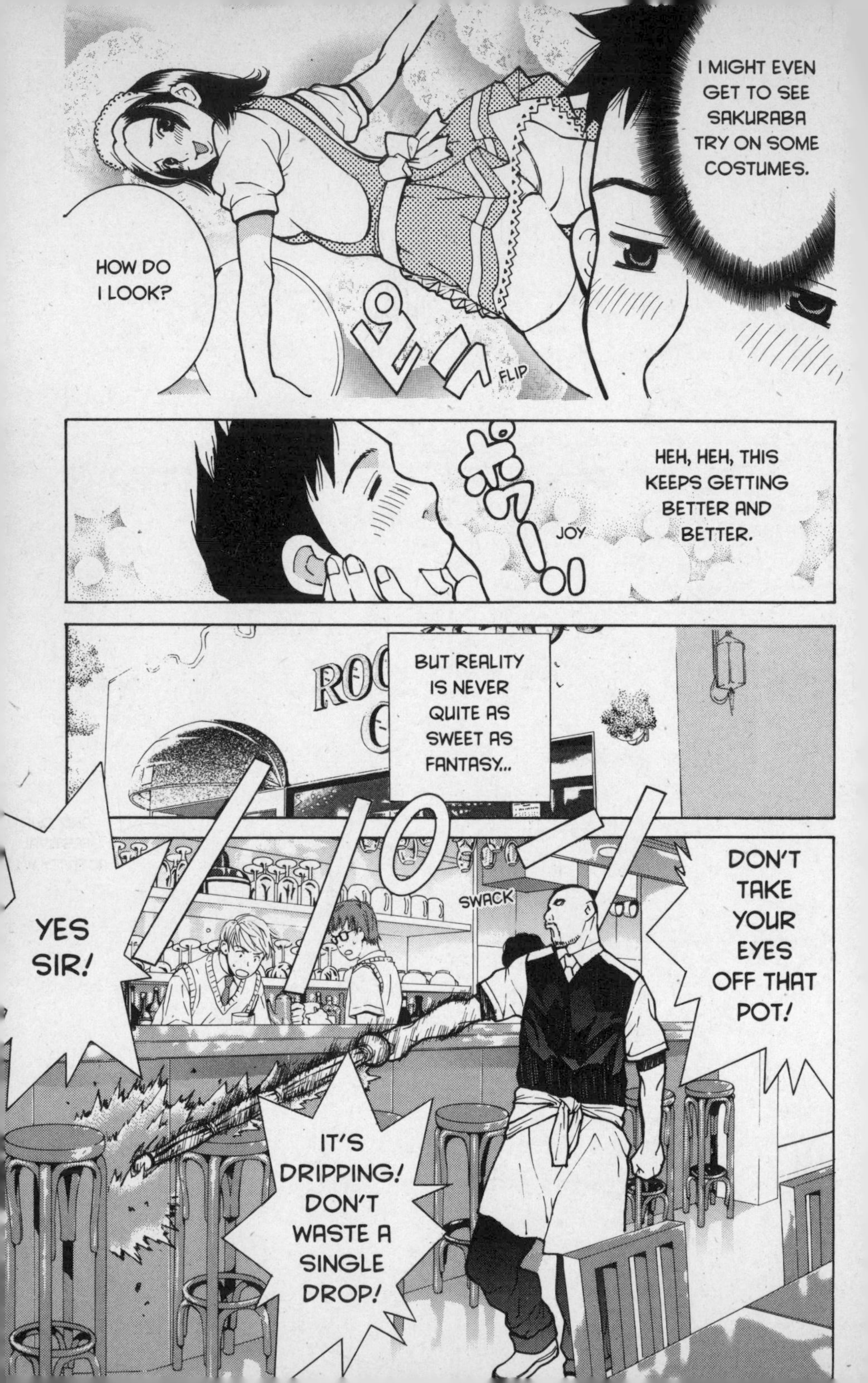
I MIGHT EVEN GET TO SEE SAKURABA TRY ON SOME COSTUMES.
HOW DO I LOOK?
FLIP
HEH, HEH, THIS KEEPS GETTING BETTER AND BETTER.
JOY
BUT REALITY IS NEVER QUITE AS SWEET AS FANTASY...
DON'T TAKE YOUR EYES OFF THAT POT!
SWACK
YES SIR!
IT'S DRIPPING! DON'T WASTE A SINGLE DROP!

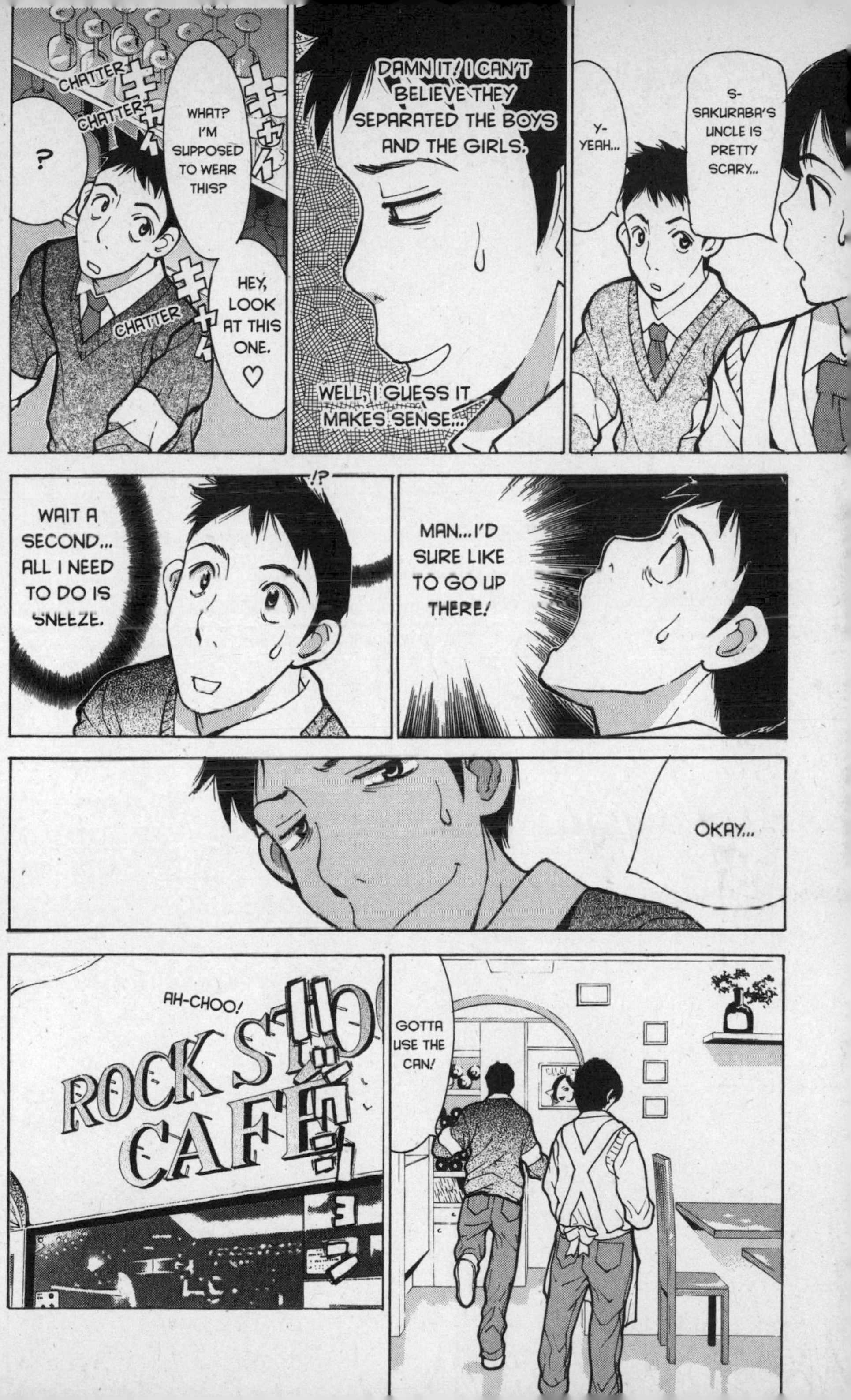
S-SAKURABA'S UNCLE IS PRETTY SCARY...
Y-YEAH...
DAMN IT! I CAN'T BELIEVE THEY SEPARATED THE BOYS AND THE GIRLS.
WELL, I GUESS IT MAKES SENSE...
CHATTER
CHATTER
WHAT? I'M SUPPOSED TO WEAR THIS?
?
HEY, LOOK AT THIS ONE. ♡
CHATTER
MAN...I'D SURE LIKE TO GO UP THERE!
!?
WAIT A SECOND... ALL I NEED TO DO IS SNEEZE.
OKAY...
GOTTA USE THE CAN!
AH-CHOO!
CAFE

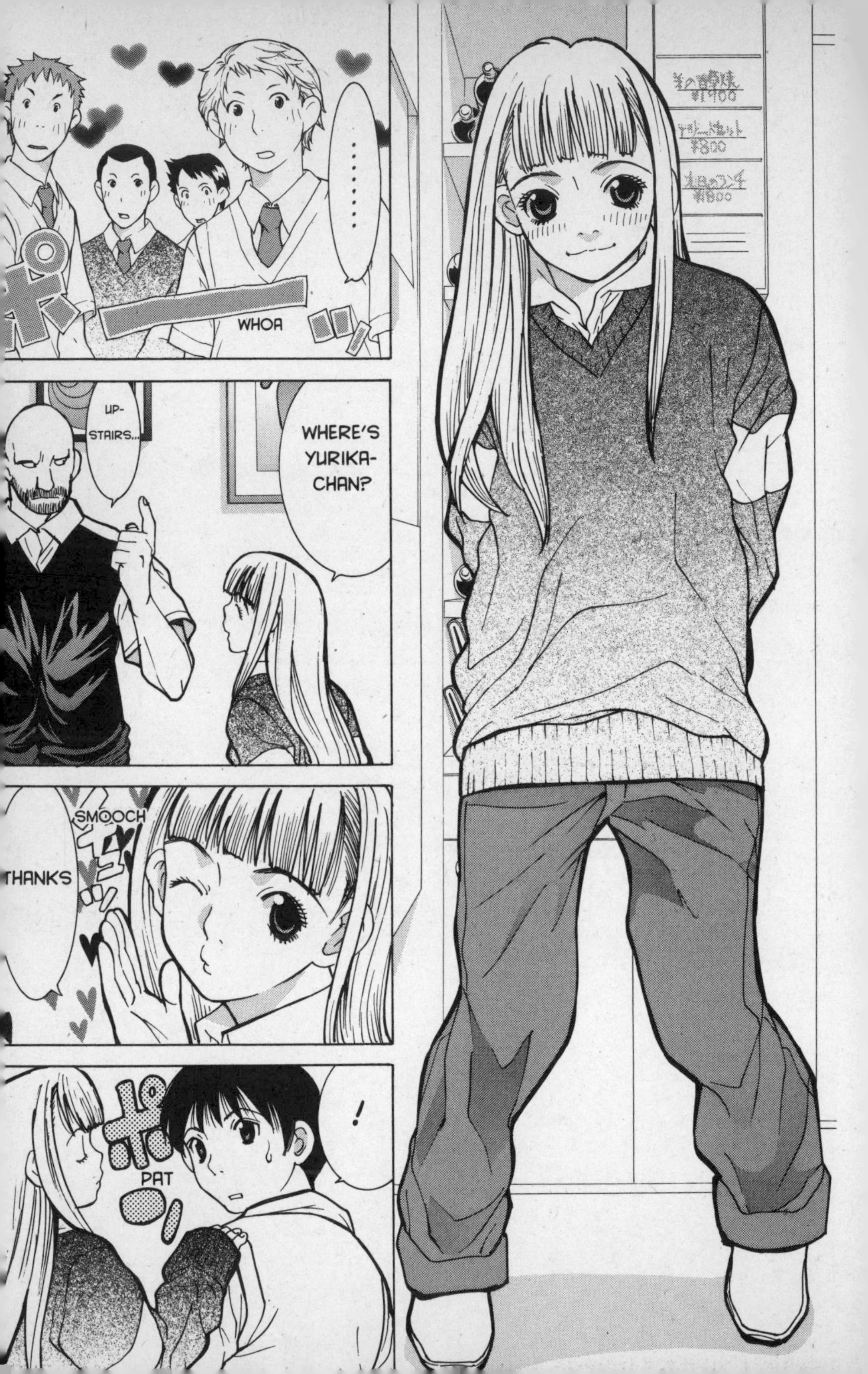

......
WHOA
WHERE'S YURIKA-CHAN?
UP-STAIRS...
SMOOCH
THANKS
!
PAT

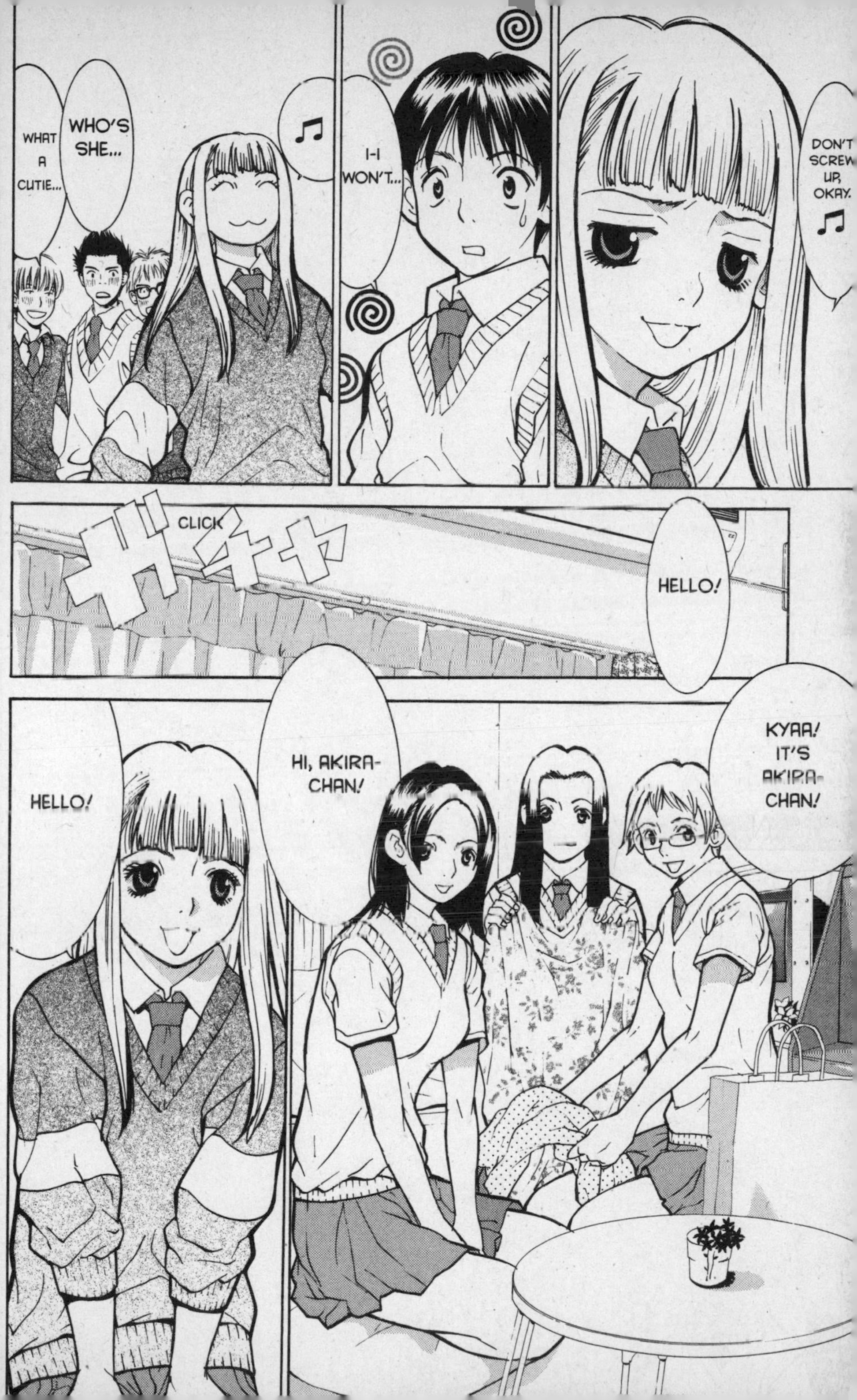
DON'T SCREW UP, OKAY. ♫
I-I WON'T...
♫
WHO'S SHE...
WHAT A CUTIE...
HELLO!
CLICK
KYAA! IT'S AKIRA-CHAN!
HI, AKIRA-CHAN!
HELLO!

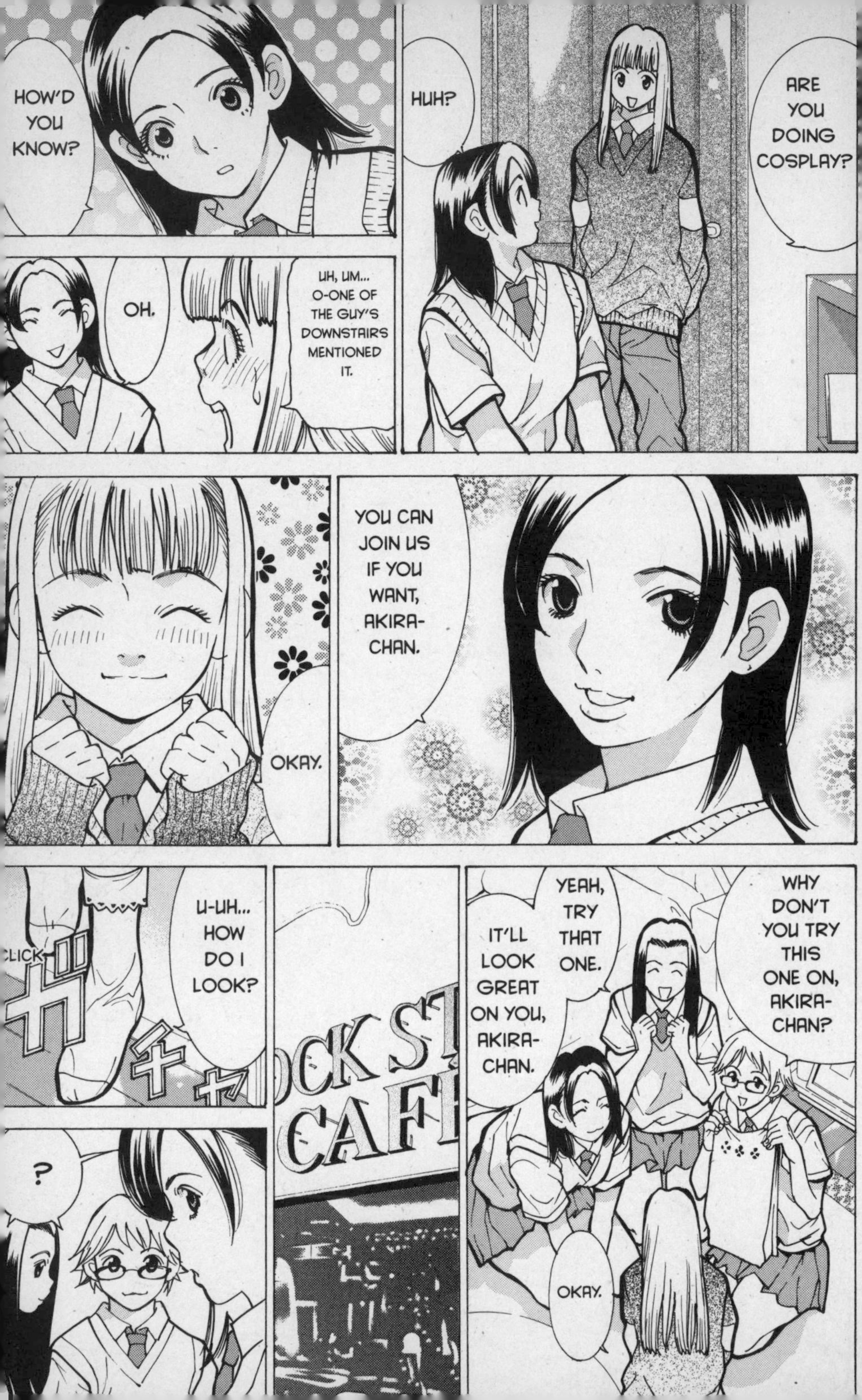
ARE YOU DOING COSPLAY?
HUH?
HOW'D YOU KNOW?
UH, UM... O-ONE OF THE GUY'S DOWNSTAIRS MENTIONED IT.
OH.
YOU CAN JOIN US IF YOU WANT, AKIRA-CHAN.
OKAY.
WHY DON'T YOU TRY THIS ONE ON, AKIRA-CHAN?
YEAH, TRY THAT ONE.
IT'LL LOOK GREAT ON YOU, AKIRA-CHAN.
OKAY.
U-UH... HOW DO I LOOK?
CLICK
?

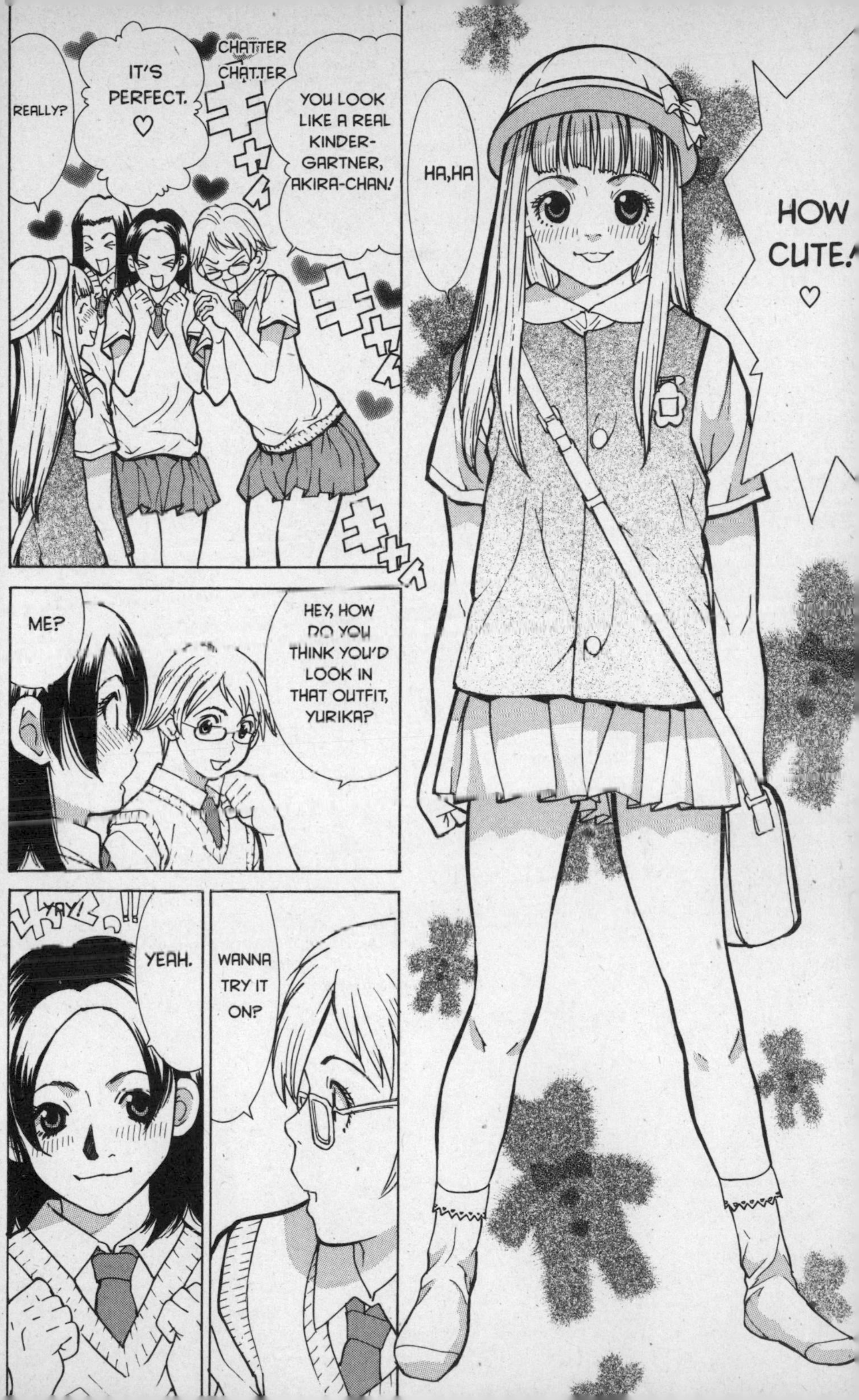
HOW CUTE! ♡
HA,HA
CHATTER CHATTER
YOU LOOK LIKE A REAL KINDER-GARTNER, AKIRA-CHAN!
IT'S PERFECT. ♡
REALLY?
HEY, HOW DO YOU THINK YOU'D LOOK IN THAT OUTFIT, YURIKA?
ME?
WANNA TRY IT ON?
YEAH.
YAY!

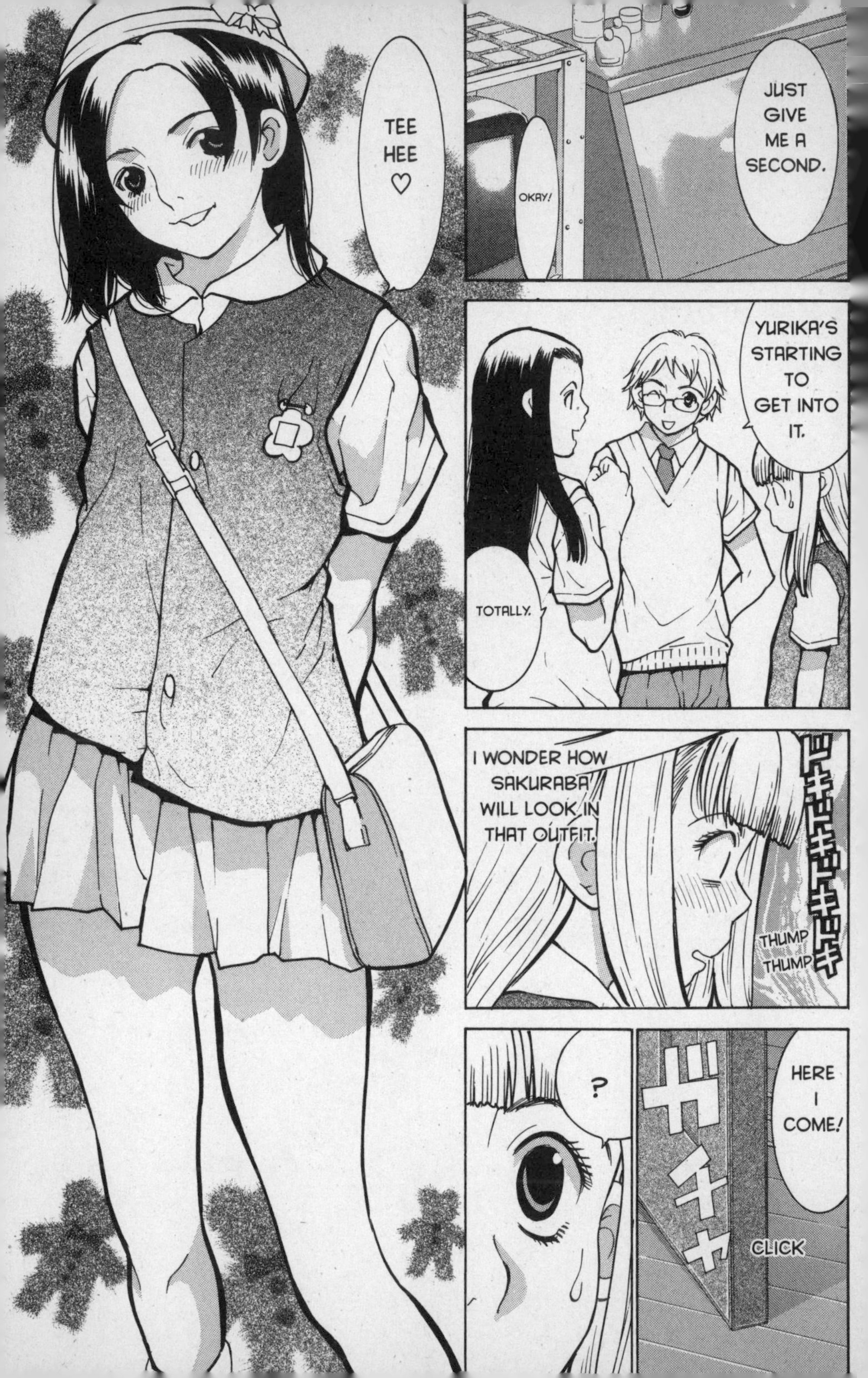
JUST GIVE ME A SECOND.
OKAY!
YURIKA'S STARTING TO GET INTO IT.
TOTALLY.
I WONDER HOW SAKURABA WILL LOOK IN THAT OUTFIT.
THUMP THUMP
HERE I COME!
CLICK
?
TEE HEE ♡

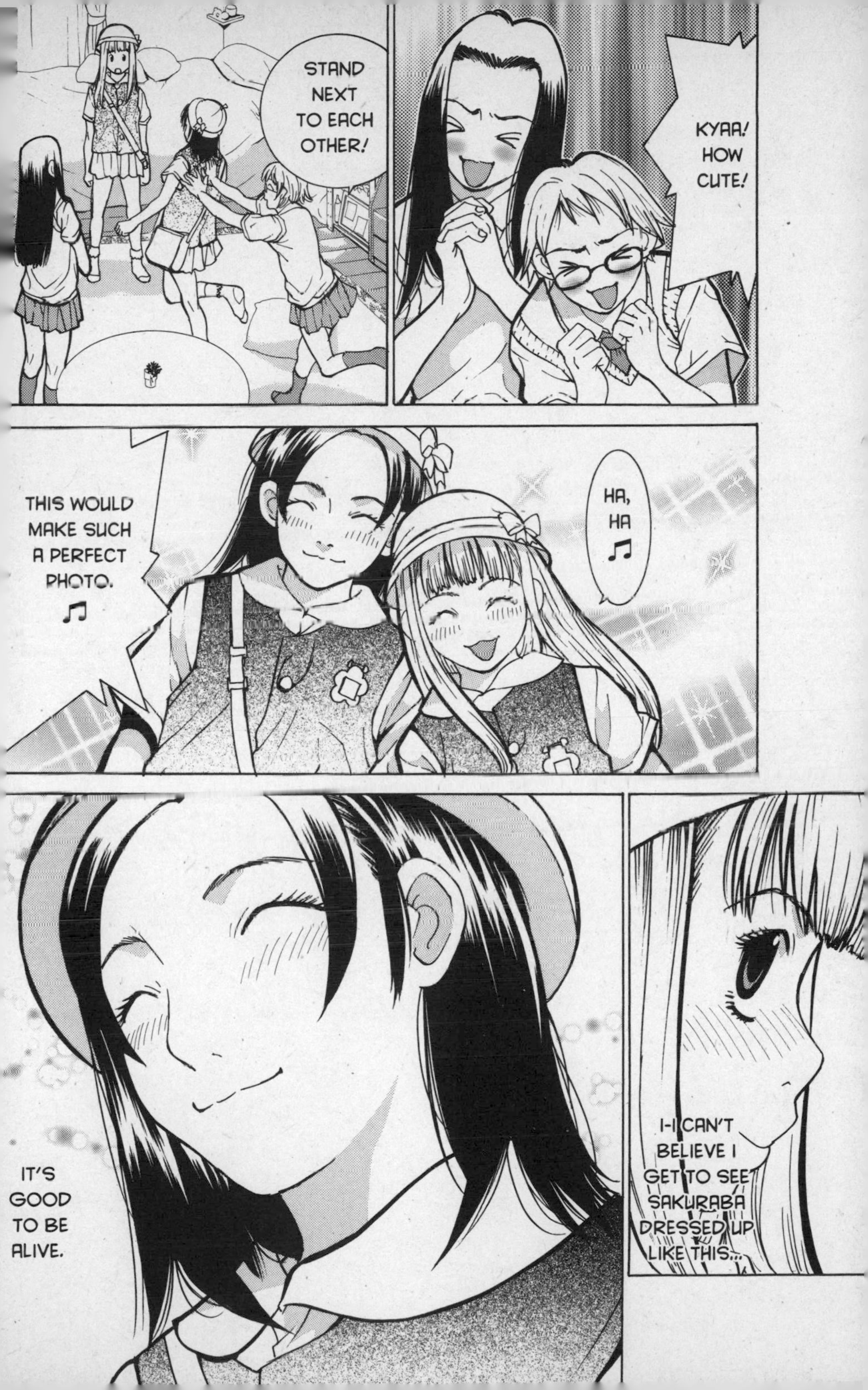
KYAA! HOW CUTE!
STAND NEXT TO EACH OTHER!
HA, HA ♪
THIS WOULD MAKE SUCH A PERFECT PHOTO. ♫
I-I CAN'T BELIEVE I GET TO SEE SAKURABA DRESSED UP LIKE THIS...
IT'S GOOD TO BE ALIVE.

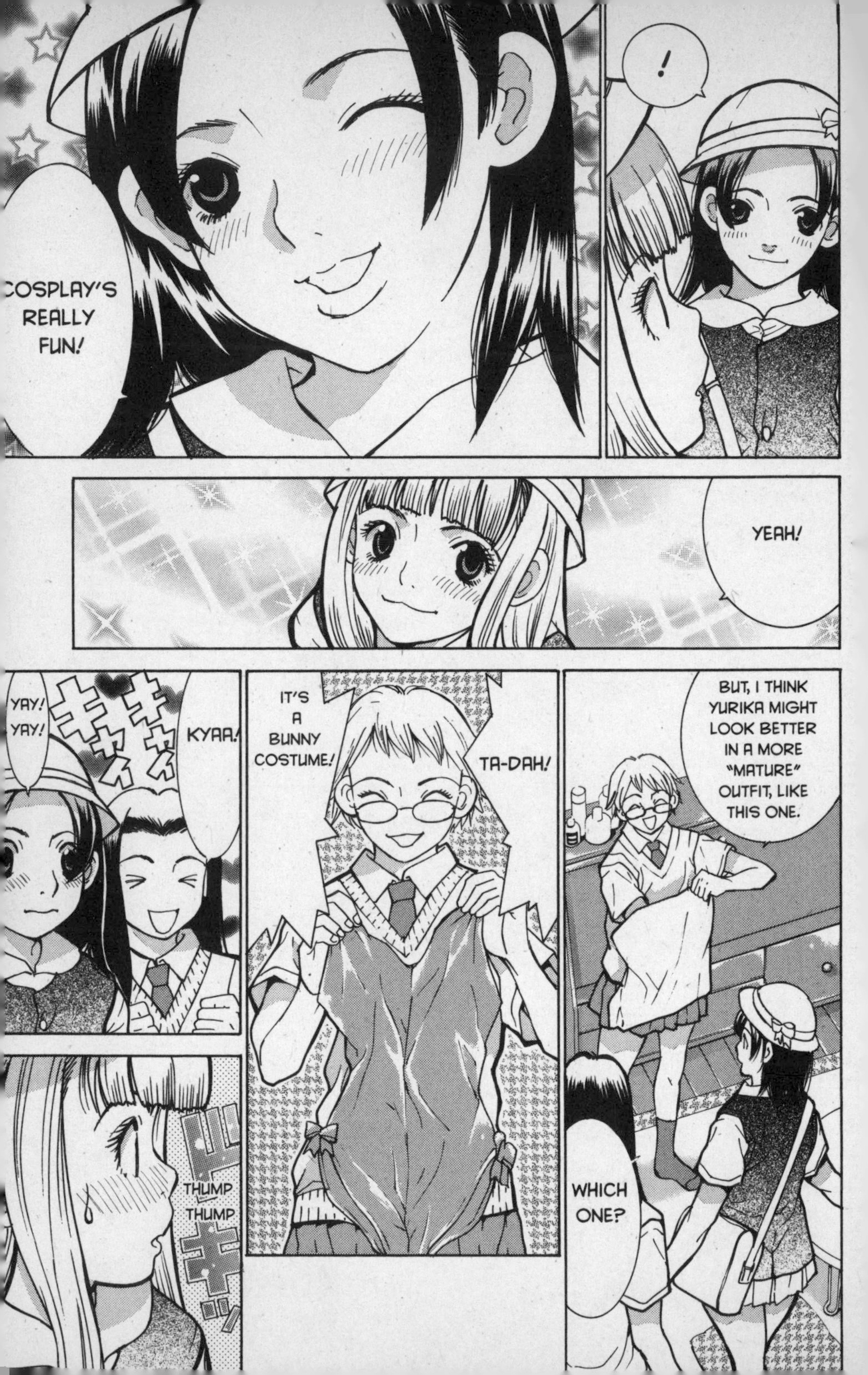
!
COSPLAY'S REALLY FUN!
YEAH!
BUT, I THINK YURIKA MIGHT LOOK BETTER IN A MORE "MATURE" OUTFIT, LIKE THIS ONE.
WHICH ONE?
TA-DAH!
IT'S A BUNNY COSTUME!
KYAA!
YAY! YAY!
THUMP THUMP

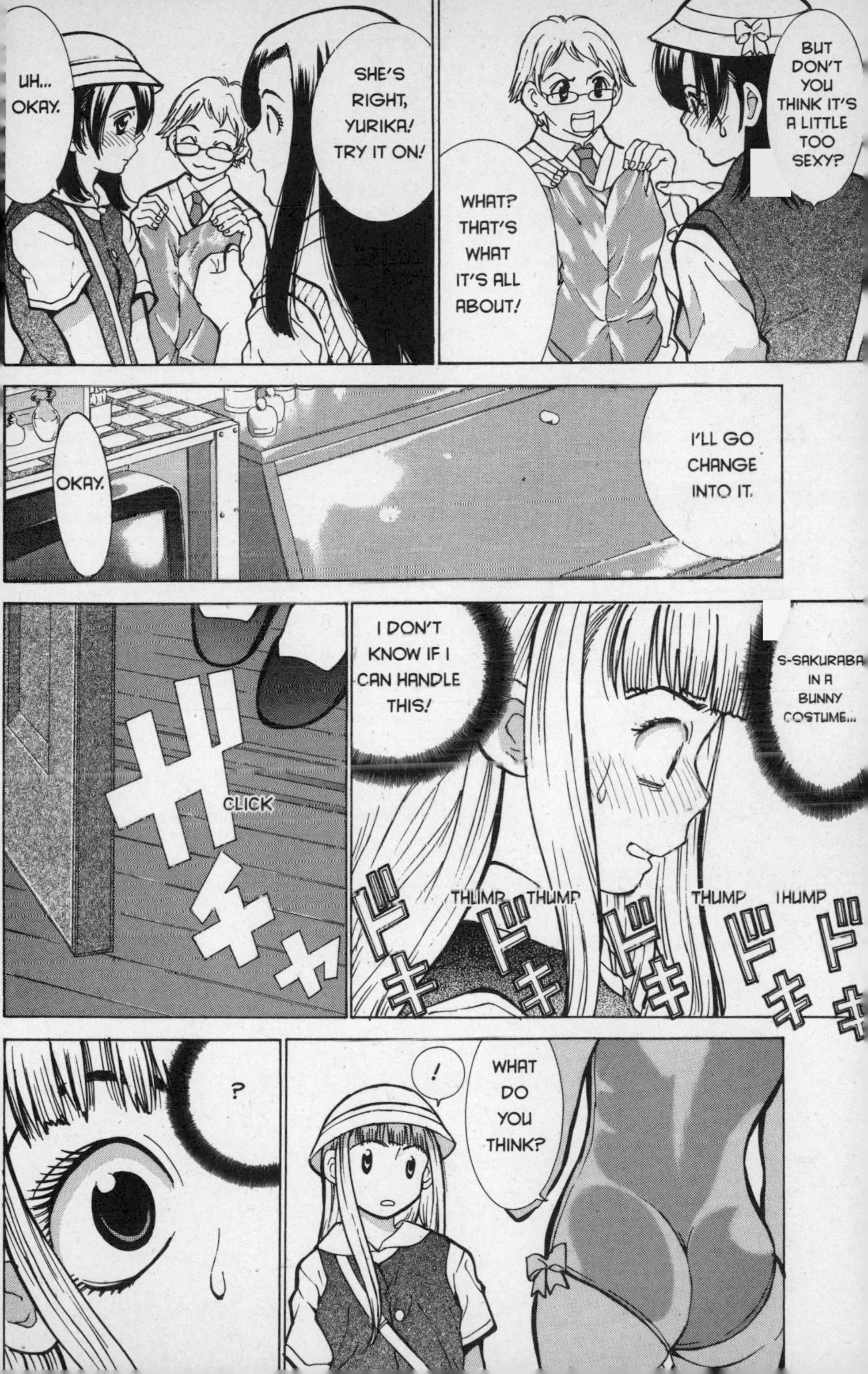

BUT DON'T YOU THINK IT'S A LITTLE TOO SEXY?
WHAT? THAT'S WHAT IT'S ALL ABOUT!
SHE'S RIGHT, YURIKA! TRY IT ON!
UH... OKAY.
I'LL GO CHANGE INTO IT.
OKAY.
S-SAKURABA IN A BUNNY COSTUME...
I DON'T KNOW IF I CAN HANDLE THIS!
THUMP THUMP THUMP THUMP
CLICK
!
WHAT DO YOU THINK?
?

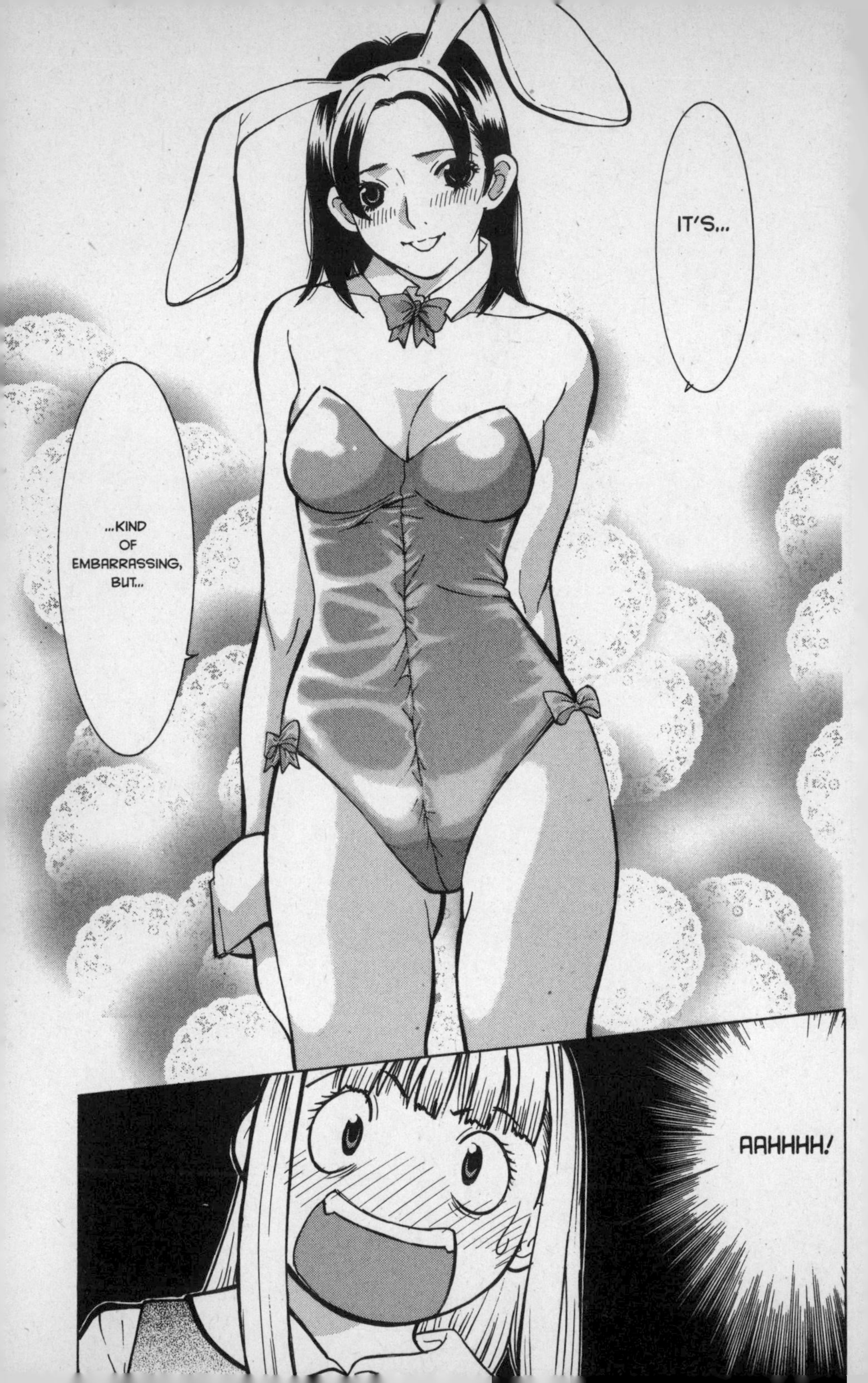
IT'S...
...KIND OF EMBARRASSING, BUT...
AAHHHH!

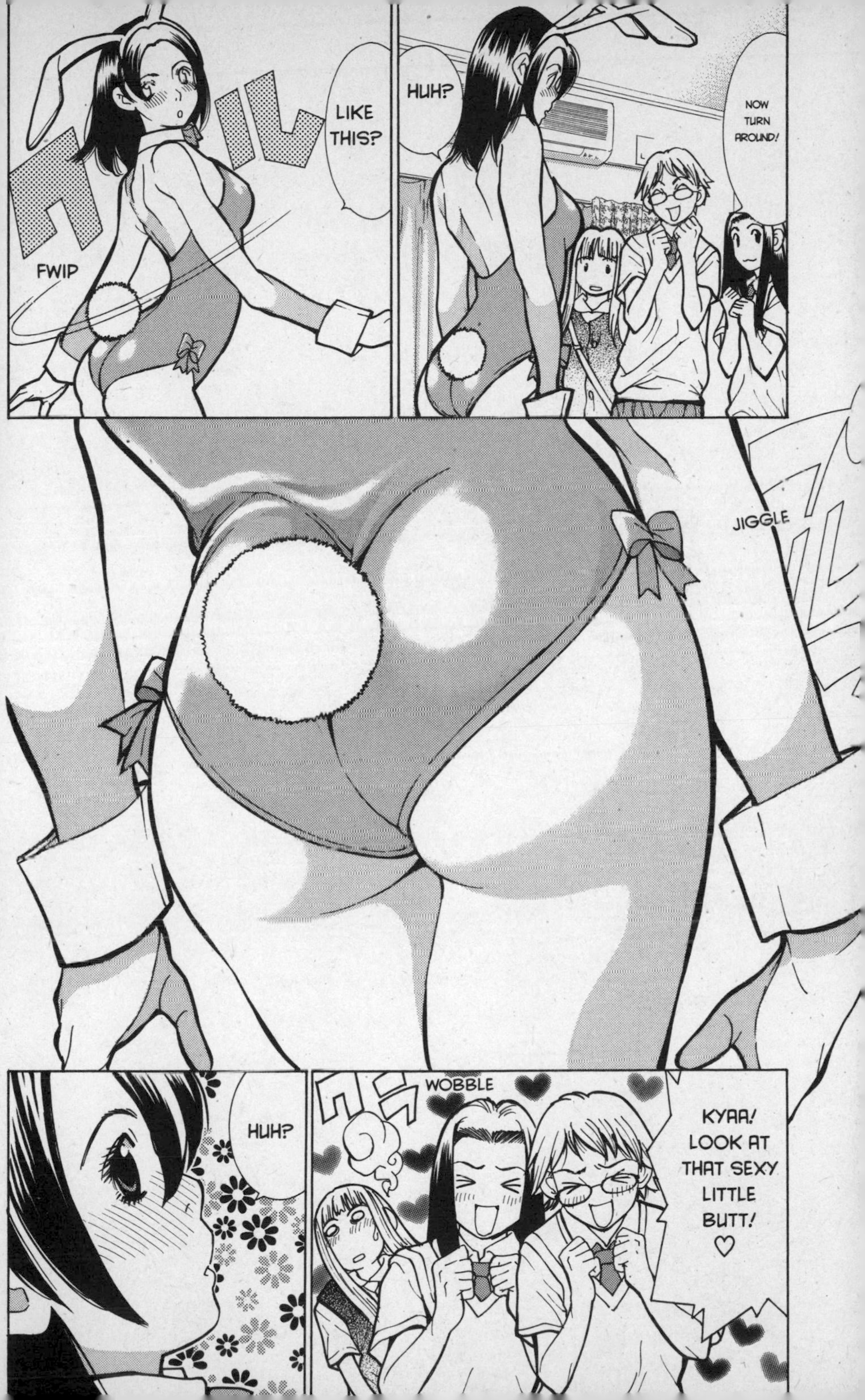
NOW TURN AROUND!
HUH?
LIKE THIS?
FWIP
JIGGLE
WOBBLE
KYAA! LOOK AT THAT SEXY LITTLE BUTT! ♡
HUH?

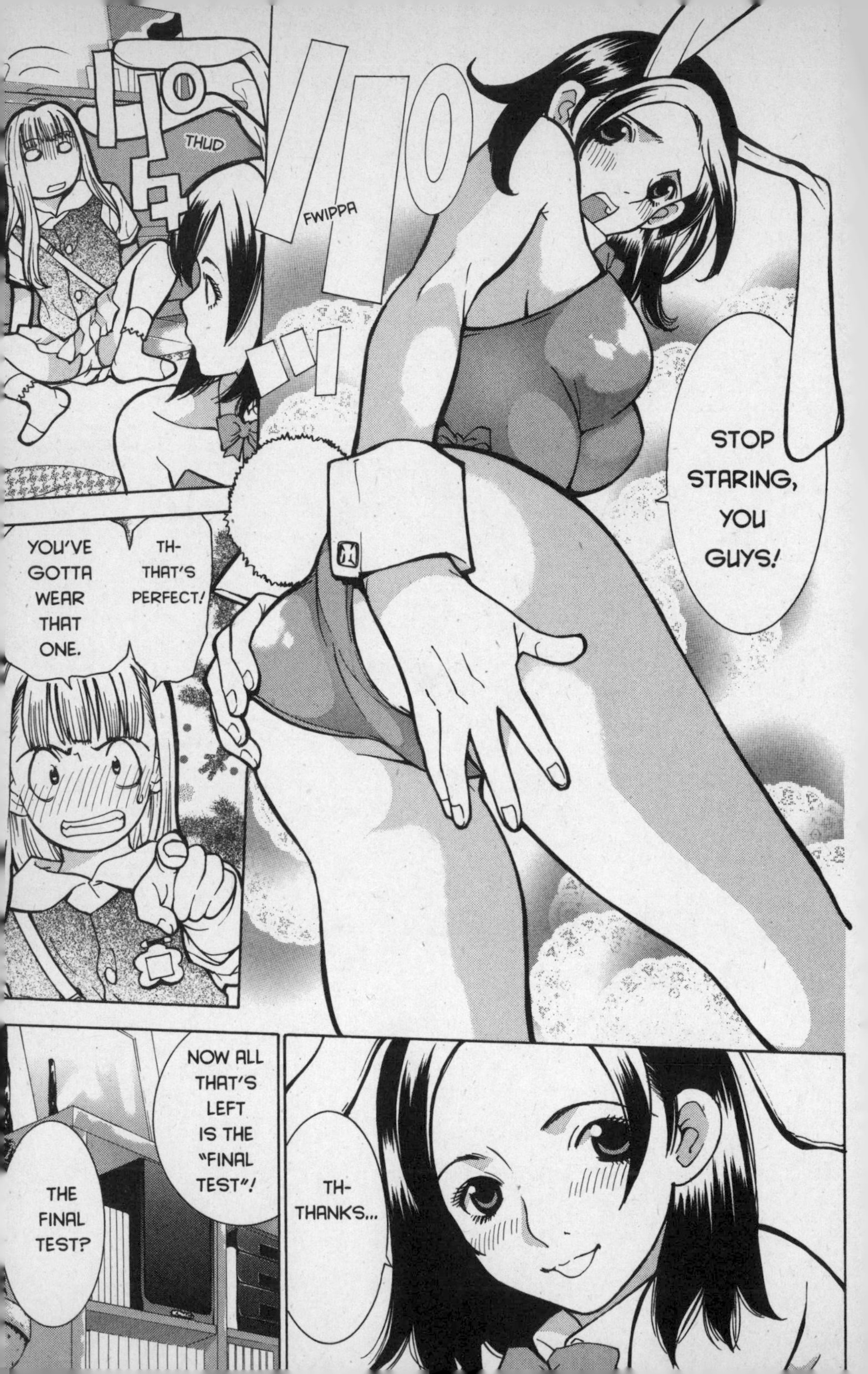
FWIPPA
STOP STARING, YOU GUYS!
THUD
TH- THAT'S PERFECT!
YOU'VE GOTTA WEAR THAT ONE.
TH- THANKS...
NOW ALL THAT'S LEFT IS THE "FINAL TEST"!
THE FINAL TEST?

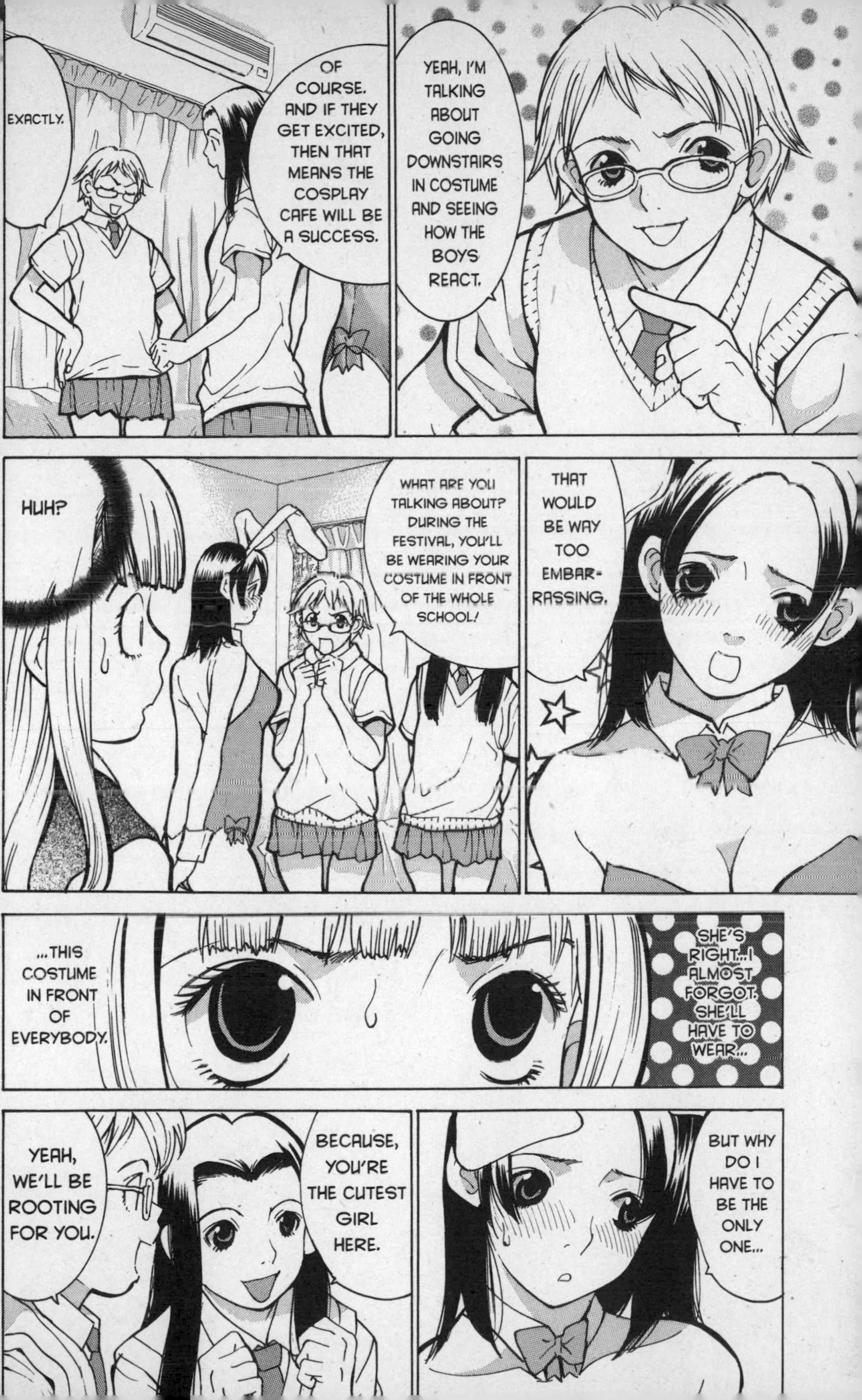
YEAH, I'M TALKING ABOUT GOING DOWNSTAIRS IN COSTUME AND SEEING HOW THE BOYS REACT.
OF COURSE. AND IF THEY GET EXCITED, THEN THAT MEANS THE COSPLAY CAFE WILL BE A SUCCESS.
EXACTLY.
THAT WOULD BE WAY TOO EMBARRASSING.
WHAT ARE YOU TALKING ABOUT? DURING THE FESTIVAL, YOU'LL BE WEARING YOUR COSTUME IN FRONT OF THE WHOLE SCHOOL!
HUH?
SHE'S RIGHT...I ALMOST FORGOT. SHE'LL HAVE TO WEAR...
...THIS COSTUME IN FRONT OF EVERYBODY.
BUT WHY DO I HAVE TO BE THE ONLY ONE...
BECAUSE, YOU'RE THE CUTEST GIRL HERE.
YEAH, WE'LL BE ROOTING FOR YOU.

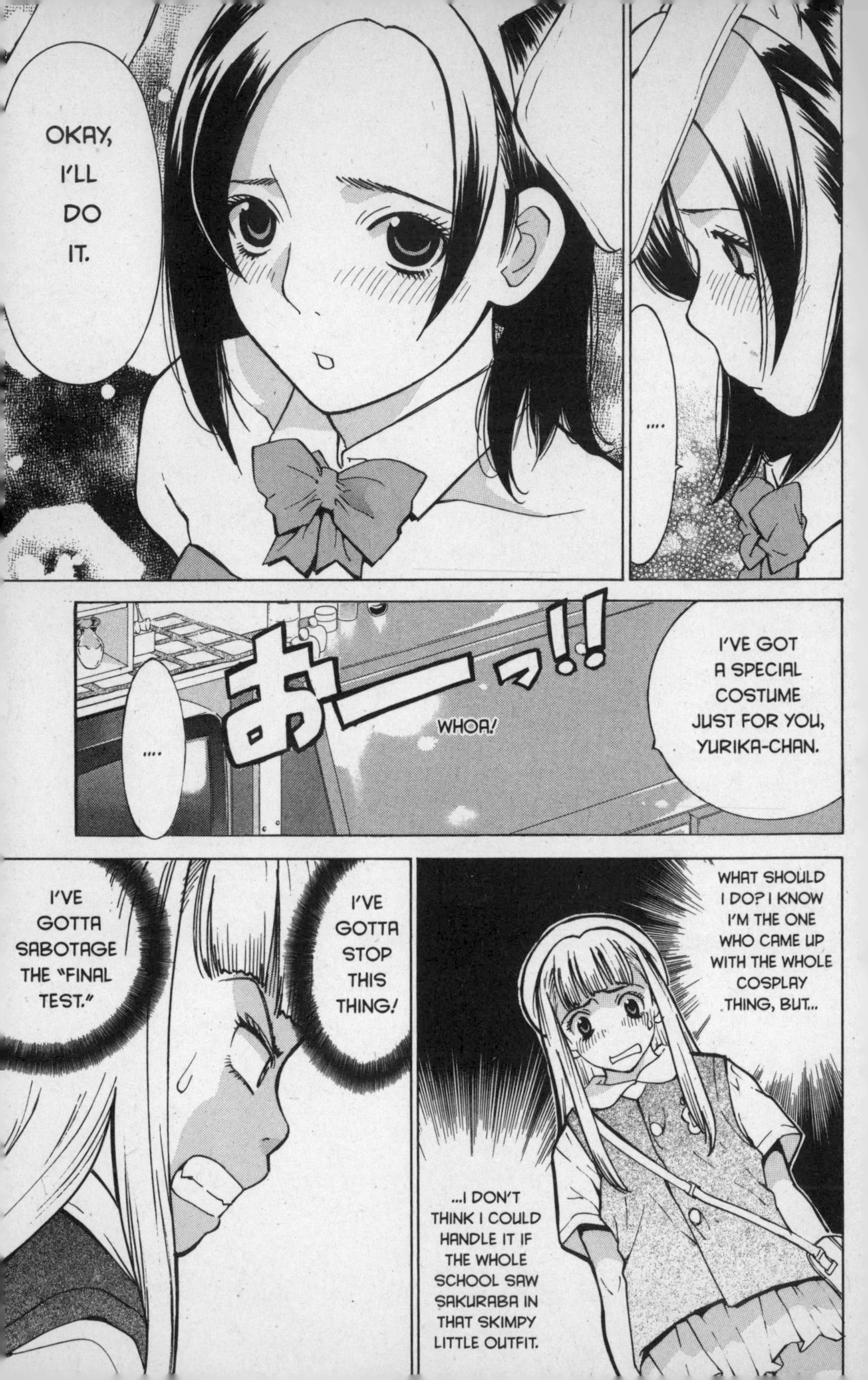
....
OKAY, I'LL DO IT.
I'VE GOT A SPECIAL COSTUME JUST FOR YOU, YURIKA-CHAN.
おーーっ!!
WHOA!
....
WHAT SHOULD I DO? I KNOW I'M THE ONE WHO CAME UP WITH THE WHOLE COSPLAY THING, BUT...
...I DON'T THINK I COULD HANDLE IT IF THE WHOLE SCHOOL SAW SAKURABA IN THAT SKIMPY LITTLE OUTFIT.
I'VE GOTTA STOP THIS THING!
I'VE GOTTA SABOTAGE THE "FINAL TEST."

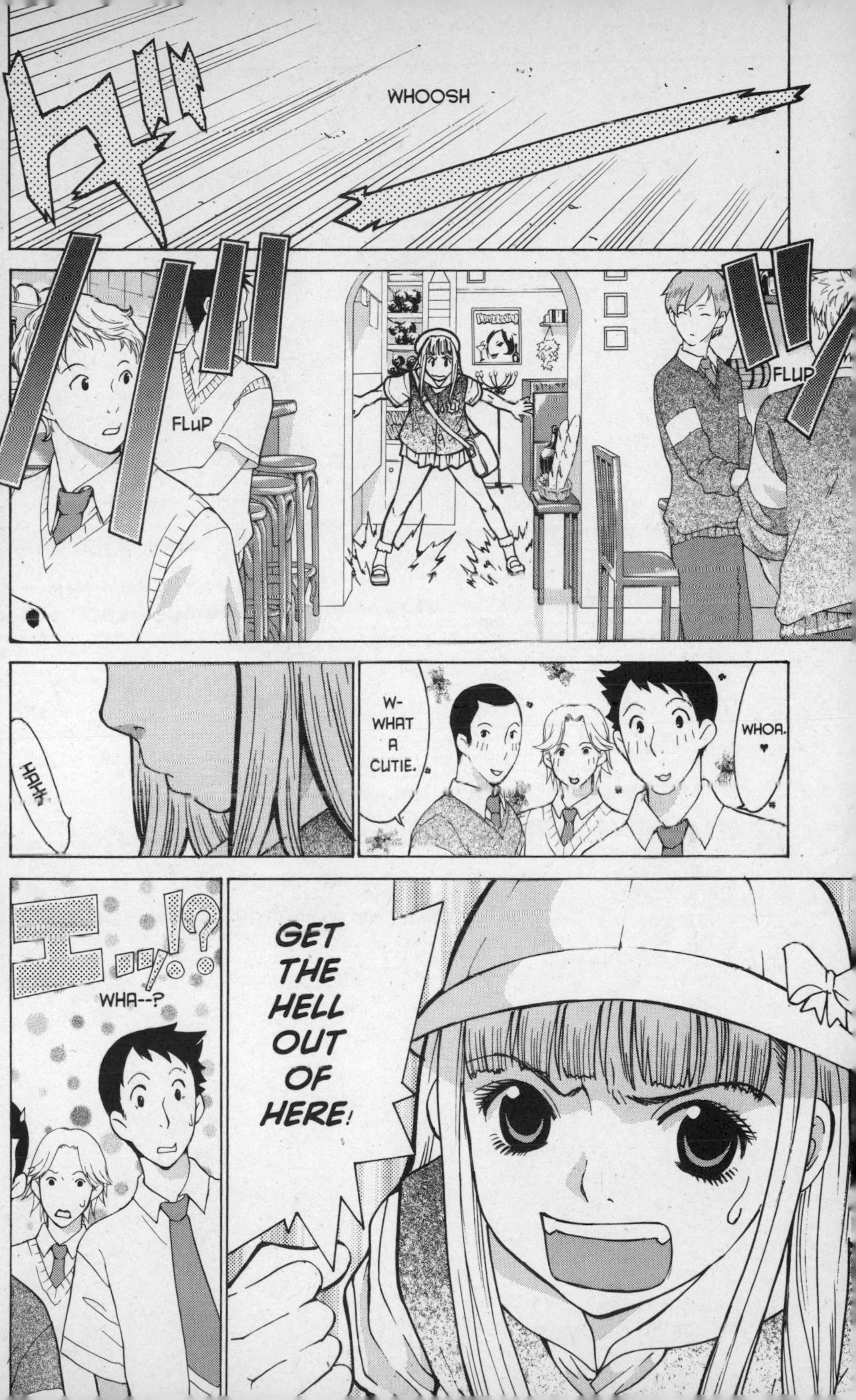
WHOOSH
FLUP
FLUP
WHOA. ♥
W-WHAT A CUTIE.
GET THE HELL OUT OF HERE!
WHA--?

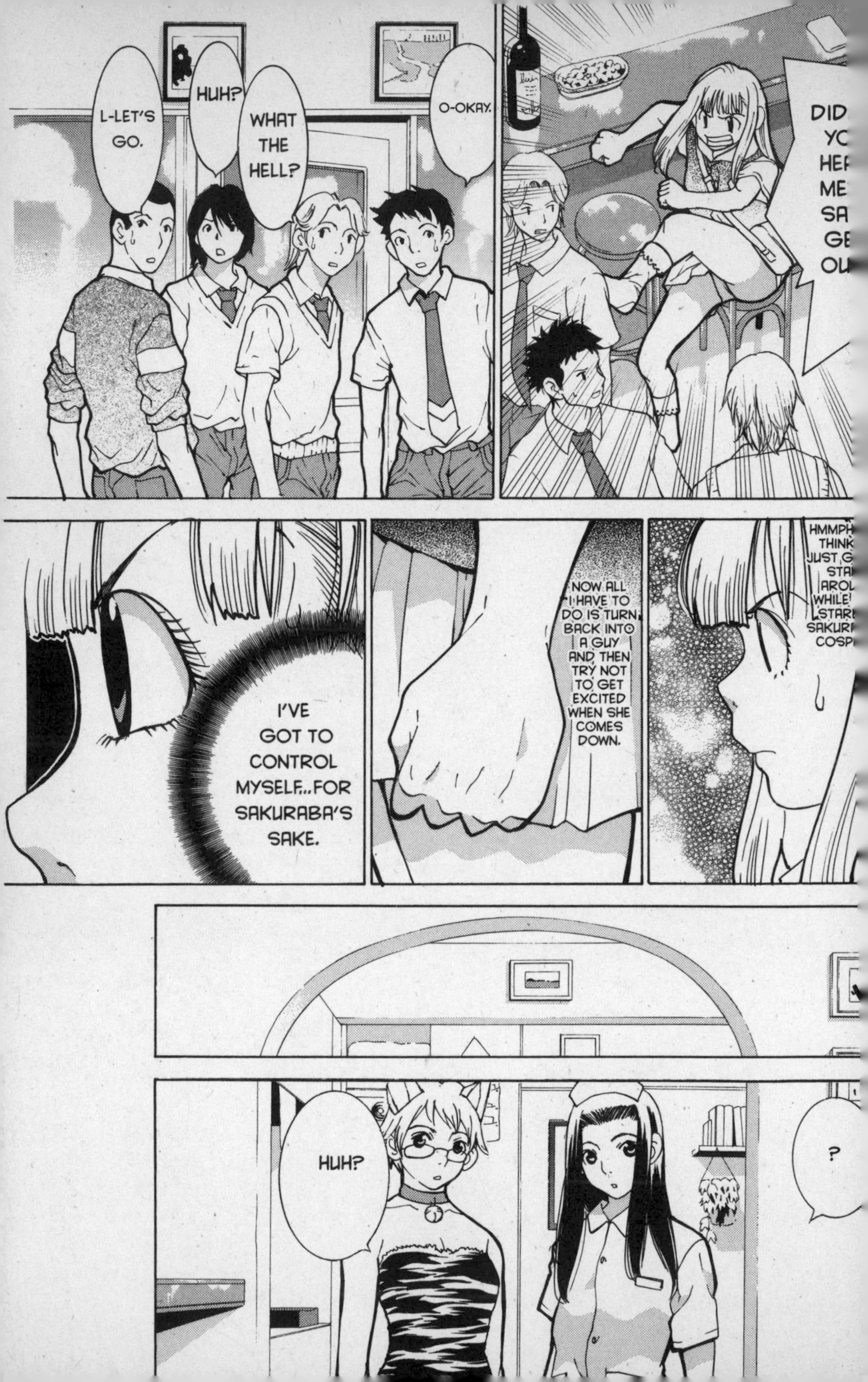
DID YO HEF ME SA GE OU
O-OKAY.
WHAT THE HELL?
HUH?
L-LET'S GO.
HMMPH THINK JUST G STA AROL WHILE STARE SAKURA COSP
NOW ALL I HAVE TO DO IS TURN BACK INTO A GUY AND THEN TRY NOT TO GET EXCITED WHEN SHE COMES DOWN.
I'VE GOT TO CONTROL MYSELF...FOR SAKURABA'S SAKE.
?
HUH?

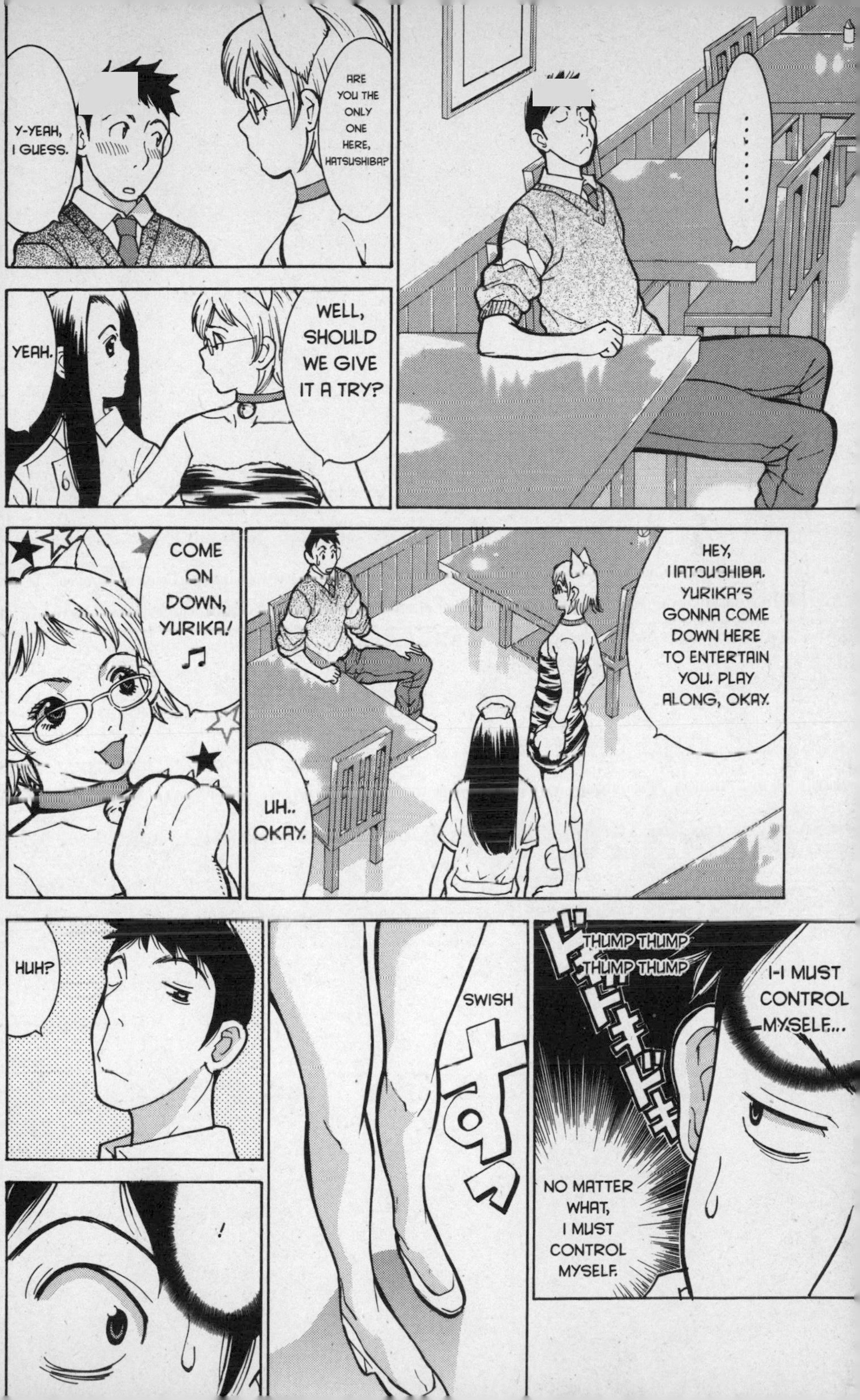
......
ARE YOU THE ONLY ONE HERE, HATSUSHIBA?
Y-YEAH, I GUESS.
WELL, SHOULD WE GIVE IT A TRY?
YEAH.
HEY, HATSUSHIBA. YURIKA'S GONNA COME DOWN HERE TO ENTERTAIN YOU. PLAY ALONG, OKAY.
UH.. OKAY.
COME ON DOWN, YURIKA! ♫
THUMP THUMP
THUMP THUMP
I-I MUST CONTROL MYSELF....
NO MATTER WHAT, I MUST CONTROL MYSELF.
SWISH
HUH?
!

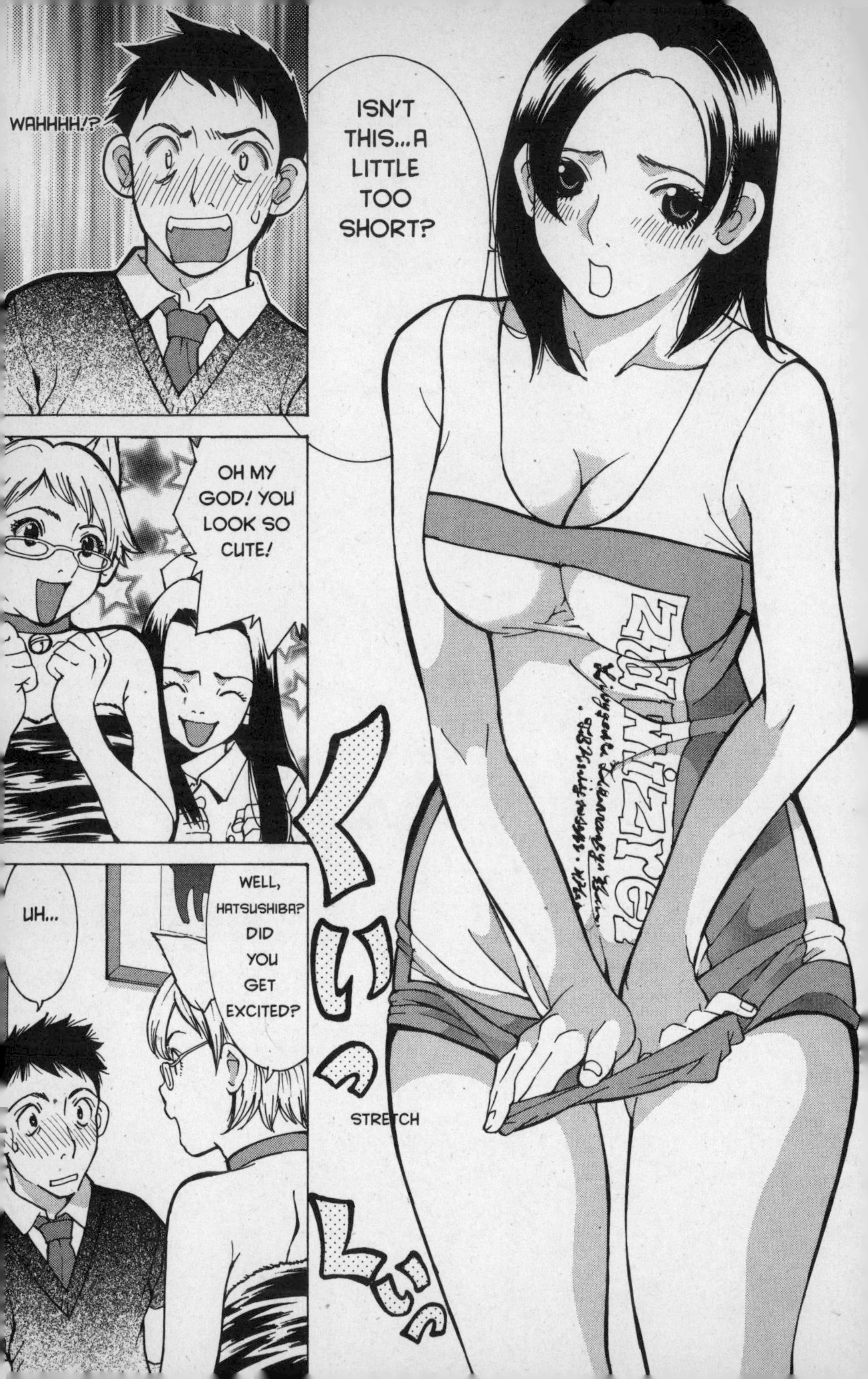
ISN'T THIS...A LITTLE TOO SHORT?
STRETCH
WAHHHH!?
OH MY GOD! YOU LOOK SO CUTE!
WELL, HATSUSHIBA? DID YOU GET EXCITED?
UH...

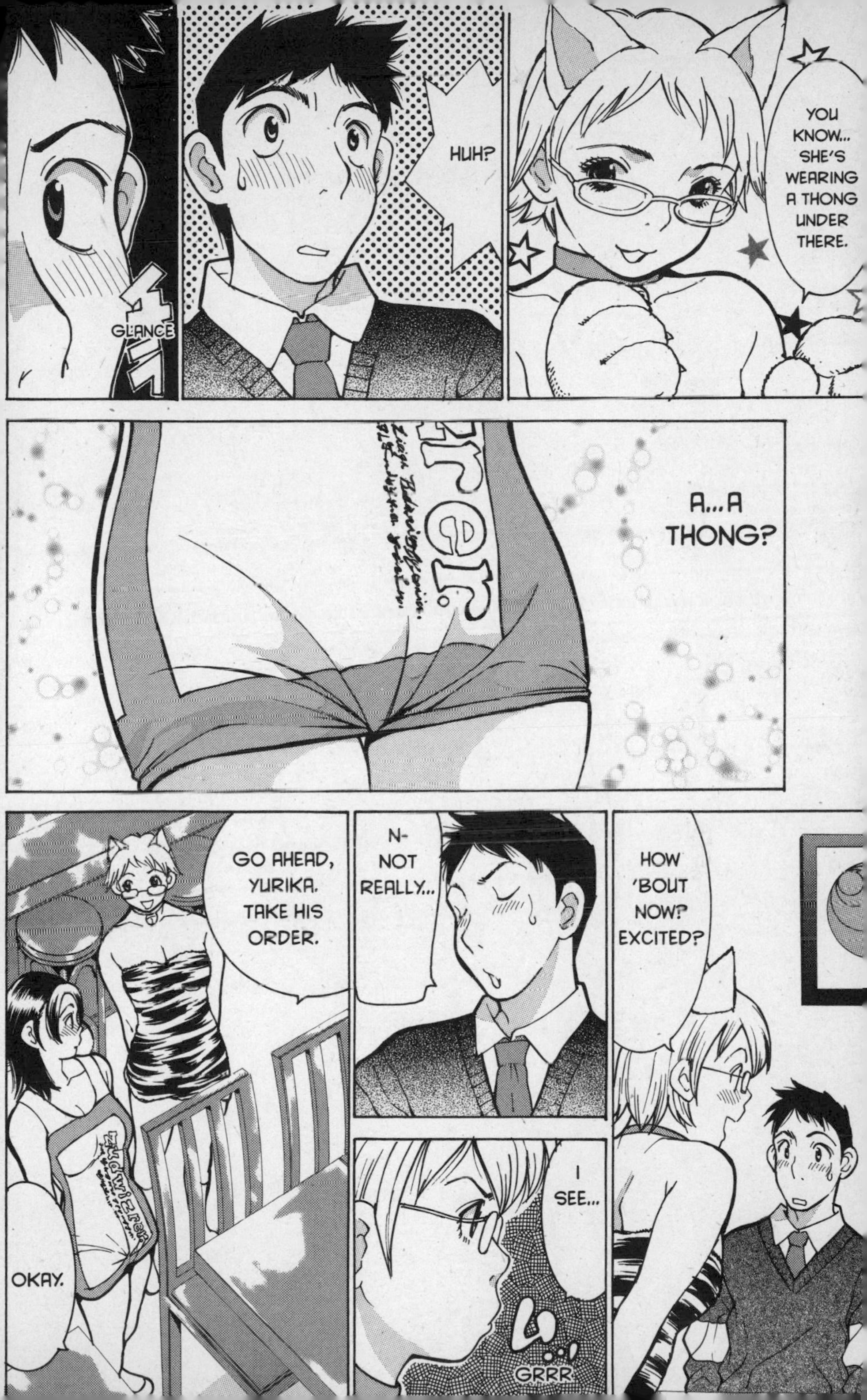
YOU KNOW... SHE'S WEARING A THONG UNDER THERE.
HUH?
GLANCE
A...A THONG?
HOW 'BOUT NOW? EXCITED?
N- NOT REALLY...
I SEE...
GRRR
GO AHEAD, YURIKA. TAKE HIS ORDER.
OKAY.

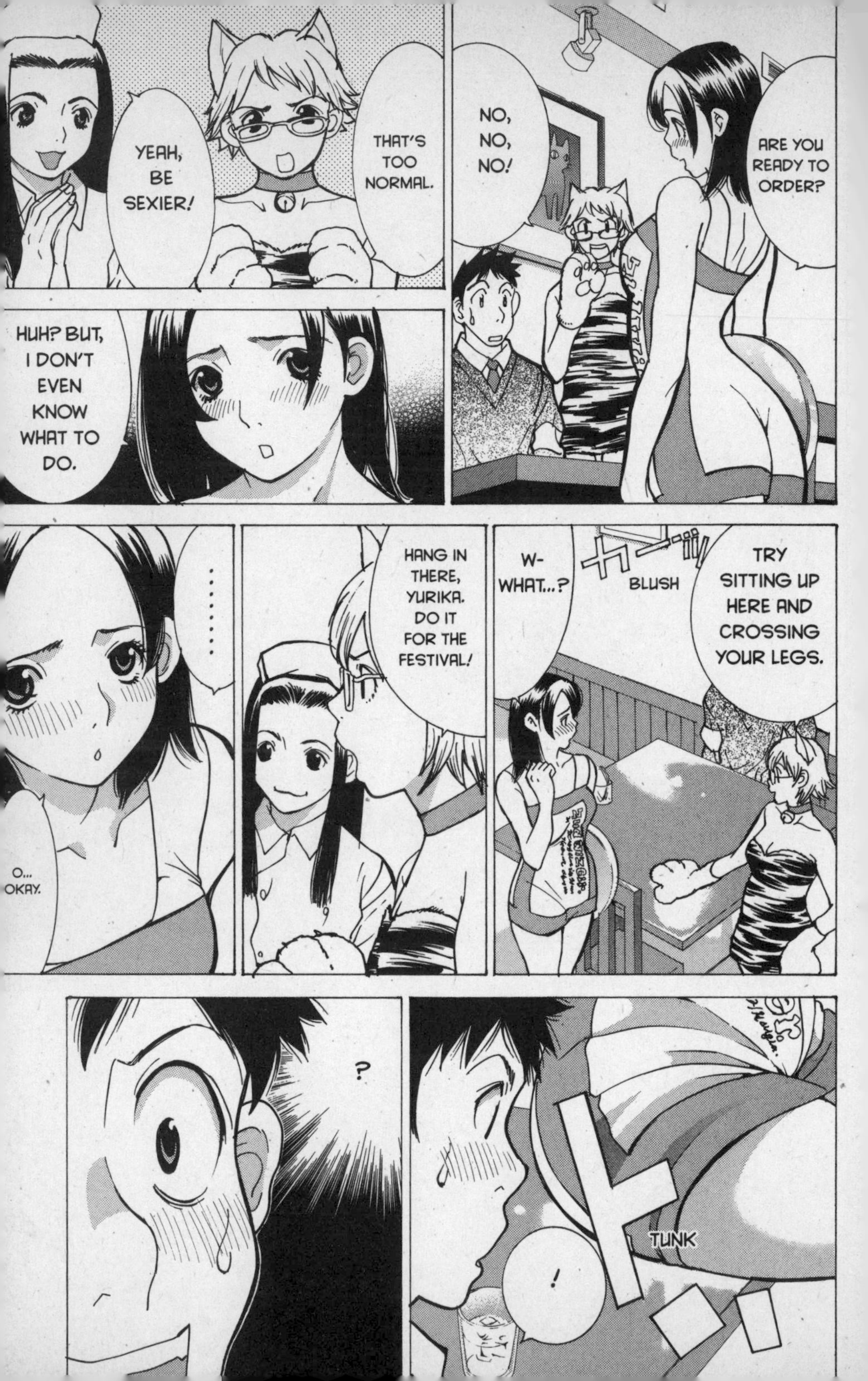

ARE YOU READY TO ORDER?
NO, NO, NO!
THAT'S TOO NORMAL.
YEAH, BE SEXIER!
HUH? BUT, I DON'T EVEN KNOW WHAT TO DO.
TRY SITTING UP HERE AND CROSSING YOUR LEGS.
BLUSH
W-WHAT...?
HANG IN THERE, YURIKA. DO IT FOR THE FESTIVAL!
......
O... OKAY.
!
TUNK
?

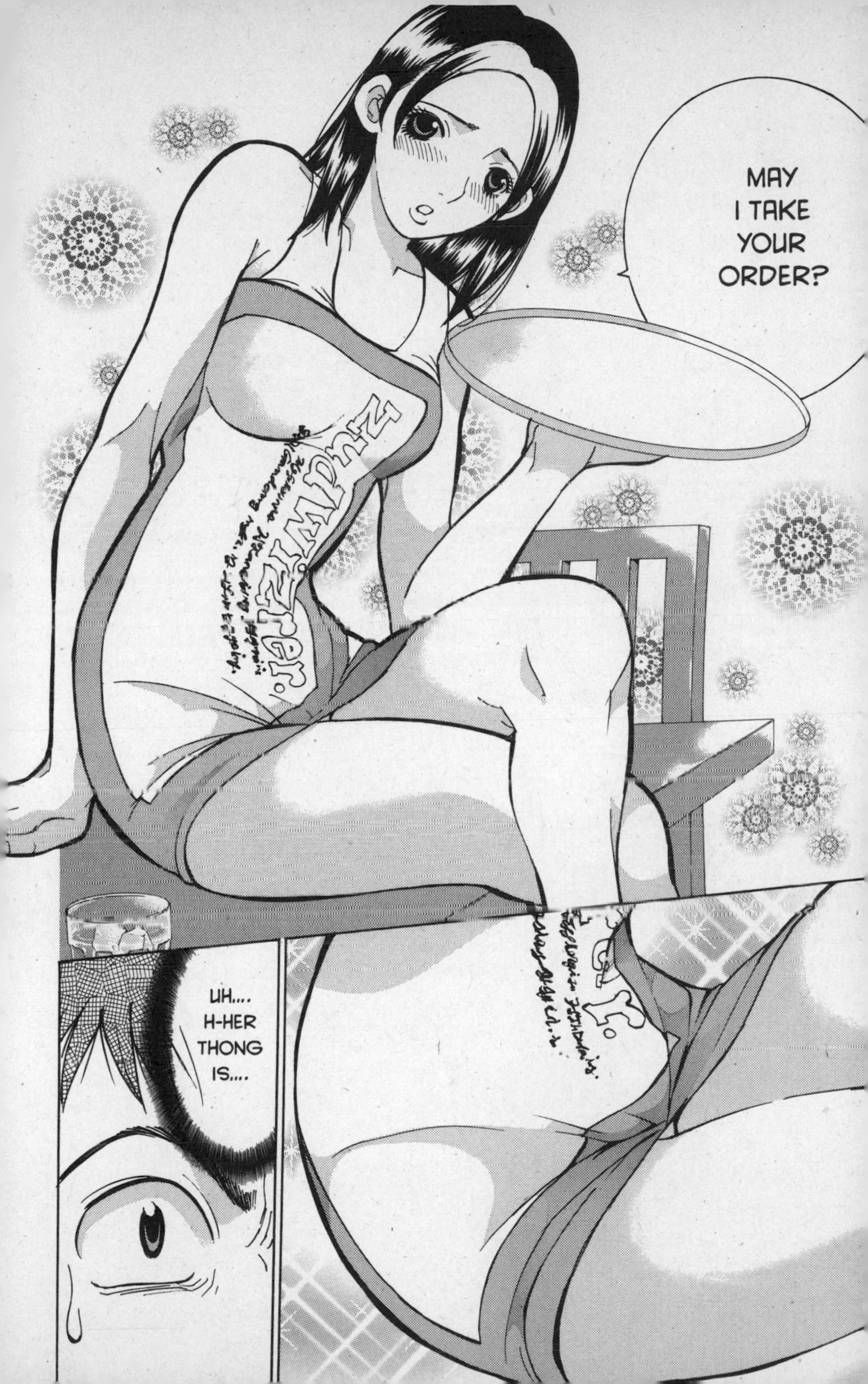
MAY I TAKE YOUR ORDER?
UH.... H-HER THONG IS....

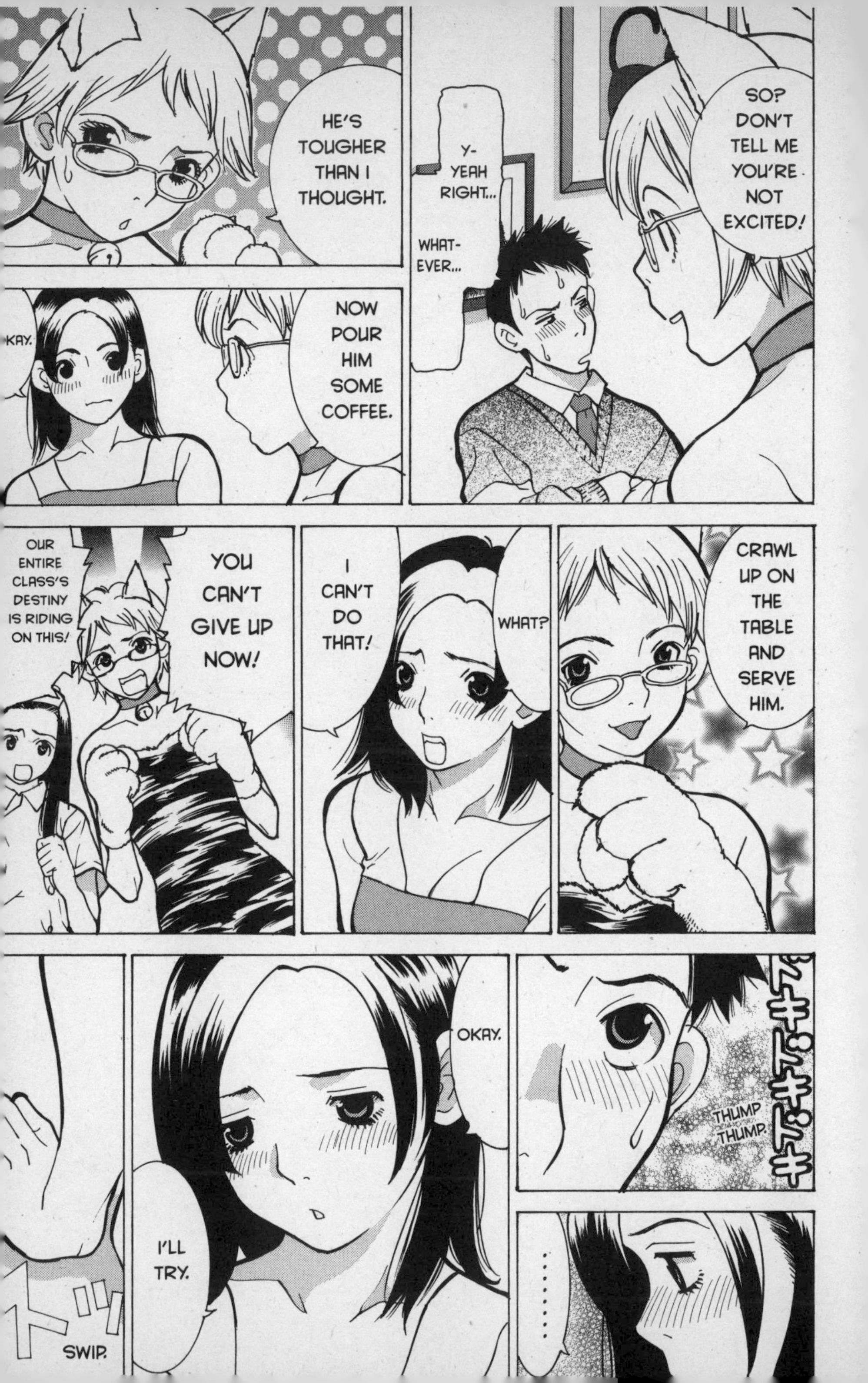
SO? DON'T TELL ME YOU'RE NOT EXCITED!
Y- YEAH RIGHT...
WHAT-EVER...
HE'S TOUGHER THAN I THOUGHT.
NOW POUR HIM SOME COFFEE.
KAY.
CRAWL UP ON THE TABLE AND SERVE HIM.
WHAT?
I CAN'T DO THAT!
YOU CAN'T GIVE UP NOW!
OUR ENTIRE CLASS'S DESTINY IS RIDING ON THIS!
THUMP THUMP
......
OKAY.
I'LL TRY.
SWIP.

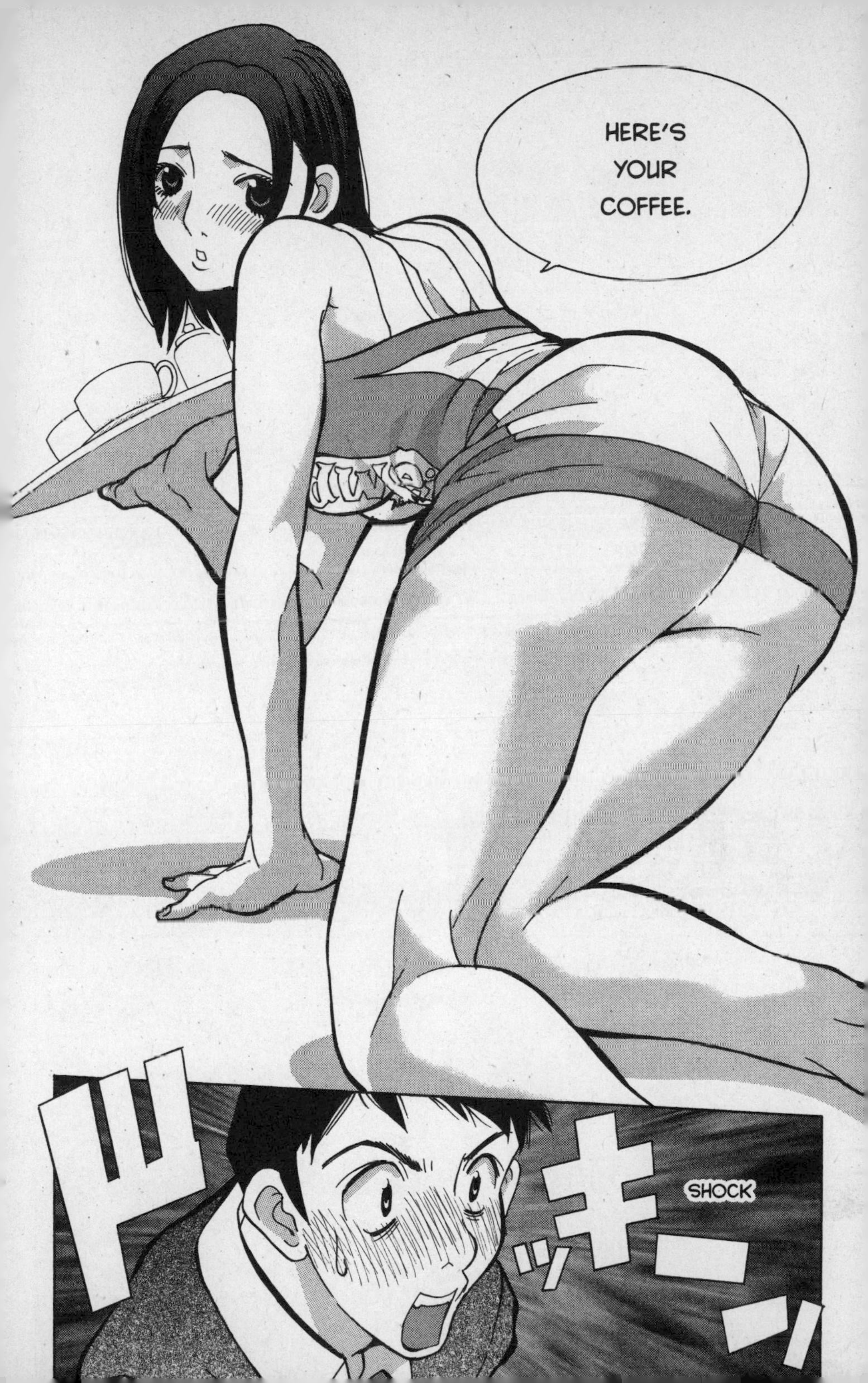
HERE'S YOUR COFFEE.
SHOCK

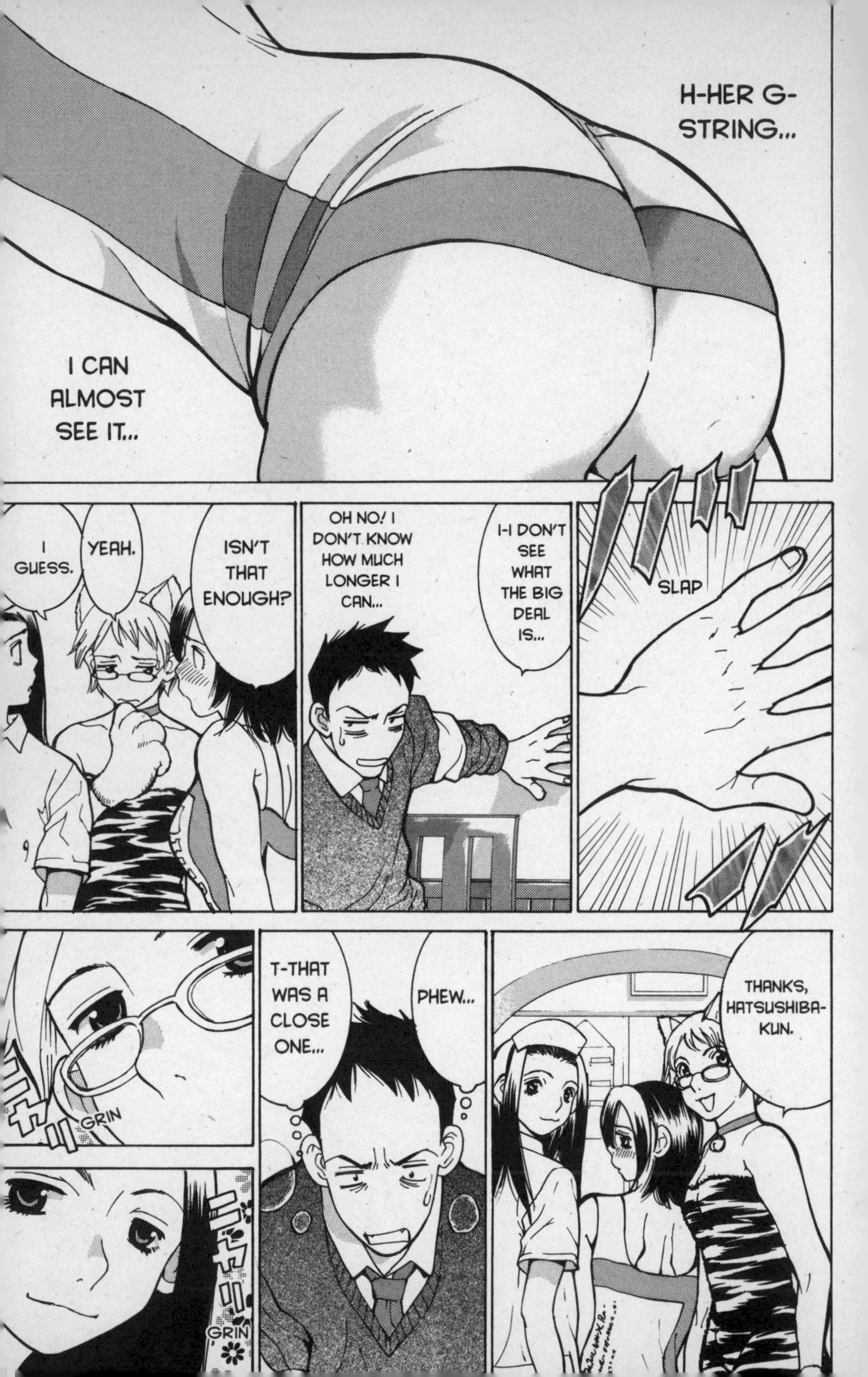
H-HER G-STRING...
I CAN ALMOST SEE IT...
SLAP
I-I DON'T SEE WHAT THE BIG DEAL IS...
OH NO! I DON'T KNOW HOW MUCH LONGER I CAN...
ISN'T THAT ENOUGH?
YEAH.
I GUESS.
THANKS, HATSUSHIBA-KUN.
PHEW...
T-THAT WAS A CLOSE ONE...
GRIN
GRIN

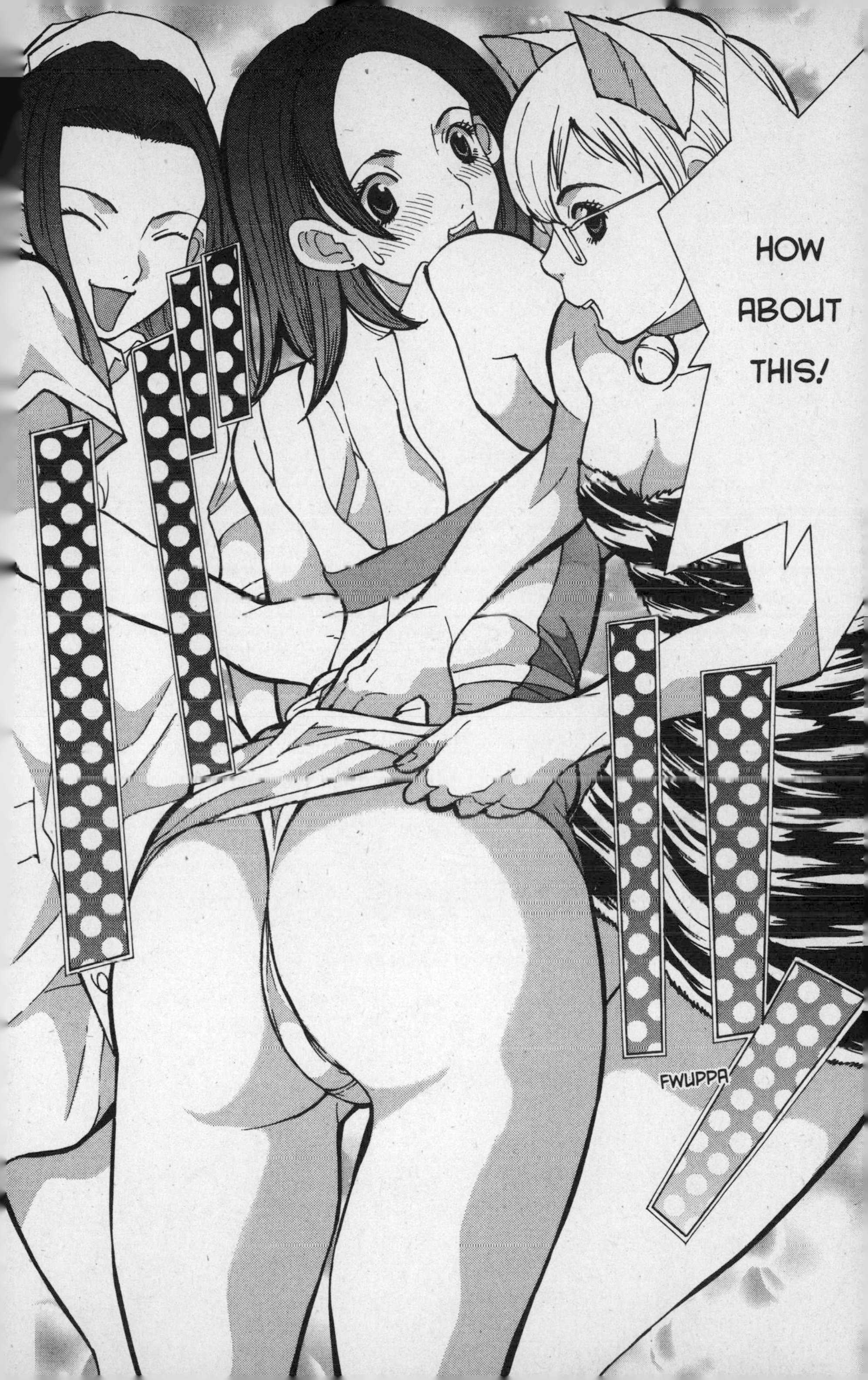
HOW ABOUT THIS!
FWUPPA

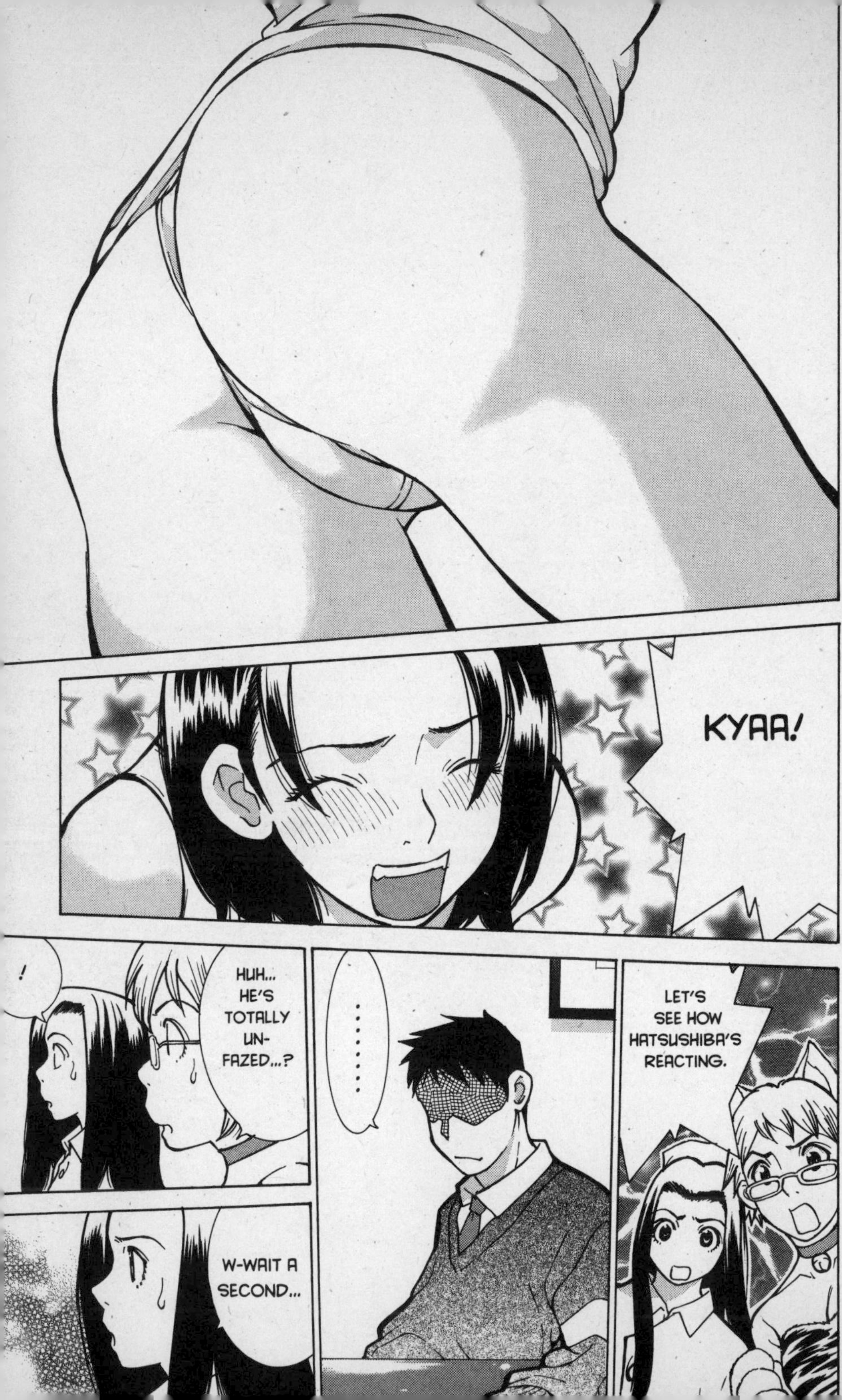
KYAA!
LET'S SEE HOW HATSUSHIBA'S REACTING.
....
!
HUH... HE'S TOTALLY UN-FAZED...?
W-WAIT A SECOND...

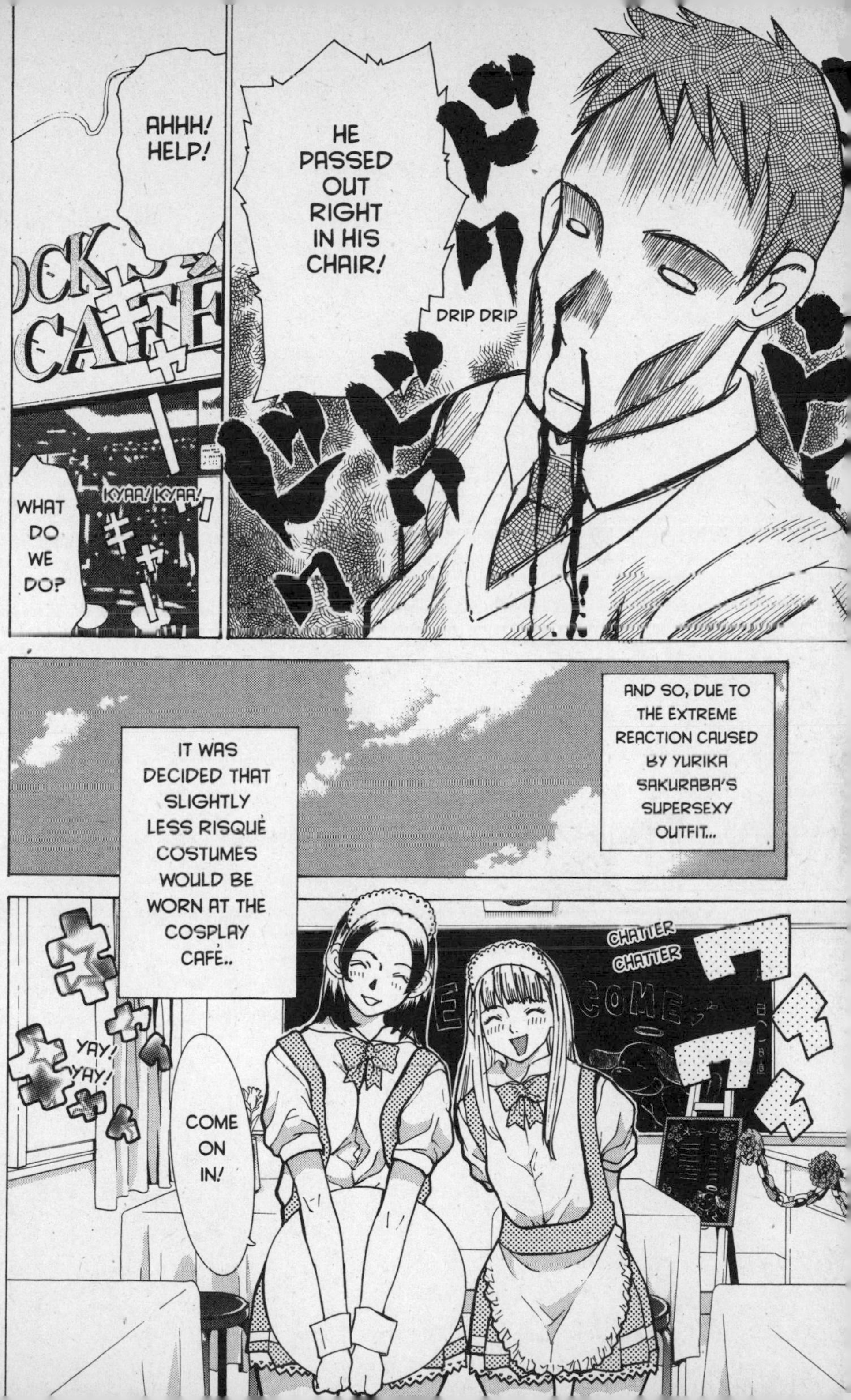
HE PASSED OUT RIGHT IN HIS CHAIR!
DRIP DRIP
AHHH! HELP!
KYAA! KYAA!
WHAT DO WE DO?
AND SO, DUE TO THE EXTREME REACTION CAUSED BY YURIKA SAKURABA'S SUPERSEXY OUTFIT...
IT WAS DECIDED THAT SLIGHTLY LESS RISQUÉ COSTUMES WOULD BE WORN AT THE COSPLAY CAFÉ..
CHATTER CHATTER
COME ON IN!
YAY! YAY!

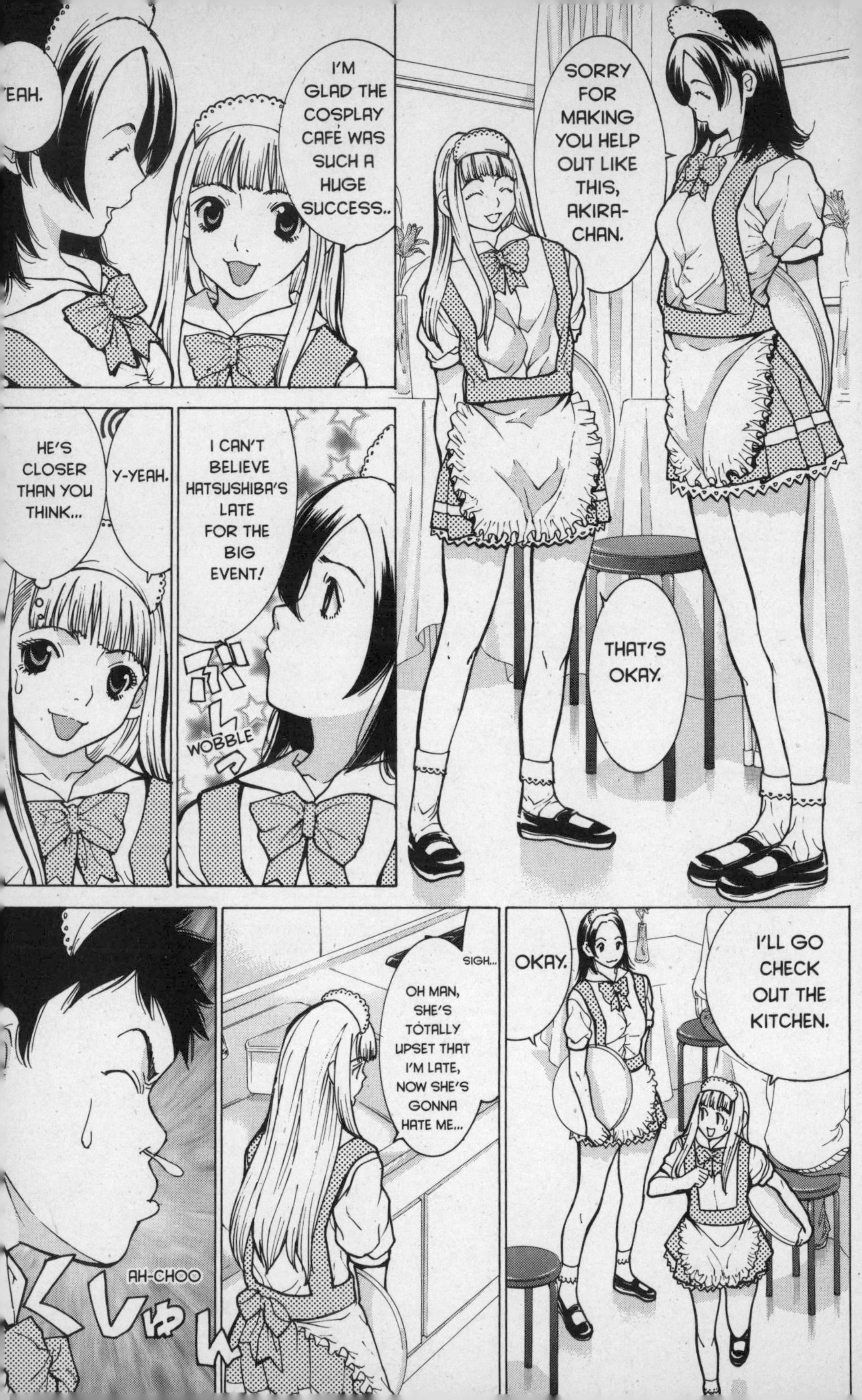
SORRY FOR MAKING YOU HELP OUT LIKE THIS, AKIRA-CHAN.
THAT'S OKAY.
I'M GLAD THE COSPLAY CAFÉ WAS SUCH A HUGE SUCCESS..
EAH.
I CAN'T BELIEVE HATSUSHIBA'S LATE FOR THE BIG EVENT!
WOBBLE
Y-YEAH.
HE'S CLOSER THAN YOU THINK...
I'LL GO CHECK OUT THE KITCHEN.
OKAY.
SIGH...
OH MAN, SHE'S TOTALLY UPSET THAT I'M LATE, NOW SHE'S GONNA HATE ME...
AH-CHOO

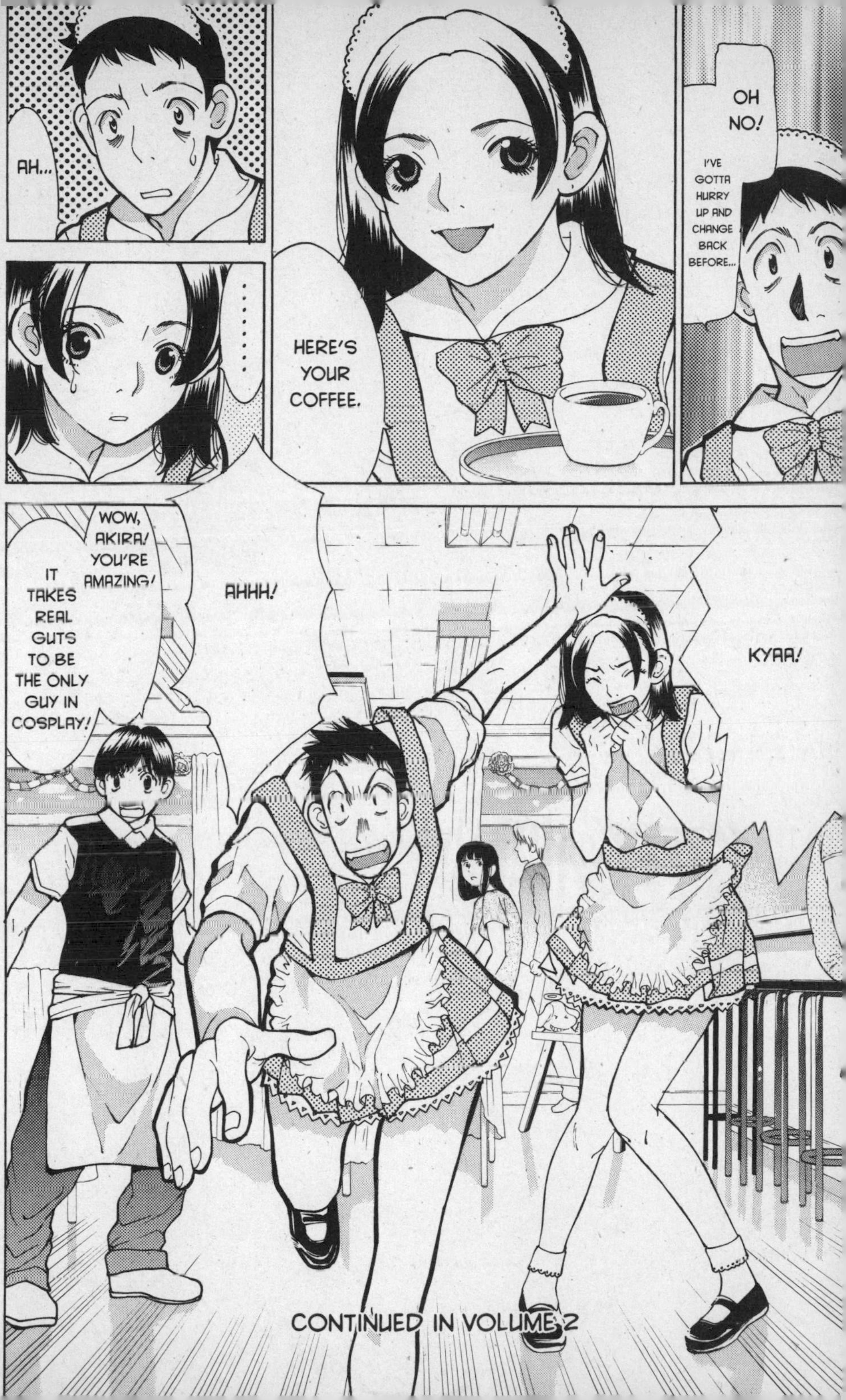
OH NO!
I'VE GOTTA HURRY UP AND CHANGE BACK BEFORE...
HERE'S YOUR COFFEE.
AH...
......
KYAA!
AHHH!
WOW, AKIRA! YOU'RE AMAZING!
IT TAKES REAL GUTS TO BE THE ONLY GUY IN COSPLAY!

CONTINUED IN VOLUME 2

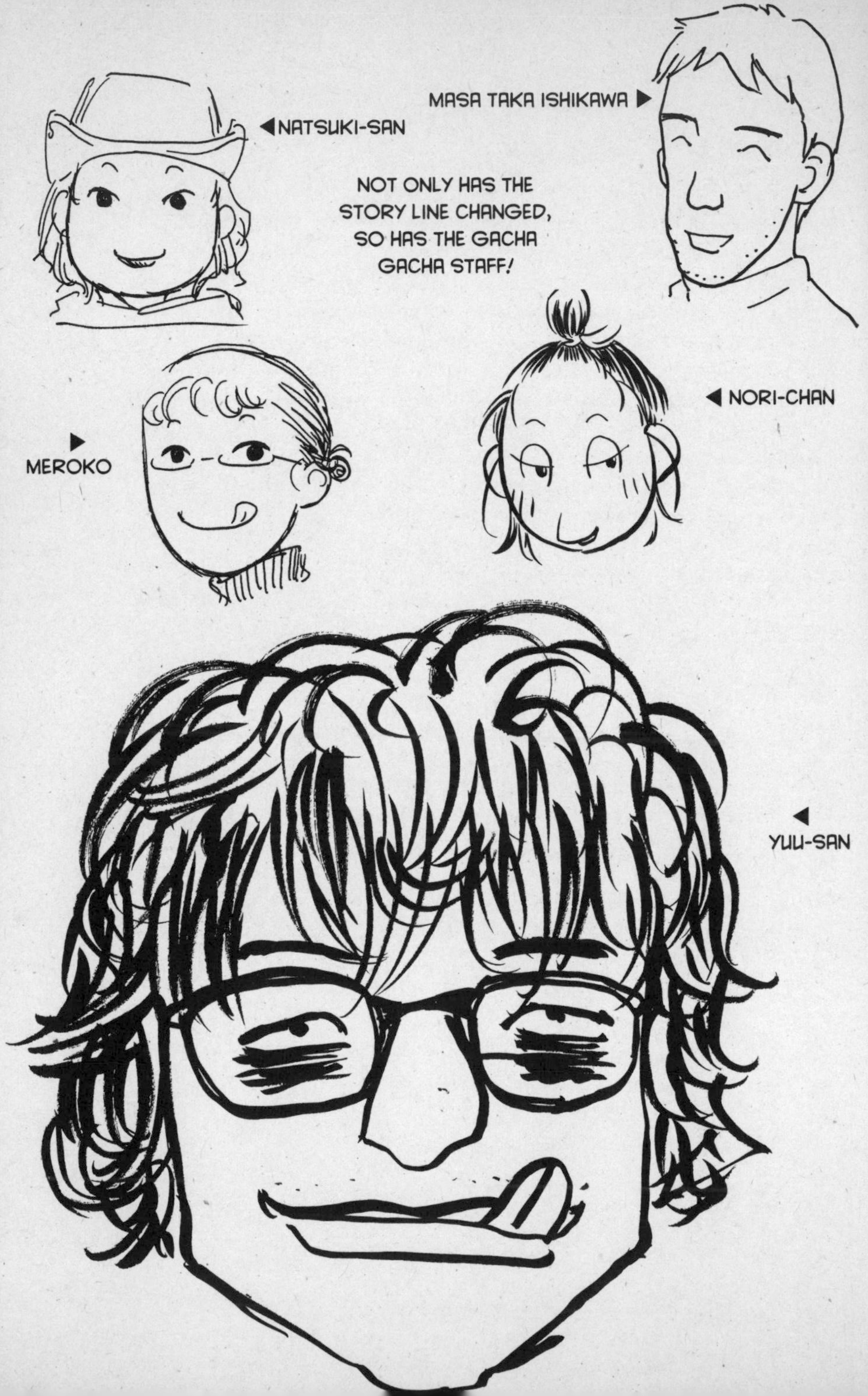
MASA TAKA ISHIKAWA
NATSUKI-SAN
NOT ONLY HAS THE STORY LINE CHANGED, SO HAS THE GACHA GACHA STAFF!
NORI-CHAN
MEROKO
YUU-SAN

About the Creator

Tamakoshi Hiroyuki was born in 1970. In 1997, he was awarded
the Fine Work Prize in the Best New Cartoonist category at *Shonen*
magazine's 45th annual competition. His previous work includes
Boys Be . . . (1991–1997), *Boys Be . . . 2nd Season* (1997–2000), and
Boys Be . . . L Co-op (2000–2001). Masahiro Itabashi was the
cartoonist of the original work. *Gacha Gacha* was published in
Shonen magazine's double issue 36–37 in 2002, and is currently in
the serial magazine started from issue 29 in 2003 with *Special No. 8*.

Comics

Boys Be . . . complete in 16 volumes.
Boys Be . . . 2nd Season, complete in 20 volumes
Boys Be . . . L Co-op, complete in 5 volumes
Gacha Gacha, volumes 1–8
Boys Be . . . 1991
Boys Be . . . 1992
Boys Be . . . 1993
Boys Be . . . 1994
Boys Be . . . 1995
Boys Be . . . 1996
Boys Be . . . 1997
Boys Be . . . 1998
Boys Be . . . 1999
Boys Be . . . 2000
Kodansha Manga Collection

Games
Boys Be . . . 1997 (PlayStation)
Boys Be . . . *2nd Season*, 1999 (PlayStation)

Favorite Mobile Suits
RX=78 GUNDAM
The strongest man in the world
Amuro Ray.
A respectable person
GUNDAM (because I want to be a GUNDAM).
PC environment
Power Mac G4 733 MHz, OS 10.3.5, 19-inch monitor.
Favorite movie
Lock, Stock, and Two Smoking Barrels.
Are you enjoying your life?
So-so.
Favorite animal
Cats, but I have a dog.
Describe yourself with a metaphor
A kettle.
Favorite animation
Evangelion and *FLCL.*

Translation Notes

Japanese is a tricky language for most Westerners, and translation is often more an art than a science. For your edification and reading pleasure, here are notes on some of the places where we could have gone in a different direction in our translation, or where a Japanese cultural reference is used.

Ore and *Atashi*, page 33

In Japanese there are certain words used only by males or females. Here, Akira uses the masculine word *ore* for I'm. The feminine equivalent would be *atashi*. This shows that Akira is struggling to learn to speak like a girl. In the following panel Akira introduces himself in a more feminine manner.

Bloody nose, page 40

In Japanese manga, a sudden bloody nose is a sign of sexual arousal.

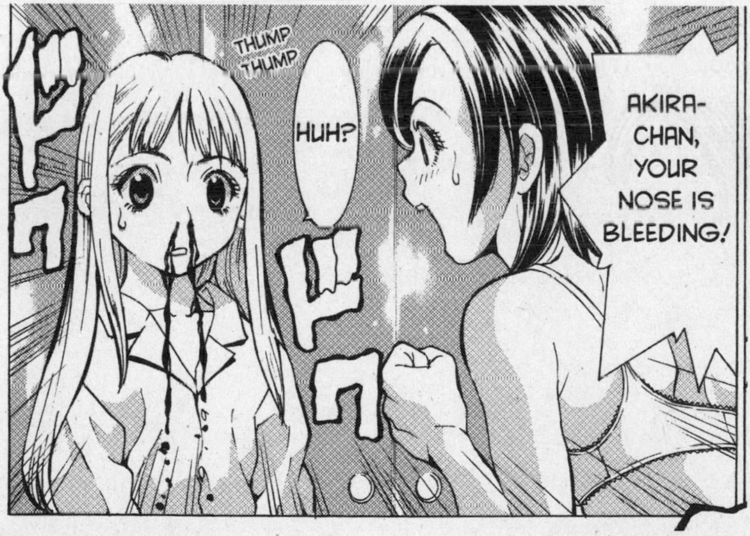
AKIRA-CHAN, YOUR NOSE IS BLEEDING!
HUH?
THUMP THUMP

Koyori, page 47

A *koyori* is a string made from wound-up pieces of Japanese paper. It's often used as ribbon when wrapping gifts.

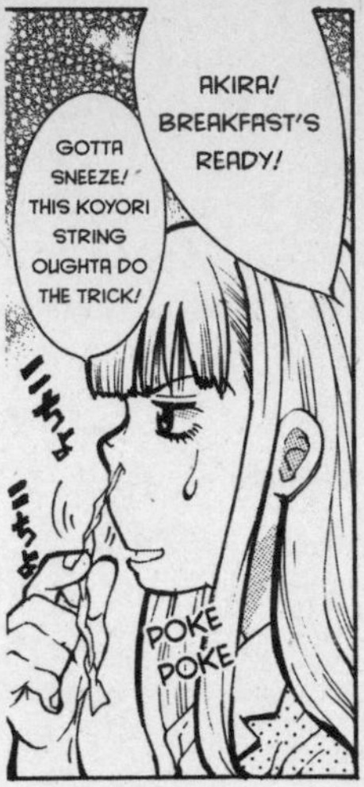
AKIRA! BREAKFAST'S READY!
GOTTA SNEEZE! THIS KOYORI STRING OUGHTA DO THE TRICK!
POKE POKE

Misebra, page 98

A misebra, or showing bra, is a bra that can also be worn as a top.

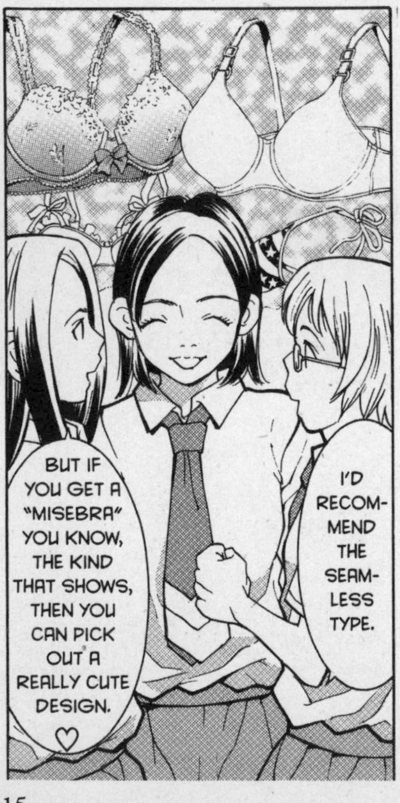
I'D RECOMMEND THE SEAMLESS TYPE.
BUT IF YOU GET A "MISEBRA" YOU KNOW, THE KIND THAT SHOWS, THEN YOU CAN PICK OUT A REALLY CUTE DESIGN. ♡

School festival, page 175

Most schools in Japan hold a school festival once a year. Usually each class organizes an activity for the festival, such as a dance or a play. Some classes open up food stalls or cafés too.

"Everybody stand up," page 175

At the beginning and end of class in Japan the students stand up and bow in unison to show respect to the teacher. Every day a different student is in charge of leading the class. Since homeroom is over, today's class leader begins the salute by shouting "Everybody stand up."

Cosplay, page 179

Cosplay, short for costume play, is a popular *otaku* pastime that involves dressing up as one's favorite manga, anime, or video game character. You can learn all about the ins and outs of cosplay in the Del Rey series "Genshiken."

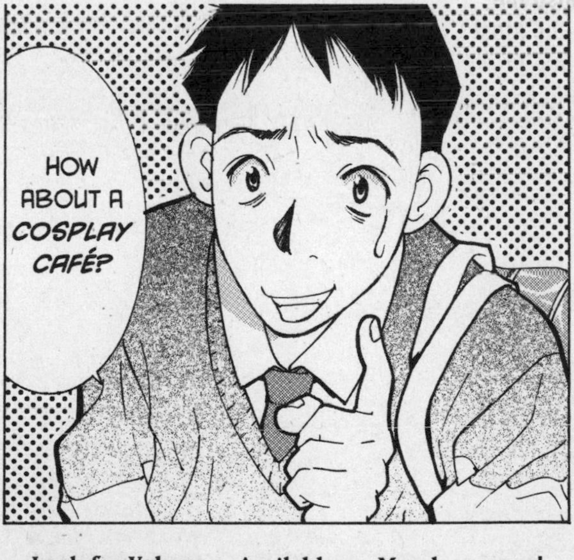
HOW ABOUT A COSPLAY CAFÉ?

Look for Volume 2, Available on March 27, 2007!

SUZUKA

KOUJI SEO

SHE'S SO COOL

Yamato is ready for a fresh start.
So when his aunt invites him to stay
rent-free in her big-city boarding-
house in hustling, bustling Tokyo,
Yamato jumps at the chance. There's
just one teensy-weensy catch: It's an
all-girl housing complex and spa!
Things get even more nerve-racking
when Yamato meets his neighbor
Suzuka, a beautiful track-and-field
star. She's not just the cutest girl
Yamato's ever met, she's also the
coolest, the smartest, and the most
intimidating. Can an ordinary guy
like Yamato ever hope to win over a
girl like Suzuka?

Special extras in each volume! Read them all!

VISIT WWW.DELREYMANGA.COM TO:
• Read sample pages
• View release date calendars for upcoming volumes
• Sign up for Del Rey's free manga e-newsletter
• Find out the latest about new Del Rey Manga series

RATING M AGES 18+

The Otaku's Choice

TOMARE!

[STOP!]

You're going the wrong way!

Manga is a completely different type of reading experience.

To start at the *beginning,* go to the *end*!

That's right! Authentic manga is read the traditional Japanese way—from right to left. Exactly the opposite of how American books are read. It's easy to follow: Just go to the other end of the book, and read each page—and each panel—from right side to left side, starting at the top right. Now you're experiencing manga as it was meant to be!